P9-ELQ-959

THE WORK OF POETRY

THE WORK OF POETRY

John Hollander

COLUMBIA UNIVERSITY PRESS   NEW YORK

Columbia University Press

Publishers Since 1893

New York   Chichester, West Sussex

Copyright © 1997 Columbia University Press

Library of Congress Cataloging-in-Publication Data
Hollander, John.
The work of poetry / John Hollander.
p.   cm.
Includes index.
ISBN 0–231–10896–6
1. Poetics.   2. Poetry—History and criticism.   I. Title.
PN1136.H58   1997
808.1—dc21   97–10041

Casebound editions of Columbia University Press books are printed on
permanent and durable acid-free paper.
Printed in the United States of America
Designed by Linda Secondari
c 10 9 8 7 6 5 4 3 2 1

FOR DAVID BROMWICH

C♀NTENTS

PART III   THE WORK OF POETS

PREFACE

The essays in this volume direct themselves to the minute particulars of particular poems and to the great particularities of particular poets. Nine of them treat of general poetic and literary matters, but most are considerations of individual writers. They were written over a considerable period (the earliest, almost twenty years ago), during which time I have been writing and teaching poetry, and they have been driven mostly by the impulse to share with a reader what I have heard or understood in these particulars and particularities. The topical studies in the first group range from questions so vast in scale that one can deal only with the tip of the iceberg each of them seems to form (like "originality") to an examination of the poetic powers in English of one tiny word, *of*, (only *I* is both shorter and more potentially metaphorical). Those in a second sequence touch, directly and indirectly, on the matter of poetic development, and they are more personal. The largest group is of observations on individual poets whose work—save in the case of Whitman and perhaps now Bishop—has not, I felt, been given appropriate contemporary notice.

Seven of these essays have never appeared in print. Chapters 11, 17, and 22 were written expressly for this volume. Part of chapter 5 was presented at a psychoanalytic conference on dreaming in Washington, D.C., in 1988. Most of chapter 8 was read at a symposium on Robert Louis Stevenson held at the Whitney Humanities Center at Yale in 1994; chapter 9 is adapted from a talk presented at Princeton University's Celebration of Contemporary American Poetry in 1994; chapter 10 is somewhat expanded from an MLA talk in 1993. The other essays have been either slightly or extensively rewritten following their original appearances, which I list below, with all due acknowledgments. A few of them appeared with footnotes, which for the most part I have included, and, save for chapter 5, I have not added any new ones and have allowed informal modes of citation and quotation to remain as they were.

Part of chapter 1 was given as a lecture at the Marine Biological Laboratory in Woods Hole, Mass., and was subsequently published in *MBL Science* 4, no. 1 (April 1990). Chapter 2 was expanded considerably from an essay in *Raritan* 2, no. 4 (spring 1983). Chapter 3 appeared in *Yale Review* 60 (winter 1981). Chapter 4, under the title "It All Depends," appeared in *Social Research* 58, no. 1 (spring 1991). Chapter 6 was printed as "Of 'of': The Romance of a Preposition" in *Addressing Frank Kermode*, ed. Margaret Tudeau-Clayton and Martin Warner (London: Macmillan, 1991). Chapter 7 was published as "Psalms" in *Congregation: Contemporary Writers and the Jewish Bible*, ed. David Rosenberg (New York: Harcourt Brace Jovanovich, 1987). Chapter 12 was an introduction to an edition of *Leaves of Grass* published jointly by the Library of America and Vintage Books in 1993. Chapter 13 was the introduction to *The Essential Rossetti* (New York: Ecco Press, 1989). Chapter 14 appeared under the same title in *Lewis Carroll: Modern Critical Views*, ed. Harold Bloom (New York: Chelsea House, 1987). Part of chapter 15 was the foreword to a reprint of Ingelow's *Mopsa the Fairy* (New York: Garland, 1977). Chapter 16 is expanded from a review in the *New Republic*, July 29, 1978. Most of chapter 18 was an introduction to a Signet Classics reprint of *Spoon River Anthology* (1993). Chapter 19 appeared under the title "Observations on Marianne Moore's Syllabic Schemes," in *Marianne Moore: The Art of a Modernist*, ed. Joseph Parisi (Ann Arbor: UMI Research Press, 1990). Chapter 20 appeared under this title in *Robert Penn Warren: Modern Critical Views*, ed. Harold Bloom (New York: Chelsea House, 1986), with some additions. Chapter 21 is expanded from a review of *Geography III* in *Parnassus* 6, no. 2 (fall 1977). Part of chapter 23 appeared in my "Poetry in Review," *Yale Review* 74, no. 3 (1985).

Over the years these pages have incurred a host of debts to friends and colleagues, including Harold Bloom, David Bromwich, John Burt, Stanley Cavell, Eleanor Cook, Angus Fletcher, Kenneth Gross, Richard Howard, George Kateb, Sir Frank Kermode, Arien Mack, J. D. McClatchy, Barbara Packer, Richard Poirier, Joan Richardson, Lorin Stein, Mark Strand, Jennifer Wagner, John Watkins, Leon Wieseltier, and Stephen Yenser. Natalie Charkow's devotion over the years of writing, rewriting, and assembling this book was crucial, as was Jennifer Crewe's patience during several years of delay in completing it.

ACKNOWLEDGMENTS

For permission to quote from material rights, which they hold, I am grateful to the following:

"For Harold Bloom," copyright © 1987 by A. R. Ammons, from *The Selected Poems, Expanded Edition* by A. R. Ammons. Reprinted by permission of W. W. Norton & Company, Inc.

George Borchardt and Carcanet Press, Ltd. for permission to quote "Soonest Mended" from *The Double Dream of Spring*, © 1970 by John Ashbery; some lines from "Grand Gallop" and some lines from "The Mythological Poet," © 1956 by John Ashbery.

Random House, Inc., for permission to quote from "In Praise of Limestone," "In Memory of Sigmund Freud," and "In Memory of W. B. Yeats" by W. H. Auden, from *Collected Poems*, ed. Edward Mendelson. Copyright © 1976 by Edward Mendelson, William Meredith, and Monroe K. Spears, executors of the estate of W. H. Auden.

Owen Laster and the William Morris Agency, Inc., for permission to quote from *Brother to Dragons*, copyright © 1953 by Robert Penn Warren; "Brotherhood in Pain," "The Garden," "Bearded Oaks," and "The Return: An Elegy" from *Selected Poems, 1923–1975*, copyright © 1976 by Robert Penn Warren; and "Part of What Might Have Been a Short Story, Almost Forgotten" from *Being Here: Poetry, 1977–1980*, copyright © 1980 by Robert Penn Warren. Reprinted by permission.

Excerpts from "Poem," "Anaphora," "The Moose," "One Art," "Crusoe in England," and "The End of March" from *The Complete Poems, 1927–1979* by

Elizabeth Bishop, copyright © 1979, 1983 by Alice Helen Methfessel. Reprinted by permission of Farrar, Straus & Giroux, Inc.

Lines from "Genesis," "In Memory of Jane Fraser," and "Of Commerce and Society" excerpted from *New and Collected Poems, 1952–1992*, copyright © 1994 by Geoffrey Hill. Reprinted by permission of Houghton Mifflin Co. All rights reserved. Previously published in *For the Unfallen* (1959). Lines from "The Mystery of the Charity of Charles Péguy" excerpted from *New and Collected Poems, 1952–1992*, copyright © by Geoffrey Hill. Reprinted by permission of Houghton Mifflin Co. All rights reserved. Previously published in *The Mystery of the Charity of Charles Péguy* (1983). Also to Penguin Books, Ltd., for permission to quote the same material listed above, as from *Collected Poems* by Geoffrey Hill (King Penguin edition, 1985), copyright © 1978 by Geoffrey Hill.

Alfred A. Knopf, Inc., for permission to quote from *In Other Words* by May Swenson, © 1987 by May Swenson; and for permission to quote "Mirror" by James Merrill, from *From the First Nine*, © 1981, 1982 by James Merrill.

Marianne Craig Moore, literary executor for the estate of Marianne Moore, for permission to reprint "Chameleon." Lines from "Marriage" and "In the Days of Prismatic Color," reprinted with the permission of Simon & Schuster from *Collected Poems of Marianne Moore*, copyright 1935 by Marianne Moore; copyright renewed © 1963 by Marianne Moore and T. S. Eliot. These extracts of poetry reprinted also by permission of Faber & Faber, Ltd., from *Complete Poems of Marianne Moore*.

"What Are Years" and lines from "In Distrust of Merits" reprinted with the permission of Simon & Schuster from *Collected Poems of Marianne Moore*. Copyright 1941, 1944 by Marianne Moore; copyrights renewed © 1969, 1972 by Marianne Moore.

Rozanne Knudson for permission to quote from *New and Selected Things Taking Place* and *Iconographs*, used with permission of the literary estate of May Swenson.

Doubleday & Co. for permission to quote from Walter Kaufmann's translation of Goethe's *Faust*. Copyright © 1961 by Walter Kaufmann. Reprinted by permission.

THE WORK OF POETRY

PART I

Poetic Substances

CHAPTER ONE

The Work of Poetry

A poet's work can appear to be very strange. It can look, for example, like a manual laborer's utter respite from work (sitting in a rocking chair, thinking, remembering, muttering, humming), even as his or her playtime manual labor isn't in fact either labor or work. And as mental work it is not institutionalized, at least in contemporary terms; when poets are asked by another kind of mental worker, such as a scientist, what their "field" is like, the question almost embarrasses, for the only appropriate answer might be "oats" (at least in re the *avena*—Milton's "oaten flute" of pastoral poetry). Among the reasons poetry isn't a field like many public and academic enterprises is this: unlike science, for instance, wherein even revolutions don't lead to Terrors and self-defeating reaction, in the realm of true poetic art there is no progress within the institution, just as there is no democracy. Or rather, art serves democracy by not being egalitarian. This is, of course, a complex issue. Poetry can exemplify a nobility of expression all the more important in a democracy that sees socially preserved, postfeudal nobility of lineage as a horrible travesty of what an evolved idea of what is outstandingly human might mean. Poetry is a realm in which elegance supplies, rather than vitiates, power of the best kind—power to make and change rather than (in the tunnel vision behind the current official talk of academic literary studies) power over people.

The view that there is no institutional or social progress in the arts was brilliantly propounded by the great essayist and social and political radical William Hazlitt in "On Why There Is No Progress in the Arts," in 1814:

The diffusion of taste is not the same thing as the improvement of taste; but it is only the former of these objects that is promoted by public institutions and other artificial means. The number of candidates for fame, and of pretenders to criticism, is thus increased beyond all proportion, while the quantity of genius [at the time this word meant "originality"] and feeling remains the same; with this difference, that the man of genius is lost in the crowd of competitors, who would never have become such but from encouragement and example; and that the opinion of those few persons whom nature intended for judges, is drowned in the noisy suffrages of shallow matters of taste. The principle of universal suffrage, however applicable to matters of government, which concern the common feelings and common interests of society, is by no means applicable to matters of taste, which can only be decided upon by the most refined understandings.

But if there is no progress in the realm of art, there is always a continuing task, and a poet is like someone in a quest story, for whom the end of the journey—finding the treasure, killing the dragon, exploring the cave, rescuing the distressed person from herself, unmasking the powerful deceiver—always results in the discovery of a new sort of task that had never been set before. To most people, it may not even look like a task. The unthinking, active person, the Alexander in us all, cuts the Gordian knot. The natural scientist in us all studies its structure, tries to conjecture the sequence of moves incurred in tying it. The philosopher may ponder the relation between those last two formulations. The poet gazes at the Gordian knot, sees that it is gorgeous, and then wonders what it *means.*

Moreover, poetry always has to struggle to shake off the mold of institutionalization that threatens to cover and poison it. It always remains a great functioning critic of what is humanly amiss in the palaver of institutions—churches, states, armies, academies, salons, convention halls, etc. It is always the best antidote to ideologies, partially because it is always insisting, with Emerson, that all sects are graveyards of the imagination. ("A Sect or Party is an elegant incognito," he says in his journal, "designed to save a man from the vexation of thinking.") This is even true of literary ideologies; Hemingway once observed that to belong to a "school" of writers is a confession of failure, and institutional enemies exist in the name of literature as they do in the name of other local deities. That is why, I suppose, the best poets of the English language from the sixteenth century on have always expressed such irritation at the hordes and schools of bad poets, who shape most readers' view of what poetry is and cause true art to be unrecognized for what it is. And that is one of the reasons many poets have thought of a history of poetry and of poetic lineage and affiliation independently of the history of literature, and of what

Matthew Arnold once wrote of as "a saturnalia of ignoble personal passions, of which the struggle for literary success, in old and crowded communities, offers so sad a spectacle."

Science, as I hope I understand it, has the continuing task of refining its formulations, so that useful, productive working hypotheses may lead to the emergence of facts that will show significant parts of those hypotheses to have been temporary fictions. This is perhaps a matter of immutable process, rather than naively construed *progress*. My late friend Irving Howe recounted in an epigraph to a book of his essays the old Yiddish story about a man who was hired by a little town to sit outside its gates and wait for the Messiah. When he complained that the pay wasn't very high nor the work very interesting, he was told, "No. But it's steady." The steady work of much human seriousness—in art, philosophy, and science—is made more interesting because of the mobs of false messiahs always presenting themselves at the gates. Poetry's steady work also involves constant walks around the periphery of the town and constant discoveries of new gates to sit at.

Poetry's steady work often involves the rescuing of the nude body of what is eternal from glitzy fashionable clothing—both Truth and Venus were represented in art as nude figures, and Truth and Beauty are always misleadingly clothed. The Beautiful, in the later eighteenth century, was in danger of being confused with the Picturesque, which had itself developed as a mode or style from the originality of earlier conceptions. A more poetic notion of the Sublime, with its built-in reminder that there had to be something a little confusing (to the senses) and a little scary—in the strictest sense of the word, awful—about Beauty, came to replace it. Their were later romantic elaborations of this notion—even to Charles Baudelaire's presentation of energetically manifest ugliness as the enemy of mere prettiness, not of true beauty.

But if a conception of beauty and its power often embarrasses modern discourse, a conception of, say, nobility fares even worse. When we hear public discourse invoking nobility, we hold the speaker guilty of being a liar, a knave, a fool, a con man, or a politician until proved innocent. But nobility is not what is represented by public statuary, flags, or statuesque oratory. Yet, as Wallace Stevens said,

> There is no element that poets have sought after, more curiously and more piously, certain of its obscure existence. . . . [And, he went on] Pareto's epigram that history is a cemetery of aristocracies easily becomes another: that poetry is a cemetery of nobilities. For the sensitive poet, conscious of negations, nothing is more difficult than the affirmations of nobility and yet there is nothing that he requires of himself more persistently, since in them and in their kind, alone, are to be found those sanc-

tions that are the reasons for his being and for that occasional ecstasy, or ecstatic freedom of the mind, which is his special privilege.

(Perhaps some of you have been mentally adding, "And science is a cemetery of truths.") The "negations" Stevens invokes are those necessary tools of the free, skeptical modern spirit. We all recognize them. But we can be trapped in their use. The American imagination is so accustomed to the creative spirit of debunking that we forget our landscape is now littered with pompous, ugly statues of that national hero, De Bunking. The little boy throwing the snowball at the top hat becomes himself in a generation or two a sacred cow. The romantic and modern antihero is now a tired figure of the heroic in our fictions and has begun to reek with the same inauthenticity against which he was originally conceived by great writers like Diderot, Lermontov, Byron, and Balzac. So that the work of poetic originality is always in some way a job of restoration.

Part of art's steady work is devoted to trying to save art from the false versions of itself that human institutions are continually spawning. Real poetry always presents the paradigm of a general human struggle to make itself understood—not in the sense that it is inarticulate and struggling for communication, but in the sense that it is not what most people will think it is. That is why there has always been a difference between poetic *rivalry* and poetic *enmity*. Poetic rivals—precursors, a few contemporaries—are in fact part of one's imaginative family. A poetic vocation consists partly in the discovery that although one has been born into a forceful and consequential biological and social family group, one is actually an imaginative foundling, or perhaps even a changeling. Indeed, as John Dryden in the late seventeenth century originally put it—and Harold Bloom with Freudian insight has reformulated it—there is a sort of family romance that embraces serious poets and their serious poetic forbears.

But a daily poetic life has nonetheless to be led among the institutions of literature, which includes, alas, the institutionalization of bad poetry. There is a powerful record of arguments against confusing true poetry with mere literature that happens to be in verse, however pretentious it may be. These have been advanced by Sir Philip Sidney, Edmund Spenser, John Milton, John Dryden, Alexander Pope, William Wordsworth, Percy Bysshe Shelley, Ralph Waldo Emerson, Robert Browning, William Butler Yeats, Wallace Stevens—great poets writing as critics. A sociologist, or the IRS, will agree that anyone is a poet who has published in some sort of journal a minimal number of writings identified only by their jagged right-hand edge—the printer's term is "unjustified," as it was the old Calvinists', but I am delighted to take it as an aesthetic one as well. A real poet will not be happy with such a convenient formulation.

But there are many sorts of legitimate difficulty with talking about poetry as an enterprise. In recent public symposiums, it counts as one of "the arts," which

I suppose it is. And yet in the United States today, public celebrations and bene-factions of "the arts" seldom involve anything involving the reading of books, let alone their knowledgeable and thoughtful consideration. Perhaps, too there is something in the relation of poetry to the other arts that is analogous to the relation of mathematics to the sciences. Bacon, in that fabulous, original grant proposal directed to the whole seventeenth century, *The Advancement of Learning,* distinguished between what were manifestly two modes of writing, but that I take also to differentiate two modes of thought:

> Methods are more fit to win consent or belief, but less fit to point to action; for they carry a kind of demonstration in orb or circle, one part illuminating another, and therefore satisfy; but particulars, being dis-persed, do best agree with dispersed directions. And lastly, Aphorisms, representing a knowledge broken, do invite men to enquire farther; whereas Methods, carrying the shew of a total, do secure men, as if they were at furthest.

A scientist might read this as a paradigm of inductive method, the "aphorism" being the imagination of hypothesis, while the process of verification is the "method." A poet might construe the terms as suggesting poetry and philoso-phy, poetry inviting imaginative and moral inquiry, raising questions about aspects of nature that never appeared to be there until they were strangely pointed out. Stevens also remarked that "a poet's words are of things that do not exist without the words." This entails a notion of the *thingness* of words that ordi-nary discourse might find peculiar. But it is even stranger than that. Poets engage words not only for what they designate but also for all the ordinarily irrelevant phenomena they exhibit, both phonologically and in their form of written inscriptions. When we use words we want them to work for us, but we are stern taskmasters and don't want to know about their lives and families and histories. That two words might rhyme, or alliterate—or that two nouns might sound as if they were the present and past tenses of the same verb—are irrelevant to what ordinary discourse, or all but poetic writing, would want to do with them.

Some of this could be put another way: suppose that every expository use of the phrase "for example" were sung to some tune or other, either well known or else so conventional in type that its character and flavor were immediately apparent. And suppose the philosopher invoking the example were unaware of this, or else, if conscious of his unavoidable singing, insisted, "Don't pay atten-tion to anything but the words."

POET: Don't sing, then.

PHILOSOPHER: (a) I'm not singing.

    or (b) I'm not really singing.

or (c) I can't help it.

or (d) Go away, don't bother me.

For better or worse, the poet's kind of attention to words is such that he always hears the melody. The chief thing Robert Frost could say about poetry was "that it is metaphor, saying one thing and meaning another, the pleasure of ulteriority." And this ulteriority starts with words themselves, and the motives for, and ways of, using them.

The education of a poet often begins with a certain kind of estrangement from his or her language itself, dialectically coupled with a certain kind of deepened attachment to it. Art in general grows out of a development of—rather than maturation *out of*—certain aspects of childhood. Just so with poetry and the language games children play: in growing up we all learn more and more how to work with language, and words become utensils for us. But for poetry, the words become, as I have suggested, a little more like people, certainly like literary—as well as merely written—"characters." It is not in an early love for truth, nor for persuasion, nor even for order, that poets emerge, but in a love of language. That, ultimately, language can be coaxed into strange sorts of truth-telling is never the point at the beginning.

"True art," wrote Proust, "has nothing to do with proclamations and is accomplished in silence." It is a silence increasingly rattled by the din of inanity, but in any case, when poetry proclaims anything, it is never in the literally hortatory mode of public proclamation—"Hear ye, Hear ye, Readers will henceforth believe in what is being chanted here." So, too, a more radical extension of this in W. H. Auden's celebrated "Poetry makes nothing happen," which is an important admission for a poet who had once been so political, and later on so homiletical. But for late twentieth-century poets as different from each other as James Merrill, May Swenson, A. R. Ammons, Geoffrey Hill, John Ashbery, W. S. Merwin, and Anthony Hecht—poets of a very different sort from Auden (and it might be added, to Auden's great credit, the poets who learned most from him were all of very different sorts)—those four words, "Poetry makes nothing happen," could mean something of another kind. Auden meant perhaps what John Donne called "an ordinary nothing," the nonentity that leaps up at us when we try to condense and make more pointed the rather bland observation that poetry doesn't make anything happen. But the "nothing" that poetry makes *happen*—causes to have occurred in the world—is the something of fictions, the stories that adhere to things and places and people in the way lasting names do, utterly changing something of their palpable natures. This comes back again to Wallace Stevens's remark about "things that do not exist without the words."

That is how *The Odyssey* comes to be as much part of the real, the natural world, as the Aegean Sea; Spenser's Bower of Bliss as present as any place where we've had sex with someone we shouldn't have and didn't realize we shouldn't have; Whitman's "Song of Myself" as much of a given as Highway I-95. But in all this, the operative words are "make happen." The "making" that poetry is— and that the word itself means in Greek—is a making of, in and out of, language. But the fiction that the made language itself makes to, causes to, happen may lie beyond that. In any event, the work of—and with—the words is always going on, in real poetry, in the service of fiction. But it is solitary, if not lonely, work and there are no palpable institutions involved.

So perhaps poetry is not a field of endeavor or an ordinary kind of enterprise at all. The question that a bureaucrat or journalist might ask, What has been happening in it? could be answered simply, I suppose: There are a number of really fine poets in the United States, all at the height of their powers—offhand, I should say about a dozen. There are also hundreds and hundreds of people who write verse, and who publish it in very little magazines often exclusively devoted to verse. The number of good readers of poetry is very small. I don't refer even to people who may buy books of poems by famous poets because they feel they ought to, or that it might help define what they might very well call their "lifestyle." Publishers know that most people who buy serious books don't necessarily read them. Although many books may be on the shelves, there is an absence of poetry in many cultural places where it used to be in evidence. University curricula in literature are increasingly uneasy about it. School-children are no longer required to commit poems and passages of verse to memory. College students are no longer trained to read it closely as a first step toward more extensive and elaborate construing of literary and nonliterary texts. University teachers-in-training in most graduate programs feel more and more that the study of poetry per se is marginal, and when poetic texts are studied, they are, like novels and plays, little blobs of condensed contextualization. For many schoolteachers and bureaucrats and poetasters outside the academy, poems are little blobs of sentiment. Criticism in the first instance consists largely now of adducing the manifest or latent evidence, in the poem, of the repressive nature of the society in which it was written. In the second, it consists too often of glossing it, in the psychobabble that has largely replaced the mildly religious popular discourse of an earlier time.

A popular error underlying this second or unacademic view has it that the work of poetry is the expression of feelings. The matter of a neoclassical ideal of representation being phased out historically by a romantic one of expression— the mirror giving way to the lamp, in the figure that M. H. Abrams made so compelling more than forty years ago, was for a time an important model for literary history as studied in the universities. I am not referring to its concern here but rather to a received view that "the truest poetry" is not "the most feigning" as Touchstone ambiguously put it, but perhaps the most complaining, or at any rate speaking for the most metaphorical or even physical pain (which may have become the most privileged and sanctified of human experiences in contemporary sentiment).

But save for *ow!* or *ouch!*—for groans of pain, grunts or cries of orgasm, gasps of fear, bellows of rage, sobs of grief, laughter of being tickled—which might conveniently be called unmediated expression of something felt, I would maintain that most of what is called expression is in fact representation. And that what we call "feelings" are often complex mixtures of physically defined emotions like those above with thoughts, beliefs, ideas, and representations of another order. A common tendency is to say that knowledge we might "have" (within us?) is *represented* discursively, but feeling is *expressed*. To say that emotions are often fictional entities, created by poetry, which have become conventionally embraced and even incorporated might sound like bargain-basement deconstruction or easy perversity. True, the icon of our conventional valentine or card-pip heart can be considered as the picture of one of the most hallowed of those fictions. But when we "express" a thought, a hypothesis, an inference, a fear, a particular pleasure, we are perhaps using the term to mean "represent." The work of poetry is not to try to say what *ouch!* or Horace's *eheu* or the Greeks' *pheu!*—or *aiai* or *oh*, or *ah*, or *oi*—"say" so purely and authentically. Poetry can be what emerges through a complex structure of channels and falls and pools carefully contrived and yet yielding always to discoveries occasioned by the act of construction. What leaks out of the helpless agent is not poetry.

True poets may nonetheless have constituencies of various sizes, and of various sorts, some embracing such misapprehensions and some not. Robert Frost, for instance, was a great poet whose large adoring audiences mostly couldn't tell what a poem was; he courted them nevertheless, by presenting his own poems to them as if they were simpler, and far less interestingly "ulterior," than they were. Wallace Stevens, during most of his life, had no constituency and a small readership. But all the important poets of the next generations were reading him all the time. "Deep calls to Deep," wrote Emerson in his journal, "and Shallow to Shallow." Any consideration of the wide realm of the shallow would be a matter of the sociology of literature, which I have not wanted to discuss. And yet that the number of serious readers of poetry should be so shockingly smaller than the number of purported and not only self- but mutually designated poets cannot really be surprising in a culture that cannot produce textual or computational literacy or the simplest grasp of geography or history in more and more of its wretched schoolchildren every year. For serious readers of poetry must have read a very great deal of it—particularly the great poetry of the past—and must have keen auditory and rhetorical perceptions; they must know and care what knowledge is; and they must on no account have a tin ear for human reality.

As will be seen—even more from the essays that follow than from the previous observations—I've always been something of a moralist. In this regard, my most important poetic "teacher"—that is, an older contemporary poet a good deal of whose work I had so committed to memory that its voice, the poems' versions of *his* voice, I carried in my head—was W. H. Auden. I remember puzzling out a difficulty none of my friends seemed to hear in a famous line of his at the very end of his important poem in memory of William Butler Yeats, written in 1939 about seven months before the German invasion of Poland and the start of World War II. (Earlier in it he says, "In the nightmare of the dark / All the dogs of Europe bark, / And the living nations wait, / Each sequestered in its hate.") The poem is full of the sense of poetry's being able to make nothing happen. It ends with the couplet enjoining the living poet he has been addressing to "In the prison of his days / Teach the free man how to praise." Why did free men have to be taught to praise, to praise anything? And if they did need to be taught, why should poetry have to do the teaching? But brooding about this led me to a half-formed conception of how "praise" had become as disfigured as nobility or beauty—that when magnified praise looked more and more in the world like thousands of Heiling arms at a Nuremberg rally, free men must find it revolting. So true praise, as a continuing human act, continuingly elevating—rather than debasing—for the spirit of the praiser, requires some imaginative reconstruction work.

I think it may be a certain inability to take many formulations of ideas at their word, so to speak—the inability not to find peculiarities, strangeness, ambiguities, even in the most ordinary words and expressions—that allows for the development of a poetic ear as a sort of compensatory mechanism. It is a machine for handling your uncertainty with. And certainly our childhoods are always alive with analogous moments—misconstruings of canonical recitations like the Pledge of Allegiance or hymn texts—that go out like the light of fireflies as we grow up. But these, along with children's word games, their first delighted grasp of disrespectful—and eventually, dirty—parodies of official, sacred, or patriotic songs, are in fact the templates for poetic art. (All poems, for example, can be considered as providing new words to an old tune of some sort, but in such a way that if the words are right, the tune will never sound quite the same again.)

As a formal—that is to say, institutional—teacher, I have come to highly regard poetry's role as an informal one. I certainly don't mean by that anything like a didactic function, although there are ancient and medieval traditions of versified treatises and instruction manuals, and early astronomical works like those of Aratus in Greek and Manilius in Latin were in epic meter. Much less do I mean some sort of literal moral treatise. Poetry teaches by parable, and, moreover, some of its parables are about itself. "Life," says Emerson in "Experience," "is a mixture of power and form, and will not bear the least excess of either."

One of the ways in which you learn this, learn the domestic economy of balances and trade-offs here, is not just from poems, but by the very nature of what poetry is. Bad poets, whether in flabby and inane free verse or uptight and inane pentameters (or, increasingly more likely, in doggerel rhymes that don't scan) are all "formalists," to this extent; even if they declare themselves to be loyalists of a Party of Power rather than of a Party of Form, their very conception of how poetic power operates and is manifested will turn out to be encoded in tired, formal gestures.

All real art provides an ever self-correcting model of what good human work is, in that it keeps faith with the spirit of play while never regressing into it and teaches by complex example and ad hoc analogue, rather than by precept. This is also true, I think, of science, and philosophy, and the writing of history, however more turned and twisted the tales of fiction may be. But not to be able to tell the truth "slant" may mean inevitable lying somewhere down the line.

The great work of poetic criticism is, I think, always to be telling the tale of that tale. It starts from the first bit of impassioned and indubitably loaded retelling or recitation of what the reading eye has seen and heard. From the point of view of humanistic scholarship this is rather like the best sort of art historian's engaged and caressing ecphrasis, or verbal description of a painting. And it remains in part estranged from the writing it attends to and in part in kind, in the best of ways like poetry itself.

CHAPTER TWO

Originality

Some thirty years ago, on Third Avenue in the fifties in New York City, there was an Italian restaurant of an older-fashioned sort—Neapolitan in cuisine, with the cooked tomato heavily in evidence—and marked by white tile and bentwood chairs that had not yet become newly modish. It was called, simply, "Joe's," and at the time I speak of, the eponymous owner (and author of the rather unoriginal name) retired. He sold his location, lease, stock, and what I believe may still be called "goodwill" to someone else, and "Joe's" continued to flourish, but without Joe. After some years of presumably unsatisfactory retirement, said Joe decided to reenter his former profession, and opened up a new restaurant, some blocks to the north of his previous one, but called, again, "Joe's." After a short time, his successor at the old place of business decided he had better annotate the text of his house's name, and changed it to "The Original Joe's." Had *Joe's* here been italicized, or enclosed in quotation marks, there would be little of interest in these events; but the ambiguity that in fact resulted (from the absence of this distinction between what the logicians call "use" and "mention") suggested that the restaurant was that named for the original Joe. The original Joe, however, was now the proprietor of simply "Joe's." When both these houses produced branches, the literary, moral, and religious problems of priority, authenticity, primacy, derivativeness, novelty—in short, of the Protean transformations of the concept of Originality itself, blossomed in low-comic profusion.

I want to raise some questions now about the several modes of originality invoked by the several Joes, and in so doing perhaps to touch on some aspects of Greatness in literature and of the nature of Tradition. I should like, in so doing, to begin at the beginning, with the Original Event, the origination of everything, but I am afraid that I neither will nor can. Will not, because it is traditional with subjects of heroic proportions to begin in medias res, in the midst of things, as do all the epics from Homer on. (And, as we shall see later on, there is some relevance here to the opening of Genesis.) Cannot, because in any case *the* Beginning is elusive in many ways—not merely because of problems of history or nomenclature involved in chickens or eggs coming first, but even more because all accounts, descriptions, analyses, let alone all fables, are doomed to start thrust, as Spenser said of it, "in the middest."

The original *Beginning*, the first word of the Bible, is a problematic one. Genesis starts out in the Hebrew with a grammatically mysterious "In the beginning of —," without any object. (The word *b'reshith* is apparently always in the construct state, as "in the beginning of the reign of —" elsewhere). This tempts translators to fill in the blank (e.g., Msgr. Ronald Knox's fine "In the beginning of time,") but one is left with a feeling that even the original Beginning of Beginnings suppresses *something*. Consider, again, the middest, in a great novelist's most reticent opening, the epigraph to *Daniel Deronda:*

> Men can do nothing without the make-believe of a beginning. Even Science, the strict measurer, is obliged to start with a make-believe unit, and must fix on a point in the stars' unceasing journey when his sidereal clock shall pretend that time is at Nought. His less accurate grandmother Poetry has always been understood to start in the middle; but on reflection it appears that her proceeding is not very different from his; since Science, too, reckons backwards as well as forwards, divides his unit into billions, and with his clock finger at Nought really sets off in medias res. No retrospect will take us to the true beginning; and whether our prologue be in heaven or on earth, it is but a fraction of that all-supposing fact with which our story sets out.

We might dispense with the problem of openings, of course; like Dr. Johnson giving what appeared to be an unproblematic kick to a palpably para-Berkeleyan stone, we might observe that *any* beginning is *the* beginning of whatever commences therewith.[1] Indeed, it is just that claim that any beginning may validly stake out, the claim to being *the* beginning—at least of whatever occupant of a space of time that beginning initiates, which lies so close to the heart of my subject, that of poetic origination. It is like the claim made by one meaning of the word *original*—the meaning that clings to our thoughts of independence, noncontingent selfhood, privacy of our own experience, creativity, some of which the eighteenth century called "genius"—to legal proprietorship of the word's extension.[2] (Most recently, in the part of the twentieth century dominated by the ideologies of modernism, a dogmatically narrow construction of "novelty" has been put on this notion of "originality.") This is a claim, too, that an older, earlier use of the word, which still hangs around for special purposes, is an unlawful usurper. For that earlier use insists that *its* meaning of the word *original*—initial and initiating, source, primary, earliest causal—is indeed, in just that proper sense, the "original" one. A *source* is, literally, a point of origin of a stream, the point at which water rises and bursts out of the ground, a fountain or spring. The water that flows from such a source is conducted along the trough of a stream and partakes not of the fountain or spring. The water that flows from such a source is conducted along the trough of a stream and partakes not of the fountainhead itself, but of its container, the banks of that stream as well as the forces acting upon it once it has ceased gushing and gone on to flow. (Even the sparkle or bubbling we see in it, even the "white water" that occasional rocks may make, is at best an artificial souvenir, a kind of inadvertent echo of the original bursting forth.)

"Origin and tendency are notions inseparably co-relative," writes Wordsworth in his "Essay on Epitaphs": "Never did a child stand by the side of a running stream pondering within himself what power was the feeder of the perpetual current, from what never-wearied sources the body of water was supplied, but he must have been propelled to follow this question by another. 'Towards what abyss is it in progress? What receptacle can contain the mighty influx?' "[3] And yet the beginning, says Plato in *The Laws*, "is like a god who dwells always with us." The literal source may not survive in the flowing stream, but we hear rumors of it in the water's noisy hearsay.

The linguistic source of our very word *origin* is in the Latin *oriri*, "to rise," used first perhaps of the sun or moon coming up; with this is connected *origo* as a source of water (whence the common phrase *fons et origo*). The etymon, incidentally, of our word *source*, *spring*, being Latin *surgere*, to "leap up," itself from *sub-regere* or "upright-going." Other streams branching out from the river of "arising" are the "orient" of the east and its originating place of the sun's shining (there is more of a sense of the German *Morgenland* for "east" in our "orient" that might be guessed), and even of the *rivus* of *stream* itself. Our metalanguage for talking of the histories of words seems engulfed in its own tropes. But certainly the phenomena of moving water retain an original idea for us, figures of spring, stream, and pool haunting our language and remaining central in our unavowed modern mythographic manuals. Originality is water coming up from underground; the sound of the flowing water is discourse, derivative both historically and rhetorically as if, in the rhetoricians' terms, *elucutio* flowed from the source of *inventio*. That noisy flow of language may become stilled in a pool of silent consciousness, with its ancillary tropes of surface and depth.

We could pursue the origin and course of all the words with which we engage on such pursuits, but we would bring back from that quest only a shadowy light to cast on our concepts of firstness. (Our necessary distinction between *literal* and *figurative* is fraught with figurative dangers.) A sense of "rule" is there in the Greek *arche*—as if the name and position, say, of an "archon" did not derive from his original power, but vice versa—but *arche* as "Beginning" is what somehow took the semantic lead. *Prime, prior, first, before* all seem to come from that Indo-European base of all those prepositions *prae, pro, per* meaning "forward" or "through," etc. Only the archaic English *erst* and later *early* arise in a hypothetical Indo-European **ayer* of "morning." Depending upon whether we privilege the phenomenology of ordinary usage or the guerdon of etymological quest, the current meaning of the etymon can be seen as figurative or literal, as original or derived. Even Samuel Johnson, perhaps the only total literalist ever to write greatly of literature, must accord to common parlance the shadowy virtue of being figurative. In his preface to *A Dictionary of the English Language* he avers that "the original sense of words is often driven out of use by their metaphorical acceptations, yet must be inserted for the sake of regular origination. Thus I know not whether *ardour* is ever used for material heat, of whether *flagrant*, in *English*, ever signifies the same with *burning;* yet such are the primitive ideas of these words, which are therefore set first, though without examples, that the figurative senses may be commodiously deduced."[4]

But all this points toward the question Nietzsche raises: "What indication of the history of the moral ideas is afforded by philology, and especially by etymological investigation?"[5] One answer would have to involve the contention for authority of two "originalities"—the prior etymon, hidden from all but the philological hero, of the fresh, present, colloquial use, the original object of language acquisition.

Yet here again we are turned back toward the very problem of our formal subject. Even etymology itself, the life cycle of words, metamorphosing from egg to larva, pupa, and the winged creatures who fly about our own speech, unfolds into the same battle between the originalities we have touched upon already. Modern linguistic theories, following Ferdinand de Saussure, distinguish between *synchronic* and *diachronic* analyses of language—building models of a language's structure either without, or with, regard to the history of that language's sounds, patterns, meaning, and uses. For example, we can analyze written English synchronically—without regard to the history of speech and writing—and observe that we have a ridiculous redundancy in that the signs *ph* and *f* designate the same phoneme, /f/, and that *ph* might well be dispensed with. Diachronic analysis adds another dimension to our model of written English and observes that *ph* and *f* inscribe two different elements, the first occurring in words imported from classical Greek only. For the diachronic eye, the difference between a word as spelled with an *f* or a *ph* covers a taxonomic distinction; for the synchronic one, spelling *fotograf* with *f*'s merely violates a convention that has been kept up by a silly code of manners. For synchrony, the structure of *what's there* is authoritative and, in our first sense of the word, "original," even as *speech* is held to be original (by structural linguists of the American school) and writing derived. For diachrony, historical priority is prime.

Diachronic or historical semantics is the mode of thought that so nobly and intricately contends with the synchrony of our own everyday experience and our sense of it. We think of a *text* as something written or transmitted with some sort of authority, but the diachronic bore sitting next to us at dinner insists that a *text* is something woven, because it descends etymologically from the Latin for *web*, something woven, the rhetorician Quintilian pointing out that it was a trope when applied to something woven out of language. Indeed the bore will go on, if not silenced, to remark that it's not in the least strained or picturesque for a critic to talk about the texture of a poem, or other literary work, even though it might seem metaphorical for us ordinary wielders of modern meanings. For journalists or writers of instruction manuals, a knowledge of a word's prior meaning and derivation would be crippling; in writing, they had best learn to forget what is known about that. Not so for poets who, if they are to be more than journalists in verse, had better contain their own boring philological dinner partner, always contending for authority with the unhistorical consciousness.

Nowhere is all this more obvious than in the poetics of proper names. Plato in the *Cratylus* treats meaning in general as naming, and yet our own narrowly synchronic relation to personal names diminishes, rather than expands, meaning for them. Giving names is essentially poetic work. Emerson in "The Poet" cites the poet as "the Namer or Language-maker, naming things sometimes after their appearance, sometimes after their essence, and giving to every one its own name and not another's, thereby rejoicing the intellect, which delights in detachment or boundary." Nietzsche sees the assigning of names as a mark of originality, perhaps as a result of being able "to see something that has no name as yet, and hence cannot be mentioned although it stares us all in the face."[6] In a midrash on Genesis, Adam's ability to do just this–what the more originally created angels fail in that story to do–is perhaps a mark of his true originality. The Hebrew Bible is full of etiological fables about naming persons and places, although in the King James Version, that seminary of our poetic language, the point of many of these are lost. For example, try to imagine the following fragment of narrative in French or German translation: "She had two sons, and she named the first one *Bill*, saying 'Here is what my husband owes me for the pain of this birth'; and the second one she called *Will*, saying 'In him is indicted the legacy of my Desire?' " The pun in the first case (let alone the overloaded doubled one in the second) would be lost, together with any higher critical supposition that the doubled Bill and Will were probably born not of woman, but of two different poetic name-fables told about one historically "original" William. (It is tempting to think of the paired invaders of Britain, Hengist and Horsa—"steed" and "horse" in modern Germanic languages—as being a bilingual gloss on the name of only one warlord.)

Mythographies have frequently performed the inverse procedure, telling the interpretive story of a name as if thereby bestowing it anew, which is essentially poetic rather than historical work. Thus some interstellar chronicler of naming, confronting that of New Haven's High Street, ignorant of the normal English prototype of its name, could suggest that it was so called because, a century or more ago, undergraduates would meet there early in the morning and greet one another with the call of "Hi!" or "Hi, there!" The Hi!-street became, through pedantic redaction, "High Street"—or some say (the chronicler might continue in the Renaissance mythographers' formula) "in some of its secluded places mid-twentieth-century students would, with the aid of various pharmaceuticals, get 'high' there." Such glosses are inherently poetic.

In romance, the occasion of naming is often a crucial piece of action. Since narratives can handle unnamed persons or places for a considerable time before having to christen them, the moment—as well as the scene—in which a name is revealed to a reader is itself potentially allegorical matter. *The Faerie Queene* overflows with such instances, and Spenser's almost Joycean interlinguistic punning is used primarily to generate complex, allusive names. For a rationalist, names are really common nouns properly designating particular persons, devoid of all powers save that of simple designation, and any ancillary qualities they possess cast shady and illusory patterns of color on reality. "Names to men of sense," says Halifax "are no more than fig-leaves; to the generality they are thick covering that hide the nature of things from them." This voices a sort of Baconian view of the traps of language generally. But another tradition dwells on the opacity of names and what they *mean* in the specific sense of what they predicate of their designees. These meanings hide in the form of a conventional name, and thus, for Cicero, the etymon of a man's name was one of his attributes as a person. But again, the purely linguistic character of names—regardless of what they might say about their givers or bearers—can give them a status of another sort. Sir Thomas Browne's burial urns cared too much for bodies and not enough for more soul-like names:

> What time the persons of these ossuaries entered the famous nations of the dead, and slept with princes and counsellors, might admit a wide solution. But who were the proprietaries of these bones, or what bodies these

ashes made up, were a question above antiquarism, not to be resolved by man, nor easily perceived by spirits, except we consult the provincial guardians of tutelary observers. Had they made as good a provision for their names, as they have done for their reliques, they had not so grossly erred in the art of perpetuation. But to subsist in bones, and be not pyramidally extant, is a fallacy in duration.

Names are clearly more original in some senses than ashes of bones in bodies. Christian names, in American English today, paint a wonderful picture of American or—as we shall shortly see—late-coming, originality.

The names we are given are transparent and empty: the meaning of a personal name is, for us, the person it designates. There are many Nancys, Sallys, Scotts, and Wendys, not to speak of people of either sex named Leslie or Wednesday. And while Miltons, Sidneys, Irvings, and misspelt or perhaps inadvertent Shelleys will perhaps suggest synchronically that the bearers represent one component of the population, and Billy-Jim another, Brian or Kevin will tell one nothing about the surname to follow, as indeed they would have forty years ago. In America, one could have in the past observed that anything ending in -a (evolving thereby a ghost of the romance second declension of nouns of the feminine gender) could be a girl's name. Now one observes that anybody can be named anything. Rather than being governed by the kind of code that prevailed in France until recently, by which one had either to name a child with one of a limited stock of traditional—usually saints'—names or (thanks to the revolution) a Gallicized form of a classical one, American naming is now totally *original*. Parents write the poems of their children's names as if there were no linguistic history—as if all names had a synchronic dimension alone, and as if awareness of what felt like "a good name" or "a nice name" were an analogue of a sense of clothing style, an eye for proper length of hemline or the cut of jeans (itself today controlled by pressures on young people to wear not clothes but articulated brand-name labels and to surrender the tiresome mental task of assessing what one might really look like *in* something).

Speaking simply synchronically, we might observe that many linguistic and stylistic conventions are like the devil—their power seems to inhere, or at least entail, the notion that they don't exist. And so with conventions of naming: the phasing-out of the many Barbaras and Shirleys of my generation, the rise of the recent Jason, not to speak of Sharons, Karens, Sherrys, Terrys, and so forth, variously spelt, seldom affects the word-hoard of parents in the act of titling, or writing an important text of, their children. They do not opt for fashionableness but, in their response to shared original stirrings, simply perpetuate its shapes. One can choose, perversely, to violate certain conventions: I once knew a cat named Fido, and there could be dogs called Bossy or horses called

Pussy, but simply as a result of their perversity, such names would be very literary and allusive.

But what happens when the shadow of the diachronic falls across the simple candor of present experience? Then we are told that *Nancy* is "really" a diminutive of *Anne*, as *Sally* is for *Sarah*; and while Bettys of the past four hundred years were made aware, as part of their cradle lore, that they were "really" Elizabeth but "called" Betty or Beth, Bess or Elspeth (thus engendering the Mother Goose riddle about the four girls who were really one), rare is the Peggy or Polly today whose birth certificate reads, as it "really" should (according to the spirit of old Originality), "Margaret" or "Mary." The awareness of *Scott, Keith*, and *Wayne* as surnames that eventually got to be so commonly applied that most people don't think of them as surnames, but rather as Christian names in their own right, is the diachronic consciousness, speaking in the same voice that tells us that "silly" *originally* meant (and came to mean)"foolish." Here again, we have the contention of the *primary* ("dammit, *Wendy* is a girl's name, period"—or maybe, succumbing to a learned impulse, "perhaps it's short for *Gwen* or *Gwendolyn*") with *prior* ("the first person ever called *Wendy* was a man, J. M. Barrie, in fact, called by the daughter of a friend [William Ernest Henley] 'Friendy-wendy' and, thence, 'Wendy'; to please her, Barrie called the heroine of Peter Pan, 'Wendy' "). Which *sense* of the name *Wendy* is really its "original" one: the primary, from which, perhaps, fussy, learned knowledge, interfering with the clarity of our conceptual morning, will "derive," as it were, a belated fable of the name's "meaning" or "origin"? or the "original" one in the older sense, the anecdote of its first bestowal? In that pure morning light, the child's sense of the *origin of Isaac* is the moment in the playground when the little boy on the swing next to him first produces his name and age.

But—it might be interjected here—not the surname: perhaps the reason for the disappearance of surnames from young persons in the past two decades has been nostalgia for the world of the playground, an attempt to regain, far too late in the day, that lost morning. Perhaps it is a repudiation of family (and hence, of the shadow of diachronic *originality*) as being in bad taste. Surname alone puts you in a historical line; Fred or Betty alone puts you comfortably in a present crowd, if that's where you feel comfortable. But in any event, as my recently-graduated-from-college daughter has pointed out to me, the reversal of familiar and intimate has taken place with first-naming (our only *tutoyer* in English): you now only learn Tom's surname after some degree of acquired intimacy, whereas in the past you got to call Mr. Smith "Tom" only at that same point. This seems to happen with bed, as well as with address: social acquaintance might, along the winding road to deep intimacy, eventually uncover an original—the old, last, original—place of meeting. Today, the last act has become a version of the original flowers and candy that each partner now gives to the other, in a dance of courtship that might lead both into a misty, visionary chamber called a "relationship." The origination of sexual intercourse has become for many merely social intercourse, an opening rather than a quested-for source.

At any rate, the origin of "Isaac" is that moment in the playground, particularly for the modern American child, whose mental life has been piously laundered of all knowledge of scripture. Thus in the sadder afternoon, he may come to make other connections: "Isaac" is—diachronically—not just *that* boy but others, occasionally, as well. If pursued sociologically, they may be of Jewish parentage; if pursued further, the "original" Isaac may enter his world, together with the Bible's etiological anecdote of his birth. *Isaac* may then come to "mean" laughter, as well as "meaning" something like "named after the biblical Isaac." Finally, curious learning will reveal that Isaac's father, named Irving, is "really" named Isaac (at least, Yitzchak in Hebrew)—that the English surname, made famous by the pen and the stage to newly arrived immigrants, seemed a better option for an "American" version of the Hebrew name than the canonical English translation, *Isaac*, either because it was unknown (Eastern European Jewish immigrants had seldom heard of the Reformation, of something called the Old Testament, which was a translation of the Hebrew Bible into vernaculars, etc.) or because Isaac was, quite plainly, an American Yankee, very Protestant name. Working through to the Original Isaac, then, involves surrendering the originality of the primary scene of naming (the playground) to the primal one (of the Bible). One might say that it involved a revisionary reading of the text of the name *Isaac*—but more of this later. It certainly illustrates once again the contention of the *primary* and the *prior*, the originalities of the *now* and the *then*.

Students of rhetoric may perceive a related question here of the contention for some kind of originality between the literal and the figurative in general. Oscar Wilde's devastating reminder of how originality and authenticity inhabit the domain of the figurative puts one view almost unanswerably: "Through the streets of Jerusalem at the present day crawls one who is mad and carries a wooden cross on his shoulders. He is a symbol of the lives that are marred by imitation." Certainly, the occasion of a sudden rhetorical revision—a moment of literalizing a figurative usage, of, in wit, reviving a "dead" metaphor—can have a quality similar to a moment when, in etymology, a prior claim to originality dawns upon the user of a word. In the episode in Genesis 18 that tells of the birth of Isaac, the Lord appears as one of three men to Abraham and Sarah in the instance I mentioned just before. But imagine that, instead of laughing— in the words of the King James version—"within herself, saying After I am waxed old shall I have pleasure, my lord being old also?" Sarah were to have said, "What a laugh! That's absolutely divine!" and one of the two angels standing there with the Lord would have responded, "Divine, indeed!" The word *indeed* means "in literal, rather than figurative, word" (deeds are words only in the Hebrew *d'varim*, not in the Greek *logos*, with fascinating consequences for poetic history yet to be mapped). The world of deed feels itself to be refined into metaphor, or generally *troped*, by the world of word; and yet how often does the dialectic not reverse itself, and the language not claim primacy, originality even, over the things?

The Marxist dogmatist has behind him a major Enlightenment tradition of grounding originality in the hard, entrepreneurial earth. A consideration of this might start with the famous series of revisions, in *Faust*, of the opening of the Fourth Gospel:

Geschrieben steht: "Im Anfang war das Wort!"
Hier stock ich schon! Wer hilft mir weiter fort?
Ich kann das Wort so hoch unmöglich schätzen,
Ich muss es anders übersetzen,
Wenn ich vom Geiste erleuchtet bin.
Geschrieben steht: Im Anfang war der Sinn.
Bedenke wohl die erste Zeile,
Dass deine Feder sich nicht ubereile!
Ist es der Sinn, der alles wirkt und schafft?
Es sollte stehr: Im Anfang war die Kraft!
Doch, auch indem ich dieses niederschreibe,
Schon warnt mich was, dass ich dabei nicht bleibe.
Mir hilft der Geist, auf einmal seh ich Rat
Und schreibe getrost: Im Anfang war die Tat! (Pt. 1, 1234–37)
[It says: "In the beginning was the *Word*."
Already I am stopped. It seems absurd.
The *Word* does not deserve the highest prize,
I must translate it otherwise
If I am well inspired and not blind.
It says: In the beginning was the *Mind*.
Ponder that first line, wait and see,
Lest you should write too hastily.
Is mind the all-creating source?
It ought to say: In the beginning there was *Force*.
Yet something warns me as I grasp the pen,
That my translation must be changed again.
The spirit helps me. Now it is exact.
I write: In the beginning was the *Act*.][7]

This ends, finally and triumphantly, in "the deed," and is quoted pointedly by Friedrich Engels: "Act comes before talk. Talk of a god shut from the whole world is a gratuitous insult to religion. In the beginning was the deed. Act comes before argumentation."[8] The crude reduction of the chain and its figurative completion occurs in the witty line from Trotsky's *Art and Revolution* (for all its brutalities, by the way, a far more human document than anything produced by the hideous engines of "relevance" and socialist realism)—"In the beginning was the Deed. The word followed as its acoustic shadow." And yet it is the Marxist dogmatist who will, when criticizing the significance of a deed—say, one of charity—imbue with an almost Platonist priority the abstract and troped march of historical necessity, saying (and perhaps some older readers may remember this *"subjectively* this is helping a poor family to survive and even improve themselves: *objectively* it is staving off a major readjustment of such matters, a mere treatment of symptom, a kind of bribe." But he will *not* say, *"literally,* this is helpful; *figuratively,* it hinders," but that is because of a commitment to a set of metaphors about what reality is.

Plato himself may in fact be the originator of the rhetorical strategy of such inversions, particularly of internalizing figuratively a quality deemed otherwise objectionable in order to legitimate a new fictional entity then declared to be the true one. The *locus classicus* of this might be Socrates's substitution (*Phaedrus* 276 A), for the inauthentic silent icon of the written word, its "legitimate brother" *(adelphon gnésion):* "The word which is written with intelligence in the mind of the learner" [Hos met epistêmês graphetai en tê tou manthanontos psuchê]. This move is recapitulated in St. Paul's "our epistle written in our hearts, known and read of all men" (KJV II Cor. 3.2)—as opposed, here, to mere actual letters of recommendation. (The almost cartoonlike eating of the scroll [KJV "roll"] by Ezekiel speaks for a cruder concept of internalization, which I shall not explore here.) And indeed, Plato's device is reflected in the whole pattern of internalization of the prior, by the latecomers claiming to restore the original, of the Reformation. In Plato's celebrated fable of writing (in the *Phaedrus*) the Egyptian King Thamus scorns Toth's gift of newly invented writing because it will, he insists, supplant memory (just as we might say that the card-size wallet calculator might destroy mental arithmetic). But this is almost like saying that figurative writing existed in memory before Toth crudely (in both senses) *literalized* it in writing, and that the internal form remained higher and preferable to its representation.

Thus finally, consider the contention between the schools of Freud and Wilhelm Reich about the metaphors of "superego" and "muscle tone"—in the language of the former, a physical matter can be the figurative actualization of a psychic one; in the language of the latter, concepts of the psyche get construed as evanescent superstructure. Even in the language of mathematical logic, ordinary readers can find this suspiciously poetic—as we shall come to see it—contention for originality between abstraction and concreteness, as in the terms *model* and *interpretation:* a set of axioms presented in an algebraic sort of nota-tion, talking only of sets and members will be a *model;* what it is true of—say, lines and points in the plane of Euclidean geometry, of a particularly constituted political party, say, with strict rules about membership on committees—would be called an *interpretation* of the model. And yet literary readers, full of com-mitment ever since Bacon to the priority of the particular and its power to orig-inate, to engender the generality, would think informally of the axiom system as an interpretation of some model minute particular, a mental portrait—and hence an interpretation—of the physical presence of the nude model of daily life. Here again, in the contention of the origins propounded by deduction and induction, we seem to find a shadow cast by our subject.

All our originations exist in the shadow of a First one. One of the ways in which the latecomer makes his claim to originality and copes thereby with the silent but immensely powerful claim of the earlier, is by a strange process—a usurpation of *priority* by a different sort of *primariness*. Consider the business firm of Bloggs and Son, established 1921 by the original Bloggs, an orphan. His son, young Bloggs, who expanded, diversified, etc., is full of entrepreneurial imagination—he brought (and here, competitors and associates all agree) an originality to what had *originally* been merely solidity and steadfastness. Not to speak of priority, of course, but it's indeed the case that we so often prefer not to speak of it. At any rate, the family firm of Bloggses suggests more interesting and complex relations than those prevailing between the two sorts of Original Joe in our earlier example. The originating Bloggs gives way to a more original conception of the nature and function of Bloggshood. We might want to observe, by way of making generational peace, that young Bloggs's originality is a version of the older one's—that he takes after his father not literally (he would himself have to be an orphan founder to do that) but figuratively. That is, he revises the original conception of the shape, size, and activity of the busi-ness, by revising, as it were, the text he inherited, by reading it in a different way. (Other theorists of tradition—those without the least desire to make peace of this sort—might want to recall the joke of a walleyed, magnificently musta-chioed comic named Jerry Colonna, who, I have heard, said, "When I was born they didn't know whether I was going to take after my mother or my father, but I surprised them. I got out of my crib and took after the nurse." Such jokes tend to have deeper thrusts of significance than appear in their tip-of-the-iceberg points: the later resembles the prior, and attempts to overtake, in order to pos-sess it—here not erotically, but self-creatively.)

The house-organ history of Bloggs and Son seems a far cry from the story of greatness and originality in poetry and art in general, my putative subject. But John Dryden, himself a poetical descendant of near and distant founding Bloggses, put the matter clearly: "Milton was the poetical son of Spenser, and

Mr. Waller of Fairfax, for we have our lineal descents and clans as well as other families. Spenser more than once insinuates that the soul of Chaucer was transfus'd into his body, and that he was begotten by him two hundred years after his decease."[9]

It might also be observed that young Bloggs, if asked to characterize his interpretation of the firm he inherited, would call it a *new* version. His father's old, surviving business associates, now put out to pasture perhaps, might ruminatively conclude that it was a *late* version. "The best is yet to be," says Browning's Rabbi Ben Ezra, "the last of life for which the first was made," thus giving to lateness a privilege that theologies accord only to last things (in the case of Logos, first and last). But we should still find it a problem to decide whether sundown is an improvement over the dawn, just as the succession of young Bloggs could move into a host of stances towards his father. Later *versions*, like Junior Bloggs, have a different mode of self-assertion from that of later *phases*, like late age or afternoon. There is a great moment in book 9 of *Paradise Lost* when Satan, descending into Paradise on a second visit that will culminate in his destruction of it for human habitation, is momentarily smitten with its beauty:

O Earth, how like to Heav'n, if not preferr'd
More justly, Seat worthier of Gods, as built
With second thoughts, reforming what was old!
For what God after better worse would build?

Notwithstanding his tragic and characteristic mistake here (what enterprising, competitive, mortal, fallen *human* "after better worse would build"—syntactically as well as temporally—save to deceive and thus build better fraud; not what *god*), I have always felt Satan's claim that Mark II is always preferable to Mark I, this year's model to last year's, rumors of the origination of all modernisms, and of the New World, America in particular. The New Law for that other great modernist, St. Paul, claims not to destroy but to fulfill the Old one. And so with all new dispensations, Junior Bloggs kicks farther upstairs to be chairman of the board and points out that he is not terminating, but fulfilling a managerial passage. The American Adam, as R. W. B. Lewis pointed out so well, is not merely a late version of the old revision. "Early in the morning," writes Walt Whitman in 1861, "Walking forth from the bower refresh'd with sleep, / Behold me where I pass, hear my voice, approach"; it is only six years later that he revises the first line into the one we know today, "As Adam early in the morning," making it not perhaps earlier in the morning, but rolling it back to the first, or original day. "Adam" is an afterthought.

It should be added that among the senses of "the prior," the *primary*, the authentically prototypical residing in "firstness," there is the more problematic notion of *centrality*. Emerson in *Nature* puts first things—by which he means central things—first; importance for a half-hidden agenda becomes primary, as well as epistemological rather than entrepreneurial, priority: "The eye is the first circle; the horizon which it forms is the second; and throughout nature, this primary figure is repeated without end"—or so the belated poet says, taking back from Copernicus an outrageous opthalmocentrism, and making larger concentricity a figure of derivation.

New, Old, Early, and Late—these notions are all crucial to poetic theories of origin, and their relations are best expressed by a dialectical paradigm. "Early" and "Late" are irreversible conditions, or states. *New* and *Old* (and I mean *old* not in the sense normally contrasted with *young*) are more like conferred titles. Unlike the other pair of terms, these partake of the rhetorical. It is almost as if the Late—regarding the Early with a kind of envy that causes it to avoid or repress or conveniently forget the whole realm of priority—translates the question into one of innovation. Late claims the *primacy* of New over Old, canceling the significance of temporal priority itself, as if the very relation of Early-Late were a contrivance of priority to make subjects of all followers. The New-Old relation is the rhetoric of lateness.

A diagram of these relations might look something like this:

NEW (fresh, "original")	supersedes	OLD (stale)
LATE (secondary, derived)	suppresses envy of	EARLY (primary, original)

What lies below the line, like all imprisoned fictions, will somehow get its own back, often with volcanic force. The more obdurate the denial of this underlying realm by what sits over it, the more shattering the return of the repressed. Nietzsche observes, in a note (translated and quoted by Walter Kaufmann): "The Germans alternate between complete devotion to the foreign and a revengeful craving for originality. . . . The Germans—to prove that their originality is not a matter of their nature but of their ambition—think it lies in the complete and obvious *difference:* but the Greeks did not think thus about the Orient . . . and they *became* original (for one is not original to begin with, but one is raw!"[10] This last suggestion about the evolution—or perhaps the gradual creation, as a work of art—of originality sounds surprisingly Wildean.

"Novelty" can refer to the condition that that "revengeful craving" has to settle for. Burke, in writing of the Sublime, nicely identifies novelty as the object of curiosity, "the most superficial of all the affections; it changes its object perpetually; it has an appetite which is very sharp, but very easily satisfied; and it has always an appearance of giddiness, restlessness and anxiety."[11] But this same restlessness, argues Burke, makes of novelty a useful epistemological stimulant.

There are for Burke no questions here of ancient/modern, old/new, original/derived, dead/remembered in the matter of novelty, however. It is this same revivifying sense of novelty that inheres in Edward Young's observation that "We read Imitation with something of his languor, who listens to a twice-told tale. Our spirits rouze at an *Original;* that is a perfect stranger, and all throng to learn what news *from a foreign land* . . . though it comes like an Indian Prince, adorned with feathers only, and having little weight."[12]

Innovation is itself an innovation of periods in our history that were aware of their forerunners. Writing amid a welter of novelties and projects, Bacon cautions the old against terror or disgust at the sight of the new: "As the births of living creatures at first are ill-shapen, so are all Innovations, which are the births of time."[13] William Blake, in one of his savage marginalia, writes next to this passage "What a Cursed Fool is this / Ill Shapen are Infants or small Plants ill shapen because they are not yet come to their maturity." Blake was a great melodramatist of priority, succession, and their wars, but in his rejection of the Muses—who, as you will remember are the daughters of Memory—for the daughter of Imagination as the source of inspiration, he was himself speaking the language of the New.

But with writers like Blake, we are not dealing with a modernist, or propounder of newness, but rather with that more dialectical descendant of any sort of Bloggs, a revisionist. A prototype for revisionism—in the culture of the English and German languages—is the Protestant Reformation, a late-coming that proclaims not that it is, like Satan's false construction of Paradise, a new and improved model but, with radical force, maintains that it is really, in the old sense, the Original religion. The Church, persisting in its misprision of the early, or true, church, became not only the false one but thereby the autogenetically "original" one—too original by half, in fact. Reformation claims direct contacts with the old, original Christianity and with its Old Testament parenthood—a direct contact through the genealogy of scriptural text begetting interpretation, begetting the truth of the text . . . and so on. The mere outward show of the laying on of hands was read as a piece of Roman theater, a false literalizing of the spirit of true derivation. (And how convenient for the English Church, in the late sixteenth century, to be able to use papal Rome, in reading the Book of Revelation, as the concrete interpretant, rather then the mere antitype, of Babylon-as-Caesar's-Rome.)

The older meaning of "forming again" gets lost in our clusters of uses of the word *reform;* and "seeing again" fades from *revision*, which we use to mean, in both higher and grubbier senses, "re-writing." All history is a more or less shared version of the fables of many writers. But if we connect these two senses of the word *revision*—a rewriting and thereby or therewith a seeing again—we begin to approach the question of original writings, or scriptures, which has been lurking beneath the surface of my observations from the outset.

In this regard, revisions can be of several types. One of these proclaims that a professed original is really only a very good copy (and hence, in the rhetoric of tradition and religion, a bad or evil one). Here an overtone of genuineness is heard, The use of *original* as a noun—as in reference to "an original work of art"—to mean a unique production rather than copies of it, which it, or other similar productions could engender, goes back to the seventeenth century. John Donne in a sermon explores the figure of "originals"—painted masterpieces (in the older sense) as against cheap prints:

> We should wonder to see a mother in the midst of many sweet children, passing her time in making babies and puppets for her own delight. We should wonder to see a man, whose chambers and galleries were full of curious master-pieces, thrust in a village-fayre, to look upon sixpenny pictures and three-farthing prints. We have all the image of God at home; and we all make babies, fancies of honour in our ambitions. The masterpiece is our own, in our own bosom; and we thrust in country-fayres, that is, we endure the distempers of any unseasonable weather, in night-journeys and watchings, we endure the oppositions, and scorns, and triumphs of a rival and competitor, that seeks with us, and shares with us.[14]

There seems at first to be no problem of relative value here: a "copy" is always, in some sense, a "mere" one, even if not a fraudulent candidate for originality. Yet an original can sometimes indeed be worth less than a copy: consider an indifferent, anonymous still life, copied by the young Picasso aged thirteen, say. We will undoubtedly look for traces of "originality" (later sense) in the copy, which the "original" (in the sense of being originative, or creative of copies, imitations, versions, and interpretations) could not have.

Acts of revisionary proclamation can be violent. Similarly, revelations of a prior originality of a very literal sort can be catastrophic for the later claimant, who may not even have been aware that there was a problem to begin with. Our fresh experience, our morning encounters with the first Isaac in the playground, seldom send to have their titles searched; and when a face turns out horribly to be mask, a name a collection of different sorts of roles and meanings, a song a coded message, a pointless tale a parable, we feel all the explosion of the sudden birth of something geologically new. The conflict of the *prior* and the phenomenologically or experientially *primary* for the trophy of *Real* is not limited, as we have seen, to etymology. An old and well-loved song like "Loch Lomond," with its sentimental injunctions about taking high and low roads, was apparently sung as a Jacobite hymn in the eighteenth century—the "low road" being death without dishonor, the "true love" never to be met with again being the king—

or the pretender if you take the high road of English—and so forth. But we learn all this with an amused shudder, as if discovering a flaw in an otherwise perfect gem of uncompromised "song."

A certain kind of poetry that we may all have known and loved as a sort of scripture can have its *originality* (not its genuineness, nor its authenticity, mind you) dissolved in an instant. I am thinking of that example of scripture that most of us who grew up in English-reading households probably share, regardless of what is nominally religious heritage. That loosely controlled and limited canon called *Mother Goose*—many of us possessed versions of this canonical collection of varied nursery rhymes, assembled on the same pages, in the same typeface, and illustrated in the same graphic style. (Indeed, seeing different illustrations in a friend's different edition of *Mother Goose* could cause minor revisionary shock.) We didn't know the authorship of "Oats, peas, beans, and barley grows" (or why one sang and danced it) nor of "Lucy Locket lost her pocket" nor of "Bobby Shafto's gone to sea," nor "Mary had a little lamb," but it was as if they were all Homeric, if indeed stitched together, then stitched together so far back that it was all one.

But then cracks appear in the integrity of the *Mother Goose* scripture. At first they are minor; a certain wonder at how Lucy Locket could lose—and Kitty Fisher find—a *pocket* is dispelled when some knowledgeable adult, or a dawning inference drawn from the reading of some historical novel, explains that, in the sixteenth through eighteenth centuries, pockets were not sewn to their plackets, or pocket-slits, but rather hung, separate purselike bags, under skirts, and could be easily lost and found. (The degree to which illustrations over the past hundred years would either mystify or explain such archaisms could be a fascinating little iconographic study.) But what were originally timeless girls of fable, Lucy and Kitty, become merely, and specifically, historical. And yet subsequent revisions would be cataclysmic: the biblical higher criticism of the folklorists, of the sort collected by Iona and Peter Opie in *The Oxford Dictionary of Nursery Rhymes*, for example, would not only reveal that Lucy Locket and Kitty Fisher were being identified as courtesans of Charles II's day as early as the 1840s (but more likely of the eighteenth century, and perhaps related to one of the heroines of *The Beggar's Opera*). It would also reveal that Bobby Shafto was a parliamentary candidate in 1761, and that if he had a predecessor of the same name, the song was at least revamped for the occasion. Oats, peas, beans, and barley may very well have been the order of crop rotation somewhere in the south of England (in which case, the "Nor you nor I nor nobody knows" has an air of vegetative mystery). The overtones of allusion to the Blessed Virgin and the Lamb of God in "Mary had a little lamb" are the casual inadvertence of a strongly Protestant Boston lady in about 1830 (rather, I suspect, than a glaring case of the return of the repressed). But the Mother Goose corpus, once the grown child is capable of scholarly scrutiny, has now become a gathering, with a textual history. In its earlier, scriptural innocence, the verse had all, had other—in the later sense, "original"—meanings. Moreover, those meanings had developed by association with the other verse, and the slowly accumulating Mother Goose canon, with editor after editor at work compiling it, interpreted all the other songs—the residues in rhyme of forgotten or abandoned or superseded matters of adult interest—by their very inclusion in the canon per se. But now, with what Wordsworth called the "fallings from us, vanishings" of knowledge, the scriptures, the secular psalms and chronicles and proverbs of childhood are revealed as literary texts; those prior, unfallen readings were themselves grounded, it now turns out, in acts of textual faith.

Now many books make scriptural claims—claims staked to unassailable originality of the prior sort. But one moment in Emerson refuses to allow this: "Every book is a quotation; and every house is a quotation out of all forests and mine and stone quarries; and every man is a quotation from all his ancestors." This even goes so far as to deny that a unique human individual, whose originality as a being one would have thought him to hold canonical, escapes allusiveness any more that a text can. So, too, Melville, in a meditation on originality in *Pierre:* "The world is forever babbling of originality; but there never yet was an original man, in the sense intended by the world; the first man himself—who according to the Rabbins was also the first author—not being an original; the only original author being God . . . never was there a child born solely from one parent; the visible world of experience being that procreative thing which impregnates the muses."[15]

But despite these insistences, and the observation in the Tunisian writer Albert Memmi's *Scorpion* that "the first text was itself a commentary," poetic tradition has always fashioned for itself a "first text," holding that there is an Original—a true scripture on whose cover is written in letters beyond the fire "The Revisionary Buck Stops Here." Such texts—Homer, and that Mother Goose-sort of anthology compiled over the centuries loosely called the Bible— are indeed our great Originals. Rousseau, Herder, and Vico on the origins of our writing aside, our poetic history all derives from these sources. But Memmi's point is not idly taken—we have to face one fact about our very greatest poems, a fact that they themselves face and evade in a complicated ballet of avowal and suppression. These all-but-originals, these most original or new or novel works, creative, innovative, powerful, and subsequently generative of later texts in their own right—these are the most allusive of our books. Two of our major biographers of fable, differing as they do on the role of hypostasized convention and unappealable will, agree on this. "Any serious study of literature shows that the real difference between the original and the imitative poet is that the former is more profoundly imitative" (Northrop Frye). "The covert subject of most poetry of the past three centuries has been each poet's fear that no proper work remains for him to perform" (Harold Bloom). The origins of romanticism's new sense of originality in conceptual history as well as in this dilemma have been brilliantly studied by Thomas McFarland,[16] and other sources in the earlier fictions of English poetry are given resonant readings in Leslie Brisman's *Romantic Origins*. But this is not a problem of romantic poetry alone: from Sappho through the present time, noble poems have been built out of poetic footnotes to what has preceded them. They are all written by Junior Bloggses, wandering far to found utterly new firms, praying at the outset that they may not founder.

Nathaniel Hawthorne, in a strange sketch called "Buds and Bird Voices" in *Mosses from an Old Manse*, reminds his readers and himself that even our most natural figure of renewal, spring, comes to us enmired in derivations. "On the soil of thought and in the garden of the heart, as well as in the sensual world, lie withered leaves." But these leaves are not merely "intermingled memorials of death" lying somewhere between those barren leaves of imaginative literature and the renewed, reimagined, and retroped leaves "of grass"—texts of bodily life—of Whitman. They are emblems of past experience and the humus of our poetic inheritance,

> . . . the ideas and feeling that we have done with. There is no wind strong enough to sweep them away; infinite space will not gather them from our sight. What mean they? Why may we not be permitted to live and enjoy, as if this were the first life and our own the primal enjoyment, instead of treading on these dry bones and mouldering relics, from the aged accumulation of which springs all that now appears so young and new? Sweet must have been the springtime of Eden, when no earlier year had strewn its decay upon the virgin turf and faded into autumn in the hearts of its inhabitants! That was a world worth living in.

But midway through this passage, the meditation rebukes itself, making an Emersonian claim that the spirit of originality turns the whole burden of the past into tropes, and lives in the reality of its own powers:

> O thou murmurer, it is out of the very wantonness of such a life that thou feignest these idle lamentations. There is no decay. Each human soul is the first-created inhabitant of its own Eden. We dwell in an old moss-covered mansion, and tread in the worn footprints of the past, and have a gray clergyman's ghost for our daily and nightly intimate; yet all these outward circumstances are made less than visionary by the renewing power,— should the withered leaves and the rotten branches, and the moss-covered house, and the ghost of the gray past ever become its realities, and the ver-

dure and the freshness merely its faint dream,—then let it be released from earth. It will need the air of heaven to revive its pristine energies.

Hawthorne's invocation to Springtime, his muse of originality, is buried within his book of "old" stories (another volume being titled, we will remember, *Twice-Told Tales*). Earlier in our literature, this summoning up of new power comes at the beginnings of ambitious works. John Milton calls up in *Paradise Lost*'s opening invocation a new, as-yet-unnamed Muse, to aid his "adventurous song" in its pursuit of "things unattempted yet in prose or rhyme" That very phrase is the opposite of self-descriptive: "Things unattempted yet in prose or rhyme" translates a line of a predecessor, Ludovico Ariosto, at the start of his *Orlando Furioso*—"Cosa non detta in prosa mai, né in rima." Moreover, Milton's line resonates with overtones of other such claims to novelty: Spenser (most immediately for him), Boiardo (most immediately for Ariosto), Boccaccio, Dante, Statius, Manilius, Horace (talking of *carmina non prius audita*), all reecho in these words.

E. R. Curtius, in *European Literature and the Latin Middle Ages*, discusses the assertion of novelty as a traditional topos of the exordium. Since I am more generally concerned with what a great writer could mean by the use of what he knows is a convention, Curtius's learned discussion, to which we are all indebted, only raises questions; the study of conventions occurs in an atmosphere of near *pudeur* about writers meaning what they say, and great poets in particular seem to elicit interpretive angst from serious and powerful critics much more than they do from trivial rhymers, producers of mere literature in verse, who are immune to the pressures and tugs of greatness because they have no imaginative bodies at all. (But see Thomas M. Greene's great study of *imitatio* in the Renaissance, *The Light in Troy*, for a masterful consideration of these matters.)

It is as if no claim to poetic originality can be made without a concomitant avowal of the impossibility of that assertion. Milton, in mentioning "things unattempted yet," is putting the words in the invisible quotation marks of learned allusion. It is almost as if he had found a word whose usual, present meaning was "new," but whose etymon, whose root, or earlier, or (dare we say) *original* meaning was "old," and thus used that word to characterize his point.

Paradise Lost is fascinating here not only because its ambition is so great. Virgil followed Homer, and the intermediate successions were only the Alexandrian epics—cyclic poems like those that the poet Callimachus so scorned in a famous epigram (echoed, in fact, by Horace in the poem quoted above). Virgil could combine the arms of the *Iliad* with the man of the *Odyssey* in his announced scheme. Milton comes later on—and in a way that cannot be mapped simply as being further on along a line. (Greatness does not appear to diminish, like light and gravity, as the square of its distance from a prime source of originality.) In the field of forces generated by the competing claims of prior and belated, or innovative, originalities, we must consider how many different family lines converge in *Paradise Lost*. There are Virgil's revision of Homer; Dante's carefully circumscribed guidance by Virgil; the tangled thicket of relations of Renaissance romantic epic not only to the realm of medieval fable but to the classical tradition; the even more dark wood of allusiveness in which Milton's closest forerunner, Spenser, sent forth his knight of errant dream. It is not only these poems but their own allusive relations to one another that constitute Milton's covert pre-text. Covert, because great poems direct attention to their manifest "subjects," or "themes," (or, in some Silver Ages, to their "styles"?). But the deep poetic question is not so much, *What* shall I do? as *How* to do this thing? and thereby generate a "subject." I suppose I am simply arguing what has already been extensively argued, namely that for poetry, the object of such prepositions as "about," "concerning," "on" *(peri, de)* is always figurative—that a prediction of theme or subject is always a troping.

But most important of all for Milton's originality is its overt text, for it is a commentary—a midrash, or interpretive fable, rather than a homily or exegesis— of the Original Story itself. The Book of Genesis is our first story of origination, of the world, of human consciousness (a central point of Milton's commentary on it) and, indeed, of originality itself, of the first false claim to self-origination. "I am Pride. I disdain to have any parents," says the personified sin of originality in Marlowe's *Doctor Faustus*. John Donne illuminates the originality of original sin, the "radical pride," with a reminder that "we know that light is God's eldest child, his first-born of all creatures; and it is ordinarily received that the angels are twins with the light, made then when light was made. And then the first act that these angels that fell did was an act of pride. . . . So early, so primary a sin is pride as that it was the first act of the first of creatures."[17]

Later in the same sermon, Donne cries out in a kind of moral fury seemingly at his very outcry of pained belatedness: "O the earliness! O the lateness! how early a spring and no autumn! how fast a growth and no declination of this branch of this sin, pride, against which this first world of ours, *sequere*, follow, come after, is opposed! This love of place and precedency, it rocks us in our cradles, it lies down with us in our graves."[18] The whole sermon is concerned with Christ's *sequere me* (as opposed to his injunction to Satan, *vade post me*—"behind" but not "after"). Milton's vast anatomy of origination lays bare a structure of derived originals and original derivations, or present *nows* and *thens* both past (like Latin *olims*) and future. His belated account unrolls for twelve epochal books before the Original People can see how "the world lay all before them," in a final avowal of a partially redeemed but contingent originality, even as the spatial sense of the preposition "before" supersedes its temporal one.

Originality

Genesis, then, is in every respect our original story of origination. It is also, canonically, our First Text. The Hebrew Bible, particularly the Pentateuch, is to our culture what *Mother Goose* was to our childhood—canonized by tradition as an Original Text, containing an account of its own origination (the revelation of text on Mount Horeb or on Sinai), and accompanied, in part of that remarkable anthology surrounding it called by Christianity the Old Testament, by another account of its own canonization.

That account of a declared textual institutionalization is found in II Kings 22, where it is related that Hilkiah, the high priest, commanded by King Josiah to repair the crumbling walls of the Temple, finds "the book of the law in the House of the Lord," gives it to Shaphan the scribe, who reads it, delivers it to the king, and reads it again before him. In Nehemiah 8, during the rebuilding of the temple, Ezra the scribe recapitulates this by reading the law before "the men and the women and those who could understand the reading." This is a scene of reading aloud and of interpretation that virtually ordains originality for scripture.

Canonizing a text may be considered a figurative enactment, claiming to be an affirmation, of its revelation. Or, indeed, vice versa: a canonization may be viewed as a performative utterance of a type that asserts Originality (rather than, as more usually, derivative authority, or even, further down the fallen scale of Lateness, mere authenticity). From such a viewpoint, accounts of Revelation of Text are fables, or narrative tropes, of that canonization. From that viewpoint, which we might call that of poetic history, the declaration of Originality and of Unity and Truth for a text is as authoritative as Revelation itself. (Whether the performative act of canonizing a text—the assertion that "this is it, and therefore *shall* be" is perlocutionary or merely illocutionary I leave to speech-act theorist and to all heresiarchs to debate.) In any event, the fable of revelation in Exodus 19–40, and the original presentation of canonical text in II Kings and Nehemiah 8, again characteristically, the historically prior one asserts literal power over the later—the Word of God is just that, not because it is said to be so but rather demands that it be subsequently proclaimed as such. For western poetic history, the text of Homer is as original, as revealed-as-it-were, as the text of scripture. The so-called stitching together of earlier lays and songs by a community of Homeridae results, so the higher critical, modern Homeric scholar tells us, in an eighth- or seventh-century official written text. But for all subsequent Greek literature, including the mighty reticent poet Plato, Homer is scriptural, and *devant lui le deluge*. Here, in place of the story of Moses on Sinai, we have the story of a blind bard—perhaps from Chios, perhaps from Smyrna or some other Ionian city. And here, too, in place of the stories of Hilkiah and Ezra, we have the account, widespread through later antiquity, of the establishment of the text of Homer, under the reign of Pisistratus in the sixth century, and the affirmation of its unity by a prescription that the poems could only be recited entire. (One can only speculate on whether it was the effect or intention to institute, by fiat and by subsequent interpretation, a scriptural unity whose separate parts of disparate composition were thenceforth not to be considered.)

Higher criticism of the Bible insisted implicitly that in the very fact of disparate composition of the text of the Pentateuch over many centuries a process of continuing witness was indeed manifesting, rather than denying, revelation. On the other hand, traditional modes of interpreting scripture have always aimed at the promulgation of the unity of what in seventeenth-century science was called "saving the appearances" but in another sense. The magnificent structure of Psalm 19 moves from "The heavens declare the glory of God; and the firmament sheweth his handiwork. Day unto day uttereth speech, and night unto night sheweth knowledge. There is no speech not language where their voice is not heard" to the astonishing conclusion from verse seven on, concerning the Law. We tend to read it as causing, like Hopkins's "Windhover," our eyes to lower from the exultation of light in the sky in praise to the textual ground; its unity is affirmed by the sentence of Kant that, I was told in my youth, Beethoven kept by his worktable: "The starry heavens above us and the moral law within us." And yet, higher criticism reveals, the two parts of the Nineteenth Psalm are—and here I hope I can use the word with some deep ironic resonance—"originally" two separate poems, stitched together under the pressure of just that interpretive unity we traditionally give it. It is not for nothing, I think, that Psalm 19 remained a kind of set piece for Judaic textual interpretation for so many centuries: it is almost as if its cracks of origination were always in evidence, and that the plastering over of these, the work of interpretation, must needs continually have gone on.

The canonical originality of scripture is like that of the world itself, which is declared in chapter one of Genesis and subjected in our time to the higher criticism of the natural sciences. These observations on authority have come down to this matter of scriptural originality, which is yet itself only a starting point. What we mean by the Bible is itself the product of so many interpretive layers and recensions—commentaries and translations by priestly, rabbinic, patristic, reforming, and higher critical scholars—that wherever one's personal creed wishes to halt the revisionary unrolling, there will remain a palimpsest of readings. Indeed, the dry-as-dust scholarly footnotes by later writers of varying degrees of knowledge and imagination have become part of the text itself. The very format of the KJV, the Vulgate, of the masoretic text of the Hebrew Bible all cast text and later annotations into the same mold. It is an instructive experience for the unscholarly but serious reader to try to glean from a modern critical text and translation of Genesis (I have used E. A. Speiser's in the *Anchor Bible*), to reconstruct a passage or two. Thus, Genesis 16 in KJV, where the rhetorical pattern Now A, and B, and C, and D, and E "proclaims the periods of one voice":

> Now Sarai Abram's wife bare him no children: and she had an handmaid, an Egyptian, whose name was Hagar.
>
> And Sarai said unto Abram, Behold now, the Lord hath restrained me from bearing: I pray thee, go in unto my maid; it may be that I may obtain children by her. And Abram hearkened to the voice of Sarai.
>
> And Sarai Abram's wife took Hagar her maid the Egyptian, after Abram had dwelt ten years in the land of Canaan, and gave her to her husband Abram to be his wife.
>
> And he went in unto Hagar, and she conceived: and when she saw that she had conceived, her mistress was despised in her eyes.

But here is the passage following Speiser:

> Abram's wife Sarai had borne him no children. Now she had an Egyptian maidservant whose name was Hagar. So Sarai said to Abram, "Look, Yahweh has restrained me from bearing. Cohabit then with my maid. Maybe I shall be buoyed up by her," And Abram heeded Sarai's plea. [Thus, after Abram had lived ten years in the land of Canaan, his wife Sarai took her maid, Hagar the Egyptian, and gave her to her husband Abram as concubine.—Ed.] He cohabited with her, and she conceived. And when she saw that she was pregnant, she looked upon her mistress with contempt.

It is by an ironic turn of historical reorigination that *Paradise Lost*, perhaps the greatest commentary on Genesis of all, should make as a point of its "no middle style" an absorption of lengthy, glossing footnotes into the fabric of the narrative, grafting onto the Homeric and Virgilian digression the precise, anxious delineations of a later biblical scribe (e.g., the fig tree out of whose leaves the prelapsarian nudity, now fallen into the first nakedness, gets covered).

This palimpsest of readings inheres in the surfaces of all our primal works. In Nathaniel Hawthorne's *Wonder Book*, a young poet narrates the Greek myths to a group of children, his younger cousins. The stories are romanticized in an Emersonian kind of way. They take on touches of allegory from the context of natural scenes in which they are told—Midas confusing the golden and the mere metallic gold, narrated under the splendid autumn leaves of the Berkshires; Pandora as a bright, bored, curious child opening the forbidden box, her story recounted in an attic on a cold, snowy day; and so forth. He is rebuked by the children's father—a classical scholar—who objects to the wit, the quirks and, above all, the hints of moralization in the tales. "Your imagination" he says (but might he not be talking thus to Ovid?) "is altogether Gothic and will invariably

Gothicize everything you touch." The effect, he continues, "is like bedaubing a marble statue with paint." There is an irony for us in the fact that we now know that the Elgin marbles and all the "marble statues" of antiquity were indeed *originally* bedaubed with paint and that, whether Hawthorne himself knew it then or not, a classical mythological text, un-Gothicized, uninterpreted, undaubed by the paintbrush of a Homer, a Hesiod, or a Pindar, does not exist.

So too with our most original account of origination. Of all Western accounts of creation, chapter one of Genesis is uniquely original in being acataclysmic—in not representing the creation of the world as a violent act in which prior forms or beings are ripped, wrenched, or broken apart, as in other Semitic and Indo-European accounts. Light is called, not torn, forth. The waters are separated benignly, and the upper ones do not preside (save in later, anxious interpretations) over those below. The so-called Priestly author of Genesis 1–2.4a himself may have written as much as five or six hundred years after the great author of the so-called J source, and perhaps even in revision of him. That is, the hexameral account, with its lovely unfolding of what comparative religion would suggest should have been a catastrophic act of creation, may itself have revised the J author's originally less "original" account. Certainly the worlds of Genesis 1 and Genesis 2—the unnamed Paradise of first harvesting as opposed to Eden's as yet unbudded spring differ as much with respect to ripeness, climate, and scene as by their differing accounts of the origins of woman. I personally like to think of the later author of Genesis 1 as living at the time of Ezra, perhaps a child held by the hand of two adults who were caused to understand the reading of an earlier text.

Perhaps it is as well that we conclude this exploration with this paradox of biblical originality—with the more "original" (in the sense of "novel") first chapter of Genesis as possibly deriving its uniqueness from a revision of some canceled original first chapter we now lack. But the necessities of *daubing* will always be with us (whether taken in its etymological sense of "whitewash" or not). The proclamation of canonical originality for a text is itself a basic undercoat of paint. It is perhaps in the nature of our greatest and most originally original text—the writing of the J author or "Yahvist"—that its very originality is too bright to bear, and that the many-colored daubs that are the history of reading so as "to give the sense and cause to understand" are the shadows and stains by means of which we can see at all.

NOTES

1. The relation of the scheme of openings in fiction to the trope of beginnings is another matter. See Edward Said's *Beginnings* (New York: Basic Books, 1975).
2. See David Bromwich, "Reflections on the Word 'Genius,'" *New Literary History* 17 (autumn 1985): 14–4.

3. William Wordsworth, *Prose Works*, 2 vols., ed. W. J. B. Owen and J. W. Smyser (Oxford: Oxford University Press, 1974) 2:51.

4. Quoted in *Samuel Johnson*, ed. Donald Greene (Oxford: Oxford University Press, 1984), 317.

5. Friedrich Nietzsche, *The Genealogy of Morals*, tr. Horace B. Samuel, essay 1, para. 17, n.

6. Ibid., *The Gay Science*, tr. Walter Kaufmann (New York: Vintage, 1974), 218.

7. Johann Wolfgang von Goethe, *Faust*, tr. Walter Kaufmann (New York: Doubleday, 1961), 153.

8. Quoted by John Brooks Wheelwright in his note to his own fine poem, "The Word is Deed," in *Collected Poems*, ed. Alvin H. Rosenfeld (New York: New Directions, 1971) 149. Wheelwright claims *Anti-Dühring* as the source for this, although I have not been able to locate it there.

9. John Dryden, "On Translating the Poets," preface to *Fables Ancient and Modern*, in *Essays*, Everyman Edition (London, 1912), 273.

10. Quoted and translated by Walter Kaufmann, *Nietzsche*, 3d ed. (Princeton: Princeton University Press, 1968), 154.

11. Edmund Burke, *A Philosophical Enquiry into the Origin of Our Ideas of the Sublime and the Beautiful*, sect. 1, "Novelty," ed. J. T. Boulton (Notre Dame: University of Notre Dame Press, 1968), 31.

12. Edward Young, *Conjectures on Original Composition: In a Letter to the Author of Sir Charles Grandison*, (London, 1759), 12.

13. Francis Bacon, "Of Innovations," in *Essays, Advancement of Learning, New Atlantis, and Other Pieces*, ed. Richard Foster Jones (New York: Odyssey Press, 1937), 70.

14. John Donne, sermon 4, folio of 1660, in *The Sermons of John Donne*, 10 vols., ed. George R. Potter and Evelyn M. Simpson (Berkeley: University of California Press, 1955), 9:8–1.

15. Herman Melville, *Pierre; or, The Ambiguities*, ed. Henry A. Murray (New York: Hendricks House, 1949), 304f. Also see chapter 44 of *The Confidence-Man*.

16. Thomas McFarland, *Originality and Imagination* (Baltimore: Johns Hopkins University Press, 1985), 1–30.

17. John Donne, sermon 72, folio of 1640, in *Sermons*, 2:294.

18. Ibid., 2:296.

CHAPTER THREE

A Poetry of Restitution

"The sole advantage," said Santayana, "in possessing great works of literature lies in what they can help us to become." Those of us who were nursed by modernist literary and artistic theory find this difficult to assent to. Not only does the "sole" bother us, but a modernist aesthetic engaged in a kind of well-intentioned witch-hunt against the didactic, and the very notion that poetry was, should, or even could be of moral importance lies somewhere between the distasteful and the dangerous. That poetry could exercise this moral function in any other than a didactic way was indeed grudgingly admitted, if only in the deep pieties of the idea of a "pure poetry," that found an exemplary, if not an otherwise instructive, virtue in the avoidance of the ethical, even as of the discursive.

So-called poststructuralist avoidances of the poetic could not even see any virtue in this, since they would hold such exemplariness to be untenable. But more recently, Richard Poirier radically shifted the grounds of what might, after all, be called the postmodern. He focused an attack not on representational or prophetic and instructive stances and functions of poetic texts themselves, but on particular ways in which they are misinterpreted and invoked in dubiously literalized arguments about literature's improving or restorative power for our democratic culture. He is surely right in repudiating such bad claims; poetry can only help us to become "something" in figurative, rather than in literal, ways. Even poems allegorize smaller elements of their own discourse, and propound parables, but not instruction manuals, from the text of their own language. Just as poems do not literally argue, give empirical explanations, interrogate, answer or command, create and so forth—as we have seen—they do not literally teach.

Robert Frost's sonnet "The Oven Bird" exemplifies the ulteriority of poetry's didactic agenda by the way in which it hides its lesson. That "singer everyone has heard, / Loud, a mid-summer and a mid-wood bird" elicits a consideration of the complexities of heralding the middle of the journey. No lark of morning—invisible sound from a great height—nor nightingale of darkness, no Hardy darkling thrush, singing at the dawn of a new century for which even two cheers would seem uncalled for, the oven bird sings of midpoints, of halfways. In the indiscernible muddles of the middles of times and places, the appropriate music is that of epistemological musing, not of fanfare or of dirge:

The bird would cease and be as other birds,
But that he knows in singing not to sing.
The question that he frames in all but words
Is what to make of a diminished thing.

But what does that mean? "What do you make of an X?" asks both how you construe X—interpret or understand it—and what you construct *with* X, or *from* it. Given the poem's concern with the bird's discourse ("in singing not to sing"— he is more of a philosopher than a poet), the two meanings of the phrase occur to a reader in just the order given above. But again, what would be a concrete instance of such a question? The old schoolroom joke about optimists and pessimists is transcended here by a meditation on the problem itself: "Is the bottle of summer half full or half empty?"—not just "anything that has been diminished" (like, of course, summer) but a *thing* that has been made less of one. The characterization of the question is itself characteristically ambiguous, for "to make of" can mean *to construe* or *to construct with,* and the question itself can be something like "At a midpoint, is the glass of summer half full or half empty?" or "Well, now, what shall we create out of *this?*" The terminal, rhyming stress-position of the word *thing* gives a kind of voice to the substantive weight of the word—its tone of meaning underneath the words, as it were—and the more casual reading ("what to make of a *diminished* thing") has to hear the reminder of "a diminished *thing.*" The poem itself is not only the interpreter of its own text, making, as Frost's best critic Richard Poirier says, "an inquiry into the resources of the language it can make available to itself" but also the teacher of its own text as well.

What the sonnet conceals, though, is the bird's precise mode of discourse, perhaps because as a poetic fiction he is a very guarded, transumptive revision of a particular earlier bird, Wordsworth's throstle in "The Tables Turned":

He, too, is no mean preacher;
Come forth into the light of things,
Let nature be your teacher.

The last of these lines is phonologically unfortunate, and its awkwardness casts modern doubt on the authenticity of the expostulation. But Frost hides the natural folklore that conventionally renders the song of the oven bird—a particularly shrill kind of warbler—as "Teacher! teacher!" (which he would not want to allow to rhyme with "preacher," in any case). Ultimately, the question framed by the poem is what to make out of what we make of our own teachers. The bird's song "in all but words" tropes speech. Poetry, in all but schools, tropes teaching.

The moral consequences of myth-making lay ignored in an overview of centrality in poetry that averted its gaze from Spenser, from Milton, from Shelley, from Browning, and that celebrated the sustaining power of irony and purification—or, in the words of Joyce's young poet seeking to escape his backward time and place, "silence, exile and cunning." I shall speak now of contemporary poetry, and, since my subject is its moral dimension, shall refrain from any further revisionist history of our poems and our theories of them. Anyone with an interest in poetic eras rather than modern modes may, I suppose, think of my observations as applying to the beginning of the period of the postmodern. I should rather present them as a meditation on three very consequential poems by three of my poetic contemporaries, written over a period of not quite twenty years.

Before we possess ourselves of these texts, however, we might consider a related matter that in the past decade has troubled the American poetic conscience. Let us start with what remains an essential and unimproved formulation of the trouble:

Though loath to grieve
The evil time's sole patriot,
I cannot leave
My honied thought
For the priest's cant
Or statesman's rant.

If I refuse
My study for their politique,
Which at the best is trick,
The angry Muse
Puts confusion in my brain.

The evil time is 1847, when "the famous States" are "Harrying Mexico / With rifle and with knife"; the place is Concord (in the only region of the nation in whose dialect *patriot* rhymes with *thought*); the voice is Emerson's, bridling at the injunctions of poetic visions itself to engage with subjects—the Mexican War, the Fugitive Slave Laws—that are bound to result in bad and possibly even meretricious poems. Like another famous poem of politicopoetical ambivalence written not quite exactly two centuries before, this one commences with its author's somewhat nervous acknowledgment that he can no longer "in the shadows sing / His numbers languishing." Like Andrew Marvell's "Horatian Ode," the irregular ode inscribed to the abolitionist William H. Channing (the "sole patriot") concludes not in fence sitting but in coming down on one side; we learn that the crossing has only been authenticated by the apparent seesawing along the way. In both poems, too, the ironies lead to further ironies—it is hard to believe that Emerson was not thinking of Marvell, whom he so greatly admired and elsewhere echoed—and the very vacillations lead to the resolutions. Emerson rhetorically demands of Channing

What boots thy zeal
O glowing friend
That would indignant rend
The northland from the south?
Wherefore? to what good end?
Boston Bay and Bunker Hill
Would serve things still;—

He concludes with an almost apocalyptic formulation: "Things are of the snake"—not just things in the nowadays of an early agricultural-military-industrial complex beginning to tear itself apart. "Things" comprise the very world of material concern and gain within those interstices meditative and even self-critical vision is afforded. In Marvell's poem, the muses appear to be forsaken at the beginning. In Emerson's, a more complex fiction is needed: the muse, confusing and confused, is angered at having to make a choice between truth and beauty, somehow aware that in choosing either, not the one rejected but the chosen value itself will be thereby betrayed. And yet, at the end of the poem, "The astonished Muse finds thousands at her side"; but we may be sure Emerson's muse could hardly be surprised that a powerful proclamation would have many adherents—rhetoric, as we know, is very gluey. Her astonishment is somehow at the poem itself, which, by the very act of questioning the relation between moral action and the visionary imagination, has managed to complete itself successfully.[1]

There surely have been great political poems, in which visions of justice, living peace, or unpolluted order have not resulted in epigrams, or even in rhymed essays. (I think these last should be all the more valuable at a time like the present, when we have no major moral essayists in prose; W. H. Auden wrote our last moral essays in verse.) When a political moment can call forth mythopoeia, the muse is neither reticent nor nervous; one need never have heard of Castlereagh's oppressions to grasp the general moral truth of Shelley's sonnet of England in 1819, with its line about "Golden and sanguine laws that tempt and slay"; nor is the continuing, merely topical applicability of that line to, say, the Harrison narcotics act a test of its truth as poetry, any more than of what we might call its poetry as truth.

What is more significant is this: If one reads the poem without the topical rubric, it seems to describe a locus of resonance, a Bad Place through which some quester must pass, and not without somehow dealing with its badness. Ruled by "An old, mad, blind, despised and dying king,—" with "A people starved and stabbed in the untilled field" and "An army, which liberticide and prey / Makes as a two-edged sword to all who wield," this sick kingdom is a paradigmatic conception of greater power than the momentary rhetorical figurations of a literal polemic might be. Despite Shelley's polemical intention, his myth-making got splendidly out of hand. It is not that (and this has been remarked of the relations between Elizabeth I and Spenser's Gloriana) this poem's realm is like Castlereagh's England, but rather the reverse. The poem's vision will continue not merely to remain "applicable" to states of affairs but to raise implicit questions for intelligent readers about the nature of such applicability. What is ordinarily called political poetry will not do this.

When morality and poetry are mentioned in learned milieus today, the question of art and political commitment invariably comes up, both as part of the subject and as a cloud in which it is wrapped. During recent decades many views both morally righteous and politically correct—for the party of what we might call remembered hope to which most American poets belonged—became incarnated in verse. Epigrams, cabaret satires, pasquinades, exhortations, and editorials proclaimed the injustices, in the late sixties, both of a war and of a peace its wagers envisioned. The authors of these verses must have been of several sorts: first, those who felt that no utterance could be a bad poem if its sentiments were correct; second, those who could not believe any poem of their own to be bad; third—and here we enter a realm of moral seriousness—those who believed with half of Emerson and most of Yeats that thrusting the muse into rusty armor might cripple her and would certainly win no battles. We can be moved, I think, by the notion of a poet who felt that the only way he could expose his "fugitive and cloistered virtue" to an authenticating trial would be in being willing to write badly, if necessary, by way of bearing witness.

But poems have a kind of life of their own. If they—rather than the citizens in whose public being their creators reside—are to bear witness, it must be a figurative bearing and an image of witnessing. I take the poems seemingly called for by crises of political morality only as extreme instances, in recent American poetry, of a more general case. Few poets who responded to the call for an antiwar poem learned much from Emerson's model, but it was a time of demoralizing pressures, and few of those same writers might have responded to public pressures for moral poems of another, more venerable sort—funerary elegies, for example. I cannot see an American poet of the 1960s being urged by his or her fellows to write a dirge for his or her own dead child (although, in the present culture of complaint, it is probably happening more and more). Poems mourning one's dead predecessors have always been another matter, and the proliferating sects of poets have always shared this most solemn of liturgical forms.

The response to a call for the imagination's moral power is one thing, and I have wanted to suggest that it is never a simple matter. But it is the poem itself that shall now concern us, the poem that, in whatever its small or cool or tinted mode of glowing, stares sightlessly out at the reader from the page until some voice—although not its own, perhaps—is heard to say what Rilke heard in the presence of his stone poem of antiquity: "Du musst dein Leben ändern" [you must alter your life]. This is not to say that poets cannot—in verses of some sort and, thereby, putatively as poetry rather than generally as exhorting men—do the work that the journalist and the commentator, given the fading away of American literacy, are less and less able exaltedly to do. Sorrow and rage at injustice, or at the chill that lasts after the fading of the pained smile at ironies that seem now to inhere in events, rather than in the tropes of the writer and thinker—producing these is the bitter work of reportage. The British chaplain De Stogumber, in Shaw's *Saint Joan*, confesses that the burning he had encouraged has altered his life: "I had not seen it [cruelty] you know. That is the great thing. . . . It was dreadful . . . but it saved me," to which the poetic ironist Cauchon must respond: "Must then a Christ perish in torment in every age to save those who have no imagination?" The relation between what Yeats called rhetoric and true poetry is in some ways like the relation between the experience of horror and true imagination in Shaw's great question, to which the answer is, alas, probably "Yes." But if we do in fact need both poetry and rhetoric, we should not confuse their functions. Poems do not urge, or propound programs of deportment, or criticize in detail those already propounded. The contemporary poem, like the Renaissance one, must ultimately do its teaching, a late time of myth-making, when instead of moralizing Ovid, it adduces new mythologies in explanation of older ones.

But in order to hear the poem's command to do something about our lives, we must place ourselves directly before it, until there is no place in it that does not indeed see us. Let us start with a beautiful poem of looking and reflecting, written about forty years ago by a poet only beginning to feel his powers. A dramatic monologue in half-evaded rhymed couplets (the second line, irregular in length, rhymes with the penultimate or antepenultimate syllable of the first one), the poem is also an emblem that reads itself for significance. James Merrill's "Mirror" is truly a speaking picture: the reflecting glass considers itself, and most importantly addresses its pragmatic counterpart, an open window opposite.

I grow old under an intensity
Of questioning looks. *Nonsense,*
I try to say, *I cannot teach you children*
How to live—If not you, who will?
Cries one of them aloud, grasping my gilded
Frame till the world sways. *If not you, who will?*

The question is not intended as a rhetorical one, but must inevitably remain just that. The mirror of art held up to nature is too wise to attempt an answer, but instead continues:

Between their visits the table, its arrangement
Of Bible, fern and Paisley, all past change,
Does very nicely. If ever I feel curious
As to what others endure,
Across the parlor *you* provide examples,
Wide open, sunny, of everything I am
Not

(and what a wicked enjambment for a mirror to employ in its treatment of what seems manifestly primary to its mere echoing answer)

You embrace a whole world without once caring
To set it in order. That takes thought. Out there
Something is being picked. The red-and-white bandannas
Go to my heart. A fine young man
Rides by on horseback. Now the door shuts. Hester
Confides in me her first unhappiness.
This much, you see, would never have been fitted
Together, but for me. Why then is it
They more and more neglect me? Late one sleepless
Midsummer night I strained to keep
Five tapers from your breathing. *No,* the widowed
Cousin said, *let them go out.* I did.
The room brimmed with gray sound, all the instreaming
Muslin of your dream.

As if to answer her own rhetorical question (and we must recognize the mirror now, I think, for what she is, gilded and elegant, an extremely wise old lady, a great Proustian aunt), the mirror remembers a death. And this is the one point in her meditation at which the continuing present tense of the verbs, synchronizing all she has seen in a reflected plane, gives way to preterites. At her most frighteningly magisterial she asserts, without undue insistence, that it was she

45

∷

A Poetry of Restitution

and not the window who abandoned the mad effort of all daughters of memory to eternize human breath. (What remains eternally puzzling throughout many readings of this poem, however, is the referent of "That takes thought"—what? setting a world in order? or embracing it without caring to? This may reflect some deep ambivalence on the part of the mirror.) We notice, too, how she remarks on "all the instreaming / Muslin of your dream." *Your* dream; the window's dream is that plangent cliché of reverie, the inblown curtains enshrined in romantic paintings of meditative room interiors from Adolph von Menzel to Edward Hopper. The mirror hears the flapping of death in the darkness; she can read the emblems of consciousness that inhere even in the objects of conscious perception as no mere window can. And this is why, and the fact of death is why, they more and more neglect her.

Years later now, two of the grown grandchildren
Sit with novels face-down on the sill,
Content to muse upon your tall transparence,
Your clouds, brown fields, persimmon far
And cypress near. One speaks. *How superficial*
Appearances are!

Indeed! But the mirror's depths, her realities, are on, or at most, she knows, *in,* her surface; she, and the poem itself, shiver at the callow beauty of the young people's discovery, and when she takes up her musing for the last time, it is with a brilliant pun, what the French call a *rime riche* on the penultimate syllable of "superficial," at first almost coarsely answering the charge with a flash of *Dasein,* a gross presence, an angel of gleaming surfacing from literal depths. But then, having surfaced, it adds its light to the surface of shining discourse that is the mirror's triumph over mere openness of window, or candor of artificial light:

>   *How superficial*
> *Appearances are!* Since then, as if a fish
> Had broken the perfect silver of my reflectiveness,
> I have lapses. I suspect
> Looks from behind, where nothing is, cool gazes
> Through the blind flaws of my mind. As days,
> As decades lengthen, this vision
> Spreads and blackens. I do not know whose it is,
> But I think it watches for my last silver
> To blister, flake, float leaf by life, each milling-
> Downward dumb conceit, to a standstill
> From which not even you strike any brilliant

Chord in me, and to a faceless will,
Echo of mine, I am amenable.

Where she—or, rather, perhaps, *it* again, for we are clearly talking of poetry itself—is most transparent, the poem is most blind. It can only reflect—this mirror of art and of our highest consciousness—when its transparency, its Emersonian eyeball, is itself illuminated from within its capacity to know, by a gleaming, a shining from behind. For poetry to be a mirror, after centuries of flaking and dimming belief in its truth, it must at the very least be its own lamp as well. The images, the patches of silvery fiction that project that light forward, fall not like leaves of romantic poetry into the broadcasting wind, but down into silent darkness. And when there is nothing to the mirror but the clear glass through which the nothingness of that dark can be read, the imagelessness of that deep truth is preserved even as the truth is presented. In the last darkness, which will not be dawned upon, the mirror and the window alike are cold, smooth, unseen glass.

Merrill's mirror reveals itself first as a novelist's figure of wisdom. Then, radiant beyond the Renaissance emblem of mimetic art, it becomes the modern poem, "the poem of the mind in the act of finding / What will suffice." It is the world mirrored in the most profound way: Hester, alone with her unhappiness and that consoling image that is the legacy of Milton's Eve, cannot but unwittingly confide in the mirror even when she is most alone. We cannot talk about our feelings—and this has been true in the case of all our poetry of love, from Sappho on—without talking about talking about them, without pointing out the peculiar ways in which we must use language in order to tell the truth. Merrill's poem remains shiny, clear, framed in a gilded, semiantique meter, not in order to be itself—even for Americans, bowed under the weight of history's injunctions to be ourselves, that is not, alas, enough—but in order to mean something. *"I cannot teach you children / How to live."* But the children's response is our own, and is the poet's own, as he was coming to knowledge of what would suffice. Modernism dictated the refusal to teach, but something at once younger and more grown-up hears the voices of the children: *"If not you, who will?"* It is that enabling climate in which Merrill's poem itself seems to grow older and wiser as we read it; from a modern poem about poetry—and therefore morally pure, unrotted by didactic intention as its surface seems unflecked by expository rhetoric—it emerges as a mirror of life after all. It is in order to reflect what the cheerful, mindless window can only helplessly reveal that the mirror *reflects upon* itself, upon its own mode of reflecting. Less solipsistic than the human children who consult it, the poem comes, by being about itself, to be about everything else outside it. *That* takes something more than thought. The romantics called it Imagination.

The lessons we learn are about time, space, and reflections. We are reminded of all the mythology that lies behind the speaking mirror—the looking glasses of the nude lady who may be Vanitas or Venus, and the one who is surely truth; the mirror—whether for magistrates, or like Hamlet, "the glass of fashion" as Renaissance model or exemplar; the mirror into which it is dangerous to gaze, lest, like Narcissus, we inadvertently heed the philosopher's injunction to know ourselves, and thereby lose everything; the strong, enabling mirror held up to the goddess by Amor, an emblem of her own power; the *esoptron* (glass) of St. Paul, by which we perceive truth "darkly" *(en ainigmati)* in the riddle and puzzle by which all the half-reliable oracles speak; the mirror of modernism, and image of paradox, reversal, self-reference, and schematic mystery; the looking glass threshold through which Lewis Carroll's Alice passes into dreamily allegorical romance; the mirrors of Jean Cocteau's *Orphée*, all of which are easily unfrozen surfaces covering the many entrances to the poet's hell of self-absorption; the mirrors of enchantment and trap in romance. And finally, there are the actual mirrors, not into which we gaze or peer for specific information about our appearance, but that mirror us inadvertently—those startling, occasional glimpses of ourselves we happen to catch are always of some stranger (as the Japanese poet Hitomaro observed in a famous *tanka*), and the troped reflection is far more magical and far more poetic than the balloons or string beans into which we are satirically turned by the distorting mirrors of a carnival.

The many pier glasses throughout Thomas Hardy's poems tell primarily the tales of Merrill's window, rather than of his mirror; even the wonderful opening stanza of "The Lament of the Looking Glass" that begins "Words from the mirror softly pass / To the curtains with a sigh" seem not to be a direct precursor text, but at the most an antithetical one.[2] For Merrill's poem is also mythopoetic, in that the mirror, the wise old presence, the almost novelistic domestication, and the confrontation with the unanswering window, leave the emblem forever transformed, materially augmented. That augmentation partially exists in the dimension of the work of reflection and memory that we do in our rereading and consideration of it. The images that, Shelley said, enable language to "unveil the permanent analogy of things" can "participate in the life of truth" by making the reader into a kind of poet as well.

Merrill's "Mirror" is by no means his best poem, but it may be a central one. He went on in subsequent books to move in a Proustian direction that was quite original, and in *Water Street* and afterward he assimilated the impulses of narrative autobiography to a commanding and continuing mythopoeia. His way has been that of the mirror, not the window. His mature poetry inhabits part of that region of emblematic tale-telling that Elizabeth Bishop for some decades before her death, and Robert Penn Warren more recently, have inhabited for their major poetry. I do not refer, of course, to what has been called "confessional," that shrill and pitiful mode of contemporary verse that, neither window nor mirror, most resembles the sound of breaking glass. We can hear it, but learn nothing from it except that some disaster has occurred and that our lives are full of woe, which it seems shocking to need poetry for to inform us. The first part of Merrill's major trilogy, *The Changing Light at Sandover,* mythologizes what is in fact the Spirit of Involuntary Memory as a psychic "control" of a Ouija board. This is partially to say that the long, astonishing poem called "The Book of Ephraim" is, in almost every way, in lieu of a novel. But the mirror poem revealed a door, a hallway, down which American poetry of the next two decades would walk, not with the purpose of leaving the house and doing something outside of it, nor indeed on a nervous stroll marked by glances out of the windows in distaste. It was a walk taken indoors in an endless house, continually being added to and restored in some of its older parts, neglected to the point of near ruin in others. But to explore it, and to map it, was to map heaven and hell, now and then, all the overlays that enable us to read the raw sense of the physical map of life itself.

Now a map of any region may show a way through it, and perhaps what there is on, and by, the way. But there are times of terror, times when not merely *things,* but everything, is of the snake, and when the spirit cries out for rescue. But where there is no palpable sublime, when there are no summits of nobility from which the imagination may come in a rush of assistance, where do we turn? The American Imagination is such a latecomer to the feast of grandeur! We have no crowns; a top hat marks merely the next man to take a pratfall. Our mythologies, the tales our grown-ups live by, tell of Founders spawned of Olympus: our mature faith is in the knowledge of Parson Weems's mendacities. Our commemorative statues are bronze gobbets of dishonor: rarely is one redeemed when the unveiling of morning shows a Chaplinesque tramp still asleep in its hard arms. For the nourishment of our minds there is still humor, but for hearts, the momentary beauty: "Dolphins still played, arching the horizon / But," Hart Crane concluded sadly, "only to build memories of spiritual gates."

So that when "things are of the snake," a second task is set for the American poem. Let us take for a second text a poem of the 1960s, one that in its modes of clarity and difficulty is quite different from Merrill's. It is a poem not overheard, but one that more dangerously responds to the request for a word at a time of disaster—a quarrel, a dish dropped and broken, both perhaps amid the barely heard sounds of distant, failing warfare. The very title of John Ashbery's "Soonest Mended" is half the proverb ("Least said, soonest mended") that it tries with self-descriptive triage to follow. It seems aware that we risk more, imaginatively, by speaking when we are spoken to than by merely being out of turn. Ashbery's opening flat, public diction, a pitch of the quotidian to which he frequently tunes on setting out, is in this poem immediately rescued—in the absence of Pegasus, in the loss even of the hippogriff of romance who replaced him—by the flapping wings of outlandish allusion. And thereby he takes seriously his three improbable opening clichés and is off on his poem in lieu of an apology:

Barely tolerated, living on the margin
In our technological society, we were always having to be
    rescued
On the brink of destruction, like heroines in *Orlando Furioso*
Before it was time to start all over again.
There would be thunder in the bushes, a rustling of coils,
And Angelica, in the Ingres painting, was considering
The colorful but small monster near her toe, as though
    wondering whether forgetting
Might not in the end be the only solution.

Allusion—here, to Ariosto—and secondary allusion (to a problematic illustration of Ariosto, itself poised on the margins of silliness) have a strange power that keep for the user as much as they give. One of Ingres's studies for the Ruggeriero and Angelica painting (at the Fogg Museum) was, until long after this poem was published, labeled "Perseus and Andromeda," the foreshadowing types of Ariosto's pair. But for the modern poet, the later figures are the fallen ones; and the losses are incurred in moving from myth to romance to gooey illustration to the contemporary moment of remembering all this in a time of need. This much the poet keeps for himself; what he gives us are the limits to the possibility of rescue. But forgetting, even in the presence of the toe of a muse imprisoned in academic painting's fini, is not only not the only solution: it is impossible. Even those of us who require wisdom seek after a sign. What next for Ashbery?

And then there always came a time when
Happy Hooligan in his rusted green automobile
Came plowing down the course, just to make sure everything
    was O.K.,
Only by that time we were in another chapter and confused
About how to receive this latest piece of information.
Was it information?

The hero astride the flying hippogriff or popping out of the rusted green automobile, unlike the "pagan in a varnished car," which Wallace Stevens had denied could descend into our lives as a capable fiction, the Imagination's rescuers dart in and out of the chapters of our daily story without the fanfare even of the certainty of their arrivals.[3] This is the residue in major American poetry of the Wordworthian view that redemptive vision will be there, when it is to be there at all, in the light of our ordinariness. The answer to Ashbery's question is that it *was* information, but could be authenticated only by having been able to elicit our doubt.

Was it information? Weren't we rather acting this out
For someone else's benefit, thoughts in a mind
With room enough and to spare for our little problems (so
    they began to seem),
Our daily quandary about food and the rent and bills to be
    paid?

That daily quandary is the high noon of our usual attention, the state W. H. Auden, whose language is indeed suggested in that last line, invoked as "the time being." It is not that succession of days from which we are, or desire, to be rescued; at the beginning of this great later poem, "Grand Galop," Ashbery makes clear that it is both *through* such a realm, as through an allegorical surrounding region, and by means of it, that the force of what we know can become the possible joy of what we do. At the beginning of a great walk through urban dreck, which yields him as many seeds of light as ever glinted out at Henry Vaughan strolling through the West Country, Ashbery's vision of desiccated spring can lead him to the horrendous sequence of days in which poetic language need only name in order to act. "The weigela," he says,

        does its dusty thing
In the fire-hammered air. And garbage cans are heaved against
The railing as the tulips yawn and crack open and fall apart.
And today is Monday. Today's lunch is: Spanish omelet,
    lettuce and tomato salad,
Jello, milk and cookies. Tomorrow's: sloppy joe on bun,
Scalloped corn, stewed tomatoes, rice pudding and milk

(not an ecstatic Whitmanian catalogue, but more like a recital by W. C. Fields, trying to incapacitate further an already nauseated bank examiner).

It is through, not from, the time of the dreadful lunches that our spirits are to pass, perhaps out into sunlight—or, at any rate, in "Soonest Mended,"

To reduce all this to a small variant,
To step free at last, minuscule on the gigantic plateau—
This was our ambition: to be small and clear and free.

In an almost cinematic movement, the poem zooms away from this innuendo of sublimity; and the next strophe of the poem (although unmarked as such typographically) acknowledges its turn away from vision with an allusive touch of older tunes in its diction. Although with a Stevensian exclamation of "Pardie!"

as unavailable to him now as a Horatian "Eheu!" the poet must minimize his wail and move immediately to a confrontation with the difficulty of making poetic arrangements in a late time:

Alas, the summer's energy wanes quickly,
A moment and it is gone. And no longer
May we make the necessary arrangements, simple as they are.

We want to ask, "But how simple *are* they?" What Ashbery elsewhere calls "Using what Wyatt and Surrey left around, / Took up and put down again / Like so much gorgeous raw material," is, after all, simple like the arrangements of the daily quandary from which poetry so differs and yet for which it stands. What is never simple is doing what we have to do at the time, at this time, whenever it is. How can fictions even less than supreme be of any importance now? How can poetry mirror what Shelley calls "the gigantic shadows which futurity casts upon the present" when the covering shade of the past makes such mirrored shadows almost unreadable? Ashbery's answer starts out with a terrifying acknowledgment of the ancestry of all our rhetorical and visionary reticence, and then moves into the central passage of the first half of the poem:

Our star was brighter perhaps when it had water in it.
Now there is no question even of that, but only
Of holding on to the hard earth so as not to get thrown off,
With an occasional dream, a vision: a robin flies across
The upper corner of the window, you brush your hair away
And cannot quite see, or a wound will flash
Against the sweet faces of the others, something like:
This is what you wanted to hear, so why
Did you think of listening to something else? We are all
        talkers
It is true, but underneath the talk lies
The moving and not wanting to be moved, the loose
Meaning, untidy and simple like a threshing floor.

This "meaning," its own chaff and fruit unwinnowed yet, is not only the meaning of our talk, our poems, our representations to each other of our lives, neat and complex as such deep structures have been held to be. It is more significantly the messy meaning of the word "meaning," the meaning of life. It is as if the poem had come upon its own central concern at the thirty-sixth of its seventy-one lines: Ashbery's resolved major theme of Getting On with It.

In "Soonest Mended" the theme manifests itself in its discovery that significances, moralizations, intentions—all the untidiness of meaning—reach out from talking to what is talked about. Specifically, in the middle of the poem, the postmeridional time in the history of poetry, in the very chronicle of imaginings, resolves itself into the time of middle age. This is a poem of being forty-two or forty-three; what one had set out upon, whether or not in response to some vocation, twenty-five years or so earlier, will have been arrived at only in a surprising way. It is not only that the time of heroic rescues is over and that one finds oneself, in middle age, in America, awakening to the condition in which all the available heroisms are part of the predicament rather than the means of its dissolution. One discovers that acts of consciousness can be great acts as well:

These then were some hazards of the course,
Yet though we knew the course *was* hazards and nothing else
It was still a shock when, almost a quarter of a century
    later,
The clarity of the rules dawned on you for the first time.
They were the players, and we who had struggled at the game
Were merely spectators, though subject to its vicissitudes
And moving with it out of the tearful stadium, borne on
    shoulders, at last.

What kind of action is it, then, to try to grasp the meaning of what had been overflowing with possible significances? All our modern kind of poetic knowledge, all the ways in which, from the major romantics on, we could possibly be instructed by our moments of vision as to how to live in between them, preclude the possibility of direct answers to such questions. The landscape or scene that is moralized by the very asking of the question, rather than, in the older poetry, an ultimately anagogic formula, returns in some hardened or reduced form as if in answer to the questioning. In Ashbery's poem, "the end that is past truth, / The being of our sentences, in the climate that fostered them" brings together our lives, what we have said of them, what we have—in both senses of the word—made of them. It is not only that men say things because they know they have been sentenced to death; what we say makes up our life sentences. What we could call "the poem of our lives" is at once the poem *about* our lives and the poem that *is* the individual life itself. What then, Ashbery goes on to ask, of the early poem when we awaken to our own request for a prose paraphrase? There is something scary about either refusing the request or trying to meet it; in any event, the early life affronts abstraction:

    These were moments, years,
Solid with reality, faces, nameable events, kisses,
    heroic acts,
But like the friendly beginning of a geometrical
    progression

Not too reassuring, as though meaning could be cast
    aside some day
When it had been outgrown. Better, you said, to stay
    cowering
Like this in the early lessons, since the promise of
    learning
Is a delusion, and I agreed, adding that
Tomorrow would alter the sense of what had already been
    learned.

"And," Ashbery continues, "probably thinking not to grow up / Is the brightest kind of maturity for us, right now at any rate."

The difference between "thinking not to grow up" and pretending not to have done so is, in a way, the difference between a trivial, reductive reading of Ashbery's lines and the full—and, I hope that I have been suggesting, fully moral—one. Politically speaking, American visions of maturity—particularly during the 1960s and 1970s—could drive the true grownup screaming to the cradle. The businessman, the governor, and the soldier, they who represented the potent maturity of being all "balls," and, alternatively, the uncooperating stud who represented the potent maturity of being all cock—these maintained a cloven fiction of manliness, of being grown-up in America, that has always existed, but that the tasks and injunctions of our earlier history put to active use. Poetically speaking, this is the problem of how to get better, how to go on in any art without merely replicating what one can do well, without producing forgeries of one's earlier genuine work. In our losses, in our sense of time promised and time past slipping away from us, we American artists cannot say with Wordsworth in his *Elegiac Stanzas,* "I have submitted to a new control"; instead, we move toward a subsequent messiness that we hope will redeem us from our successes.

For Ashbery in this poem, the dilemma about what to do with our beginnings resolves in the very act of contemplating ourselves as we are now. The astonishment at the realization of having arrived makes for a pause, but not a lack of motion. Life and art come together again in the lesson to be learned: our poems must get better, and we must all keep going. "And you see," he continues,

      both of us were right, though nothing
Has somehow come to nothing; the avatars
Of our conforming to the rules and living
Around the home have made—well, in a sense, "good citizens" of us,
Brushing the teeth and all that, and learning to accept
The charity of the hard moments as they are doled out.

Ashbery's continuous clarity makes us overlook the way his poetic surface is occasionally so beautifully wrought—I am thinking here of the precise and powerful definite article in "living / Around the home" (just "home" would give a sense of "hanging around," while "the home" makes it a purposive center of life). Similarly, "brushing the teeth" seems a powerful and delicate alteration of the more Audenesque "our teeth," the combined "our" of prayer, the editorial, and the nursery. If we think of the "hard moments"—difficult, windowless, durable in the memory—as being those of Ashbery's hard poem, we can understand how, in that poem, they are the moments of life itself. The difficulties of, and in, our fictions recapitulate those of the rest of our lives. Ashbery's final, firm, almost measured lines conclude his poem with a substitute for the traditional openings-out of landscape, or closings-in of shadows, which the visionary lyric in English derived from Virgil's eclogues and made its own. The conclusion they draw, in an expository sense, is a substitute for heroic resolution, or reductive hope, or a tired, tragic commitment to keeping the inner beasts of disorder chained up as well as one can. The poem has acknowledged its response to the truth about lives to be "a kind of fence-sitting / Raised to the level of an esthetic ideal"; how can it draw itself to a close? Ashbery's measured appositives to "not being sure" hide their startling revisions of the ordinary language—even the cliché—of resolution almost until they have themselves drifted by:

For this is action, this is not being sure, this careless
Preparing, sowing seeds crooked in the furrow,
Making Ready to forget, and always coming back
To the mooring of starting out, that day so long ago.

One of these revisions accounts for the deep resonance of "making ready to forget"—not making ready to forget life, making ready to live and to be living. The other brings about the apparent oxymoron of "the mooring of starting out." Not only is there an alteration of the expected "the morning of starting out." There is also rather a matter of condensation than contradiction; at a more purely Stevensian rhetorical moment in his work, Ashbery might have glossed his image more by playing about with the consequences of the metaphor. "It's not that starting out on artistic and, indeed, generally human courses of wisdom is a matter of cutting loose from moorings—no complex consciousness could without the crudest of ironies utter 'I'm adrift, I'm adrift' in avowal of its uncertainty. It's only that the starting out itself, the vocation, the initiation of serious life, is all that we can be, or authentically *be said in a real poem to be,* moored to. The trope of moorings and the sea voyage of life can only apply when troped itself." Something like this, in dialectic but certainly not in language, might have provided a passage of an earlier style of American poetic meditation. The very difficulty of this kind of poetry is the difficulty of having it be true of our lives, of having its art unfold in wisdom.

This is a very different kind of poetic difficulty from that of modernism, some of whose obliquities and ellipses of the expository have already become conventional idiom, but whose other mode of allusive elusiveness, of mandarin closure, functioned as a kind of *trobar clus,* as the troubadours called it, a rhetoric that would lock away the expression of perhaps common feelings from the understanding of the vile and the base. There is some deep justification for this hermetic impulse when one is writing of love: announcing a desire for a particular person—or, perhaps even more emotionally dangerous, announcing the condition of one's inner states to the degree of saying "I love you"—both depend upon the same words that *anybody* will use. And yet, Eros being most blind of all to its own lack of specialness, the poetic impulse to say "I don't mean what they, the others, mean by this: I mean *you* and *me*" is one of the most venerable. To extend this to all poetic expression was a different matter. Contemporary poetic difficulty in America (and we are flooded now as always with bad, easy poems, as easy to read as not to read, and probably easy to write—as Karl Kraus said of aphorisms, poems are easy to write when you don't know how), contemporary poetic difficulty in America, at its most important, results from our own critique of our sense of uniqueness, our distrust of the forms of affirmation that belie its continuing necessity. Ashbery has said that all his poems are love poems, but this is not because the name of a beloved is coded in a pseudonym, or that desires and the sad knowledge we have about desires are clothed in trope or clouded in scheme. He is concerned, as I think all our important poets are now, with what our imagination makes of our ordinariness, with what the possible rescuers are actually like. He starts with a rusty old saw that rebukes all poets, all talkers, with the advice to "shut up and then everything may be O.K." He chops it in half, and then says most. Ashbery's poems are full of the unspecial: stretches of banal phrases that stumble against peaks of visionary image, faceted clichés in the ordinarily cheap settings of inverted commas. But to confuse this use of the givens of our lives (as some of his sillier admirers have done) with what has been called "pop art" is a little like confusing Emerson with Mary Baker Eddy. The banalities are hard; the difficulty of the poems as poems is the difficulty of making sense out of our lives. "Reality," noted the young Wallace Stevens in a letter, "is so Chicagoan, so plain, so unmeditative," and yet it alone must bear the weight of all our unfancying meditation. In this sense, the truest poetry is New Yorkean, complex, reflective.

But this does not mean its mode must necessarily be urban: "the need of being versed in country things" is as much a need of being versed, of being mythologically prepared to read any region of experience, as of the mind's hunger for rural truths. In an astonishing little one-line poem, Emerson once implied that poetry associates the extra-urban scene with the broadcasting of knowledge that in the city is kept pent: "A man tells a secret for the same reason that he loves the country."[4] Emerson's image is the exultant yell of openness here, but it must not be mistaken for an echo of the country's own voice, which broadcasts nothing in the way of truth. Like the urban scene, it presents emblems to be read, and it presents the general enigma of emblem—of making sense out of what we know we are amidst. Whether for Whitman's great ode of the mockingbird's loss, or for the guarded Frost, not even inquiring of this long scythe (in "Mowing") whether it knew the relevant text in Deutero-Isaiah, the voice of nature could only come in a whisper.[5] Straining to hear that whisper has been a major American poetic act always, just as squinting at our scenes for the shadows cast upon them by our lives has been one of the major visions of "that wilder image" (as William Cullen Bryant called it) of our painting. In one sense, the poet should not want to have nature's voice, for no matter how mighty in decibels the roaring wind, it is a philosopher with laryngitis; the truth of audibly moving water can only be hearsay. And yet the poet's longing for nature's way of making things, and of making things happen (beyond breed to brave Time when he takes you hence), reflects so many of our general longings for authenticity in the manufacture of our lives.

A. R. Ammons is a poet who strains for whispers and squints, not so much for the shadows as for what hides in them and how they appear to lengthen and deepen apart from the time of day. As a poet of nature he walks in the country accompanied by the moving shadow cast by the light of his own consciousness. More than a reader of emblems, more than an epigrammatizing biologist or even a chanting thanatologist, he engages the countryside with the powerful hands of awareness in a working of the land that is also a playing with it. Santayana warned that "if we do not know our environment, we shall mistake our dreams for a part of it, and so spoil our science by making it fantastic, and our dreams by making them obligatory." He was talking of a culture that has gone well on its way toward doing just that; but there is the internalized civilization of the individual imagination, which provides us with exemplary states of consciousness, and in Ammons's poetry, the mythology of structure and function in plant and animal flowers all year long.

The last of the poems to be confronted here is perhaps atypical of Ammons's meditations on a site or sample, but representative of the American poem of longing for natural power. It is a text of the 1970s, marked by a somewhat deceptive rhetorical ease and, unlike "Mirror" and "Soonest Mended," standing clear of the shifting tract of memory. It is the set of dedicatory verses to Ammons's long poem *Sphere*. More than some of his rightly best-known meditations on radiance and clarity such as "Gravelly Run" or "The City Limits," it points to the question of our own naturalness. The poet starts out from a familiar point, the mountain top from which both classical and biblical visions are vouchsafed:

I went to the summit and stood in the high nakedness:
the wind tore about this
way and that in confusion and its speech could not
get through to me nor could I address it.

But the summit of what? There are several kings of mythical mountains. Olympus as a region, seat, or dwelling place of the gods; Parnassus as a scene of specifically poetic elevation; Sinai as a high point of revelation and transmission of holy law; Pisgah as a supreme point of overview, of what can be vouchsafed in vision but not directly possessed or inhabited; Spenser's Mount of Heavenly Contemplation, his beautiful Acidale, his part-local, part-universal Arlo-Hill; Milton's Niphates upon which Satan alights and the pinnacle of the other mount from which the other Satan (in *Paradise Regained*) "smitten with amazement, fell." All are paradigmatic of later mountains (as indeed the earlier ones in this list are of those at the end of it) in subsequent poetry. (Only Ararat seems a nonce occurrence—a point whose height does not reach toward a higher realm, or provide views of the lower one, but that becomes, at the subsiding of the Deluge, the new First Ground. And, at the other end of the list, there is Thomas Mann's *Der Zauberberg,* in no way a typical revision of any of these.)

But the first *modern* summit is probably that of Mont Ventoux, which Petrarch attained in April 1336, partially on the original grounds that "it was there and so I had to climb it," partially because of the injunctions of biblical and classical story. He ascended to the very windy summit, accompanied by a beloved brother, ignoring the aged shepherd "in the folds of the mountain" who tired to dissuade him from the climb, and most important of all, carrying with him a pocket-size manuscript of Augustine's *Confessions.* At the summit, by a kind of *sortes,* he opened his codex to a text that indicated that men go to admire high mountains, the sea, the great rivers, the stars, and thereby desert themselves. What Petrarch discovered on the windy mountain was about the height and scope of consciousness; never again would summits be the same.

Ammons's unnamed, general summit does not afford him the opportunity for discourse, much less communion, that Whitman might have felt there, and having been brought to where he stands by personal history, and by the history of poetic art, he can only examine nature's inability to reflect, or to echo:

still I said as if to the alien in myself
I do not speak to the wind now:
for having been brought this far by nature I have been

brought out of nature
and nothing here shows me the image of myself:
for the word *tree* I have been shown a tree
and for the word *rock* I have been shown a rock,
for stream, for cloud, for star
this place has provided firm implication and answering
    but where here is the image for *longing*.

What Ammons, what we all, have inherited from our meditative tradition is a
way of reading parts of a world for the whole; his summit-climber finds at the
top of contemplation the signatures of the diving words in the things that
embody, or image, them. But what had led him to try for heights remains unrepresented in the vision those very heights afford. Neither would natural philosophy afford him that, nor would the most profound caressing of the phenomena themselves, rather than an unpeeling of them in quest of the structures
that produce those appearances. Ammons continues, in the next lines, to maintain this, starting with an important echo of Whitman's syntax:

so I touched the rocks, their interesting crusts:
I flaked the bark of stunt-fir:
I looked into the space and into the sun
and nothing answered my word *longing*.

And again, his final exhortation to an unlistening nature sings a tune sadly playful in a Whitmanian way at first—

    goodbye, I said, goodbye, nature so grand and
reticent, your tongues are healed up into their own element
and as you have shut up you have shut me out: I am
as foreign here as if I had landed, a visitor.

As if the tongues by which nature could speak to Wordsworth, or to Emerson,
had been wounds of some sort? The single word "element" is isolated in its
verse, free of local syntax, as if thereby to represent its silence. The art that must
speak for nature, as, indeed, for all the rest of our silence, must come from some
other, unsublime "element," and Ammons's climber descends to baser ground,
to muck around in the Adamic mud and shape a new piece of natural history. It
will not be a mere filling of a void, no fantastic substitution for the longed-*for,*
but, of necessity, a human image of another sort.

    I took the image to the summit: first
I set it here, on the top rock, but it completed
nothing: then I set it there among the tiny firs
but it would not fit.

Unlike Wallace Stevens's jar that "did not give of bird nor bush / Like nothing else in Tennessee," Ammons's image completes nothing because it answers to no longing of the hilltops, to nothing in rock, tree, stream, cloud, or star that has ever quested after a greater naturalness or hearkened after a prior voice. This is not the complaint of the First Shaper that his human creation would not fit in Paradise, not that of some human simulator of forms that his golem would not play properly and quietly in the back yard. I suppose that it is possible to imagine the "image for longing" as a woman or a beautiful youth—an image *of* (but not, in Ammons's richer sense, "for") a longed-for object of desire. But in this case, it would be the image of an image, and the longing of the poet-climber for the intercourse with mute nature would be troped by the absence of a beautiful body. Nor would a reflexive emblem satisfy the conditions of the poem—a modeled image of a man modeling an image of what or of whom—he desires. One need only think of the Creator, contemplating his garden with a sense of distance from his own creation and setting amid its rocks and trees an image of himself, in order to decide what sort of figure Ammons's image for longing makes.

But its appearance is not in fact the problem. It is a question of the ecology of significance, of what in this poem is spoken of as a setting. Even the poem that would complete the silences of nature must seek out the city of understanding. And "so" says Ammons,

I returned to the city and built a house to set the image in
and men came to my house and said
    that is an image for *longing*
and nothing will ever be the same again.

And to do that to everything was why the poet came. Perhaps this ends with the same ambiguity of syntactic closure that makes us wonder, in the absence of canonical punctuation, about who is saying exactly how much at the end of Keats's poem on the urn; despite its present tense, is the last line only what the others say in recognition of the image? Is it not part of the testament of the poem? The time of poetic vocation that lies in the distant past of Merrill's mirror, unremembered or, at any rate, unrecalled, and that Ashbery continually reinvokes, is here memorialized as a bardic anecdote. The image completed nothing in the wild that called forth the need of it; the maker had to return to the ground to gather the element of such an image, and to return to the city to build a house that the image might complete.

In one sense, "I Went to the Summit" is the poem of the First Poem, both in the poet's history and in that of the world. A parody of Creation, it reminds us of the Original Trope (and, perhaps, causes us to linger for a moment over the identity of that trope: is the relation of Creator to Man one of metaphor? irony? synecdoche? metonymy?). But in its parody, Ammons's tale avoids the confusions of the uninspiring winds that tear about the summit. If at a lower altitude they would whisper of death—that message that is our imagination's overload always—at the privileged, high place that seems to point toward transcendence, there is nothing to be understood. In all our general American longings, our uneasy quest for "firm implication and answering," it is so easy to pretend to understand the wind in the high nakedness, and to descend, ever to echo its roaring. But the poet will not have that, nor will, by extension, the unpublishing poet who fills every wise, passionate consciousness. He must make an image for longing, and then build a house of life for which that image will remain the *lar familiaris,* as the Romans referred to it, the household spirit.

Every stage of life has its losses, and every age of culture its own longings. Now to avow these will probably not lead to the making of poems that command us to change our lives, poems imbued with what D. H. Lawrence called "a passionate, implicit morality, not didactic." Much well-intentioned verse that, as we have seen, can respond too directly and too trivially to the violences from without remains, in Ammons's myth, the equivalent of carefully worked samplers hung on the walls of a house not even built for them, but inherited. (Were I to have been discussing style here, I might have added that during recent decades it even became fashionable for the samplers to present their ABCs and their pieties not in the careful fancywork of long tradition, but overwrought instead with the *fausse-naive,* misshapen and tearstained as if by an incapacitated or miserably unwilling child.) But the true poems that embody images for the losses as well as the longing cannot merely *be* homely wisdom. They must reinvent wisdom and even homeliness itself.

To this extent, then—that at the end of every true poem "nothing will ever be the same again"—the problems of American affirmation, of modern heroism, and of the apparent impossibility of wisdom seem part of the same condition. Like the medieval *chansons de geste,* the heroic poems that flowered in times of treasons, stratagems, and spoils, and the *chansons d'amour* that filled in with language the space created by absence, our poems of love and deed at once blossom only in our own late aftertime. After the originations of nature, our images of rocks and trees are not enough, and it is only in our poems of awareness of this insufficiency that we can live our imaginative lives. Such poems fill in the spaces vacated by the ever-vanishing hope of our ever *being* our models, our heroes, our images of the good, original life, and aid us to become them, by, and within, ourselves. In an America past the time of its own youth, promise, and capability, it is not for a major poetry to mourn the time of year, but to provide images for *imagining.* If a man, to be greatly good, must indeed "imagine intensely and comprehensively"—if, the more complex his nature, the more dialectic, the more historical vision, and the more humor he must be able to exercise—then it must be such poems that will nourish the imagination, if only by forcing the reader to cooperate in their creation. We may want verses to touch, to tickle, to caress, to remind, to wound us; the many modes of sermon, editorial, and epigram contrive to do that and more. In the absence of wisdom, the poetry of modernism informed us, there is only the sad knowledge of that absence and a way of putting what we know in "a series of isolated perfections" perhaps. Our epigrams continue in that task. For the larger questions, our late epics, our derived romances, our scriptures and their commentaries, come more and more to be scattered among the leaves of our meditative lyrics.

We can agree with Richard Poirier that literature cannot restore or improve what has gone wrong with our own and with society's lives.[6] But as enlightenment is a trope of improvement, and one colloquial use of the word "realize" (for an act of consciousness) figuratively enacts what is envisioned by the other use (for a reification, physical representation, or even an institutionalization), so restitution stands in for restoration. It is these poems that have come to be our poetry of restitution—for local and for general losses; for the exhausted powers of private and public language (and when the sword avers the pen to be mightier, let us beware, for that will only occur in a police state); for vanished emblems of wisdom, ever needing replacement; for the vacancies left by modernist poetry's view of its own history; and for the continuing American task of self-invention—a burden as cruel as that of the demand for originality that modernism has thrust upon all poor artisans—if not even half completed in a summer of national power, then perhaps to be continued in a brave autumn of decline.

NOTES

1. But see David Bromwich, "Emerson and the Ode to W. H. Channing" in *A Choice of Inheritance* (Cambridge, Mass.: Harvard University Press, 1989), 133–44.

2. Thomas Hardy, *Complete Poems,* ed. James Gibson (London: Macmillan, 1976), 674. Also see "In the Room" by James Thomson ("B.V."), which Merrill had almost certainly read.

3. Stevens's line from *The Man with the Blue Guitar,* sect. 10 ("The approach of him whom none believes, // Whom all believe that all believe, / A pagan in a varnished car") is itself a revisionary, transumptive second coat of gloss of the Homeric *eukestos,* "well-polished," "well-planed," for Olympian chariots, and most likely via Milton's "Heav'n's youngest-teemed Star / Hath fixt her polisht Car" ("Ode on the Morning of Christ's Nativity" [ll. 240–41]), given the obvious transumption by Milton of the Homeric phrase. Stevens also plays with the archaic and modern meanings of *car* (as chariot, railroad carriage, automobile).

4. Emerson, Journal E, 152 (1840), in *The Journals and Miscellaneous Notebooks of Ralph Waldo Emerson,* ed. A. W. Plumstead and Harrison Hayford (Cambridge, Mass.: Harvard University Press, 1969), 7:361.

5. Frost's line is "My long scythe whispered, and left the hay to make," where I now think that "make" is both the rural colloquially intransitive and the Greek *poiein,* the "making" of "poetry." The biblical passage is at Isaiah 40.6. On Frost's poem, see Richard Poirier, *Robert Frost: The Work of Knowing* (New York: Oxford University Press, 1977), 285–90.

6. In the opening section of his *Renewal of Literature* (New York: Random House, 1987), 3–66.

CHAPTER FOUR

What You Mean by Home

"It all depends on what you mean by home." Mary, the farmer's wife in Robert Frost's "The Death of the Hired Man," may as well raise one of our central questions for us. We will remember that, in the poem, a former farmhand—and one of variable efficiency—who had left their employ in somewhat strained circumstances, shows up at the house in extremely debilitated condition:

"Warren," she said, "he has come home to die
You needn't be afraid he'll leave you this time."

"Home," he mocked gently.

              "Yes, what else but home?
It all depends on what you mean by home.
Of course he's nothing to us any more
Than was the hound that came a stranger to us
Out of the woods, worn out upon the trail."

This occasions that celebrated exchange between man and wife that used to be so well known to readers of my generation; the husband's formulation—

"Home is the place where, when you have to go there,
They have to take you in."

is followed by his wife's rejoinder:

"I should have called it
Something you somehow haven't to deserve."

At first glance, the dialogue seems to privilege the contrast between these views—the husband defines home with respect to the responsibilities, specifically of the other persons who constitute a household, while the wife talks the language of rights, rather than responsibilities, and of a possession, a place in particular. Frost himself, amusingly and quite trivially, highlighted this difference by giving it a reductive reading of his own:

> In "The Death of the Hired Man" (he remarked in an interview with his greatest critic, Richard Poirier) that I wrote long, long ago, long before the New Deal, I put it two ways about home. One would be the manly way: "Home is the place where, when you go there, they have to take you in." That's the man's feeling about it. And then the wife says, "I should have called it / Something you somehow haven't to deserve." That's the New Deal, the feminine way of it, the mother way. You don't have to deserve your mother's love. You have to deserve your father's. He's more particular. One's a Republican, one's a Democrat. The father is always a Republican toward his son, and his mother's always a Democrat.[1]

But the art of this poet has been ultimately to make us hear these definitions as profoundly complementary. The husband's remark unfolds in a line of monosyllables, with displaced syntax, slowly and as if framed with some difficulty; his wife's answer completes a half line and trips musically along. She has the last word; but her "I should have called it . . ." might ultimately just as well be put as "That is to say, it's / Something you somehow . . . ," for they are ultimately paraphrases of the same notion. You have to get taken in by them whether you deserve it or not; you don't have to deserve to be there (and consequently, oblige them to acknowledge this by taking you in). This complementarity, rather than a more aggressively arrayed antithetical quality, marks the relation of the masculine and feminine definitions. Poirier has remarked on how these two are like Milton's Adam and Eve—but, we should add, before the Fall (in *Paradise Lost,* book 9). Afterward, their debate might have been trivialized, and the fallen Eve, now a merely human housewife, might have muttered in return, "I know, and we're / The 'they' who're always stuck with having to" or even (he) "Home is the place where, when I finally get there / My supper will be hot." (she) "And yet Shaw called it / 'Home . . . the girl's workhouse and the woman's prison.' " Yet in this antithesis, the caustic force of the last word is primarily directed not toward what's wrong with having a home, but with a false or partial way of construing it. One bad construction deserves another. But let us return to the prelapsarian one.

"Something you somehow haven't to deserve. . . ." Therefore not an earned right, or desert, but a natural one, to be acknowledged along with one's personhood or humanity. Still, "it all depends on what you mean by home," and thereby some home, somewhere, or any particular home. (This might certainly lead to conflicts, if two people claim the right to the same home, like some sort of extension of rights to and in one's body? An entity one claims as one's home may indeed coincide with some particular piece of property, rights in which, by law, one has in some way to deserve.)

But this is surely not the point. The ultimately unspecified, not-quite-repressed definition of home evoked by the end of "The Death of the Hired Man" is as the human point of ultimate return. Perhaps the poet-in-the-reader might add, "I should have called it / The place you always come to when you die," the grave being what figured, in the King James Version's queer translation of the great passage in Ecclesiastes (12.5) about the decay of the body: "and the grasshopper shall be a burden, and desire shall fail: because man goeth to his long home, and the mourners go about the streets." And to that extent we are all delinquent farmhands of the earth, coming back to it when we return in the cyclic movement of dust (primordial mud and/or adamic clay) to dust. We will return to this text a bit further on, noting only at this point a particular central instance of one way that we use the word *home* in modern English to mean "a place of origin returned to." I cannot help but notice the name of the Macintosh function key in front of me, pressing which will take me back to the top of my document: HOME. In the more profoundly general case of death, the English language reinforces the sense of a particular enclosure with two associated names with the rhymes—almost a commonplace in the Renaissance—on *womb* and *tomb* (as if the *-omb* were the general human home).

"It all depends on what you mean by home." This central issue—as I take it to be—for today's observations can apply variously to the word and the concept, to a matter of linguistics in English and to a matter of deep human consciousness. I wish to consider the ways in which these are interestingly related, but from the outset we may feel the latter of these plagues the process of definition. My self, my body, my home—I don't know if this series should show some intervening terms; but it is clear that "home" belongs toward the very beginning of it, rather than toward the end occupied by "my favorite chair," "sandwich," "my [half-read] newspaper." But "it all depends on what you mean by home" could also be a lawyer's remark, in re, say, the law's word for *home*— not unoccluded access to a somehow privileged place nor the acknowledgment of its privileged relation to you by others, but where simply you are at legally, as a citizen, as a social agent.

The active word here is *domicile. Domicile* is defined by *Black's Law Dictionary* as "that place where a man has his true, fixed, and permanent home and principal establishment, and to which whenever he is absent he has the intention of returning." The permanent residence of a person, the place to which he intends to return—perhaps marked by possessions left at a residence with intent to return to them—is crucial to the legal notion of *necessary domicile,* "that kind of domicile which exists by operation of law, as distinguished from voluntary domicile or domicile of choice."[2] In other words, "Home is the place where, for its jurisdiction / A court says where you're from." The "domicile of choice" alluded to is what we construe a home to be: "Home is the place where, when you want to stay there / They have to say you are." For the law, necessary domicile can frequently prevail over domicile of choice, and in a larger sense, we might say that our bodies-in-the-world are our domicile of choice. (This is vainly opposed to Nature's overriding claim that we are mere sojourners in them, merely residing there, while our true domicile is the earth.)

Also to be distinguished are two more metaphorical instances of legal home: *Corporate domicile,* "the center of corporate affairs and place where its functions are discharged" (corporations "have" homes in a very different sense from persons having them), or—to follow the paradigm—"Home is the place that's haunted by that ghost / We call a corporation." More relevant to the present discussion perhaps is that other institutional concept, *matrimonial domicile,* "Wherever either one may be, home's where / The marriage always is" (perhaps it's more a matter of *in rem*).

And finally, there is that most mythologically pregnant among the distinctions drawn by legal language, the *domicile of origin,* defined as "the home of the parents," or "Home is the place which you were born into / Wherever else you go." The ways in which domicile of choice ceases to be coextensive with domicile of origin are part of the story of the developing and growing self in modernity. Many of our modern fables deal with the child's need for a domicile of choice, however small, located within the larger circumference of the parental home; in the past, when reading led to both knowledge and imagination and hence to freedom, the child's own home was often the place where he or she could be alone with a book, a place both walled in with privacy and far outrunning, in imaginative space and possibility, the walls of the household that could protect but not contain it. The central dialectic of the wall as boundary (rather than as bearing structural member) involves the price paid, in the hard cash of being walled in, for walling out the unwanted. Here emerges the important relation of safety and freedom that Simon Schama aligns, in his discussion of seventeenth-century Dutch culture, with the concept of home and world.[3]

Many of the questions of "what you mean by home" depend upon specification of locus and extent, in what might be likened to a set of Emersonian conceptual concentric circles. The outermost one, for the time being, let us call the surface of the planet, which can certainly qualify as being home realm—what in

German is called *Heimat,* or native land—enough for any returning astronaut. The law's "necessary domicile" will almost invariably designate a state or a county in the United States, without specifying any smaller enclosure or space, rights to use that space (acquired by ownership or rental or whatever), etc. Construing "home" often entails considering concentricities radiating outward, starting from a smallest self (indeed, perhaps even a temple of that self, built to enclose its cult image) instead of, as in orthodox Christianity, a sort of prison farm that one's soul didn't own but was forced by nature to rent. It is only with Descartes that modern skepticism starts wondering just what sort of knowledge of, control over, housekeeping skills and responsibilities for—indeed, even what sort of possession of—its bodily home consciousness may be said to have. And indeed, the cessation of prolonged but temporary pain, partial paralysis, or muscular dysfunction makes us feel as if we had been somehow displaced in our bodies, to which now we had returned home.[4]

This range of concentricities is interestingly marked in German by the range of senses of the word for *home, Heim,* from the widened boundaries of *Heimat* to the extremely extended form *Geheim.* The feeling that one's home is itself really the center of a series of radiating circles of hominess becomes most apparent when we consider how one returns to a slightly different sense of *home* from the one that one ventures forth from. The Greek word *nostos,* meaning a homeward journey, probably derives from an Indo-European base that means only "a safe return"; it survives on loan to English only through the interestingly distorted "nostalgia." This word originated in a Swiss medical treatise of 1688 as a translation of the Swiss-German *Heimweh,* considered as a mode of something like melancholia.[5] We designate by it not literal "homesickness" but a strange and perhaps not quite legitimate extension thereof, a longing for a time and not for a place, and perhaps a time that one knows like E. A. Robinson's Miniver Cheevy (who "loved the Medici, / Albeit he had never seen one; / He would have sinned incessantly / Could he have been one"[6]) from literary or historical hearsay. But in the *Odyssey,* the *nostos,* the journey toward and arrival at home, almost becomes an end in itself, and we find Odysseus on Calypso's pleasure isle wanting "to reach my house and to see the day of my return" [oikade t'elthemenai kai nostimon hêmar idesthi, 5.219–20]. Elsewhere, too (5.115), "to reach his high-roofed house [oikon es hypsorophon] and his native land [patrida gaian]" we feel that to translate *oikos,* "house," as "home" might be almost allegorizing. (To feel how this can be true, one should imagine the word "homecoming" as if it meant what it does to us, but without there being any English word "home" at all, and that its first syllable designated nothing.)

Or our own word *home* we are led to observe here that the sense of *nostos* as a return to a point of origin inheres in some of our modern derived uses of our word, whether in the homely baseball designation of a home base, which one contrives, even strives, to leave only in order to complete a *nostos,* or in the further extended sense of a goal or *telos* of target of activity, whether in the instance of an arrow or a rhetorical point "hitting home" or, as early as 1625, in Bacon's epistle dedicatory to his *Essays,* where he remarks that now that his newer and revised essays have been published, thereby "as it seemed they came home to Mens Business, and Bosomes."

The necessity for revising or redefining the locus of one's own home is important in many central heroic stories we have told about our origins. We are all the children of Adam and Eve, who were at home everywhere there was for them; it was only by losing this privileged human place forever that they entered a world in which they would have to internalize, and go on successively internalizing, the place-of-being-at-home, as it were. At first, this is literally a matter of technology, for which there was no more need in the Edenic environment than a fetus in utero "needs" a prothesis. It is only after the fall from perfection into nature that "being-at-home" could ever be localized in something like a house. What Joseph Rykwert has so revealingly written about "Adam's house in Paradise" applies to the visions and desires of fallen, natural human consciousness.[7] Even the crucial distinction inside/outside had not become so invested with human hopes and fears, and the consequent dialectic of walling-in and walling out I alluded to earlier; it remained in Paradise no more than a possible option of pleasant pattern and playful design. From the Edenic standpoint, Adam and Eve had no house because they were so purely at home.

Milton in *Paradise Lost* (book 9) implies that the very first bit of technology to ward off homelessness occurs even within Eden: with the first flush of sexual guilt and of feeling not at home in their bodies, Adam and Eve "with what skill they had" (9.111–12) housed their shame in fig-leaved dress. Even more remarkably, Milton seems to sketch out the entire subsequent history of the conceptualization of home, from a concrete locus in a hut of some kind, built "with what skill" the historical moment had, to a fully metaphoric transformation. Just before the expulsion, Adam is told that ultimately he will "possess / A paradise within thee, happier far" (12.586–87; and note that "possess" means, all too literally, to contain). And Eve reciprocally redefines home not as a sheltered or contained place, but as the presence of the only other person: "In me is no delay; with thee to go / Is to stay here; without thee here to stay, / Is to go hence unwilling" (12.615–17), she says to Adam as they are about to set forth, with the world "all before them," into natural history. It is almost as if, for Milton, the essence of the original, paradigmatic condition of being-and-feeling-at-home consisted in the unfallen matrimonial domicile, that the relation between two persons generated a space and an enclosure that superseded literal emplacement. They leave their lost Paradise bearing the invisible germ of at-homeness that will flower when they have by hard labor wrenched, urged, twisted a place of dwelling out of the earth.

In another sort of heroic tale of departure from home, Abram leaves the northern land of Hur to find and make a new home that will be (and for this he is renamed *Av-raham,* "father of multitudes") a future *Heimat* but only after long years of being not at home. The outward journey of Exodus is neither a *nostos* of return, nor a circular, continuing nomadic motion; it is rather a directed wandering, a quest for a single original tribal one. Virgil's Aeneas bears his father on his back out of the burning ruins of their old home of (not so much "in") Troy to find and found a new Troy in Italy, dispossessing its older inhabitants by conquest. Even as his precursor Odysseus eschews a number of wonderfully comfy or elegant or exciting places of sojourn for his true royal home of Ithaca, so Aeneas moves on ruthlessly past the various attractions of What Might Have Been. In his study of the ways in which Old English literature constituted its culture's history, Nicholas Howe has explored the relevance of Exodus to the stories by the Anglo-Saxons of how they "were a chosen people to whom a promised land had been entrusted by virtue of their migration."[8] But from the picaresque tale through the nineteenth-century bildungsroman to major modern romances like *Moby-Dick, Huckleberry Finn, Kim,* and countless others, the contingent heroes of bourgeois modernity have left the homes they felt were no longer truly theirs to wander in search of a home not for a future nation of multitudes but for their own multitudinous selves. Our stories, then, tell us we have all been Bedouin at some point; it is as if the abstract "home" we carried with us in our wandering—the way Aeneas was said to have carried his original Penates, or household gods, out of Troy with him—could possess and inhere in the actual houses we built, as if they were thereby somehow ensouled.[9]

I wish to consider now another aspect of the problem of "what you mean by home," that is, what our English word "home" really means. It is possible that the very agenda of this entire discussion could not be framed in anything but English, German, Dutch, or another Germanic language. The relation between "house" and "home" has become complicated in contemporary usage by a number of ironic reversals of original meaning. The common—and, unlike many common expressions, vulgar—use of "home" as a euphemism for "house" is by and large the linguistic waste product of the American real estate industry. Literate people can be reminded of how continually we repress our disgust at this particular vulgarity as when, for example, a student of mine recalls a Chinese emigré academic, who had taught her in college, reading aloud in disbelief an ordinary sign: "Homes for Sale? How can you buy or sell a home? Home is [and he groped for the formulation] . . . memories."

There were probably two pressures at work on the replacement of *house* by *home* in the real estate business. One is simply hyperbolic and more benign: as early as 1835 the celebrated versifier Felicia Heman's immediately and subsequently famous lines about "The stately homes of England! How beautiful they stand" still referred to ancestral houses, but easily shifted its ambience to bourgeois aspirations. And thus, an account in *Harper's Magazine* of 1882 refers to "a lovely drive . . . bordered with homes, many of which make pretensions to much more than comfort," while seven years later a real estate advertisement in the *Kansas City Times and Star* boasts "for rent, a fine home at 1223 Broadway." On the other hand, the euphemistically shortened form "house" for "whorehouse" or "house of prostitution" undoubtedly urged the substitution as well.[10] It is perhaps with a sense of this developing substitution that Edgar A. Guest, the popular homely versifier of the *Detroit Free Press,* had even before World War I been able to proclaim that "It takes a heap o' livin' to make a house a home."

Needless to say, ordinary users of *home* = *house* are today unaware of how strange the equation might seem. I remember myself, as a child of Manhattan, referring without question or wonder to my parents' or a friend's parents' apartment as "my (or Billy's) house," but only in the sense of say, *chez moi (ou Billy).* One may nonetheless observe how the multiple resonances of the word *home* may possibly confuse purely practical argument, for example, the debate among various reformers as to whether homelessness is simply houselessness or something more abstract—institutionally or spiritually. If a "home" is something you can buy, then that appears to be all there is to it. In any event, there is no word so loaded as "home" in the Romance languages, and English (or German, etc.) sentences containing the word are always variously translated.

It is particularly interesting in this regard to observe the role of the Latin word *focus,* meaning "hearth" or "fireplace," which even in classical times serves as a metonymy for "household" or "family." In Romance languages, the *focolare domestico, le foyer familial, el hogar,* perhaps the Portuguese *lar,* all retain this sense.[11] But certainly the hearth as the center or focus of the home is notable in literature: from Athena's remark to Zeus at the beginning of the *Odyssey* (1.58–59) that Odysseus longs "to behold if only the smoke springing up from his land" [kapnon apothrôskonta noêsai / hês gaiês] through its recollection by the Renaissance poet Joachim Du Bellay in a canonical locus of nostalgia.[12] "Quand revoiray-je, hélas, de mon petit village / Fumer la cheminée: et en quelle saison, / Revoiray-je le clos de ma pauvre maison / Qui m'est un province, et beaucoup d'avantage." (Although this mode of preferring one's Local to the culture's Central gets short shrift from Robert Burton, in his *Anatomy of Melancholy,* who declares that " 'Tis a childish humour to hone after home, to be discontent at that which others seek.") In many of our representations of our lives, home is where the hearth is, just as the other element of Du Bellay's longing, the homeliness and lowliness of home contrasted with the grandeur of, in his case, Rome, shows up continually in our literature, the central American text probably being the aria from Sir Henry Rowley Bishop's opera of 1839, *Clari, of the Maid of Milan,* which begins " 'Mid pleasures and palaces tho' we may roam / Be it ever so humble, there's no place like home." Only in English, it will be noted, is *home* not only homonymous with *Rome* and *roam,* but lurks in the name of the eternal domicile of origin of all our literature, Homer.

We know that words are used without regard to their own origins save by pedants and sometimes poets, but it is instructive when considering linguistic and social constructions of "home" to consider the etymologies of some common words that touch on it. From the (hypothetical) Indo-European base *weik,* designating a clan, a social unit above that of the household, we get not only the Greek word for *house, oikos,* but the Latin *villa,* a country house or farm, and *vicus,* meaning a quarter or neighborhood in a city. The familiar *domus,* conversely, possesses and generates all those meanings of house and household that become even more independently manifest in Romance languages, and on loan in English from *domicile* and *domestic* to *dominate, dame,* and *domain* — in modern Western languages, both dominion and economics begin at home.[13]

Our resonant Germanic word *home* (*Heim, ham, heem,* etc.) seems to derive from an original Indo-European *kei,* implying lying down, a bed or couch, and something dear or beloved, which also yields *haunt* and even *cemetery* (from Greek *koiman,* "to put to sleep"). The metaphorical implication of the semantic change is that home is a place to lay your head. And yet the Anglo-Saxon *ham* that is the ancestor of our word designates a village or town, an estate or possession. It is rather the word *house* that has always had the sense of "home" embedded in it. *House* (with its cognates) itself is strange in that it has no base in Indo-European, but belongs to that group of Germanic words of no known origin and that have always apparently meant exactly what they now mean — words like *arm* and *sea,* for example. A house was always a building for human habitation, and most often the dwelling place of a family; all the subsequent extensions of the term to cover various sorts of public buildings arise, not unsurprisingly, in the fourteenth century and after.

The semantic energy of the English word *home* has been charged particularly in the last three centuries by the interanimation of the various instances of "what you mean by home." That extended sense of the legal "domicile of origin," of home as the end as well as the beginning of all journeys, resounds through the phrase from Ecclesiastes mentioned earlier, "and man goeth to his long home." This translates the Hebrew for "eternal dwelling" [*beit olamo: bayit,* designating a house or housing, sheltering structure, generally gets extended to mean various sorts of private or public buildings but, in another direction, to mean a household or a family). And as is frequently the case with the poetic texture of the King James Version, an inadvertent ghost metaphor arises from the modern reader's misconstruing of the earlier English. *Long* thus becomes dimensional rather than durational, and *long home* the final, horizontal dwelling of the grave, the place of dust returned to, the place that really was our home all along.

On the other hand, we may remember Wordsworth's skylark, in his sonnet, who flies so high that the poet first wonders whether its "heart and eye" are with some ultimate vanishing point or with its nest on the ground; but he then concludes that the bird, as an emblem of wisdom—but we might rather say of fully self-conceived life—confounds the question, in being "Type of the wise who soar, but never roam, / True to the kindred points of Heaven and Home."[14] The implication that a home, and an inconceivably distant point toward which imaginative energies and enterprise aspire, are somehow kindred suggests an important parable of modernity: the journey out is as much part of the heroic *nostos* as the journey back. This formulation may be more interesting than the mere Neoplatonic reversal of the "Heaven, which is our home" (that is, the soul's; the body's remains, as it were, "Dust, which is our home") of Wordsworth's earlier great "Immortality" ode.

An individual's idea of his or her home can embrace so many of the different senses touched on above. At the same time, any one of them may seem on one occasion or another to be more essential: Is home the place where you lay your head, eat your supper, do your work, ignore your work, make love, experience being greeted, if only exuberantly by one's dog, problematically by one's cat, or even more mutely by one's possessions, feel safe, feel well, instruct one's children? For Georg Simmel, making a home is a unique piece of women's work, bringing into being something both concrete and institutional, rather like a work of art: "The home is an aspect of life and at the same time a special way of forming, reflecting, and interrelating the totality of life."[15] It will also be remembered how a specific local home may cease to be a place one feels at home in; this may entail reinterpreting it as a mere "domicile of origination," and then making one's own private versions of a biblical or Virgilian quest for a new, or true, one.

The world of nature does not necessarily owe us homes. We must in fact construct them, even if only by—in that other sense of the word—construing some bit of naturally afforded shelter as our home. In this, I suppose, cats are our great domestic teachers. Whereas our dogs inhabit our lives, our cats inhabit our dwellings, and are constantly making themselves at home in all sorts of regions and spaces, conforming and causing to conform in ever-renewing instances. But we moderns talk as if we feel that the world of other people does indeed owe everyone a home, or at least some material object to house a home in. And it may be that being a person entails being able to be, and having to be, at home, in the world at large and, by extension, in a successively narrowing set of loci.[16]

In this regard, it might be observed that another important characteristic of home is that "Home is the place where when you have to go there / The way they talk is yours." The matter of language cannot be overlooked, and here again the outwardly radiating circles of enclosure of different spheres of homeliness move out from the idiolect of the household—its private nuanced version of the most local language, which would include both the allusive modes and the allusive materials of its forms of talk—to the dialect of the tribe, as it were. But being at home in, and with, a language is a most complex matter: it may be that certain modes of periodic estrangement from certain aspects of one's native speech can occasion poetry in it, for example. The whole question of language in, and as, home is one whose importance can only be acknowledged, rather than detailed, here.

"Home" can perhaps be construed even as the site, and the seat, of civilization itself. Plato, who seems to want the citizen to be at home only in his *polis,* and who prescribes in the *Laws* (8.848) that every inhabitant of his Just City have a country house and a town house, would not want to associate our Germanic sense of "home" with its withdrawals into the safe houses of our dwellings or, even further, of our post-Cartesian bodies with the houses, which are more for him counters in a game of just allocation.

This brief exploration of some of "what you mean by home" should also acknowledge "home" as the very place of such explorations, the thinker's and writer's home. The cloister and the cell as home places of meditation and work are reflected in secular modernity by the idea of the writer's home, characterized by Montaigne as that *arrière-boutique,* or storeroom, to which one retires from the outside world of family, bed, and board of the rest of his house. The young European or American bourgeoise might be said to retire in sequence from the household to her room to the pages of her dear diary. Ultimately, we can see what looks like a conscious revision both of this and of Montaigne's notion in T. W. Adorno's implication that the ultimate home or study of the deracinated modern writer and thinker is not only on the pages of his text itself but in the matter inscribed there:

> In his text, the writer sets up house. Just as he trundles papers, books, pencils, documents untidily from room to room, he creates the same disorder in his thoughts. They become pieces of furniture that he sinks into, content or irritable. He strokes them affectionately, wears them out, mixes them up, rearranges, ruins them. For a man who no longer has a homeland, writing becomes a place to live. In it he inevitably produces, as his family once did, refuse and lumber. But now he lacks a storeroom, and it is hard in any case to part from leftovers. So he pushes them along in front of him, in danger finally of his filling his pages with them.[17]

But we might best conclude with the high household of philosopher-nobles that we might all be, in Emerson's wonderful appraisal of the economy of material and function and how it runs out of hand. This great passage from his essay

"Nature" also constitutes one of the best comments I know on the complex relations between the means and ends of material "house" and more transcendent "home." It propounds thereby a fitting cautionary parable for our very proceedings in our public discussions, which require a place to house them, but must escape the bondage to materials, constructions, and artifacts that those requisites all too easily afford—we do need to hire a hall, but we had damned well better say something worthwhile there:

> This palace of brick and stone, these servants, this kitchen, these stables, horses and equipage, this bank stock, and file of mortgages; trade to all the world, country house and cottage by the waterside, all for a little conversation, high, clear and spiritual! Could it not be had as well by beggars on the highway? No, all these things came from successive efforts of these beggars to remove friction from the wheels of life, and give opportunity. Conversation, character, were the avowed ends; wealth was good as it appeased the animal cravings, cured the smoky chimney, silenced the creaking door, brought friends together in a warm and quiet room, and kept the children and the dinner table in a different apartment. Thought, virtue, beauty were the ends; but it was known that men of thought and virtue sometimes had the headache, or wet feet, or could lose good time whilst the room was getting warm in winter days. Unluckily, in the exertions necessary to remove these inconveniences, the main attention has been diverted to this object; the old aims have been lost sight of, and to remove friction has come to be the end.[18]

Emerson implicitly reminds us of how humanly insubstantial our constructions of localization may be, and that placing, locating, housing are by no means necessarily homing.

NOTES

1. Richard Poirier, *Robert Frost: The Work of Knowing* (New York: Oxford University Press, 1977), 234–35.
2. Domicile for purposes of jurisdiction of a court would be an instance of this. Thus (from *Mas v. Perry*, 489 F2d 11396 95th Circ., 1974) a woman who formerly lived in Mississippi goes to Louisiana to graduate school, then moves to Illinois; she intends to move back to Louisiana so her husband can complete a degree and has no idea where she will live after that. The court holds that she is domiciled in Mississippi, for all that. Or, hypothetically, X moves from his home in New York to California to be with a terminally ill parent, renting an apartment nearby, hoping to stay there until the parent's death, then return to New York. But he is necessarily domiciled in California, since he can't predict the exact date of the death and of his consequent return.

3. Simon Schama, *The Embarrassment of Riches* (New York: Knopf, 1987), 375–480.

4. But to push this one step further and suggest that one cannot be at home in one's mind goes past the point of functional agency here. I think that one must be oneself in order to feel at—be at—home, where safety, privacy, etc., are characteristic of the ambience. In other words, I have only been talking about relatively sane persons throughout.

5. Johannes Hofer, *Dissertatio de Nostalgia oder Heimweh* (Basel, 1688). A good discussion of some of these feelings about exile, enforced or elected, is in Alan D. McKillop, "Local Attachment and Cosmopolitanism—The Eighteenth-Century Pattern," in *From Sensibility to Romanticism*, ed. Frederick W. Hilles and Harold Bloom (New York: Oxford University Press, 1965), 191–200.

6. Edwin Arlington Robinson, "Miniver Cheevy," from *The Town Down the River* (1910).

7. Joseph Rykwert, *On Adam's House in Paradise: The Idea of the Primitive Hut in Architectural History*, 2d ed. (Cambridge, Mass.: MIT Press, 1981).

8. Nicholas Howe, *Migration and Mythmaking in Anglo-England* (New Haven: Yale University Press, 1989), 180.

9. The name "Penates" derives from *penus,* or "storehouse," and in the most ancient times had been, according to Michael Grant in *Roman Myths* (New York: Scribner's, 1971), 79, "the principal objects of the cult maintained by every Roman household, in which they represented the forces or powers that each family honoured to make sure it had enough food every day."

10. In ironic contrast with this is the early instance of "home," in the 1830s, apparently referring to a barroom or tavern or public house, probably to avoid a tavern tax on entities so named.

11. The modern uses of *focus* in English, involving a center of attention, a sort of internal cynosure of, indeed, what has been "homed in on," all seem to derive from Kepler's first use of it in geometric senses in 1604, although he may have been influenced by an earlier use of it in connection with a parabolic mirror, whose "focus" is at its hottest point (and thus the connection with fire).

12. The famous sonnet from his *Regrets,* beginning "Heureux qui, comme Ulysse, a fait un beau voyage."

13. The trace of a sense of **weik* in one extended use of our very different word *house* can be seen in the English phrase "house of X," meaning patrilineal line, whether of kingship, lordship, or bourgeois possession of a business. The Russian *rodia* (= mother- or father- or birth-land, ancestral land, etc.) deriving from *rod* (= kin, kind) is opposed to *dom* (= house) and is even more strongly differentiated from *priut* (= asylum, shelter). In these brief observations, I have not been able to touch on anything beyond the Indo-European, but it might be noted that these derivations move in various directions. I am told that the

modern Turkish *yurt* (= rent) contracts down from the wider reaches of the Old Turkic word for "country" or "fatherland."

14. William Wordsworth, "To a Skylark" (1825).

15. Georg Simmel, "Female Culture" in *Georg Simmel: On Women, Sexuality, and Love,* tr. and ed. Guy Oakes (1911; New Haven: Yale University Press, 1984), 93–94. Here also he observes more generally, "At least within the more advanced culture of Europe, there is no interest, no gain or loss of either an internal or an external sort, and no domain affected by individuals that does not, together with all other interests, merge into the unique synthesis of the home."

16. I wonder here, though, at the implications of William James's observations, of which Richard Poirier reminds me, that "All 'homes' are in finite experience, finite experience as such is homeless" ("Pragmatism and Humanism," in *Pragmatism* [Cambridge, Mass.: Harvard University Press, 1978], 125.)

17. T. W. Adorno, *Minima Moralia,* tr. E. F. N. Jephcott (London: Verso Editions, 1974), 87. But also see Adorno's remark earlier (39), to the effect that "It is a part of morality not to be at home in one's home."

18. Ralph Waldo Emerson, "Nature," in *Essays and Lectures* (1844; New York: Library of America, 1983), 552.

CHAPTER FIVE

Dreaming Poetry

Dreaming and poetry have been traditionally related in a variety of ways. Dreams, prophetic visions, *furor poeticus* imagined places are similar yet clearly different epistemological derangements all leading to verbal fictions of a peculiar kind as they are reported. Aside from reporting—narrating, describing, invoking—particular dreams, poetry can engage dream in ways more general or oblique. It can celebrate acutely privileged normal states—"the glory and the freshness of a dream"—of Wordsworth's "Immortality Ode" 's conception of the consciousness of childhood—or propound puzzles like Novalis's remark to the effect that we are close to waking when we dream of dreaming (and is that about the physiology of sleep? or is it about metaphor?). There are dreams in and out of poems, poems in and out of dreams. There is the common and interesting challenge that both poems and dreams pose to the idea of intentionality; both the dreamer and the poet could be said to will elements in each of these, but unwittingly. (One thinks of elements of organization, complex trope, overtone, or echo, for example, that a critic might detect in a poem and its author refuse to acknowledge were intentional; the critic might then ask the poet to recall a recent dream of his or hers, and inquire, "Did you *mean* to dream just that?) Certainly, since Freud first showed how dreams should—had to—be read as seriously as poems, ways of viewing this relation between the two have changed. We are in some ways more intensely ourselves while dreaming and perhaps more original than in a world we share with others; as Robert Herrick put it (the thought came from Plutarch quoting, he said, Heraclitus) "Here we are all, by day; by night we're hurled / By dreams, each one, into a several world." All sleepers are poets while they dream; the envisioned metamorphoses and uncanninesses of dream are parallel to, and often emblematic illustrations of, the wordplay of wit and trope in poetry.

In the following pages I touch on some of these questions in the course of looking at a few poems in English written over several hundred years. I deal with modern considerations of dreaming. No matter how a poet might want to write about some aspects of the complex relation between poem and dream, however unwilling or unable he or she is to write as a theorist of any kind, one must start with Freud. I particularly want to start by remarking that the central term for one of the major operations of the dream work itself embodies an agenda. *Verdichtung*—translated by Strachey and thereafter as "condensation"—comes from the old Germanic etymon that is cognate with English *thick*, and to translate it as "thickening" would not be misleading at all. But it accidentally falls together with another word, one of Latin origin (from *dictare*), *Dichtung*, which means "poetry." From my point of view, the word *Verdichtung* in *The Interpretation of Dreams* is extremely well chosen, and is perhaps itself not only allusively *dicht*, or dense, but perhaps *überdeterminiert*, overdetermined for its author as well. Rather than cross-matching (in the manner of Frenchified literary theory following Lacan) oneirocritical condensation and displacement with rhetorical metaphor and metonymy, and so forth, I shall prefer simply to deal with such matters as the *Dichtung* of, and in *Verdichtung*, as well as the rhetorical *Verdichtung* that is as essential to the pointedness, the intensity, of poetry as is its version of *Verschiebung*, or displacement.[1]

I also ask leave to become, at a certain point, personal and even anecdotal. This is partially because the only dreams I can feel—and I feel I deeply know—to exist independently of hearsay—or rather, since I mean someone's report of them, seesay—are my own. The dreams of others are inferences drawn from other people's works of oral or written literature, usually of a genre defined by openings such as "I dreamed *of* . . ."(an older convention) or "I dreamed that [or, that I] . . ." (rather newer, perhaps). The inquiry into a poem is another poem, assert radical theorists of criticism from Oscar Wilde on. "The inquiry into a dream is another dream," maintained the seventeenth-century aphorist Lord Halifax. But that other dream, embodied—as inquiries are—in language, can perhaps cross over and be a poem. Since I have discussed in detail elsewhere the role of certain dreams in poems of my own, I introduce only one instance at the end of this discussion.[2]

We only know about the dreams of others from their verbal performances about—not "of "—them. Frequently in the past these have occurred in—or in the form of—poem or fable. Two issues might be distinguished here: accounts of dreams occur *in* literature before nineteenth- and twentieth-century psychological discourse separates them from fiction; on the other hand, "scientific" accounts of dreams in the last hundred years have continued to reveal their poetic form, and it is only with Freud's great book that every dreamer was revealed to be a far better poet than a prophet. But I suppose the formal literature of dream report is at first a separate matter.

Accounts of dreams and their consequences range throughout literature, starting with the famous biblical ones. There are Jacob's dream of the ladder and, later on (in Genesis 31:10) of the rams, "ring-straked, speckled and grisled"; Joseph's patently prophetic dreams of his own advancement, which he naively— or perhaps not—tells his brothers, and which are followed by his unveiling of the oracular prophecies in the four dreams of the Egyptians; Nebuchadnezzar's dream and the dream of its interpreter, Daniel. Then in Greek tradition there is in the *Iliad* the personified Dream who takes the form of Nestor, and who is sent by Zeus to Agamemnon. More characteristic of the poetic complexities of romance is Penelope's dream, in the nineteenth book of the *Odyssey,* of the eagle killing her wheat-eating household geese. It occurs in a scene of interpretative density: the dream itself contains its own explanation, the eagle telling her that what is happening is all not a dream, but a true waking vision *(ouk anar, all'hupar),* and that he, the eagle, would return as her husband, Odysseus, to dispatch the suitors. But Penelope narrates this to the still-disguised Odysseus who has not yet revealed himself to her. He argues for the eagle's reading (his own, of course, in two senses) of the meaning of the dream. She counters by saying that not all dreams are true ones; and it is here that there is propounded the great fable of the two gates of sleep, of ivory and of horn, through which dreams both true and false pass into the world. The two puns on *keras* (horn)—*krainô* (fulfill) and *elephas* (ivory)—*elephainomai* (deceive) are untranslatable, as they were even for Virgil, who in book 6 of the *Aeneid* removes his account of the gates from Homer's intimate scene of interpretation and surrogacy and domestic disguise. The *Aeneid*'s gates of horn and ivory instead become part of the very landscape of the underworld of Virgil's own poetry, whose protagonist needs a golden bough to enter it and who, in order to leave, must pass out through the ivory gate of fiction and false dreams, rather than that of prophecy, of fulfillable vision. (It is only in book 7, in Turnus's dream of the fury Allecto, that the *Aeneid* returns to the mode of the *Iliad*.)

When a historian of poetry thinks of dreaming a poem, he or she will first consider what is in fact a purely rhetorical convention, often referred to as the medieval mode of dream vision or dream allegory. Although it has its roots in Cicero's *Somnium Scipionis* (from his fragmentary *Republic*) and, particularly Macrobius's elaborate commentary on that text (ca. A.D. 400) the most familiar instances of it for English readers will be William of Langland's *Piers Plowman* and Chaucer's *Book of the Duchess, Parlement of Foules, House of Fame,* and *Legend of Good Women*.[3] The convention is fairly simple: in a first-person narrative account, the poet finds himself in some *locus amoenus*—a lovely garden or pleasant wood—usually in springtime.

Falling asleep to the sounds of a stream and the song of birds, he dreams either of personified abstractions or of more plausible personages behaving in ritualized or symbolic fashion. In some instances, the dreamer may be a reader, falling asleep over a book; but in any case, the matter of literary convention tends to obscure matters of dream work. Two exceptions might be briefly noted in passing, though: one of these involves the dreamer's knowledge of the (frequently allegorical) name of a personage from the outset; the other is that in the occasional work of genius by a poet like Chaucer, the poesis of the fiction itself will suggest the ulteriority of dreaming.

Chaucer's *Legend of Good Women*, for example, starts out from a promise he had made at the end of a previous work, the long *Troilus and Criseyde*, for a poem in praise of virtuous women like Penelope and Alcestis, as a kind of penance. His poem opens in praise of first books, then of the spring flowers for which he abandons them, in particular the "flower of all flowers" the daisy (its English name invoking the "day's eye," because the flower closes up at night). The poet spends the day in the fields, in adoration of the flower; when it folds up, he returns to his bed, strewn with flowers, and goes to sleep. His dream is of the God of Love, appearing to him holding by the hand some queen, dressed in green, with a white crown, which "made her like a daisy to behold" (I modernize Chaucer's Middle English here). She is "Alceste the debonaire," the meek Alcestis (who, it will be remembered, offered to die in place of her husband Admetus, did so, but was rescued from Hades and returned to Admetus by Heracles). She comes to the poet's defense, and as a consequence of this, he resolves to write in praise of virtuous and heroic women, thus framing the separate narratives that follow. Having preferred daisies to women, as one critic remarks, he now dreams of a daisy-woman who is herself the queen of womanly virtue. (Meredith Skura, in her fine book on psychoanalytic process and literary interpretation, elegantly compares this fictional dream, highly conventionalized as it is, with Freud's analysis of his own "Dream of the Botanic Monograph," and I shall not go over that matter here.[4])

Even more interesting for a number of reasons is the strange account of the dream that constitutes Chaucer's aforementioned remarkable early poem, *The Book of the Duchess*, written in consolation of John of Gaunt for the death of his wife, Blanche, Duchess of Lancaster, of the plague in 1368. The poem starts out with the narrator reading a medieval romance version of Ovid's story of Ceys and Alcyon, in which a mourning woman's drowned husband returns to her in a dream, his body having been animated by Morpheus, god of sleep and of dreamed human shape. The poet then falls asleep and dreams that he awakens to birdsong on a May morning, followed by the sound of hunting horns; he goes out onto a field where a noble emperor is hunting a great hart. He is then led into a phantasmagoric wood by a little dog who eventually runs away from him. In the wood, his back against an oak tree (associated with death in medieval tradition), is a man dressed in black, reciting a conventional poem of medieval complaint. The dreamer, not understanding that the poem is literal utterance, and that the man in black really means that death has taken his wife away, asks him what makes him so woeful.

Throughout the poem, in which the Knight in Black tells the whole story of his love, from first meeting to her death, the dreamer continues to ask stupid questions—for example, when the Black Knight says he'd played chess with Fortune, and Fortune had taken his queen, the dreamer, dumbly and literal-mindedly, voices disbelief that so much sorrow could accrue from the loss of a chess piece. Only after the Knight in Black has completed his tale is the dreamer's last uncomprehending question answered with an unequivocal "She is dead." "Nay!" he replies. The Black Knight: "Yes, by my truth." "Is that your loss?" responds the dreamer, "By God, it's a pity." And with that, all the mourning comes to an end, and the "hart-hunting," with its appropriate pun, as well; the dreamer follows the emperor to "a long castle" with white walls, on "a rich hill" thus inscribing into the dream, and into the poem, the name of Blanche (white), and John of Richmond (rich mount) Duke of Lancaster (long castle)—her grieving husband.

The seeming stupidity of the dreamer is considered by scholars to be the first instance of Chaucer's use of a fictitious narrator from whom he as author is keeping an ironic distance. But we might observe here that such apparent stupidity occurs all the time in dreams totally uninfluenced by the conventions of medieval poetry. And we should have to say that Chaucer's remarkable poem incorporates dream work independently of its framing fiction: the hunting of the hart-heart as pursuit of a love utterly lost, and the rebuslike punning on the name of the allegorically invoked Duchess, are both the stuff of poem work in medieval and Renaissance verse. The seemingly uncomprehending repetitions by the narrator-dreamer of a question with an obvious answer are the stuff even of modern dreaming. (The whole question of the poem's unacknowledged ironic reversal of the sexes of the mourners in Ovid's story and in the dreamer's response to it touches on both realms. The literary device of the reversal is the work of a strongly original poet, but the lack of acknowledgment of it is both strangely modern and clearly dreamlike.) And yet I would hesitate to say that Chaucer's invention had either (a) employed memories of some of his own dreams or (b) somehow prophetically anticipated by sheer imagination a pattern in dream experience, which could not itself become noticeable until the invention by Freud of modern oneirocritical writing, and the narrative style of the examples in *The Interpretation of Dreams,* in particular.

Chaucer's great poem seems trivially connected but strangely related to what is perhaps the greatest and most celebrated dreamed poem of the seventeenth century, and that may deserve some attention here. It is John Milton's twenty-third sonnet, recording a dream of the return to him of his deceased wife, dressed in white, her face veiled; when she bends forward to embrace him, he awakens but—as a totally blind dreamer inevitably must—to darkness.

Methought I saw my late espoused saint
  Brought to me like Alcestis from the grave,
  Whom Jove's great son to her glad husband gave,
Rescued from death by force though pale and faint.
Mine as whom washed from spot of childbed taint,
  Purification in the old Law did save,
  And such, as yet once more I trust to have
Full sight of her in heaven without restraint,
Came vested all in white, pure as her mind:
  Her face was veiled, yet to my fancied sight
  Love, sweetness, goodness in her person shined
So clear, as in no face with more delight.
  But O as to embrace me she inclined
  I waked, she fled, and day brought back my night.

The poem has traditionally presented an apparently insoluble difficulty for scholars, but before going into this central matter, I would like to observe that the very opening phrase of the sonnet is at once almost formulaic and yet allusively dense. "Methought I saw . . ." appears to signal for late sixteenth and early seventeenth century English poetry the onset of a dream report. We can find its post-Miltonic use in, for example, Shelley's "Triumph of Life," linked as much with medieval dream vision as with Milton ("This was the tenour of my waking dream. / Methought I sate beside a public way"). And indeed, its first occurrence, as far as I know, is in the poem of Chaucer we have just been considering. The dreamer starts the narration of the dream in *The Book of the Duchess* by saying "Lo, thus it was, this was my dream; / Me thought thus: That it was May," etc. (And again, fifty-odd lines later, "Me thought I heard a huntsman blow / To test his horn.") Nowhere else does Chaucer use "Methought I—" to introduce a dream account.

The phrase surfaces again at the opening of Sir Walter Raleigh's dedicatory sonnet (1590) to Spenser's *Faerie Queene*. It starts out with a purely fictional dream that makes clear the author's feeling that the true Muse-Heroine of Spenser's poem has replaced their great precursor Petrarch's famous Laura:

Methought I saw the grave, where *Laura* lay
Within that Temple, where the vestal flame

Was wont to burn, and passing by that way,
To see what buried dust of living fame,
Whose tomb fair love, and fairer virtue, kept,
All suddenly I saw the Fairy Queen.

Shakespeare's Bottom in *A Midsummer Night's Dream* (V.i), awakening from
sleep after the ass's head has been removed from his own, convinced that he has
dreamed it all (and just after Demetrius has said "It seems to me / That yet we
sleep, we dream," and led the courtly party off with the suggestion "And by the
way, lets recount our dreams"), utters his resonant "I have had a most rare vision.
I have had a dream, past the wit of man to say what dream it was. Man is but an
ass, if he go about t' expound this dream. Methought I was—there is no man can
tell what. Methought I was, and methought I had—but man is but a fool, if he
will only offer to say what methought I had." The formula occurs elsewhere in
Shakespeare (in *Richard II, The Tempest, Hamlet, Cymbeline,* and *2 Henry IV.*)

Indeed, the translation by "R.D." of the first part of Francesco Colonna's
Hypnerotomachia Poliphili entitled *The Strife of Love in a Dream* (1592) starts out
with the narrator being full of sorrowful thoughts, lying sleeplessly "in the high
cogitations of love," then falling into a "heavie sleepe": "Methought I was in a
large, plaine and champion place, all greene and diversly spotted with many
sorted flowers, whereby it seemed passingly adorned." Other instances of the
"methought" formula for introducing dream reports abound: Eve's "me-
thoughts" in telling of her dream in book 5 of *Paradise Lost* and Adam's "Abstract
as in a trance methought I saw" in book 8 are echoed by his nonformulaic, pre-
sent-tense "methinks," for example. There are occurrences of it in *Comus* and in
Areopagitica. Worth considering for a moment is Eve's account of her dream in
Paradise Lost 5.35–36: "methought / Close at mine ear one call'd me forth to
talk"; likewise its parallel in book 8.295 when Adam reports that "One came,
methought, of shape Divine." But the centrally relevant repetition of the phrase,
I feel, is in a passage a bit further on (8.460ff):

Mine eyes he clos'd, but op'n left the Cell
Of Fancy my internal sight, by which
Abstract as in a trance methought I saw,
Though sleeping, where I lay, and saw the shape
Still glorious before whom awake I stood.

The syntax is fluid and ambiguous ("where I lay"—a scene, a placement—is the
object of "methought I saw," and yet it seems to modify "though sleeping" as
well), underlining the contingency of the "methought" vision.

The formula reoccurs in Dryden's *Annus Mirabilis,* "Christabel," *The Prelude,*
"The Fall of Hyperion," and "The Triumph of Life," these later instances perhaps

being derived from Shakespeare and Milton. I cite these prior uses of "Methought—" for "I dreamed that" to suggest that Milton's phrase is allusively overdetermined in the way that so much in poetry always is; in particular, the association with the dream of the mourner in Chaucer, and of a Muse's tomb in Raleigh, not to speak of the deep consequences of Bottom's skepticism about the possibility of any sort of dream account (after all, he *hadn't* been dreaming) all seem at work in the very framing of the report of the dream in Milton's enigmatic poem.

The enigma turns on the identity of the "late espoused saint" here (and let us remember that the word "saint" in sixteenth- and seventeenth-century English can mean a soul in heaven). It could easily refer to Milton's first wife, Mary Powell, or to his second one, Katharine Woodcock. Mary died, three days after the birth of a daughter, in May 1652; Katharine died in 1658, more than three months after the birth of their daughter. The lines about the "spot of childhood taint" refer to the "old Law" of Leviticus 12:4–8 specifying that, after the birth of a girl, a woman shall be unclean for two weeks, and must continue her period of purification for thirty-six days. Mary Powell died before being washed of that spot, Katharine did not. Yet the veiled figure in the dream appears "as whom washed, . . . etc.," which could mean the returned wife was Katharine (the word *katharos* meaning "pure" in Greek). Mary Powell was his wife before his final total blindness; he never saw Katharine. The veiling of the figure is a complex matter. Alcestis herself was veiled on her return from the underworld, but a veil could be part of a dead woman's shroud, or associated with a ceremony of thanksgiving after childbirth in the English Church. And veiled figures are crucial in two central episodes in Spenser's *Faerie Queene,* a poem that always meant a great deal for Milton. In both cases the veils cover the faces of figures assumed to be female—Nature, sitting at an important trial, and a figure of Venus set up in her temple—and in both cases Spenser implies that the veil prevents a viewer from determining whether the figure is really female or male. The effect in the dream is certainly to hide the face, and perhaps the identity, of the wife, however much it may function as a displacement of Milton's own blindness, in the case of Katharine whose face was figuratively always veiled to him.

Scholars of Milton's work have sought to identify the veiled figure as either Mary or Katharine, and to treat, almost with some irritation, the poem as being biographically veiled for them.[5] Unfortunately, there is one external indeterminacy. It is most probable that the poem was written between 1658 and 1660: the copyist in whose hand we have the manuscript of the poem worked for Milton between those years, and while he might possibly have been making a fair copy of something composed earlier, it is most reasonable to assume the later date of the poem. But it might possibly have been written earlier, before Katharine Woodcock's death. Yet in that case, the final line would merely echo an easy

Petrarchan sonneteer's paradox ("dreaming of you makes night day, and awaking from the dream into mere daylight is a dark night," etc.). But it is so characteristic of Milton to work a deeply revisionary turn on poetic conventions that one may almost assume that in this poem, the familiar sort of paradox is resolved by a terrible literalism—"and day brought back my night" not only tropes the loss of the dreamed presence in a return to the darkness of absence— for the vanishing of the dream figure doubles the loss of both wives by death once again. But it additionally describes a totally blind man awakening from a vivid dream. I think the assimilation of the two wives—the as-yet-unpurified Mary (her name significant here too, perhaps) and the pure but unseen Katharine—is inescapable, and the purely poetic devices of the opening and ending aside, the poem does indeed report an actual dream. And yet the *Verdichtung* of the figure of the "late espousèd saint" is augmented by the *Dichtung* of the association with Alcestis, the dual dreamt and alluded-to function of the veil, and so forth.

It is with respect to this conventional literary fiction of the text of the poem as literal transcription of a dream—and hence given the complex rhetorical authority mentioned earlier—that I introduce the following dream. Or, perhaps, joke. It was reported to me more than fifteen years ago as a comical but factual anecdote—perhaps more of what Freud distinguished as *ein Scherz* rather than *ein Witz*—of the kind in which nature is doing the work it has learned from art. I do not recount it here as the text of an interpretable dream. This would be grossly irresponsible, in view of two lacks of qualifications: my own, for this sort of work, and the dream's, because only the barest facts about the dreamer are known to me (it was reported to me by a close confidante of a friend of hers). Please consider this story, then, only as a joke about the myth of Coleridge's "Kubla Khan" and its tribe, yet perhaps a joke whose punch line sheds some lingering light along with its loud report. I acknowledge the risk of having it greeted—by hardworking, street-smart, *Traumpilizei* who have heard it all—with yawns, and adduce it only as a story that poets, variously concerned with getting access to knowledge of their own that they are not aware of, have found hilarious.

The dreamer was, in this case, a somewhat thoughtful person in the world of broadcasting, at a period in her life marked by considerable anxiety about her own effectiveness and abilities as well as by other concerns.

The Dream of the Magical Utterance

> She is at a cocktail party with a lot of very chic people [she tends always to feel madly unchic at such gatherings]. She enters the room, and starts up a conversation with one of the guests; after a brief time, they are joined by another, and successively another and another, etc. By the time there are five or six people, they are all pressing in upon the dreamer, accusing her

of incompetence, particularly in discourse; she remembers that she is told many times that she cannot "get her facts straight." She is unable, finally to talk at all, and the others back her into a corner of the room, to her great consternation and anxiety. But there suddenly occurs to her a wonderful, powerful, effective thing to say, an almost magical utterance, at which they all simply fall away, and the dreamer immediately awakens.

The dreamer, being habituated by whatever form of psychotherapy it was to keeping a pad of paper by her bed, immediately upon awakening transcribes the utterance, being certain that she will forget its exact form in the morning. Upon awakening later, remembering the dream and the inscription, she rushes to read it. On the pad she has written "Go away!"

For poetry, the double irony is not only in the explosive demystifications (1) of the imaginative and prophetic privilege of ancient and outmoded conceptions of dreams and their nature and (2) of overly simple conceptions of what verbal magic is. It also involves a return to the beauty and magic of the residual words. If one were, indeed, in perfect command of him- or herself, and one's words were, indeed, *epea pteroenta,* the "winged words" that Homer keeps referring to, then, indeed, a well-directed "Shut up!" would have all the effective power of muttered witches' spells, or the Original Imperative, the divine "Let there be light." And, ultimately, this may be a joke about dreaming poems.

The whole question of poetic dream transcription, then, involves something as close perhaps to re-dreaming a dream as it is to working through an interpretation of it. For a poet, too, the language in which a vision is framed constitutes much of the vision itself, and frequently the structure and allusiveness of the language of the narrative will exhibit many analogues of language in dreams themselves. Major original poems will frequently echo other poems, in a curious version of the allusiveness of dream work; I have discussed this in detail in a little book called *The Figure of Echo,* and I shall only observe here that poetic dreams often echo other ones.[6] The dream of the Arab presenting a stone and a shell to the dreamer in book 5 of *The Prelude* certainly echoes Descartes's famous dream of the books, for example. The very modes of transcription may be, as we have seen in medieval poetry, conventionalized. And a poet's insistence that he or she has dreamed a particular account of a dream always must be a manifest fiction, for clearly, metrical schemes and patterns, rhymes, rhetorical conventions, are part of the language of transcription. Asking whether, in a particular patient's narrative account of a dream, the "And then . . ." used at a particular moment were part of the content (as opposed, say, to simply a "Then . . . ," which might have been used) opens up the matter of the warp of necessary discursive convention upon which the fabric of the dream report is woven. But a poet's dream will seldom have occurred "in" the verse form, rhyme scheme, rhetorical framework, etc., within which it is transcribed. (I except from this, actual auditions in dreams of utterances cast into verse; I have myself "heard" single lines of iambic pentameter, if not in full dreams, then in hypnogogic or hypnopompic occurrences during very light sleep.) And yet the poem of dreaming will frequently appear to insist that it has been dreamed as a very utterance. And this is a poetic convention of its own.

I might note the following, though. The poet Vicki Hearne has on several occasions literally dreamed a poem in the sense of dreaming a text. A typeset page would appear, with words in line and stanzas (and on one occasion, a recognizable typeface [Bookman]), but with the bottom part of the page tilted slightly so as to be blurred and illegible. Upon awakening she copied out the text and then, as it were, "supplied" the illegible part, although the process of that composition was as tentative and fraught with crossing out and revisions as a draft of any of her poems. And yet the dreamed material is not in the least dreamlike—which is to say that it partakes in no way of any of the various literary conventions of dream report. In one such poem, "The Absence of Horses," from her 1983 volume of the same name, the dreamed section begins

Action is love. Once stillness
Is lost, once the surface blurs
And the lake heaves with the stone
In its heart, action failing
Is love choking and stillness
Becomes a putrefaction

and ends

     Action is speech
(Not speech action) the utter
Parole, its benevolence
A fusion.
    *[and here the text became illegible, and
thus the completion of this last line—the missing 7 syllables—and the continuation
were all done in order to "save" the poem]*[7]

The author, by the way, makes no claim to having, in some romantic sense "dreamed the poem," but rather, far more pragmatically, only to having "dreamed that she had written, and was now reading, the poem on the partially legible page before her."

Christina Rossetti, now being regarded again as a poet of great imaginative power, writes rather conventionally of dream, waking, and desire in the third sonnet of "Monna Innominata." But she deals with dreaming much more powerfully and problematically in a strange poem called "My Dream," which begins

Hear now a curious dream I dreamed last night,
Each word whereof is weighed and sifted truth.[8]

Her language here is sufficiently ambiguous, in the way of poems, as to beg
central questions: a dream, the words "whereof"—that is, words *about* the
dream, its narration with whatever built-in secondary revision occurs, etc., or
the dream's own words, as if, for a poet, it had been built of language alone.
Every real poet's words are "weighed and sifted truth," not because they are
used in logically determinate propositions, which may be synthetically or ana-
lytically "true," but because they are true as *treu,* as keeping faith, and consistent
with the poem's own conception of language and what can be done with it. It
is significant, then, that the claim of authenticity for the dream report is implicitly hedged in this way, unlike Samuel Taylor Coleridge's famous—even canonical—account, purely fictional but offered as truth, of the genesis of his "Kubla
Khan" in an opium dream. The transcription of this, it will be remembered,
started immediately upon awakening, was interrupted by the celebrated person
"from the neigbouring village of Porlock" who thus, according to Coleridge,
caused the truncation of the dreamt poem.

Whether the identification of a poem as a dream is ancillary—epigraphic,
glossorial, anecdotal—to the poem itself is of some interest. Such an identification may be part of the text itself—and thus a candidate for figurativeness,
rather than being a lie or a mistake. A fruitfully problematic marginal case is that
of Emily Dickinson's disturbing tale (no. 1670) of the worm in her room
("Pink, lank and warm") that is subsequently doubled by "A snake with mottles
rare" who speaks in the tones more of Milton's Satan than of the serpent of
Genesis. The narrator flees this uncanny encounter, ending in an alighting that
is often a trope for awakening:

Nor ever ceased to run
Till in a distant Town
Towns on from mine
I set me down
This was a dream.

But the status of the final assertion is ambiguous: the poem seems to conclude
with the rhyming quatrain—*Town / down* provides some kind of terminus to a
tale of fear and flight, so that the last line may be a postscript in authorial metalanguage. And yet, given the loosely occasional rhyming pattern of the whole
poem, the pararhyme *down / dream* can provide a mode of closure of its own,
and the poem could include the dream attestation for its own governing tropes.

But let us return to Rossetti's dream. It is of the river Euphrates, out of
whose "myriad pregnant waves there welled / Young crocodiles." The preg-

nancy of the waves with crocodile young is simply Renaissance mythological folklore, ubiquitous in poets like Spenser, and if "each word" of this report were indeed "weighed and sifted truth," it should have to begin: "I dreamed a scene from one of the older poets, like Spenser." But no matter. The dream continues with an account of how one particular crocodile, larger and stronger than the rest, lording it over them, eventually ate them all up. (This seems very much in the fashion of one of the Egyptian dreams that Joseph interprets — the one prophetic of famine, in which lean cows eat up fat cows.) Then the surviving crocodile "dwindled to the common size," and a winged boat appeared that

. . . levelled strong Euphrates in its course;
Supreme yet weightless as an idle mote
It seemed to tame the waters without force
Till not a murmur swelled or billow beat:
Lo, as the purple shadow swept the sands,
The prudent crocodile rose on his feet
And shed appropriate tears and wrung his hands.

What can it mean? you ask. I answer not
For meaning, but myself must echo, What?
And tell it as I saw it on the spot.

Christina Rossetti echoes more than her fictional questioner here, for the dream itself is a strangely rewritten version of a remarkable dream that occurs in Spenser's *Faerie Queene,* book 5, canto 7. The heroine, named Britomart, a female knight usually disguised in armor as a male one, enters a temple of Isis, where she sees an image of the Egyptian goddess standing with her foot on a crocodile, identified with Osiris. (Isis is also associated in this region of the poem with Equity, and Osiris with Justice.) Britomart falls asleep beside the altar and dreams that she is herself a priestess of Isis, making an offering that is interrupted by a tempest that rages through the temple (the near-pun is operative) and a fire that threatens to destroy it. This awakens the crocodile at the feet of the image of the goddess; he devours the flames and the storm and then turns on the dreamer to devour her, but the goddess beats him back with her rod, at which he becomes docile and loving. The dreamer accepts his love, and he then draws so near her "that of his game she soone enwombed grew, / And forth did bring a lion of great might." She awakes, frightened and "doubtfully dismayd" (and here Spenser puns on dis-maided, or devir-ginated). The priests of Isis console her by interpreting the crocodile in the dream as being her lover (whom they do not know, whereas the reader already does — he is Artegall, patron of Justice); they similarly identify Isis's crocodile as Osiris, so that her lover and Justice are connected through the dream by interpreters unwitting of the allegorical connection in the story-world that frames them all.

Rossetti knew Spenser well (a year or so before the composition of this poem, in 1854, she had been doing some scholarly research on *The Faerie Queene*), and the dream in her poem may be a reworking of Britomart's dream vision in just the way poems—often very original poems—revise earlier ones.

The ironically moralized ending breaks the mythopoetic context to the degree that the surviving crocodile becomes simply the proverbial one, shedding "appropriate," that is, "crocodile," tears. This is a far cry from the fulfilled prophecy at the end of Spenser's episode (the Tudor lion being in one sense the progeny of Britomart and Artegall, who are perhaps also conjoined in a dream-like way, by the final and initial syllables of their respective names, as a Britomartegall). On the other hand, one of Christina Rossetti's literary biographers has reasonably argued that her crocodile may have been *her* friend, the painter William Bell Scott.[9] The ultimate aftermath, for our concerns, is the author's notation, several decades later, on a printed text of the poem; it reads, "not a real dream." But even in view of what is clearly a poetic allusiveness in the structure and content, I am not precisely sure how much this inscription closes down the problem of the relation of dreamed fiction and fictional dream in this rather remarkable text.

Space does not allow me to yield here to the temptation of discussing in any detail a number of fascinating instances of dreamed poem or poemed dream— as it were—that suggest themselves. A full account of Eve's dream in *Paradise Lost* book 5 would require many pages. The complex admixture of possible actual dream report and notional one—as well as the matter of some actual or fictive aftermath—marks James Merrill's dream episode ("Last night I dreamed the dream called Laundry") in his poem called "The Mad Scene." The celebrated dream-within-a-dream of Lermontov's *"Son"* ("The Dream")—in which a dying soldier in a dale in Daghestan dreams of a young woman who is dreaming of a dying soldier in a dale in Daghestan—seems to exemplify one aspect of Novalis's aphorism quoted at the beginning of these remarks. A brilliant play on the transition of dream to awakened reality considered as Ovidian metamorphosis occurs in a poem by Robert Herrick called "The Vine." The speaker dreams that he is changed into a vine and overgrows and surrounds his "dainty Lucia" so entwining about her "that she could not freely stir. / All parts there made one prisoner." The poem ends with a metamorphic extension of the dream (and/or of a trope) into the waking state, here precisely that of waking with an erection:

But when I crept with leaves to hide
Those parts which maids keep unespied,
Such fleeting pleasures there I took

That with the fancy I awoke,
And found (ah me!) this flesh of mine
More like a stock than like a vine.[10]

And John Donne tropes dreaming/waking more generally as perfection/truth in the first strophe of "The Dream," in which, being awakened by his lover from a dream, he avers that she had awakened him

. . . wisely; yet
My dream thou brok'st not, but continud'st it,
Thou art so truth, that thoughts of thee suffice,
To make dreams truths, and fables histories;
Enter these arms, for since thou thoughtst it best
Not to dream all my dream, let's act the rest.

An unusually well-edited collection (by Stephen Brook) of texts in *The Oxford Book of Dreams* contains hundreds of passages recounting dreams, ninety-six of them in verse. A rhetorical taxonomy of dream report might easily start with a discussion of its pages alone.

I conclude these observations with a slightly more unusual instance of coping poetically with the stuff of dream. It is that of a poem of mine from the fall of 1975, called "The Angler's Story."[11] It actually recorded no particular dream at all, but embodied—in what I now realize is something of a dreamlike way—my concern about my own articulateness during a somewhat agitated period of my life shortly after my first wife and I had separated. The dreaming involved was all actually hypnogogic material: for about a month, while staying at a celebrated colony for artists and writers, I became briefly obsessed with the idea that my speech had become slightly incoherent—that I was stumbling over polysyllabic words from time to time, that I was producing spoonerisms and other strange locutions. As it happened, I had found most of the other people silly, ignorant, and insufficiently intelligent and interesting for the degree of vanity they exhibited. But before I realized that I had best leave this unrewarding place and return to my home and friends in New York City, I experienced a strange transformation in the fringes of dreaming, the hypnopompic foyer, and the hypnogogic realm from which we keep awakening with fragments of material. (In my experience, these are not narrative situations—one truly dreams "of" something, rather than "that" something, for example. It is a condition in which one might be said to dream an emblem, rather than a place, an occasion, an event, and in which one is not present as subject.) In this instance, these fragments were all auditions rather than visions; and although I have always had these, awakening to a phrase or sentence, rather than to a visual presentation, in the present instance, these auditions were confused and incoherent. They were, I later realized, extreme—almost caricatured—representations of what I had falsely fancied was occasionally occurring in my actual speech. But they only added to my disturbance at the time. Some months later I tried to write of this. The poem that finally came about may be relevant to some of what I have been considering, precisely because, although dealing in some way with dream material, it records none of it, and yet seems to have the form and content of a dream report itself. (This is also something I did not realize until long after the poem was published.) At the time I was simply addressing the metaphor of vertical layers of sleep and consciousness—of surfaces and depths—as well as trying to deal with the problem of how all those jumbled syllables and words and phrases were not part of something happening to me, but something I had, as it were, "come up with." This immediately established the whole framing metaphor of the poem. (The form of the poem, by the way—a sonnetlike pattern of fourteen lines of fourteen unmeasured syllables, unrhymed—was simply given by my mode of working at the time. There are other verses of mine in the same and related patterns.)

The Angler's Story

I let down my long line; it went falling; I pulled. Up came
A bucket of bad sleep in which tongues were sloshing about
Like frogs and dark fish, breaking the surface of silence, the
Forgetfulness, with what would have been brightness in any Other element,
    flash of wave, residual bubbling,
But were here belches of shadow churned up by the jostling
Tongues from the imageless thick bottom of the heavy pail.
I could not reach into that fell stuff after them, nor fling
Them back into night like inadequate fish; nor would they Lie flat and silent
    like sogged leaves that had been flung under
Mud, but burbled of language too heavy to be borne, of Drowned inflections
    and smashed predications, exactness pulped
Into an ooze of the mere desire to utter. It was
My bucket, and I have had to continue to listen.

Fish stories are lies or exaggerations, and I was consciously propounding a fiction here. I had not "dreamed" any of these images, but rather, poetically, "dreamed them up." And not "out of thin air," but rather in the imagination's thickened one. The figure of depths and surfaces figured as a pond or pool is an old metaphor for the mind, the consciousness, which has surfaces and depths, and I was deliberately engaging it. Perhaps all I can add here is that one word occurring right in the middle of the poem, "imageless," resonated with a half-conscious allusion to Shelley, in *Prometheus Unbound*. The personage called Asia, descending into a kind of underworld to consult a strange being called

Demogorgon, receives from him the knowledge that "The deep truth is image-less." I suppose that what I had done in the poem was to construct a dream that I had never had, but dealing with a problem of incoherence that I fancied I had. And I suppose that the concluding sentence concerns the general mandate, handed to one by one's dreams, to continue to interpret, to take some kind of responsibility for what waking consciousness insists one is not responsible for: "It was / My bucket, and I have had to continue to listen."

NOTES

1. On the question of translating some of Freud's terms into English, see Bruno Bettelheim, *Freud and Man's Soul* (New York: Alfred A. Knopf, 1983), 65–108 in particular. He comments on, among other matters, *Die Traumdeutung* as being echoically parallel to *Sterndeutung;* also on *Deutung* vs. *Erklärung.* The most frequently commented on translations are, of course, *Ich* = ego; *Es* = id; *Trieb* = instinct (or, later, drive), etc. But no he does not discuss *Dichtung-Verdichtung* here.

2. The role of dreams in my own poems is discussed in an essay called "The Dream of the Trumpeter," *Dreamworks* 1 (summer 1980): 101–5.

3. Chapter 3 of Macrobius's celebrated commentary is important for its taxonomy. It distinguishes five different kinds of dream, each with subtypes: enigmatic *(somnium),* prophetic *(visio),* oracular *(oraculum),* nightmare *(insomnium),* and apparition *(visum)*—prophetic dreams are like oracular ones, but in them the premonition turns out to have been true (as if this were part of the typology of dream itself). See *Commentary on the Dream of Scipio,* tr. William Harris Stahl (New York: Columbia University Press, 1952), 82–93.

4. Meredith Anne Skura, *The Literary Use of the Psychoanalytic Process* (New Haven: Yale University Press, 1981), 142–60.

5. See the discussion of sonnet 23 in A. S. P. Woodhouse and Douglas Bush, 4 vols., *A Variorum Commentary on the Poems of John Milton* (New York: Columbia University Press, 1972), 2:486–501. Since the present essay was written, there has appeared Eleanor Cook's brilliant and definitive article on the early and later uses of the term, " 'Methought' as Dream Formula in Shakespeare, Milton, Wordsworth, Keats, and Others," *English Language Notes* 32, no. 4(June 1995): 34–46.

6. John Hollander, *The Figure of Echo: A Mode of Allusion in Milton and After* (Berkeley: University of California Press, 1981).

7. Vicki Hearne, *In the Absence of Horses* (Princeton: Princeton University Press, 1983), 53.

8. Christina Rossetti, *Poetical Works,* ed, W. M. Rossetti (London: Macmillan, 1904), 315; William Michael's note is on p. 479.

9. Lona Mask Packer, *Christina Rossetti* (Berkeley: University of California Press, 1963), 94–98.

10. "If we must find a probability test for the bizarre imagery of seventeenth-century poetry, let us ask, not 'What would it be like to see this in actual fact?' but rather, 'What would it be like to dream this?' " A. D. Nuttall, *Two Concepts of Allegory* (New York: Routledge and Kegan Paul, 1967), 88. Not unrelated to this question would be the rebuslike pictorial punning ubiquitous in devices on arms and in northern Renaissance art, as well as the fascination, through an association with Freudian analyses of the dream work, of surrealism with Renaissance and baroque emblems and devices.

11. In my *Selected Poetry* (New York: Alfred A. Knopf, 1995), 170.

CHAPTER SIX

Of of: *The Poetics of a Preposition*

For poetry in English, prepositions may be the most private parts of speech. They carry no manifest freight of reference and thus cannot easily be misapplied for figuration without falling into the kind of solecism that even far-fetched tropes escape. For example, "Give it back of me"—for "Give it back to me"—sounds only like bungled English, whereas "Give her back to the grass," say, or the notorious pseudopredication of Chomsky's "colorless green ideas sleep furiously" would not. They would only sound figurative. (In this latter case, as Frank Kermode pointed out in the instance of an exemplary phrase used by John Searle, there are allusive dimensions to the total rhetorical activity of the sentence.[1]) The romance of nouns, then of verbs, at various periods in the history of meditative grammar has been discussed by linguists,[2] and the implicit nonliteral predications of adjectives and adverbs are acknowledged by rhetorical theory.

It is less common to observe that the senses of prepositions may be transferred to some of the same effect as those of other parts of speech. Dickens's celebrated zeugma in *The Pickwick Papers,* "She went straight home, in a flood of tears and a Sedan chair," is not usually analyzed, for example, as turning on two different senses of the preposition "in." And yet there is only one sense of "arrive" employed here. (On the other hand, by that magnificently revisionary use of a mere comma—where a grosser spirit might have employed the rib-elbowing dash—in Norman Douglas's *South Wind* [in re a questionable priest] "He was a fisher of men, and of women" the invitation is extended to take "men" in its more limited, gender-bound sense; the prepositions remain fixed in their use.)

I have suggested elsewhere that one of the great sources of difficulty in Emily Dickinson's poetry is her use of prepositions in ways that are, at more than merely first glance, quite opaque[3]. Sometimes it is merely a matter of a sort of prepositional trope involving the substitution of one for another, as in poem 1745: "Uncertified of scene / Signified of sound," where *of* = *by* at a first reading; the additional resonances of similar constructions ("neat of dress," "tall of stature") only clouding the syntactic clarity later on. On the other hand, take the third line of poem 1569, "A Vagabond for Genesis" (whether or not it is appositive of "Some schism in the Sum" in the previous line—the syntax is quite ambiguous, too), the preposition is itself much harder and more unyielding than the elusive but inviting pairing of the nouns it relates. A vagabond *from* (the land of) Genesis? (Unwittingly) headed for it? Wandering within it? A vagabond aimlessly, or even methodically, revising or misdoing the work of genesis? Or again, the "by" in "Eternity by term" (no. 615): does this mean "what is termed Eternity," whatever it is we call by that name or (perhaps necessarily) pseudonym? Does it designate a contingent Eternity, one that indeed has a finite term? Or do both readings command our attention in that strange way of great poetry, wherein the relation between the two (what we call X is a contingent X, or possibly even, because it's contingent we call it by the name of the real thing, etc.) comes into play? One feels that Dickinson's *for*'s and *by*'s are being pressed into multivalent service of the kind we often see at work with the preposition *of*.

This may be the most modest of our prepositions; like *by* and *for,* it lacks the active directedness of all those others that occur in pairs that help map their roles: up/down, in/out, to/from, over/under, before/after, before/behind, for/against, etc., all of which provide fundamental categories for the construction of tropes of lyric and romance. Unlike *by* and another sense of *for,* its phonology is pale and unmarked: with no initial consonant, our most reduced vowel, unstressed *schwa,* and a final voiced labial fricative, it becomes easily elided in speech (thus slightly archaic *o'* as in "Clock o' Clay," or, in modern American fiction's ad hoc mode of transcription, simply *a* as in "cuppa cawfee," or the British Dairy Board's advertisement of twenty years ago, "Drinka Pinta Milka Day," which plays wittily with it in the middle term).

But *of* is grammatically complex, both from a synchronic and a diachronic viewpoint. The sixty-odd types of sense that the OED distinguishes aside, in the paradigmatic English phrase *the X of Y,* it can serve the variety of conceptual masters—possessive, objective, qualitative, definitive, material, partitive—that the Latin genitive does, as well as a locative one. At the same time, it apes the French *de,* and provides a simple alternative to the purely Germanic construction, *Y's X,* and a whole range of more ambiguous ones to the equally Germanic mode of compound, *the YX*—thus the two different operations *of* performs in "piece of cake" and "peace of mind" can both potentially be handled by "cake-piece" and "mindpeace," although the former feels much more awkward and less likely than the latter. At two different times in the history of our language (and in a more or less continuous way since the second one), *X of Y* was used as a calque on many French phrases, thus, for example, "the poison of choice" (say, for adolescent suicides) is a calque on the French *(quelque chose) de choix*—thus *article de choix* = *choice article,* or *Hommes de choix* = *picked men*—whereas "this is a matter of choice" is clearly not.

Sometimes this could have the result of further mystifying an English word with its cognate, but cognitively dissonant, ghost. Thus in "marriage of convenience," *of* derives its strange associative power—not possessive, locative, partitive, causative, etc.—from *mariage de convenance* (= *arranged marriage*); but in no case does *of* work here as it does generally in English, as in, say, "a marriage of convenience and elegance." A more sensationally modish example, adduced by and in the name of modern Parisian theorizing, is of the bivalent role of *de* in "désir de (X)," where, say, "le désir de Vénus" could designate the goddess' wish for Mars, or Mars's wish for her (let alone with regard to the general term, desire, which is always "of Venus" in some of the more complex allegorical English senses—Desire is her realm, her creation, her instrument, the consequences of her activity, she is of its essence or it is of hers). But in any case, the immense variety of ad hoc uses of *of* in idiomatic English helps to destabilize its precise operation in certain phrases even more, and to infect clearly marked and more regular ordinary uses of the preposition with strange auras. This is certainly not true of ordinary usage. But for the poet, whose relation to his or her native language is always one of wonder born both of the deepest familiarity and the most puzzling sort of estrangement, the fruitful ambiguities of the *X of Y* construction are a matter of intimate knowledge.

I don't want to suggest that no other English prepositions exhibit a variety of phrasal behaviors. *By* has instrumental and locative senses—"Go by car, along the road by the brook"—but they rarely present ambiguities. *In,* as was observed in the example from Dickens cited earlier, has an interestingly bidirectional force: we might ourselves observe that old Dorrit was in despair, debt, and a room in the Marshalsea prison. The sequence of locations moves outward from an "inner" state (although the despair is "in" one), through a condition (debt) that feels more like an implicit physical confinement than the condition of the soul does, to a literal physical enclosure. When persons are *in X,* X can be, if a "state" or "condition" in the person, in our standard modern mythologies of the psyche. Milton's Satan, a great rhetorician full of the sense of "The Hell within him, for within him Hell / He brings" melodramatizes this dialectic of the inner/outer, formerly a fashionable topic of academic concern, in a powerfully poetic way. Internalization is still contingent with him, and with

Hell; whereas in the case of Adam's arisen form of "Paradise within thee, happier far," there is no question of a dialectic: without Paradise, it can only lie within. It might be thought that the enrichment of *of* by means of various calques and analogies would lead to nothing more than the possibility of occasional witty zeugma as well—"He was free of debt and spirit" (where *from* is meant in the first instance, and a linkage of compounding in the second), or "I am of Ireland, and of dubious sobriety."

But I believe this is not the case. So many instances of the *X of Y* in our poetry depend for their force upon a simultaneous use of different prepositional modes, that it almost seems to be a characteristic trope-enacting scheme in English poetry from Milton on. Meredith's (not Milton's) Lucifer confronts "The army of unalterable law,"[4] and it is not that we must correctly construe the phrase to decide that "unalterable law" is (a) a domain, (b) a ruler, (c) a general, (d) the entire personnel and materiel of the army itself, or (e) the characteristic behavior of the troops. It is rather that just here we cannot reject any of them, and the encompassing power of the phrase is thereby underlined. The reader's resolution of the prepositional mode by some pernicious casuistry would be as interdicted by the unalterable law as would Satan's victory in dubious battle. Blake's "Give me my bow of burning gold, / Give me my arrows of desire" follows the purely material genitive *of* in the first phrase with a mixture of (strangely) material, partitive, qualitative (arrows being generally desirous of their marks) possessive (the arrows were originally those of Classical Desire, or Cupid, although Blake might have wanted that thrown out with the rest of the rubbish of the Daughters of Memory). Bacon's "Idols" of Cave, Marketplace, Theatre, etc.—however problematic the sense of "idol" as *eidos,* or graven image, or both, may be—instance a locative *of,* but strongly reinforced by possessive and qualitative senses.

Tennyson's title *Idylls of the King* employs only that special, most interesting, sense (OED class 7 = "concerning," *about*) that I shall discuss later, but it is instructive to consider the way in which Wallace Stevens carefully cuts this sense away from a primarily partitive one in "The poem is the cry of its occasion, / Part of the res itself and not about it" ("An Ordinary Evening in New Haven," 11), however complex "cry" may be (= outcry or vendor's or huckster's cry). Stevens often depends upon the complex *of,* as in the resonant phrase from "The Man Whose Pharynx Was Bad," "The malady of the quotidian," wherein he invents, on the analogy of the archaic medical terms "tertian fever," "quartan fever," etc., a sort of "quotidian fever" that peaks every day. But is this the malady that the quotidian brings with it? The malady that the quotidian suffers? The malady that the quotidian *is?* Here the inability to choose among these constructions, and the fitful grasp of the presence and interrelation of all their consequences in the elevated pulse of the humdrum, is analogous to the situation in the last line of Meredith's sonnet.

Another celebrated case—actually, two related instances are cited here—of an intense ambiguity is usually considered in its epistemological context, but the muddying of its waters depends upon the fluidity of *of*. In "The picture of the mind revives again" (from "Tintern Abbey") the question is whether the mind is painter, collector, etc., or the *subject* (and hence, in another vocabulary, an *object*), but the possessive sense remains dominant; analogously, Mount Snowdon seen as "The perfect image of a mighty mind" (*The Prelude* 1805, 13.68–69) demands at first that the possessive be suppressed, only to return somewhat furtively after all.

For the poet's sense of language, words are not merely things, utensils, but beings, and those that relate are no less full of matter than those that designate. Since words live and move and have their being in phonology, it is a matter of poetic importance that (in a particular sort of nongenitive use), *of* and *love* rhyme. Moreover, the very relations enacted by, say, prepositions, themselves can be momentarily privileged in poetry. William James wrote most interestingly of this, in a passage pointed out by Richard Poirier:[5] "If there be such things as feelings at all, *then so surely as relations between objects exist in rerum naturâ, so surely, and more surely, do feelings exist to which these relations are known.* . . . We ought to say a feeling of *and,* a feeling of *if,* a feeling of *but,* and a feeling of *by,* quite as readily as we say a feeling of *blue* or a feeling of *cold*."[6] Nathaniel Hawthorne fancied in his notebooks how he might personify even the meanest parts of speech ("To personify If—But—And—Though, etc."[7]), and Emily Dickinson comes close to doing just that with the modal auxiliaries (her acknowledgment of two senses of "may" involving logical probability and social possibility being of particular interest):

There are two Mays
And then a Must
And after that a shall
How infinite the compromise
That indicates I will?

no. 1618

And while there are no odes to *of* that I know of, its ability to play so many positions in the game of our speech becomes for the poet a resource for word-play at another level. Whereas a French pseudophilosopher might ascribe all sorts of universal situations to what he or she might call the epistemological consequences of the grammar of *désir de,* a poet writing in English will make a strong point turn on an acute instance. The particular matter can be made even more complex, and, indeed, rendered far less arbitrary. Consider Pope's "The love of Comfort, and the love of Sway," where women desire both of these and execute both, as in their love for men when they simultaneously give comfort and manipulate. Even more fruitful in this respect is the celebrated opening line of Shakespeare's Sonnet 144, "Two loves have I of comfort and despair." The original complexity comes from the formulation itself: I have two loves that, separately or because there are two of them, both comfort me and make me despair. On the other hand, they can be thought of as two loves, one that comforts, one that makes me despair, or is itself despair*ing* (as the other may be comfort*ing*). Yet again, the "loves" are (a) faculties, in which case the French sort of *désir de* problem arises, and (b) the objects of those very faculties, jointly or respectively. And yet again once more, the comfort and despair may be the material of either the faculties or the objects.

It seems momentarily useful to invoke some conceptual pattern, like that of the scholastic four causes, in which to array the various operations of *X of Y*. For example,

Material Cause: "cup of gold," "cloth of gold" (but not, of course, "mother-of-pearl")
Efficient Cause: "cup of Cellini's," "Toccata of Galuppi's"
Formal Cause: "cup of oval shape," "coat of many colors"
Final Cause: "cup of vows" (but not, really, "cup of tea," which caps purpose with fulfillment—this tends to be true in all cases where *X* is container and *Y* thing contained: the pattern is asymmetric with respect to the appropriate term here, "teacup" (= cup for tea).

On the other hand, these could easily be mapped on the modes of the Latin genitive, for example. The point, however, is that while ordinary discourse has no problem with these, and while wit can call sudden attention to the difference between the functions with, say, a clever zeugma, poetry may want to suggest, and perhaps to employ, two or more of them at once. The various functions exist for the poet, perhaps, as rhyming words and homonyms do—not just as potential material for wordplay, but with any one of them (pairs of homonyms, rhyming morphemes) being permanently affected by the existence of the other.

When the *X of Y* is further complicated by an X or Y with more than one sense, the grammatical functions can help deploy them in the entire phrase. Britomart's spherical mirror, in book 3 of *The Faerie Queene*, in which she sees her future husband Artegall is like "a world of glass" in several senses, some simple (where *world = terrestrial globe*, for example, or where *glass* is simply material), some not (as when *glass = mirror*).[8]

The most celebrated example would perhaps be the title of *Leaves of Grass*. This is a phrase so rich and strange to begin with—it runs immediately counter to the idiom "blades of grass" and demands that "leaves" be taken as "pages" (perhaps taking a look back at Wordsworth's "Those barren leaves" with a view to greening them?). The material, efficient and formal causes are all at work here and, most particularly, the designative function (= about) as well. But both X and Y invoke previous tropes: *leaves* = *pages* aside, the figure of leaves-as-lives that runs from Homer, Virgil, Dante, and Milton to Shelley and after, and that originating in Isaiah and Psalms, of human bodies as grass to be mown in (and, later, by) time. Given these, there is a strong implication in the title of what the poetry itself confirms as a major trope, a sense of "leaves (lives) *as* grass (bodies)." That the (botanic) leaves and the (codex) leaves are somehow proleptically (although anachronistically) associated in the scattered prophecy of the Cumaean Sybil comes only as long afterthought. So does another resolution of the *unheimlich* quality of *leaves* used for "blades" of grass; the Old English root of our *leaf,* unlike the more generally Germanic *blade* (etymologically related to *blossom,* Latin *folium* and *flos,* etc., with a central sense of "bloom"), may have an Indo-European origin with a basic sense of breaking off (as if the essence of a leaf was to fall). Also, our sense of the word, innocent of the etymon or the cognate, would lead us—as it would the child who brings the poet the grass in section 6 of "Song of Myself"—to think of grass blades as perhaps being a transfer from sword blades (not as it is, of course, the other way around). And although in other Germanic languages, leaves are blades (German *Blätter*), in the English of Whitman's poem, even the blades of grass are (falling) leaves renewing themselves.

It may be argued here that the figurative overdetermination of the particular X and Y here, and the fact that *leaves* = *pages* can easily be *of* Y by being *about* it, clouds the issue of the *of.*

But the subsequent section (or, poem) title, "Song of Myself," presents similarly interesting problems. A "Song of Y" could be about Y, composed by Y, composed of Y, from (the land of) Y, etc. In this instance, "of myself" resonates also with the idiomatic "by myself." It is as much the dynamic ambiguity of the phrase function as the recurrently fascinating problem of the relation among the senses of *ipse, se,* and *ego* (or the French *le moi*) in the English word *myself* itself that makes this title appropriate for a poem in which there are at least three "selves" as major agents.

Sometimes, indeed, it may be useful to think of the preposition as playing an ancillary role, either placing the Y-noun on some figurative stage or urging us immediately to search for another use (this may be another way of saying the same thing). Scott in *Guy Mannering* calls attention to this rather elegantly, referring to "Hazlewood-House and the House of Hazlewood—meaning by the one, the mansion-house of my family, and by the other, typically, metaphorically, and parabolically, the family itself" (whereas the literal or first sense of "house" might enter grotesquely into the phrase here, such as "My people built our house of hazlewood," or "Our family house stands in the middle of

Hazlewood forest," or even "Sir Hazlewood Hazlewood rebuilt our house after the original one; the House of Sir Walter [Hazlewood] that he built of stone, was wrecked in a siege").[9] But perhaps this is only to say that the paradigmatic *House of Υ* can itself be deployed in a variety of ways, from *House* (more literally) *of God, Houses of Parliament* to all the immense array of allegorical *Houses of Υ* in romance fictions. Whether these denote what, with regard to Spenser, Angus Fletcher has termed "temples" or "labyrinths," their use of *House* oscillates between two senses of *House:* what we encounter merely as "Hazlewood House" becomes for us, after we enter it, "the House of Hazlewood" itself. Moreover, in poetic topography, partially as the result of a scheme to be considered shortly, *Place of Υ* tends to become allegorical ("House of Holiness," "Bower of Bliss," "Slough of Despond" help shade the senses of "Hall of Justice," "Land of Heart's Desire," perhaps even "Houses of Parliament," where the Y almost evaporates into the "parleying" of the legislative body).

But for an exhaustive taxonomy of the arrangements of what she calls "The Genitive Link," the reader should turn to Christine Brooke-Rose's *Grammar of Metaphor,* chapters 7 and 8.[10] Except to praise its incisiveness, I shall remark here only on the representative grammar of the book's own title. Were it used in the kind of English and American poetry I have in mind, the phrase might be deeply and systematically ambiguous. It might partake not only of what its author calls a double genitive link—in this case, a reciprocating one, of the kind that might be underlined by a sort of Jakobsonian construction, *The Grammar of Metaphor and the Metaphor of Grammar.* In addition, all the senses of metaphoric "grammars," an alternative sort of grammar composed of metaphoric substitutions or displacements or condensations or whatever, a grammar (= an abstract structure to be inferred from the phenomena of utterance) of metaphoric instances, a grammar (= a sort of analytic book about a language that invites you to learn it, and of it) might be present, and even working with, and not against, one other. Finally, I refer the reader back to William Empson's fine pages on the paired linkages in Shakespeare that he calls "the A and B of C," although it is primarily the interaction of *and* and a partitive sort of *of* that he discusses.[11]

The case of Lysimachus's "deeds of darkness" *(Pericles* 4.6.30) for "dark deeds" (= fucking) presents another aspect of the question of *X of Υ,* one that involves the connection of an abstract Y and a concrete X. This is ordinarily an instance of *of Υ = Υ (adj.) X.* Frequently, though, there is great pressure on the reading of Y to become genitive; it tends to become allegorized, to develop an initial capital and preside over the X in a multiplicity of ways. "Dark deeds" are one thing; those "of Darkness" are another—where Darkness may be, for example, a kind of ultimate, necessary demon who does one's dark deeds for one whenever one thinks one is doing them oneself. The reason for this lies not merely in the variety of colloquial uses of *of,* but in one particular textual tradition that has permeated English usage and that I now propose somewhat briefly to consider.

It comes from the English Bible. I might have introduced it by citing a line of Robert Frost's from "Directive"—"A brook that was the water of the house" (where a paraphrase of "a brook that was the running water they had" will clearly not do). Why it is that it won't not only involves the history of quasi-allegorical instances of "house" that lie behind the phrase, but a biblical commonplace as well. Or, again, Christina Rossetti's subtitle for her "Monna Innomninata," a group of fourteen sonnets: "A Sonnet of Sonnets." Here the material genitive *of* names the poem as a sort of super-sonnet, made up of sonnets for lines, as well as a sonnet made up of the trope of sonneteering, yet also, as a sequence written by a woman who is usually the clichéd sonneteer's Muse, here "drawn not from fancy but from feeling." Or it is a sonnet *about* sonnets. But however we construe the phrase, the sense of some sort of metasonnet inheres in the paradigm that lies behind it, *the X of X's*. Which, again, is biblical.

The particular prototype here, "Song of Songs," is an instance of the standard translation of a common construction in biblical Hebrew. A singular noun in the construct state with its own plural simply indicates a superlative: X of X's = Best of all X's, *Shir ha-shirim*, or "Supreme Song." (Marvin Pope in his remarkable edition for the Anchor Bible gives "Sublime Song."[12]) Thus all the other resonant occurrences that have become rhetorical commonplaces: "King of Kings" (Daniel 2.37); "vanity of vanities" (Ecclesiastes l.2); Canaan as "servant of servants" (Genesis 9.25), etc. The Vulgate translates these with the flexible genitive, whereas the Septuagint interprets this particular construction with a dative (e.g., *canticum canticorum*, but *asma asmatân; rex regum*, but *basieleus basileón; servus sevorum*, but here, simply *oiketês*, "slave"; etc.). But the English translations, using the multivalent *X of Y*, allows other senses of the construction to becloud the intended literal one. There is no sense of the partitive in the Hebrew (i.e., X of X = one of many X's), but it presents itself in the English as a sort of synecdoche. (It is amusing to note, however, that the commonplace "Holy of Holies" [Exodus 26.33], for the Hebrew *kodesh ha-kadashim*, occurs nowhere in KJV, which translates quite accurately "most holy place"; the popular English phrase itself translates the Vulgate's *sancta sanctorum*.)

But it is the problem of nouns in the construct state in general, aside from this particular usage, which so enriches the English phrase that was drafted so early into its service. In general, two nouns in the construct state in Hebrew (in the form *X the Y*) may usually be most easily translated into English as the noun-noun compound, *the YX*. The construct binds nouns in a variety of ways like the Latin genitive, but it lacks a primary possessive sense. For example, the modern Hebrew word for school, *bet ha-sepher* (house the book) should be rendered "the bookhouse" (= school). But the English Bible's inevitable construction, "the house of the book" raises, and contributes to, all the complexities of *of* under consideration. The pressure on "book" to become "Book" and, particularly in American English, so shaped by radical protestantism, to invoke *the* Book (the Good Book = Scripture) would be very strong. "The House of [temple of?] the Book"—consecrated to? enclosing? belonging to? comprised of? it, perhaps—seems poised by its very grammar on the brink of allegory.

All those wonderful cases where the simply adjectival sense of the Hebrew original becomes, in its English *X of Y,* another sort of creature, provide, for English writing up until the phasing out of the English Bible as a common text, a store of rhetorical matrices. The "multitudes, multitudes in the valley of decision" (Joel 3.14) are in the Hebrew *b'emek hecharutz* (in Septuagint, *en tê koilathi tês dikês*—the ordinary construct is there translated, as in Latin, by the genitive; in Latin, *in valle concisionis*). In English it should be "Decision Valley" (like "Death Valley,"); but what happens in KJV is similar to what might happen if "Customs-House" were ordinarily designated "House of Customs," although it is partially the mythopoetic work of Hawthorne's introductory chapter to *The Scarlet Letter* to work through just such a quasi-Spenserian conception. In the phrase from Joel, there is the lurking notion that to have to make certain kinds of crucial decisions is always somehow like being in a valley, with a lot of other people—too many, perhaps—having to do the same thing. The mountain of Decision is a *very* different sort of place, and one would probably be up there alone, which would be scarier. And yet the Valley seems insufficiently comforting. Perhaps all biblical valleys are infected with what ails the "valley of the shadow of death" (Psalm 23.4), which itself exhibits a complex doubling of the phrase that combines a *(place) of Y* with a *(representation) of Y,* each of which has an allegorizing thrust of its own. (I discuss this particular figure elsewhere in this book.[13])

And so with "wine of astonishment" *(yayin tarelah)* of Psalm 60.5; given the archaic "astonishment" for "staggering" (= intoxicating), we half expect an allegorical efficient cause (the wine brewed by a witch named Astonishment), or a formal one (the vintage pressed from the grapes of astonishment, rather than of wrath), etc. Or again, sometimes an accidental allusion can be pointedly engaged by the simultaneous prepositional functions, as in the frequently occurring phrase "the apple of [his, thine] eye" (as in Deuteronomy 32.10, where the Lord guarded Jacob *c'ishon eno*). It means, simply, "eyeball," but "apple" is so redolent in English Christian tradition of the original fruit of the Fall that it tends here to suggest "the object of the eye's desire" to the unlearned but attentive ear, especially when it becomes a commonplace in quotation.

One of the most celebrated of such phrases arises from no translation of Hebrew—indeed, it is a N.T. rubric—but which remains current only in misconstruction: the designation "the Whore of Babylon" occurs as the running head on chapter 17 of the Geneva Bible (GGgiiii: the previous recto has the phrase "the Fall of Babylon," and, ramifying the paradigm, is the mutually invoked "the Tower of Babel"). Often misconstrued by a literalizing temperament in popular homily as a locative (i.e., "Babylonian Whore") instead of the allegorical figure of Babylon as whore, derived from the prophetic trope of wicked city as harlot, it ends up pretty much that as a rhetorical commonplace. But the very construction of the rubric almost seems to have the translators' sense not of Greek, but of the Hebrew paradigm behind it.

But the very strength of biblical English is often to iron out linguistic and rhetorical differences between O.T. and N.T., as well as between their individual "books." So that in the "pearl of great price" (Matthew 13.46), the ordinary function of the Latin genitive of quality (used only when the quality is modified by an adjective) moves vaguely toward some attributive sublimity, as if in any scriptural *X of Y*, the concrete X and the abstract Y formed a kind of recurring *figura* of their own.[14]

It is interesting to consider, too, such permutations as *X of Y, X of W, X of Z*, etc., and to observe the shift of prepositional function as one moves from, say, "work of thy hands" (Psalm 43.5 passim) to "work of one day" (Ezra 10.13), to modern colloquial "work of art" (complex—a skillful act becomes its product) "work of charity" (also as currently distinguished from "labour of love"?).

But all these occurrences sing their various roles in a strange chorus of voices, and the cup of *of* is filled with possibility. It is a matter of verbal moments in Scripture receiving overlays, because of linguistic change and the coloring of analogies, that render them opaque and even slightly mysterious, somewhat in the way Kermode has demonstrated for narrative moments.[15] And even when Milton, fully aware of Hebrew grammar, uses the construction somewhat problematically, it is hardly a case of merely hoisting the stylistic standard of a Hebraism. Satan

Led Eve our credulous Mother to the Tree
Of prohibition, root of all our woe.

PL 9.645–46

Milton's implicit construct, "tree the prohibited" (= prohibited tree) engages, as the language of *Paradise Lost* so often does, the true ambiguity it generates. The Tree is the sole focus and instance of Prohibition in Paradise; its ramifications, if misused (treated as if it were part of an orchard, rather than contemplated as an ever-present emblem), will reach into the realm of *all* myriad prohibitions that will test fallen virtue. Particularly in the complex cross-predications of tree/prohibition : root/woe that Christopher Ricks suggested so long ago.[16] The biblical "tree of the knowledge of good and evil" itself, especially in contrast with the "tree of life" (Hebrew *etz hachayim*) of Genesis, itself a complex term, presents its genitive possibilities. And Milton makes the most of these.

I have been suggesting that the biblical formula provides, particularly for poetry, the bases for an array of ad hoc calques, mingling and coexisting with a host of others. The last one I shall consider occurs when, as evidenced previously, the X term names some discursive entity or representation in general (*Book of, Tale of,* etc.), so that the formula engages the use of *of* for *concerning*. That is, I should like to conclude the discussion of *of* with something about *about*.

The OED sense 7 of that preposition—not its locational meaning of "around"—is designated as "touching, concerning, in the matter of, in reference or in regard to. The regular preposition employed to define the subject matter of verbal activity, as in to speak, think, ask, dream, hear, know *about*." (In all these instances, it will be observed, *of* could be substituted; but the list continues:) "to be sorry, pleased, perplexed *about*"; (where *of* can't be used) "to give orders, instructions, information *about*"; (likewise?) "to form plans, have doubts, feel sure *about*." Here, in these last two cases, "doubts *about* X" and "doubts *of* X's Y" are different, and perhaps to be noted in connection with the general density of the functions of *of*.[17]

The use of *of* for the Latin and Romance *de*, and for the *about* that seems almost a calque on the Greek *peri* (the German use of *über* for this purpose feels too lofty for discussion here), occurs in the absolute from *of* X in rubrics and titles. Bacon's essay titles ("Of Truth," etc.) probably following Montaigne's give the feeling of a slightly different sense of aboutness from the one engaged by, say, Hazlitt's "On Gusto," etc.; his "Of Persons One Would Wish to Have Seen" is quite rare for him. But "On Sitting for One's Picture" tends to suggest, as do perhaps most instances of *on* X when X is a present participle, an ellipsis of "on the occasion of X."

Generally, the implication is that specifying "the subject matter of verbal activity," even of a piece of complex writing, is easy enough to do, and perhaps even that the claim to have done it is easily verifiable. This may indeed be true in some instances, and in some of these *of* and *about* might seem to function slightly differently. A: "He spoke of X." B: "No he didn't—I was there all night and he didn't mention her once." This does indeed seem a case for verification. But then, A: "He was talking about X." B: "Not actually—he was really talking about Y all the time." Here it is a matter of validating an interpretation, and A can easily reply, "No he wasn't," without any hope of further confirmation either way. In short, "X is about Y" most often behaves, as a proposition, like "X is like Y": the answer of "No it isn't" will not settle anything. Likeness surfaces in assertions in the form of similes, which look as if they might be open to question. When collapsed into tropes, their expository candidacy is withdrawn. And so, perhaps, with aboutness, which seems to point to some topicality, some essentiality, with an implicit sense that the mode of essentiality and the immediate instance of it will both be acknowledged. I find a remark of Paul de Man's rather puzzling in this respect: "Language can only be about something, such as man, but in being about man, it can never know whether it is about anything at all including itself, since it is precisely the *aboutness,* the referentiality, that is in question."[18] Forgetting that language can't be said to *know* anything, one might observe that there is much more to *aboutness,* and even the aboutness of some strange abstract entity called "language," in which I could mention and designate X, be arguably speaking "of Y," and perhaps submit to the charge that I was really talking "about either Z, or myself," etc., than referentiality.

To claim that an utterance or text is "about X," then, is more like a trope itself than our usual way of thinking of it admits. And an "of X" that is synonymous with it, particularly when it enters into an *X of Y* formula can be very figurative indeed. And from this perhaps derives some of the force the most resonant "of" in our literature. Milton could perfectly well have started out on *Paradise Lost* without a preposition: Virgil's accusative object of *cano* could have been matched by a nominal object of the Heavenly Muse's singing. Indeed, Milton's very English precursor in singing of first things, Caedmon, is commanded by his audition only to "syng [me] frumsceaft" (or "creation," in the Old English translation of Bede's Latin). The "of" of the openings of Italian romance had of course been attempted both in prose and rhyme, but Milton's presentation of his great argument as an *of X, and Y whose A did B until C,* etc., is as *peri,* as around and about as one can get. It can hardly be said to pinpoint a topic in any but contingent and expositorily incidental (but poetically substantial) ways— the spatial, syllabic centrality of "disobedience" in the first line, for example. Its mere aboutness seems to get drowned in a flow of possibility: human subject, action, object, source, consequence, ultimate consequence of consequence, all run into each other. The Muse will, in the vocalizations of the poem, sing *of* all this, and the poem will be a poem *of* so much that a merely topical discourse *about* a subject—say, Sir John Davies's *Orchestra, or A Poem* of *Dancing*—could never be. Its opening "of" is full of itself.

NOTES

1. Frank Kermode, "The Plain Sense of Things," in *Midrash and Literature,* ed. G. H. Hartman and S. Budick (New Haven: Yale University Press, 1986), 192.
2. In particular, Edward Stankiewicz, "The Dithyramb of the Verb in Eighteenth and Nineteenth Century Linguistics," in *Studies in the History of Linguistics,* ed. Dell Hymes (Bloomington: Indiana University Press, 1974).
3. In a symposium on Emily Dickinson, *PEN Newsletter* 68 (May 1989): 9–10, 13.
4. George Meredith, "Lucifer in Starlight," l. 14.

5. Richard Poirier, *The Renewal of Literature* (New York: Random House, 1987), 15–16.

6. William James, *Principles of Psychology* (Cambridge, Mass.: Harvard University Press, 1983), 238.

7. Quoted in F. O. Matthiessen, *American Renaissance* (New York: Oxford University Press, 1941), 244.

8. Interesting in this connection is Emerson's quatrain, "Nahant": "All day the waves assailed the rock, / I heard no church-bell chime, / The sea-beat scorns the minster-clock / And breaks the glass of Time," where the pressure of the various *X of Y* possibilities makes the literal hourglass double with its trope (glass used as mirror and perhaps even vessel).

9. I quote from the Riverside Edition, 2 vols. in 1 (New York: Hurd and Houghton, 1877), 2:212.

10. Christine Brooke-Rose, *A Grammar of Metaphor* (London: Secker and Warburg, 1958), 146–205.

11. William Empson, *Seven Types of Ambiguity,* 2d ed. (New York: New Directions, 1947), 88–101.

12. Marvin H. Pope, *Song of Songs* (New York: Doubleday, 1977). See his discussion of this construction, 294–95.

13. See chapter 7, "Hearing and Overhearing the Psalms."

14. The KJV phrase "Ancient of days" (Daniel 7.9, 13, 32) is significant in this respect, a somewhat misleading rendering of the Aramaic *attik yomin* and *attik yomayya*. Here the weight of mystification is on the X term (not "the Ancient" who might then be thought of as the God of Time, etc., but one who was old in days [= years]). In the *Encyclopedia Judaica* article on the phrase, H. L. Ginsberg remarks that the phrase in English "has a solemn and singularly beautiful ring." Its ring comes from the intricate alloy of rhetorical metals in which it is cast.

15. Frank Kermode, *The Genesis of Secrecy* (Cambridge, Mass.: Harvard University Press, 1979).

16. Christopher Ricks, *Milton's "Grand Style"* (Oxford: Oxford University Press, 1958), 75f.

17. I should note one use of what looks to be *of* but is in fact a solecism. Early twentieth-century American writers of *verismo* fiction would often indicate that a speaker was semiliterate or otherwise uneducated by a trick of spelling. The canonical and correct contraction "should've" or "would've" for "should have," etc., was spelled "should of," etc. (as if to represent how the speakers would themselves have spelled what they were saying). This strange fiction (very often little else in the speech was distorted) was used rather than writing "shoulda," "woulda," etc., which would have been more of the usual attempts from Mark

Twain on to represent allophonic variations among dialects. But increasingly among generations of writers who were taught no grammar at school, "he would of gone" has lost its distinguishing feature and is employed—admittedly, only in dialogue of first-person narration—almost as if it were an idiomatic use of *of,* of the the sort I have been examining here.

18. Paul de Man, *Allegories of Reading* (New Haven: Yale University Press, 1979), 161.

PART II
Poetic Experiences

CHAPTER SEVEN

Hearing and Overhearing the Psalms

For a long time there was only one psalm. I can still hear the tones of my father's voice identifying a puzzling string of utterances: "That's the *twenty-third* psalm," stressed just like that. It seemed the name of only one thing, and since I didn't know what the set "psalm" comprised, the poem remained sui generis. By then I was just beginning to learn that what in the world was called "the Bible" existed, in its Jewish part, in Hebrew (which I wasn't beginning to learn just yet). It would be some years before I could put together the cadences of the English Bible (the King James Version [KJV])—sections of whose Psalms and Proverbs were still read aloud in public schools, to the unwitting profit of many of those who were bored by their recitation—with what went on in synagogue, occasionally "on Sabbaths" and always "on festivals." Even though the language of the part of the liturgy that was recited in English (my family attended Conservative services) was usually a corrected pastiche of KJV English (whether translations of Torah, of *piyut*-liturgical-devotional poetry, or whatever), it would be decades before I would come to grasp the complex relations between the Hebrew Bible, the strange and powerful tendentious reading of it called the Old Testament, and the various vernacular translations.

For a modern reader, the language of KJV is inherently poetic primarily because of the relation between its high, condensed diction and the impenetrability of so much of its language, caused by semantic change since the early seventeenth century. I suppose that a poetic childhood consists in misunderstanding a good bit of what one hears and sees, in being too reticent to ask for the solution to puzzles of pattern and meaning that adults must know are silly, and in then resorting of one's own private versions of what was meant. (Mis*construings* and re*constructions:* these terms for analysis and building derive from the same Latin one.) And I suppose the inability to put away such childish things may attune the attention to the still, small tones of a vocation. "My knowledge was divine," wrote a seventeenth-century English poet and parson; "I knew by intuition those things which since my apostasy I collected again by the highest reason." He was speaking of childhood's innocence generally, but with just enough of a specific epistemological interest to seem pre-Wordsworthian. And so it is, particularly with objects of language. The child in the American joke who innocently deforms Psalm 23's penultimate verse, assuring her adult listeners that "Surely good Mrs. Murphy shall follow me all the days of my life," will only learn with "a later reason," as Wallace Stevens called it, that she was getting *something* more profoundly right about the line, the psalm, and poetry in general than any of her correctly parroting schoolmates. For the "mistake" personifies the "goodness and mercy"—the *tov vachesed* of the Hebrew—as a beneficent pursuer (the Hebrew lines imply that they are the poet's only pursuers, dogging one's footsteps, perhaps, but never hounding). Good Mrs. Murphy following the child about like a beneficent nurse is a more viable, powerful homiletic reconstruction of what had otherwise faded into abstraction than any primer's glossing. The child rightly attended to the trope set up by the intense verb "follow me" and supplied an appropriate subject for it, thereby turning mechanical allegory into poetic truth. Losing, in mature literacy, the ability to make such mistakes can mean being deaf and blind to the power of even the KJV text, let alone that of the Hebrew. One's reading slides over the figuration, and thereby over the force of the line of verse. Thus in Psalm 85.10, "Mercy and truth are met together; righteousness and peace have kissed each other" (KJV), the state of affairs being described (for all sorts of reasons, it might well be translated with verbs in the future tense—it is not our state of affairs now) points up sharply what is wrong with the present relation of the paired concepts in each case: mercy (again, *chesed,* translated "lovingkindness" or however) and truth *(emet)* do not, in fact, meet together. Nor do righteousness *(zedek)* and peace *(shalom)*—in our lives, each is usually achieved at the expense of the other or the other's terrain. They are zealous warriors against their particular enemies. But in their zeal they must necessarily compromise their fellow active virtues, revelations of truth frequently being merciless, acts of mercy involving the comfort of falsehood, peace being attained only at the expense of some wrong being righted, and the righting of wrongs requiring strife. Not getting the equivalent of the "good Mrs. Murphy" out of these lines is not getting the poet's moral point, namely that when "glory may dwell in our land" (Psalm 85.9), then virtues will not conflict, but that *they do now,* and not to notice this is moral torpor.

My own initial childhood contacts with Psalm 23 were full of small good-Mrs.-Murphy's. "I shall not want"—the intransitivity wasn't a problem so much as learning from this clause alone the older meaning "lack" or "need," instead of the more colloquial American "desire." But perhaps the contemporary reader, who may not have these precise phrases and cadences by ear (is "by heart" better?)—given that young persons are no longer required to memorize verse and prose at school, and that various insipidly "corrected" versions have replaced KJV in all public institutions save those devoted to the study of literature—might be reminded at this point of the text:

A Psalm of David

The Lord is my shepherd; I shall not want.
He maketh me to lie down in green pastures: he leadeth me beside the
    still waters.
He restoreth my soul: he leadeth me in the paths of righteousness for his
    name's sake.
Yea, though I walk through the valley of the shadow of death, I will fear no
    evil: for thou art with me; thy rod and thy staff they comfort me.
Thou preparest a table before me in the presence of mine enemies: thou
    anointest my head with oil; my cup runneth over.
Surely goodness and mercy shall follow me all the days of my life: and I will
    dwell in the house of the Lord for ever.

Simply having the memorized text, possessing it without fully understanding it, allows one's attention to caress its frequently opaque locutions and cadences. I suppose that I was introduced to trope by this psalm, as much as by any other poem: I knew that the authorial "David," the young harp-playing shepherd from my illustrated *Stories from the Bible,* didn't mean to say that he felt comfortable partially *in that* his cup was spilling onto the floor (a dreaded commonplace of the nursery). I knew that the line about the table and the enemies meant *something* beneficent, but couldn't figure out what. I didn't know what "the house of the Lord" actually was (churches were "houses of God," but I knew synagogues weren't—I'd been taught that a *shul* was a place of assembly, a *bet haknesset*), but I fancied that it designated something very general. The "paths of righteousness," the "valley of the shadow of death," the "house of the Lord"—I began to savor the rich ambiguity of those constructions, which can indicate so many syntactic relations, possessive, instrumental, causative, attributive. It would be many years before I knew enough Hebrew and enough about English to understand that KJV's peculiar way of translating the Hebrew construct state led to all sorts of latent allegorizing. The paths of righteousness, what were they? Were they the paths that led to a place—alas, somewhat distant—called Righteousness? Were they the paths someone called Righteousness used to take, striding along on business or taking his ease, and where, with proper guidance, one might get to walk, too? Were they the paths he still patrols? Were they paths across Righteousness's property or territory? Will these crooked, difficult paths, if one is led along them properly, make one righteous?

All these ambiguities characterizing the *X of Y* construction, examined in detail in chapter 6, in the English came to *feel* biblical for me. As I grew older, it kept appearing everywhere in the fabric of the poetical grammar of the English language. (It is amusing to note now how I could not know then that "green pastures" and "still waters" in that beautifully rhythmic couplet were moments of correct translation of the original, the *benot deshe* and the construct state of the *mei mnuchot,* "grassy pastures" and "tranquil streams," which would ordinarily have become "fields of verdure" and "waters of tranquillity," had the usual strategy been adopted.)

Again, the "rod" and the "staff" simply blended into some notional shepherd's crook for me (I didn't—rightly or wrongly—think then that the pastoral conceit had vanished by the third verse). Only after I knew the Hebrew—and knew something of the mysterious ways of the parallelistic line of Hebrew poetry and how it works in far more than mere decoratively varied repetition— could I realize what the slight archaism of the English words had veiled. The "rod" of "spare the rod and spoil the child," a proverb acquired a bit later on, and the staff (as "cane," "alpenstock," "staff" of Father Time and of life, as bread in another commonplace) eventually did diverge into the complimentary sticks of weapon and prop or support. Likewise, the cadential phrase "for name's sake," which seemed only to make sense in its more usual role of expletive (often of parental annoyance—"For God's sake, can't you . . ." combined with "What in the name of God have you done with your . . .") here played a strangely quiet, though darkly forceful, role. And again, only later learning would allow the less mysterious but conceptually plausible "as befits his name," for the *l'ma'an sh'mo* of the original, to operate. But, as in any riddle, the solution effects a loss even as it enables gain, and the "explanation" or "answer" explodes fiction created by the enigma, and the literal triumphs in the end. So it is with the vanishing of all the good Mrs. Murphys with the coming of the dawn of learning.

Coming to linguistic terms with the half-understood English text, then, marked the growth of my inner ear for poetry. Even the rhythmic component of the KJV psalm was fecund with incomprehensibles. Nobody had ever explained the principles of biblical verse to me, and I construed the unrhymed but closed lines as versions of accentual metrical schemes. The rough pentameters, frequently dactylic, of "Yea, though I walk through the valley of the shadow of death" (with the assonantal pattern of the last phrases pointing up the stresses), of "thou anointest my head with oil; my cup runneth over," and the final couplet made of lilting fourteener and pentameter: "Surely goodness and mercy shall follow me all the days of my life: / And I will dwell in the house of the Lord forever"—these cadences were always alive in the language for me. And puzzlingly so: why did what sounded like the beginning of a stanza (of, in my childhood vocabulary, a "verse") then break away form its scheme into something uncountable by ear? Was that part of the strangeness of the language? The three hemistichs of 2 and 3a seemed to make up a little stanza of their own, for the ear, at least:

He maketh me to lie down in green pastures,
He leadeth me beside the still waters,
He restoreth my soul.

Doubtless, the anaphora in all three lines, and the rhythmically identical (and grammatically similar) pair "lie dówn in gréen pástures: besíde the stíll wáters," as well as the undeniable effect of the "past́ures . . . st́ill . . . rest́oreth" sequence, all were bolstering my ear's little misreading of the metrical scheme, on the basis of the unintended and ad hoc—for the Jacobean translators—occasional rhythm. What my ear took in and remembered I could not, of course, have explained in this way at that time. But there always remained for me this singular rhythmic presence, underscoring all the memorable phrases that I subsequently acquired from the rest of the Book of Psalms like familiar melodies.

Thus, for example, with the resonant opening of Psalm 24, which for a long time I knew by opening alone: it sounded as if it scanned in a half-quatrain—

The earth is the Lord's, and the fulness thereof;
the world, and they that dwell therein

as if implicitly to continue—

In oceans below and in mountains above,
the tall and short, the thick and thin

or something like that. And then, having teased one out of prose, as it were, the psalm's voice abandoned one's expectations again. Actually, the phrase "the fulness thereof" had its own rhythm of mystery; my ear took it in as designating the stuffed, filled quality of the well-fed ground, something like Yeats's "mackerel-crowded seas," which I wouldn't encounter for a good many years. I could not yet realize that the words mean not *pleroma* (as, indeed, the Septuagint Greek has it), not the condition of being filled, but, rather, that which does the filling—the stuff, not the stuffedness. But the enigmatic beauty of the phrase haunted me much more than the palpable strangeness of gates being called on to "lift up their heads" later on in the psalm (not once, but twice).

And so it would be with all the constantly quoted, reechoed, half-revised phrases from the KJV psalms that kept emerging in all my reading. They seemed to be part of the very idiom of written English, along with the folk proverb and the occasional bits of Shakespearean tag. That so many of these words have lived a strange but long life, out of their context and themselves the product of the English translators' own inadvertent good-Mrs.-Murphy-making, was of no matter. There they were, "Out of the mouths of babes and sucklings hast thou ordained strength" (Psalm 8.2) and, a few verses later, the wonderful "What is man, that thou art mindful of him? and the son of man, that thou visitest him?" (Here the puzzling beauty lay in the loss of the older meaning of *mind = remember,* preserved colloquially only in proverbial admonition to mind p's and q's and manners. The Hebrew, of course, has the verb *zakhar* [remember].) "The apple of the eye" is paired with "the shadow of thy wings" in Psalm 17.8: the literal "eye-ball" yields a figure so compelling as to be used to denote, out of context, some cynosure, some lovely prize of the eye, rather than the prized organ itself, the second phrase being so ubiquitous in the psalms (e.g., 36.7, 57.1, 61.4, 63.7, 91.4). The "fire and brimstone, and an horrible tempest" shall be for the wicked "the portion of their cup" (Psalm 11.6). The "strong bulls of Bashan" that "beset me round" (Psalm 22.12) are also familiar. The opening simile of Psalm 42.1, with its mistranslation of male deer for the female that the Hebrew verb requires, gives the naive listener some of the same punning flavor ("hart" / "heart") that was so dear to the early seventeenth century: "As the hart panteth after the water brooks, so panteth my soul after thee, O God." We so often refer to the longed-for "wings like a dove" of Psalm 55.6 and the whole reverberant opening of Psalm 90

Lord, thou hast been our dwelling place in all generations.
Before the mountains were brought forth, or ever thou hadst formed the
     earth, and the world, even from everlasting to everlasting, thou art God.
Thou turnest men to destruction; and sayest, Return, ye children of men.
For a thousand years in thy sight are but as yesterday when it is past, and as a
     watch in the night.
Thou carriest them away as with a flood; they are as a sleep: in the morning
     they are like grass which groweth up.
In the morning it flourisheth, and groweth up; in the evening it is cut down,
     and withereth.

—and the later, sadly canonical "the days of our years are threescore years and ten" (Psalm 90.10). These all underline the purported authorship in the rubric of this remarkable poem, "A Prayer of Moses the Man of God," which has its legacy in Isaac Watts's "O God our help in ages past," so ecumenical as to seem almost secular. The mapping of God's dominion "from sea to sea, and from the river unto the ends of the earth" in Psalm 72.8 seemed, when I first encountered it, to be quoting from its figured paraphrase by Katharine Lee Bates ("From sea to shining sea"), until I thought for a bit.

And so many more: the mention of them "that go down to the sea in ships, that do business in great waters" (Psalm 107.23); "sing unto the Lord a new song" in Psalm 96.1, itself an old song, perhaps a quotation from Isaiah; "they that sow in tears shall reap in joy" in Psalm 126.5; the "twoedged sword" of Psalm 149.6, "my days are like a shadow that declineth" in Psalm 102.11, a haunting trope of a shortening life; "in thy light shall we see light" in Psalm 36.9, which I would encounter in the Vulgate on my university's seal while at college *(In lumine tuo videbimus lumen)* and in paraphrase in the college song ("In thy radiance we see light"); the "green bay tree" whose spreading is like that of the wicked (Psalm 37.35); the canonical statement in the psalms, as in Isaiah 50, of the herbal topos, in Psalm 103.14–16 (itself seeming to echo the passage from Psalm 90):

For he knoweth our frame; he remembereth that we are dust.
As for man, his days are as grass; as a flower of the field, so he flourisheth.
For the wind passeth over it, and it is gone; and the place thereof knoweth it
  no more.

The opening four verses of Psalm 114, the Exodus poem, became familiar to me early because of the psalm's role in the *Hallel* sequence of the Passover seder:

When Israel went out of Egypt, the house of Jacob from a people of strange
  language;
Judah was his sanctuary, and Israel his dominion.
The sea saw it, and fled: Jordan was driven back.
The mountains skipped like rams, and the little hills like lambs.

Growing up literate in English, one could not avoid encountering these and so many other tags of psalms, so that reading through the Book of Psalms itself as I got older meant encountering many commonplaces in their uncommon original. Along with the variety of the psalms, their inconsistencies of length and degrees of familiarity, their range of tone, their problematic ascriptions of authorship, all made the Psalms a very strange sort of biblical book. First of all, there were the mysteries of the title. "Psalm," from the Greek word for a song sung to a plucked string instrument, better translates the Hebrew *mizmor*, or "accompanied song," a word used only in the subtitles of many of these poems to further specify something like their genre, or occasion for performance. I think that as a child I made some kind of vague connection between "psalms" and "psalteries." It was only at eleven or twelve years of age, when, during the synagogic *longeurs*, I would search through the *siddur* or *machzor*—the daily and festival prayer books—for bits of lore in the annotations, that the Hebrew title began to bother me. *Tehillim*—praises. Before I knew enough grammar to catch the *hallal* root prominent in Hallel and "halleluya," I could still wonder why *tehilla,* a feminine noun, should have a masculine plural, rather than *tehillot.* In any event, it seemed a strange title for an anthology of hymns of praise, songs of personal lamentation and national mourning, odes of thanksgiving and royal lyrics (like the marriage song of Psalm 45, subtitled *al shoshanim*—probably "to the tune of the Lilies"—and *shir ydidot*—a song of loves). The midrash on psalms starts out by asserting a parallel of ascriptive authorship—"As Moses gave five books of the Torah to Israel, so David gave five books of psalms to Israel"—and it goes on to list the five divisions, each book ending with a doxology, although only the first two (up through Psalm 72) containing "psalms of David." The subtitles themselves were so enigmatic: what was a *maskhil?* a *shiggaion* (Psalm 7)? What, indeed, did the grammar of the frequent *mizmor l'david*—a song of David—mean: a song about, or by, or to, or for David the shepherd and/or king? "Song" was itself a strange term, for what I encountered in Hebrew was itself sometimes sung, although the cantillation of psalms, of the Pentateuch, and of parts of the liturgy, including blessings and prayers, all ran into one another for me as a generic kind of unaccompanied *shul*-singing—unaccompanied because we were a Conservative congregation with no organ. (Today I should venture that our word *lyric,* still echoing with the name of the Greek musical instrument, manages to indicate that the word *mizmor* has a similar resonance.)

And here again the psalms were beginning to lead a mysterious life for me in their variety of musical identities. The actuality of biblical song is mostly lost to us, and all the liturgical cantillation observant Jews encounter is of relatively recent origin (medieval). It is also itself unaware, as setting, of the structural principles of the verse it set, and on the basis of which one can be fairly sure that the original levitical performances of the psalms had been composed. And what about the elusive instruments mentioned in the Bible, the *kinnor* and *nevel,* both usually translated as "harp"? Was one small and private, like the Greek *lyra,* and the other large, public, and used to accompany choral song, like the Greek *kithara?* "Lyric" means solo song, and so, I should guess, does *mizmor,* and yet the musical life of the psalm texts has been in liturgy, Judaic and (now taking the Psalter as part of the Old Testament) Christian. But all those layers of interpretation of the poems, their use in the second temple, their refigured role in the religious practice of the realm of the synagogue, turn the solo song into public chorale.

Overhearing (and then, when I was older, beginning to participate in) this choral singing was part of my preliterate introduction to Hebrew. But, again, this was as problematically fraught with variation as all the other aspects of the psalms themselves. My father made Friday night *kiddush,* or prayers, in his own Ashkenazic and with one kind of *niggun,* or melody. Our synagogue used Sephardic, which was how my mother pronounced Hebrew, and when I finally learned to read a little, it was that Sephardic pronunciation I was taught.

Fragments of the psalms I first heard sung without knowing the meaning of the words returned to me in their context only later in life. At school I might have sung, to the "Old Hundredth" tune of the Geneva Psalter,

O, enter then his gates with praise,
Approach with joy his courts unto;
For why, the Lord our God is good,
And it is seemly so to do

or verses 4 and 5 of Psalm 100. (Separatism would not have allowed the doxology, usually sung in American Protestant churches to that tune, into the public school music class. It was with some surprise that I discovered, only when slightly older, that its text was more canonically associated with the melody than even the metrical version of the psalm for which the melody had been composed.) I had no idea at the time that the last two lines were, in Hebrew, so full of commonplaces that even my limited vocabulary could grasp them—"ki tov adonai l'olam chasdo / v'ad dor vador emunato"—and that, perhaps the following week, I would incomprehensibly be singing at a Passover seder the opening of the so-called Great Hallel, Psalm 136, "hodu ladonai ki tov / ki l'olam chasdo" (the latter three words repeated as a refrain twenty-five times), finding it strangely domesticated from its role in the morning synagogue service. Or my mother's voice—I still remember it—singing the opening words of the first of that mysteriously named group of fifteen psalms starting with number 120, "shir hama'alot / 'l adonai." I did not know, even as the words and melody sank into my memory, that these words were not lyric praise, but some editor's parenthetical subtitle, "A Psalm of Degrees," as the KJV gives it. (Actually, that mystery remains one, there being no scholarly agreement about what "ascents" or "degrees" refers to. The term is an open trope, like the whole body of the psalms: are these the fifteen psalms that were—or were written to be—sung by the Levites standing on the fifteen steps that the Mishnah was assured led up to part of the temple? Are they lyrics of the sublime? Do they embody a spiritual ascent of some kind—as one reading of Psalm 121.1 in KJV, "I will lift up mine eyes unto the hills, form whence cometh my help," might suggest?)

The Passover *Haggadah*, the ritual book, was, in general, a wonderful scene of discovery, providing some elementary commentary and significant identification of texts at the very scene of musical intonation. I knew that the *hallel* were a sequence of psalms (113–18, the so-called Egyptian Hallel) started before the seder meal and finished after it. I had heard the exultant 114th (which I quoted earlier) sung before I could linguistically and conceptually put the left- and right-hand pages, the English and the Hebrew, together, as it were. For in the cases of the psalms that were at all familiar liturgically (29, when the Torah scroll is returned to the ark; 92, read responsively in English in Saturday morning service at summer camp; 30 at Chanukah; 95; 99), they occupied a different corner of my inner library and record cabinet from many of the others, which were themselves repositories of memorable phrases.

Meanwhile, however, the musical versions of these poems came at me from all directions. Nobody can know and love Western music of the sixteenth through the twentieth centuries without being drenched in settings of the psalms. My very first contact with the ubiquitous Vulgate versions was, again, at grade school, where the same music teacher who taught us "Old Hundredth" gave us the Elizabethan canon on the lines that I would not for many years be able to put together with those that followed on the filling of the fourth cup of wine at seder: "lo lanu adonai lo lanu / ki-lshimkha ten kavod / al hasdkha al-amitekha." What we sang at school, in the Latin I had not yet learned any of, was those lines in translation: "non nobis domine, non nobis / sed nomini tuo da gloriam" (Psalm 115.1). By the time I reached college, the Vulgate Psalter was ubiquitous in my musical world. Vivaldi's "Beatus vir" setting of Psalm 112— "Beatus vir qui timet dominum / in mandatus eius volet nimis"—which I read through and wrote liner notes for while at Columbia; all the motets I ever remembered any part of; the texts in Stravinsky's *Symphony of Psalms,* which I sang often in a college chorus: all these texts were as new ones, each was a *shir hadash,* or new song. I think particularly of just those lines from Psalm 40 in Stravinsky's setting:

> Exspectans exspectavi Dominum: & intendit mihi. Et exaudivit preces meas. . . . Et statuit supra petram pedes meos, & direxit gressus meos.

These were sung slowly and calmly, up through *preces meas,* the patience of "I waited patiently for the Lord; and he inclined unto me and heard my cry" expressed in the reduplication of *exspectans exspectavi* just as it is in the *kavo kiv-iti* of the Hebrew. The fugal texture gets denser and denser, the singers' own feet get "set upon a rock," and the music, as well as the Lord, are "establishing their goings." And then, after an instrumental interlude, the percussive force of the now homophonic texture at the words "Et immisit in os meum canticum novum." The familiar, old formulaic *shir hadash* of the Hebrew had never meant this, and any singer of the Stravinsky literally feels the presence of some kind of new song in his or her mouth at just that point in the setting. The composer's translation of the Latin has turned it into a praise of singing, even as the last section, with its setting of the "laudete eium in chordis et organo," develops under-tones of self-reference. But generally it was *singing* the Latin psalms, rather than listening to them, that brought yet another psalter into my possession.

Nor should I neglect my strange but nonetheless telling outsider's sense of the chanted psalms in the Book of Common Prayer. When young, I courted a young lady who sang in the choir of the college chapel, whose denomination was acutely Established, and I would often "to church repair / Not for the doctrine, but the music there" (as Alexander Pope disparagingly puts it, but that for me is always authenticating, the only true "doctrine" being music). I thus got to know yet another version of the psalter, the psalms in Miles Coverdale's wonderful early sixteenth-century English (the prayer book of the English Church antedating the KJV, of course, by three-quarters of a century). Psalm 47 begins "O clap your hands together, all ye people: O sing unto God with the voice of melody," the *kol rina,* or resounding-cry voice, of the Hebrew getting nicely interpreted as "voice of triumph" in KJV, but more rich and strange, and off the mark in a relevant direction (given the etymology, probably) in the original. Later on, in verse 5, we have "God is gone up with a merry noise: and the Lord with the sound of the trump," for the more sober exultation of "God is gone up with a shout" of KJV. For British schoolchildren who would brood over what they had half heard, the corners of the church must have reechoed, over the centuries, with good Mrs. Murphys. But knowing and singing Thomas Weelkes's marvelous polyphonic anthem on this text, for example, gave me "God is gone up . . ." on an ascending fifth in the bass part, and imprinted the translation as if I had been taught it at school. On the other hand, when, at sixteen, in a blaze of literary piety, I committed vast acres of *The Waste Land* to memory, the allusion of line 182, in "The Fire Sermon," "By the waters of Leman I sat down and wept," to Psalm 137 was one I heard. But the mystery of why it was the *waters* and not the *rivers* of Babylon that were being refigured bathetically (and with no gloss in the celebrated and evasive notes) was only resolved when I could conclude that the English Church's prayer book provided the canonical text for Eliot: "By the waters of Babylon we sat down and wept: when we remember'd thee O Sion. / As for our harps we hanged them up: upon the trees that are there-in." The Coverdale psalms are full of treasures, not of quaintness but of true power, and almost any familiar text will blaze forth anew in it. I might only add the beginning of Psalm 19 (a psalm I discuss later in this chapter). In the Book of Common Prayer it goes:

The heavens declare the glory of God: and the firmament showeth his
    handy-work.
One day telleth another: and one night certifieth another.
There is neither speech nor language: but their voices are heard among them.
Their sound is gone out into all lands: and their words into the ends of
    the world.

These poems, then, spawned versions of themselves, and gradually coming to terms with them all and putting them into poetic perspective has been something of a synecdoche of my life as a reader and writer. To have been able to repossess the ars poetica of the original, coming back from all the misconstrued good Mrs. Murphys of English to realize that the original is itself full of them, has been to grasp something essential about biblical poetry in general—namely, that it exists in and for its interpretations, and that some archaeological reduction is all the authenticity one needs. By the poetics of the psalms, I mean not merely the structural wonders, say, of Psalm 42, with its pattern of five verses plus refrain, five verses plus refrain (and with Psalm 43, a supplement, confirming this), or of the wordplay in the original. That wordplay is usually displaced in translation anyway—for example, in Psalm 122.6, "Pray for the peace of Jerusalem: they shall prosper that love thee" (KJV; more properly, "let them prosper"), there is a fortuitous, faint pattern of alliteration in the English, but the Hebrew is denser: "sha'alu sh'lom yrushalam / yshlayu ohavayikh." The first four words, seemingly connected semantically, are all quite distinct in meaning, and it is as if the name of Jerusalem were derived from the words for *ask, peace,* and *prosperity*—such is the momentary etymological fiction set up by the wordplay. Sometimes the effect is more fleeting, as in Psalm 102.11, mentioned earlier—"My days are like a shadow that declineth; and I am withered like grass" (KJV)—where, in the second half-line, "va'ani ca'eshev ivash," the last two words ("like-grass," "dry-up") are made to sound inevitably connected in the Hebrew.

In short, losing the mysterious poetry engendered by mistranslation, or even by distance from the English usage of a much earlier text, is compensated for many times over by reentry into the original. Confronting the psalms in yet another identity, decked out and bejeweled by linguistic and homiletic commentary, has been an activity of my later life. More and more mysteries open up in these versions as well. For example, back in Psalm 23.4, the famous crux of "the valley of the shadow of death" comes from a tendentious repointing of the word *tzalmavet,* which could mean either "deep shade" or "death shade," and probably the former. In any case, the line means "dark valley"; the two construct states piled on each other—"valley *of* the shadow *of* death" in the traditions of English—pile near-allegory on near-allegory. It is not usual in the psalms to find "shadow" a menacing notion; and although only in Hebrew, among languages I know something of, does morphological ambiguity provide any glimpse of "dead" lurking in "shade," only in this psalm did the early editors conjure it up. (This reading is there in the Septuagint, and must have been there before.) But knowing all this in no way makes the poem shed its outer garments for the sake of a naked linguistic truth, and the various translations and versions and misprisions all coexist, and inhere in every phrase.

Whole poems of various genres from the Book of Psalms, such as the storm ode of Psalm 29 and the terse, powerful personal lament of Psalm 130—with its famous *incipit* in the Vulgate, "De profundis clamavi" [Out of the depths have I cried unto thee, O Lord]—the splendid sequence of Psalms 102–4, the brooding over the ruins in language, which some scholars feel to be akin to that of the Book of Lamentations, of Psalm 74, all continue to call up possible applications in Judaic tradition alone. The reinterpreted Psalms of the Christian Old Testament add more; and even the kind of liturgical use to which these versions have been put—for celebratory or congregational use in various traditions—have in another sense constantly been reinterpreting, reallegorizing, the nature of the "I" of the psalmist. To that extent, all the different kinds and occasions of musical setting have become as much part of the surrounding frame of annotation as any scholarly conjecture about a single dot of vowel-pointing.

The great Psalm 137, *al naharot bavel* [by the rivers of Babylon], is for me one of the very greatest. It has suffered an ironically amusing metamorphosis in English tradition, not merely in the translation—this is a minor matter—but in the adaptation, in the seventeenth and eighteenth centuries, in the versified versions, growing out of the so-called metrical psalters used for congregational singing in the English Church, written by so many English poets. The famous opening (KJV) speaks of a condition of exile:

By the rivers of Babylon, there we sat down, yea, we wept, when we
    remembered Zion.
We hanged our harps upon the willows in the midst thereof.
For they that carried us away captive required of us a song; and they that
    wasted us required of us mirth, saying, Sing us one of the songs of Zion.

The power of the refusal to perform for the captors grows during the subsequent verses. Hanging the harps, *kinnorotenu,* on the trees, abandoning familiar and consoling music, is actually a violent gesture of refusal—it is a slamming down of the piano lid, or a closing of the instrument case. With the memory of the lost home that follows, the almost violent power continues:

If I forget thee, O Jerusalem, let my right hand forget her cunning.
If I do not remember thee, let my tongue cleave to the roof of my mouth; if I
    prefer not Jerusalem above my chief joy.

The KJV "forget her cunning," for the Hebrew *tishkach,* "let forget," is one of those wonderful glossings—suppose it had the form "forget [e.g., her cunning]"?—which seem forever to inhere in the poetic text of the psalm *for* English.

The violent conclusion of the psalm with its curse against *bat-bavel,* the "daughter of Babylon" (meaning the city itself, not one of its wretched and synecdochal inhabitants), has been generating throughout the poem. But in English Protestant tradition, the opening image became more and more languorous, and the memory of Jerusalem engendered by the scene more and more nostalgic. Thomas Campion, around 1614, versifies the lines about the harps hung on the trees as

Aloft the trees that sprang up there
Our silent harps we pensive hung

with a lovely and delicate attention to the etymon of *pendere,* "to hang," in "pensive," but making it poetically and deliberately ambiguous whether the harps or the hangers of them were pensive, and in what sense. Richard Crashaw, in 1646, has

On the proud banks of great Euphrates' flood
There we sat, and there we wept:
Our harps that now no music understood
Nodding on the willows slept.

And Thomas Carew, around 1655, talks of

Our neglected harps unstrung,
Not acquainted with the hand
Of the skillful tuner, hung
On the willow trees that stand
Planted in the neighbour land.

Sir John Denham wrote, sometime before 1668, "Our harps to which we lately sang, / Mute as ourselves, on willows hang." The unfolding theme of abandonment and neglect, rather than positive, outraged refusal to perform, is far from the point of the Hebrew poem, but moves toward the generation of a new trope, the association of the instrument and the singer: they become each other. Such a version could only occur to poets.

I close these remarks with a look at what may be the greatest psalm of all, and one whose greatness resides not in spite of but within and because of its deeply problematic character. It is the heavenly hymn 19, so celebrated in paraphrase (Addison's "The spacious firmament on high / With all the blue Etherial Sky"; "The Heavens are telling the glory of God, / The Wonder of his work displays the firmament" in the text of Haydn's *Creation*). It starts out with a vision of the animate coherence of the created heavens, starting from 2 (KJV):

Day unto day uttereth speech, and night unto night sheweth knowledge.
There is no speech nor language, where their voice is not heard.
Their line [should be "call"—a mispointing of *Kavam*] is gone out through all the earth, and their words to the end of the world. In them he hath set a tabernacle for the sun,
Which is as a bridegroom coming out of his chamber, and rejoiceth as a strong man to run a race [*orach,* should be "track"].

The Hebrew has the "yom l'yom, vlaila l'layla," which Jerome's Latin ("Dies diei eructat verbum: & nox nocti indicat scientiam") and all the good English versions until such as the New English Bible ("One day speaks to another") retain. Since the point of the lines is that the communication is soundless and, indeed, nonlinguistic, the effect in English of the "day unto day / night unto night" is to underline the unmediated quality of the connection.

But the really deep problem comes with verse 7. Following on the little allegory of the sun as hero, picking up after the last part of it (6),

His going forth is from the end of the heaven, and his circuit unto the ends of
    it: and there is nothing hid from the heat thereof

we get,

The law of the Lord is perfect, converting the soul: the testimony of the Lord
    is sure, making wise the simple.
The statutes of the Lord are right, rejoicing the heart: the commandment of
    the Lord is pure, enlightening the eyes.
The fear of the Lord is clean, enduring for ever: the judgments of the Lord are
    true and righteous altogether.

The leap from the matter of the heavens to the perfection of the Torah *is* the story of the poem. And yet, originally, these were two different texts, yoked together not by violence but by interpretive connection. That is, if the first part, about the heavens, is made part of a parable, then the other part is the remainder of the psalm, up to and including the final verses of what one might call prayer and metaprayer, the psalmist concluding with a supplication, and then a supplication in re that supplication:

Keep back thy servant also from presumptuous sins; let them not have
    dominion over me: then shall I be upright, and I shall be innocent from
    the great transgression.
Let the words of my mouth, and the meditation of my heart, be acceptable in
    thy sight, O Lord, my strength, and my redeemer.

Even the pairing of the more concrete *words* and the heart's *musing* (with its punning overtones in English of silent *music,* also perhaps lurking in the Hebrew *hegyon,* used at this point) seems to recapitulate the relation between the two parts of the combined poem: what's out there, communicating without text, what's down here, communicating by text.

The consciousness in rabbinic tradition that these may indeed have been two separate poems is manifested, as frequently is the case, by the mode of its repression. I have heard that Psalm 19 was often set as an exercise for interpretation, the injunction being to read over the seam, to assert the unity of the psalm. That parabolic unity—the relation between the wonders of the sky and the wonders of Torah—*is* the psalm. Once established as an agenda, it lights up points in the text. For example, rabbinic commentary might draw attention to the word used about "the commandment of the Lord" in verse 8, "mitzvat adonai bara," the word *bara* (pure) showing that it is used of the sun in Song of Songs 6.10. The poem's lyric action could be shown to be that of a movement from looking *out* to looking *in,* or from up to down. Immanuel Kant, evidently meditating on this famous psalm, produced his (in turn) famous assertion about the connection in wonder between the starry heavens above us and the moral law within us.

Such textual assimilations, separations, revisions, occur throughout the Hebrew Bible, and the interpretive tradition, in general, tendentiously tropes the resulting text with the impolitic injunction to consider it as having been revealed/composed in just that way. It results in the final and monumental good Mrs. Murphys, and Psalm 19 is a superb instance of this. Every reader has to put Psalms 1–6 and 7–15 together in a new way, making his or her own kind of sense out of it, in a larger instance of having to come to terms with the KJV locutions like "night unto night" or even the now largely revised out "their line is gone out through all the earth" (Coverdale and the Vulgate get "call" right). This requires an ad hoc trope of a "line" of communication—some pretechnological telephone to make sense out of. The layers of misreading and rereadings are part of the poetry of the text itself in the poetic portions of the Bible. And the problems and puzzles of the psalms will remain eternal occasions for the reader's negative capability as well as for the interpretive wit that turns every reader into a poet, if only momentarily.

CHAPTER EIGHT

On A Child's Garden of Verses

Robert Louis Stevenson is an author who has become newly interesting for the period of literary sensibility that some like to call postmodern. Certainly, as a writer of romance rather than novel (although *The Master of Ballantrae* is as much a novel—and as much a romance—as Scott's *Guy Mannering*) he could thereby seem more of a neglected precursor; and Jorge Luis Borges's profound admiration of Stevenson could itself propound, for readers of thirty-five years ago, a kind of puzzle in itself.

Except for the marginalized (male juvenile) *Treasure Island* and *Kidnapped,* the short fiction, considered as insufficiently modern thrillers, was not read much after World War II. But I have been continually surprised to discover how many college students among those who have taken writing courses from me at Yale remember the experience of encountering, and many of the texts themselves, of Stevenson's *Child's Garden of Verses*. It has remained canonical for three quarters of a century, although in a haunting sort of way; turning back to it recently has produced some unexpectedly spooky encounters for me. I had also been reading through Stevenson's considerable body of verse generally. This was not only to reacquaint myself with the few old favorites I had known before—the charming sonnet in couplets to Henry James, for example, or the fascinating if not wholly satisfying experiments in vers libre that may have come from his friendship with William Ernest Henley; it was also to explore the entire range of his verse, within which to consider the poems for children and the remarkable influence on subsequent writers I feel they have had. The spooky encounters included coming across such lines as the lovely rondeau-like reworking of Théodore de Banville's verses based on a children's game, "Nous n'irons plus aux bois" that I had known both in the original and in A. E. Housman's adaptation ("We'll to the woods no more, / The laurels all are cut"). It begins

We'll walk to the woods no more
But stay beside the fire
To weep for old desire
And things that are no more.
   The woods are spoiled and hoar,
The ways are full of mire;
We'll walk the woods no more
But stay beside the fire.

I had written a poem of my own, with the Banville in mind but diverging from it, only to find that it had been more traveled by than I had known. More determinedly spooky was the realization that other moments in my poetry of the past twenty years may have resounded with some of what I'd actually remembered from the children's verses—it now seemed, for example, that a bit from the rhyme called "The Swing" had certainly crept into my extended mad-song called "The Seesaw."

But going through *A Child's Garden of Verses*, Stevenson's remarkable volume of 1885, has produced some ghostly moments of another sort, reencounters with verses I had grown up with, some of them well remembered, some of them perhaps unread even then, some of them half remembered. And some, undoubtedly, fruitfully repressed under less than dire pressures, only to return unwittingly in my own writing. Moreover, the adult reader now reads them not, as the child had, for what in life he or she recognized, but for what the writer had been doing and, additionally, for what the reader found in prior reading. (A favorite example of this is rereading Hans Christian Andersen's *Mermaid* after you have known Blake's *Book of Thel*.) Robert Schumann composed his wonderful set of *Kinderscenen (Op. 13)* in 1838; they are romantic and thus somewhat ironic evocations of "scenes from childhood" for adults to play (and too hard for all but a few advanced children). His *Album für die Jugend (Op. 68)*, published a decade later, was a much larger collection of pieces written for children to play. If we put "read" or "comprehendingly hear" for "play," we have the difference between the child-speakers in some of Blake's or Wordsworth's shorter poems, and Jane Taylor's rhymes written for children. I shall among other things consider here a wonderful Album for the Young reconsidered as the Scenes from Childhood they had become, and argue that, indeed, this is what they always were, the later adult poetry speaking in the children's verses.

My actual return to Stevenson's poems for children was perhaps heralded by my hearing one day last summer on my car radio an unannounced voice on NPR reading an unannounced text:

Whenever the moon and stars are set,
  Whenever the wind is high,
All night long in the wind and the wet,
  A man goes riding by.
Late in the night when the fires are out,
Why does he gallop and gallop about?

Whenever the trees are crying aloud,
  And ships are tossed at sea,
By, on the highway, low and loud,
  By at the gallop goes he.
By at the gallop he goes, and then
By he comes back at the gallop again.

I shivered somewhat, having forgotten the poem and the way it haunted me as a child with the all but erotic excitement that latency period is so full of, with its puzzling indeterminacy: who is the man? is he driven by the wind? driving it? I was too young for serious personifications, so the possibility that man might be the storm wind itself was deferred until, some years later, I read *The King of the Golden River* and encountered South-West Wind, Esq. (I do remember at the time—because my mother when I was quite young liked to sing, unprofession-ally but with some understanding, Schubert *Lieder* while my father played them—vaguely associating the wind-rider with the opening of *Erlkönig: Wer reitet so spät / Durch Nacht und Wind?*)

  The unidentified voice turned out to be that of Robert McNeil, of the PBS nightly news report, talking about his boyhood in Canada, and particularly about his reading. He had, both somewhat uncannily and, on present contem-plation, unsurprisingly, wondered about the poem in some of the same ways I had. I can now recognize the particular moves of ars poetica that were respon-sible for some of these effects and the delight one could take in them without even realizing what one was noticing: the "Whenever . . ." quatrain, concluding in the three pounding dactyls of the couplet that reinforced the opening d'*dah* da rhythm of "Whenever"; and then, again, in the initially linked second stanza, the idiomatically innocent passing-move of "by" in the "riding by" of the first one becomes a major question. To "ride by" in the absolute (instead of, say, "riding by my house") is the essence of this windy spirit, and the "by" keeps coming up (as if the very word were like a bell to toll you back again outside the house) in insistent anaphoric repetition, throughout the stanza.

It was interesting to discover that Stevenson himself had previously dealt poetically with the matter of the storm rider in a more ambitious way. The first of two free verse poems, "Storm," is quite Whitmanian in tone—praising the sublime energies of the tempestuous seashore, and hailing the "big, strong, bullying, boisterous waves, / That are of all things in nature the nearest thoughts to human" but not in form (the free verse is of the short-lined mode, its line breaks marking clear syntactic periods). The second, "Stormy Nights," is a precursor of the later children's poem; it is a meditation on the gains and losses of maturity that comes right from Wordsworth's Immortality ode:

I was then the Indian,
Well and happy and full of glee and pleasure,
Both hands full of life.
And not without divine impulses
Shot into me by the untried non-ego.

And indeed, at the end of the poem, he breaks out, again in the cadences of Whitman, "Why do you taunt my progress, / O green-spectacled Wordsworth! in beautiful verses, / You, the elderly poet?") The central scene from the childhood that he "Perfectly love[s], and keenly recollect[s]"—but that he interestingly remembers without wanting to "recall" even if he could—is the night-riding storm going

. . . by me like a cloak-wrapt horseman
Stooping over the saddle—
Go by and come again and yet again,
Like some one riding with a pardon,
And ever baffled, ever shut from passage.

The repetition is of import here, as it will be in the less violent and menacing *by*'s of "Windy Nights," even as the more menacing storm has been transformed into the less violent wind, mysterious rather than directly terrifying.

It is not terror, but rather wonder, that marks *A Child's Garden of Verses*—a pastoral world (*et in arcadia vixi*, he later wrote of his own childhood days at Colinton Manse, and near the Water of Leith, whose remembered stream would emerge from time to time among its flowers). I myself recall encountering this in "Bed in Summer" the book's opening poem. It was my generation's own introduction, too, to the great problematics of reading. I didn't dress by yellow candlelight, but rather, electric light; on the other hand, in summer, I did indeed "have to go to bed by day"; and dealing with this puzzle in a very Emersonian sort of ad hoc way, I think I concluded that the winter part of the paradox covered fictional experience—from books, and requiring corrective historical adjustments—whereas the summer part spoke to my own experience in an unmediated way. I wonder now how it was to function as the introductory poem, with delicate allegory providing an argument for the book it led off—like Frost's "Pasture"—rather than explicitly, like Herrick's opening catalogue of what his Hesperides would be about or Ben Jonson's "Why I Write Not of Love." The speaker's wonder at a paradoxical reversal invites the reader to follow it into meditative reflection and projective imagination; as a child, I did not need to be told "you come, too." The book that follows deals with many objects of wonder: shadows inside a house at night, the totally different companion-cast shadow of the child himself; the domestic and the foreign; the fleeting vignettes through a railway carriage window; the fireplace-meditation. . . . Even more, though, the adult reader may see the poem's day-night reversal as figuring a complex dialectic of projected adulthood and recollected childhood that underlies the whole volume.

In the course of gently but firmly contradicting the perplexing casuistries of her adult interlocutor, the "simple child, / That lightly draws its breath" of Wordsworth's "We Are Seven" asserts that her two dead siblings are indeed present and accounted for: "Their graves are green, they may be seen" she says, and goes on to report that

. . . often after sun-set, Sir
When it is light and fair,
I take my little porringer,
And eat my supper there.

We might feel that no child would say "my little porringer," any more than "my little shoes"—this is a normatively large adult talking. Yet in Stevenson's "Land of Story-Books," the speaker can speak of his trek of escape from adult evening pursuits ("They sit at home and talk and sing, / And do not play at anything")

Now, with my little gun, I crawl
All in the dark along the wall,
And follow round the forest track
Away behind the sofa back

and, even more implausibly, can say of the imagined hunter's camp he reaches, "These are the hills, these are the woods, / These are my starry solitudes." And yet, in the case of this speaker, a post-Wordsworthian poet whose discourse we shall be examining, we may be less disturbed, partially because the rhetoric of Victorian adults, of English poets generally, of elegantly expressed feelings of acutely remembered childhood experiences, all come together in what I think is a unique poetic language that, I shall suggest, has had considerable consequence. Another, crucial matter is that Wordsworth wasn't writing for children to read and listen to; children spoken *for* in these lines respond directly and innocently to the adult language, and accept it as a representation of what they have noticed or felt.

The imagined voyage or trek is central to many of these poems. "Travel" has overtones of the imaginative nocturnal activities of "Il Penseroso." And I must call attention here only to its remarkable little episode in which the child, imagining his Asian and African travels, comes to a vision, in some fancied *Arabia deserta,* of a distant and later condition that is able to contemplate the realm of childhood only through souvenirs as images:

Where among the desert sands
Some deserted city stands,
All its children, sweep and prince,
Grown to manhood ages since,
Not a foot in street or house,
Not a stir of child or mouse,
And when kindly falls the night,
In all the town no spark of light.

The child reaches in his journey the house of childhood to find nobody home. (Whether this poem underlies Frost's "Directive" might be interesting to contemplate.)

The "North-West Passage" sequence, with its little journey upstairs to bed at night being mapped on a little pattern of quest-romance—I always remembered the stanza from it that I could only decades later come to feel as almost Marvellian:

Now we behold the embers flee
About the firelit hearth; and see
Our faces painted as we pass,
Like pictures, on the window-glass.

The hearth-meditation, so important in a line that runs from Coleridge through American poetry of the nineteenth and twentieth centuries, is further exemplified by "Armies in the Fire"; in its second stanza, the relation of literature to imagination—here, imagined armies moving among burning cities—is gently touched upon, through the agency of reflected firelight:

Now in the falling of the gloom
The red fire paints the empty room:
And warmly on the roof it looks,
And flickers on the backs of books.

And it is perhaps significant that this poem follows the one called "The Land of Story-Books." But it is the final stanza

Blinking embers, tell me true
Where are those armies marching to,
And what the burning city is
That crumbles in your furnaces!

The answer can only come to the adult writer, who has no doubt been thinking of the last quatrain of Shakespeare's great autumnal sonnet 73, "That time of year thou mayst in me behold"

In me thou seest the ashes of such fire
That on the ashes of his youth doth lie.

If this is childhood itself, slowly being consumed "with that which it was nourished by," its name and nature are necessarily enwrapped in veils of the oracular for the child, who is still, as Ben Jonson would put it, a "spectator" rather than an "understander."

A variant of the overland trek is the sea voyage, as in "My Ship and I," in which the child is

. . . the captain of a tidy little ship,
  Of a ship that goes a-sailing on the pond;
And my ship it keeps a-turning all around and all about;
But when I'm a little older, I shall find the secret out
  How to send my vessel sailing on beyond.

The only sailor aboard is a doll figure; and the speaker resolves, in a marvelous inversion of growing up and being able to make adult journeys, one day to shrink to the size of the doll, now quickened to life. The two of them may then stop sailing around in circles in the narrow confines of the pond, "to voyage and explore." Pond-sailing and voyaging, circling and navigating, seem here to trope play and work—but the work is itself figured as higher play—the speaker will grow down in order to play better at the grown-up voyaging. The innocent speaker can't grasp some of the complexities of the experienced reading of such poems, but I think the figurative topoi—such as the voyage of life here—are better learned obliquely than when parable, proverb, or whatever plainly propound them.

There is also the "Pirate Story," with its meadow-as-sea, and the bed-boat, to which I shall return. I think in this connection of "Where Go the Boats?" with its introduction of the river of time topos

Dark brown is the river,
  Golden is the sand,
It flows along for ever,
  With trees on either hand

and the subtle but available music of the syntax itself that takes the young reader or listener sailing on a voyage accompanying the one made by the floating leaves construed as boats—

On goes the river
  And out past the mill,
Away down the valley,
  Away down the hill.

Away down the river,
  A hundred miles or more,
Other little children
  Shall bring my boats ashore.

The passage from *On* through *away . . . away* comes to rest at the final slightly different *away* (it is no longer where the river *goes,* but where it is). In another poem, "The Cow," the big hit for me as a child was the third line of stanza 1 "The friendly cow all red and white, / I love with all my heart: She gives me cream with all her might, / To eat on apple-tart"—all children must know there's something wonderfully and benignly strange about putting it *that* way, even if they're city children who don't know from direct observation that whatever might is expended in the process is that of the hands and arms of the milker.

This is not whimsy at all, I think. It marks one rhetorical point along an interesting range of attitudes and distances implied by what the child-poet of the book notices and cannot notice about what he is in fact saying. The poems are neither naive nor sentimental, as it were, but move across a spectrum of these. They are not arch, although Stevenson had indeed previously written, and designed some woodcuts for, arch, half self-mocking moral emblems whose tone prefigures that of Belloc's cautionary verses. Aside from instructive moral rhymes by Isaac Watts (and, indeed, some fine epigraphic poems by Jean Ingelow in her children's romance *Mopsa the Fairy* in 1869), *A Child's Garden of Verses* may be the first book of poems for children by an otherwise accomplished adult writer—in this sense, a parallel to Andersen, Hawthorne, Ruskin, and Kingsley. Perhaps James Hogg's "A Boy's Song" might be mentioned here; Stevenson echoes his fellow Scot in "The Dumb Soldier" about a toy soldier buried in a hole in the grass

When the grass is ripe like grain,
When the scythe is stoned again,
When the lawn is shaven clear,
Then my hole will reappear

(and there are Whitmanian overtones here as well, I think). More interestingly, as a book, *A Child's Garden of Verses* engages not so much the matter of whimsy, or of the cautionary, but of romance—in this, being akin to *Treasure Island* and *Kidnapped*. The speaker is the child himself throughout—and here perhaps is to raise the point about how this book is mostly *pueris sed non virginibusque*—(although John Bunyan had some two hundred years earlier produced a collection of moral emblems specifying plainly in its title *A Book for Boys and Girls*). A sole exception, perhaps, is the "Marching Song" with its bouncy trochaic rhythm:

Bring the comb and play upon it!
  Marching, here we come!
Willie cocks his highland bonnet,
  Johnnie beats the drum.

Mary Jane commands the party,
  Peter leads the rear.

And, in the last stanza

Here's enough of fame and pillage,
  Great commander Jane!
Now that we've been round the village,
  Let's go home again.

But it may be supposed that Jane gets to command by virtue of her age on the one hand and the extreme youth of her valiant warriors on the other. (In this regard, by the way, I note that Charles Robinson's first and canonical 1896 illustrations showed as many girls as possible when the lack of gender specificity in a particular poem allowed it.)

At least one contemporary reviewer quoted the well-known couplet called (with some delicate irony, perhaps) "Happy Thought" as instancing puerile thought and puerile expression. You may remember that it goes "The world is so full of a number of things, / I'm sure we should all be as happy as kings." This is certainly not a simple matter. The pastoral dialectic of childhood remembered and expressed in adult language breeds strong ironies. James Thurber used the ultimate line in his own debunking moral to one of his wonderful, adult fables for our time ("The world is so full of a number of things, / I'm sure we should all be as happy as kings, and we all know how happy kings are")—and, indeed, this is just the point: in an almost Blakean way, the child of the poem doesn't know the darker side of what he is saying; the adult reading it to a listening child does, and indeed may mutter Thurber's addition as his or her own afterthought. But the child in the verse-garden is saying something else as well: the plenitude he beholds is the demesne of his attentiveness, not a realm over which he wields the kind of repressive power that is the only sort that may be correctly addressed in universities today. (I can't help but recount how my poetic contemporary,

Richard Howard, told me that in his first-grade class—in Cleveland in the mid-thirties—his teacher, remarking that many residual kings were currently being shoved into exile or otherwise attended to, asked them to memorize her emended text—"I'm sure we should all be as happy as birds." Such a devout literalist would be at home in most university English departments today.)

Stevenson's child is, in fact, as well as in figure, monarch of all he surveys only because he can notice it with active pleasure and control it benignly in his imagination. And thus "richer than untempted kings" he can indeed feel. It is for this inherent sense of the dialectic of childhood pastoral (which Empson first identifies with Alice, and which continues in another mode here), with Blake lurking at the borders, that one might recall Stevenson's remark in a letter to William Ernest Henley in March 1883, to the effect that "Poetry is not the strong point of the text, and I shrink from any title that might seem to claim that quality; otherwise we might have *Nursery Muses* or *New Songs of Innocence* (but that were a blasphemy)." But Stevenson indeed knew well what true poetry was. He entitles his collection of 1887 *Underwoods,* the title Ben Jonson gave to a selected portion of his oeuvre; in his epigraph to that volume, Stevenson acknowledges the borrowing, at the same time showing that he is eminently qualified to do so:

Of all my verse, like not a single line;
But like my title for it is not mine.
That title from a better man I stole:
Ah, how much better had I stol'n the whole!

which itself is a perfect pastiche of Ben Jonson. Many of his own poems have premonitions of Hardy—the Hardy he could probably not have read yet, *Wessex Poems* being first published in 1890, and certainly of many Georgian poets like de la Mare. What keeps surprising the adult reader of the poems in the *Child's Garden* is how full they are of the stuff of true poetry. One quick instance here: in "Escape at Bedtime," a poem about being outside one's house at night, a brief catalogue of the constellations certainly invites the young reader's reminders of his or her own wonder at the stars:

The Dog, and the Plough, and the Hunter, and all,
  And the star of the sailor, and Mars,
These shone in the sky, and the pail by the wall
  Would be half full of water and stars.

But a present delight at the hidden zeugma of the last line, ("of" being literal in the case of the water, figurative in the case of the stars, reduplicating another figurative "of" if the water is full of stars too—how we must labor to represent our intuitions! how free the child is of the need to do so!). And it is in the first apprehension of such patterns and devices that the young reader, unknowing of their names and identities—let alone their venerable literary history—can encounter them as found natural objects, like shells along a shore, and keep them among other treasured souvenirs.

Suffice it to say these verses have played a remarkable role in the education of writers in English since they first appeared. (They may even, for a brief while, continue to. In a Yale College verse-composition class one fall, seven out of sixteen students had grown up with some or all of them, although only two evinced any acquaintance whatsoever with either KJV or even the New English Bible.)

Earlier I quoted a line from Cowper's Alexander Selkirk poem ("I am monarch of all I survey"). It makes a kind of subliminal return in what is one of the central poems of the collection, "The Land of Counterpane." The child remembers an occasion when he "was sick and lay a-bed," his head propped up by pillows, and how he deployed his playthings—toy soldiers, houses and trees, ships—on the field of his bed's coverlet. It is, like a very few others, in the past tense, so that the child-narrator seems almost to double with the adult speaker (the verbs' past tense being perfect for the child, imperfect for the adult poet). It concludes:

I was the giant, great and still
That sits upon the pillow-hill
And sees before him, dale and plain,
The pleasant land of counterpane.

Joan Richardson, in her biography of Wallace Stevens (1:219) suggests the importance of this poem for the later poet, invoking "land of counterpane with its little, sick hero fantasizing himself 'atop a hill.'" Certainly the topos is a venerable one. The visionary prospect from a height, of what one cannot literally enter, stems from Moses on Pisgah at least through Adam on his high hill in *Paradise Lost,* combines in modernity with Petrarch's view of his own world—able to be reentered after having been seen from above—from the top of Mont Ventoux.

This seems to be one of the two central fables of the *Garden,* the other being the solitary trek. Let us consider some of its occasions; for example, these lines from "The Swing":

Up in the air and over the wall,
 Till I can see so wide,
Rivers and trees and cattle and all
 Over the countryside—

or "Foreign Lands," which begins

Up into the cherry tree
Who should climb but little me?

[and here, the Dorothy Parker (b. 1893) agenda? the smarty-pants send up of
it—we wait for the smartass second couplet]

I held the trunk with both my hands
And looked abroad on foreign lands.

I saw the next door garden lie,
Adorned with flowers, before my eye,
And many pleasant places more
That I had never seen before.

I saw the dimpling river pass
And be the sky's blue looking-glass;
The dusty roads go up and down
With people tramping in to town.

One of the things this can do for an imaginative child reading it is to acknowledge and somehow license his or her own private fancy of just such a kind. The
adult world is full of suppressions and restrictions of just such fancies and discoveries (admittedly, inventing the poetic wheel), as Wordsworth indeed
understood. Poetry is an important bivalent connection between childhood and
maturity, privileging neither, aware of the ways in which growing up can be a
kind of growing down.

In poems presented to children, this link can often run along an axis of this
kind of recognition. And it can talk to children, for themselves and for the
poet's—or at least, the romantic and later poet's—reconstruction of his or her
own childhood. What helps to make Stevenson's verses into true poetry of a kind
is this dark conceit running through them: the book's child-poet speaks in the
language of English poetry and, reciprocally, introduces his very young listen-
ers/readers to poetic form and trope and mythology, so that in some way, for
many generations of middle-class children (as well as working-class ones still fortunate enough to have been schooled before 1960 or so), future writers were
being secretly educated. It would be amusing to search the compass of the *Garden*
for subsequent echoes or even topoi, all the way from Wallace Stevens to the resonant last line of "Singing": "The organ with the organ man / Is singing in the
rain," in Arthur Freed's (b. 1894) celebrated lyric of the popular song of 1929.

In *A Child's Garden of Verses* the visionary prospects need not always be
revealed from a literal height. The child conjures up pageants and parades. One
such poem chronicles a visionary parade of "every kind of beast and man," when

All night long and every night,
When my mama puts out the light,
I see the people marching by,
As plain as day, before my eye.

They start slowly, gather speed, and are followed by the child "Until we reach the town of Sleep." Children acknowledge such an experience—it is very common—and grasp that final conceit. The title, "Young Night-Thought," is half for them, and half—the allusively part-joking, part-serious half—for the adult, well-read reader, who, while not having gone through the ten thousand or so lines of Edward Young's *Night Thoughts on Life, Death, and Immortality,* would at least have known of it and its tediously extensive agenda.

Another actual height is that of "The Hayloft," with the mown grass piled up "in mountain tops / For mountaineers to roam"; these are named with great pleasure and seriousness

Here is Mount Clear, Mount Rusty-Nail,
  Mount Eagle and Mount High;—
The mice that in these mountains dwell,
  No happier are than I!

There is an echo here, incidentally, of Lovelace in "To Althea from Prison"—"The birds, that wanton in the air / Know no such liberty"; there lurks in Stevenson's poem the issue, although not the cadence, of the final occurrence of Lovelace's refrain "Angels alone, that soar above, / Enjoy such liberty." But indeed, seventeenth-century poetry resounds through *A Child's Garden of Verses:* "Auntie's Skirts" is Herrick's "Whenas in silks my Julia goes," with the substitution of the excitements of general sensuous wonder for those of eros:

Whenever Auntie moves around,
Her dresses make a curious sound,
They trail behind her up the floor,
And trundle after through the door.

And in another poem the eponymous gardener himself ("Far in the plots, I see him dig / Old and serious, brown and big")—perhaps a secret surrogate for the poet-gardener of the garden of verses—gets unwittingly likened to the Aesopian ant being rebuked by the Anacreontic grasshopper of Richard Lovelace's poem:

Silly gardener! summer goes,
And winter comes with pinching toes,
When in the garden bare and brown
You must lay your barrow down.

Well now, and while the summer stays,
To profit by these garden days
O how much wiser you would be
To play at Indian wars with me!

Lovelace's grasshopper suffers the Aesopian fate in winter ("Poor verdant fool, and now green ice"); he is a singer, not a provider. But the gardener, a worker, is for the young speaker—for whom play is serious and labor a distraction—frivolously improvident. There is perhaps something Blakean about this dialectic, and it appears in other places in the book. (One might consider, for example, a phrase in "At the Sea-Side" that seems to govern the rhetoric of the whole little poem: "When I was down beside the sea / A wooden spade they gave to me / To dig the sandy shore." The "they gave to me" momentarily turns the speaker into a strange kind of figure, half-emblematic, half a Blakean innocent speaker shadowed by the dark consciousness of the adult reader.)

I conclude by returning to a personal observation about the importance of this book for me. Tags and phrases from so many of these poems have rung in my head since the age of four or five, some as I first heard them, later as I began to read them. I know how I tried to live for a while myself in my own Land of Counterpane, even though I'd had to figure out dimly what sort of coverlet constituted it, and even though at first the final lines, "And sees before him, dale and plain / The pleasant land of counterpane," puzzled me in that dale and plain I wanted to hear both *dale* and *plain* as somehow adjectival—a "dale" vision being perhaps a clear or radiant one. My own night journeys were on shipboard—the "My bed is like a little boat" was a very resonant topos for me, and I note the return of it in a prose poem from a sequence called "In Place"; "The Boat" begins, "It took him away on some nights, its low engine running silently on even until he was too far out to hear it himself. It was as dark as the elements of night and water through which it moved. It was built for one: he was helmsman and supercargo both." And it ends with what I now realize is a consideration not just of the bed-boat, but of the whole scene of childhood, and of the relation between memories of it and allusions to what was for me one of the great texts of childhood, as seen with what Wallace Stevens called "a later reason": "It was out of service for some years, after which he came to realize that his final ride on it, some night, would not be unaccompanied, that the boatman on that voyage would stay aboard, and that he himself would disembark at last."

CHAPTER NINE

My Poetic Generation

To speak of my own poetic generation in the United States poses a number of problems, some I think interesting beyond matters of personal taste. (The issue of speaking *for* it—metonymically—will not be at issue here. In one sense I wouldn't ever presume to act as a self-constituted representative; in another sense, I couldn't help but speak, however unwittingly, as a part of it.) A historian or sociologist would be totally responsible to institutional considerations and would determine the contents of such a thematic box by consulting the usual sorts of *Who's Who*—anthologies, reviews, and so forth, and a poet is not needed for this. A good critic's construction of a literary generation can sometimes be valuable and revealing; and for such a view of the poets about whom I am writing, I refer you to the incisive and elegantly terse article on American poetic schools, to be found in the supplement to the enlarged edition of *The Princeton Encyclopedia of Poetry and Poetics,* written jointly by a poetic and a social critic—it is the best brief account I know of.

On the other hand, a poet's sense of his or her generation is to some to degree a poetic conception itself. Poets will always want privately to flee the spider's web woven of affiliations spun by others—sociologically minded others, in particular, with no aesthetic and moral agendas. Frequently this flight will take them into intended or unwitting evasion, idiosyncrasy brandished like a standard, sanctuary taken in a position that being acknowledged as *making*—to invoke W. H. Auden's triad—redeems one from the impure necessities of *knowing* or *judging*. Writing here as a maker, about—and in some sense, for—some fellow makers, I shall avoid either a dispassionate chronicle or an impassioned solo aria.

Defining any poetic generation, let alone specifically circumscribing one's own, is more of a problem. For twentieth-century poetry in America, a central issue is that of high modernism and one's relation to it. There is perhaps an analogue of first, second, and third immigrant generations in degree of chronological, historical, and personal distance from the old country of what Hugh Kenner has narrowly defined as the "Pound Era" (and what a sensitive younger scholar, Langdon Hammer, has mapped more interestingly, through the different constructions of what modernism was that Hart Crane and Allen Tate were propounding at a time of their close association). Of the generations before ours—not so much our fathers as perhaps two cohorts of older brothers and sisters—comprised the most interesting and in many ways sadly tortured group of poets—Bishop, Roethke, Lowell, Jarrell, Berryman, Schwartz. (A particular generational anomaly here is May Swenson, whom I have felt for more than thirty years to be among the finest of my contemporaries; she was born in 1913, only two years later than Bishop, but did not publish a book until 1954, and gave her age as being six years younger in any case.) The second cohort—Richard Wilbur, Howard Nemerov, Howard Moss, Robert Duncan—all published books of poems before 1950, and I have thought of my own generation as being drawn from those writers whose first book of poetry was published after 1950. I suppose that for a list of names of that generation one could well turn to the list of forty-one poets (it should be forty-two, but he excluded himself) that Richard Howard dealt with in his energetic and often splendidly idiosyncratic essays that comprise the revised (1980) edition of his *Alone with America*.

I could, for example, identify our generation in particular as being the one for which Wallace Stevens was first acknowledged as a central giant (*Transport to Summer* was published in 1947), and who could feel neither that Hart Crane's was an impressive but incoherent talent that never concentrated itself properly nor that Marianne Moore was an angel of quirkiness. In any case, it would only be information about myself to list the double-handful of those poets whose work has personally meant the most to me and in whose company I would most want to count myself. But that ten or a dozen could not be defined by the criteria that publicists of so-called literary scenes would invoke to classify groups. I suppose I think first of metrical and rhetorical modes, perhaps because of the loud but to me frivolous anthology-war around 1960, which included or excluded poets according to whether they wrote free verse or not. And yet it is only those who are not true poets, or themselves writers of badly and unwittingly imitative verse, who would think that anyone's own, private, personal construction of a formal mode at a time when the major decorum is eclecticism could be a matter of literary political correctness. Real poets have too much respect for the almost magical power of a personal mode of poetic voice to summon up knowledge to allow one to think that someone else's mode, institutionalized, should be worn like a club tie.

But, in fact, the matter of vers libre as opposed to "formal" verse is an ignorant and self-condemning description. In the first place, all good poems in free verse have form, and make use of formal sub-elements as well as apparent containers. So that to call all but vers libre "formal" indicates a profound ignorance of what verse is, and does, in poetry. Modes of free verse are as various as purely syllabic, purely accentual, and a traditional accentual-syllabism operating in verse in Germanic languages for half a millennium. I have discussed this matter in detail in a previous chapter, and shall only remind the reader here that poetic "form," even in the deepest and most complex sense of that term, isn't of the essence, but the ideologues of form have tended to know least about it—about its way of framing trope, its ability to work for every individual poet as a kind of charm or spell for summoning up knowledge you don't know you have. Form is the only bucket that will bring up what's in the Muses' well; but of course, without being properly used there, it will remain nothing but empty.

Yet there is a matter of some importance here—having nothing to do with any subsequently constructed literary politics of form—as it applies to my generation. I think it is this: We all started writing in the shadow of Edmund Wilson's strange essay (in *The Triple Thinkers* [1938]) entitled "Is Verse a Dying Technique?" This title is ambiguous. What Wilson meant was that great books could no longer be long poems but that prose fiction would have to do what long poems once did in trying to be great and central, and that verse was dying in that it had no longer the power to do *that*. But the title can also mean that verse was dying because people couldn't write it—(as Yiddish, say, is a dying language). This is another and most interesting question: if you mean by "verse" only accentual-syllabic verse—the mode of the English language from Chaucer through Yeats, Frost, Stevens down to my contemporaries Merrill and in England Geoffrey Hill—then in that sense he was proleptically right. It will be remembered that by *verse* I do not mean *poetry:* though all poetry is framed in some kind of verse (and even what is called prose-poetry is formally distinct from exposition or prose fiction), all verse is not poetry; again, for example, "The couplet I've just written here / Should make this matter very clear." Verse, which attends to and organizes matters of linguistic sound that we usually ignore in ordinary usage is, like prose, one of two modes of eloquence. The ability to write good or even extremely well-turned literary verse was in the past not the province of poets, but of good writers generally. But poets do as much *to* and *with* verse as they do to and with meanings of word, and forms of written and spoken discourse generally, by playing around in and with them.

Now, verse was still part of our verbal culture. We all knew a good deal about verse, and whether we wrote free verse or not, it all came from choices made in light, not in darkness. By this I mean that an ear for various modes of English verse could allow one to tune in on one's own rhythmic wavelength. Not so subsequent generations. Now we are in a time rather like the hundred years before Surrey—when Chaucer's pentameter line had been forgotten, and tone deaf attempts to write it produced with tin ears. The computer on which I have been writing these remarks establishes, under the heading "style," a typeface it calls "the default." In generations subsequent to ours, all but some of the youngest of poets today write in a default mode; they are bound to free verse because they can hear nothing else, rather than coming to it—and to a mode of it all their own—by knowledgeable choice. This is one of the reasons why poetry has gotten so toneless, save at its very best. We all knew that our precursors such as Eliot, Stevens, Lawrence, Crane (with only Frost and Williams as poles, perhaps) had often written both vers libre and accentual-syllabic and, in Moore and Auden, pure syllabic. This is why, for example, the powerfully original and totally idiosyncratic free verse modes of, say, Ashbery, Merwin, and Ammons could only come from a deep culture of verse and poetry generally. And why Kenneth Koch has not hesitated to speak in *ottava rima* when it was specifically appropriate. And W. S. Merwin could write, a few years ago, a touching ballade (a *ballade!*—) on his missing pet dog.

I will dwell on the nature of this culture for a moment, for it transcended divisions of wealth, region, and so forth. We all grew up, whether in public or private schools, reciting and memorizing and hearing verse read aloud. We also, incidentally, heard a lot of plain prose, clearly enunciated and sanely intoned for the sake of syntactical and rhetorical sense by competent announcers on the radio. The issue of the speaking voice, so blustered about as an item of high modernist dogma by Ezra Pound, had indeed a larger resonance. This was the whole matter of "the sounds of English making sense in verse" (and notice how, without my design, this notion fell into a pentameter line lying somewhere between Browning and Frost in its framing of the speaking voice). There was also the aural presence of the English Bible (still, in those days, "appointed to be read in churches" as the Jacobean translators had introduced it). It was in our heads and could be alluded to with a nevertheless ironic kind of allusiveness— not mostly as part of a Christian or Protestant sermon on Scripture but as part of the fabric of the language by which parables were being preached on the general scripture of reality. And, of course, there was the secular equivalent of hearing the lesson read in church to be found in performances of Shakespeare.

I hardly wanted to dwell on the issue of form to the exclusion of other questions, but I think it was exemplary, if not central. There are a number of other issues I might bring up with respect to defining and characterizing our generation. Some of them had to do with its distance from the high modernism in which it was indeed educated. One obvious but by no means trivial aspect of this was the matter of erotic explicitness. It was while most of use were in our late thirties or forties that gradually evolving standards of sexual explicitness seemed suddenly to have shifted. The first printing of a celebrated book of verse published in the mid-1950s still had by law to substitute asterisks for the word *fuck* on several occasions. Concern with sexuality, hostility to *pudeur*—these had been ideological matters for most highbrow literature, continuing to define itself against the true vulgarity of middle-brow constructions of the "vulgar." To some degree, verbal reticence, whether imposed by law or already deeply internalized, called up and kept in working order many of the resources of indirection, of telling it all, as Emily Dickinson put it, "slant." And indirection is the soul of poetry. It was most interesting when an elite regard for openness and specificity no longer paid any great price and, in fact, became easy, general, and perhaps in a new-old sense, vulgar after all. This general cultural movement may have had some effect on diction and on those less important matters of sub-genre and what not-very-interesting critics of poetry might call "themes." It may also figure in the background of the rise of excessively literal—and this is by no means to say necessarily *truthful*—versified autobiography called by the literary journalists "confessional" poetry.

Another issue was that of poetry and a number of different matters that have all been called "politics." Born before the outbreak of World War II, we had in our literary background the following: Auden's elegy for Yeats; the very text of Eliot's politics and the paradoxical taking up of the cause of modernist literature and modernist poetics by the anti-Stalinist American left intelligentsia; the crystallization, during the Vietnam war, of the issue of politics in verse yet again arising. Might it not be that a poet's supreme sacrifice could be to abandon his or her art for polemic, for literal statement, no matter how high and deeply felt the sentiments? Was the model of creative reaction to be official verse—no matter how belligerently directed against official officialdom—like, say Yevtushenko's *Babi Yar*? For most American poets, the very different model of Celan's great and in no way official *Todesfugue* was less available. A general point was that many of our generation had been raised on Shaw and Orwell as well as Auden, and for them the experience of ideological complexity was at least there, albeit to be confronted or shunned. There was a central lesson about this, waiting to be read, in Emerson's great "Ode" (the one inscribed to Channing, who had just urged him to write a poem against the Mexican War), which I have previously discussed as a case of how a poem legitimately about the problem of writing "about" the war can end up by indeed being about it, and poetically, not editorially. Poetry can be *about* the realm and condition of the political; it can deconstruct and transcend and otherwise deal with ideology. But when it decays into the substance of what it should be troping, it stops being poetry. Poetry, in other words, can be precisely metapolitical. But all this is itself a dense and broad issue, to which I can't do any justice now.

Another question now more modishly prominent is that of gender. Richard Howard's study of our generation, *Alone with America,* considers six women among forty-one men, or 14.6 percent. (*Poems of Our Moment* [1968]—not U.S. but Anglophone generally—considers four out of thirty-four, or 11.7 percent.) If he, or I, were putting together today a list of poets of the age of forty-five or younger of equivalent accomplishment and power (and I'd guess that forty-five was the median age of the poets in Howard's first edition of 1969), probably half of them would be women. This is perhaps not surprising. But I consider that of the poets in the Library of America's *Nineteenth-Century American Poetry* the population of women poets is 12 percent in the first volume—poets born before 1819—and double that, or 25 percent, for those born after that date, and have to conclude that there may have been something of the post-World War II redomestication of women in America. For example, in Harriet Monroe and Alice Corbin Henderson's important 1917 anthology of British as well as American modernist verse (in it are celebrated poets like Hardy, Eliot, Frost, Stevens, H.D., and Williams, and many now unknown ones), women compose 33 percent of the total. But now I am edging into the sociology I have neither the credentials nor the temperament to explore.

Then there was the question of the relation of poetry to criticism. Our generation also began—and continued to do—its writing throughout what Randall Jarrell called "an Age of Criticism," half complaining that for too many young people aspiring to be writers, it was not the novel or story or play with which they wished to discover their writing selves, but the brilliant or definitive critical essay. But this was in good measure beneficial, for it implied that there was a legitimate genre, and perhaps a *techné,* or particular set of skills, that writing in it necessitated. (There is a conventional mode of authorial blustering against criticism—"What do critics know, anyway? If they're so smart, why don't they write themselves?"—the answer to these being "Quite a lot, if they're good at their jobs," and "They do indeed write.") Criticism is not parasitic upon literature. The relation is rather symbiotic; true criticism is written out of the greatest literary sensibility, with an intellectual agenda, whether theoretical, moral, aesthetic, or sophisticatedly political, an agenda that supports it but does not smother it. This kind of criticism can be poetry's best friend, the kind of best friend that we as persons need to love us, care about us, and show us things about ourselves that no moral mirror of our own could allow us to see, such as the effect we may be having on other people, the misdirections of some of the stories we tell ourselves about what we are up to, and so forth. Good criticism is as good a friend to good poetry as other good poetry. And in addition, it can deal openly with a great enemy—bad poetry—in a way that good poetry cannot, but must only defy by example and in secret, coded messages.

There were, when we started writing and pretty much up through the mid-1970s, a good number of critics of poetry who were often not poets themselves, who knew vast amounts of poetry of the past and present, whose love and knowledge and understanding and impulses to explain and demonstrate, all manifested themselves in penetrating and stimulating critical writing that was of aesthetic and moral value in itself, and whose function was not primarily to praise or blame but to interpret and, in a way, to teach. Good poets benefited from such writing in a great number of ways; but ultimately it was the security of knowing that there were standards, themselves implicitly acknowledged by other standards, that made so much critical writing about all poetry worth paying attention to. Critical discourse of a knowledgeable and uncrabbed kind helps keeps poets from wondering whether they are crazy or not to care about the things they do. Such criticism, by the way, flourished both within and without the universities.

But this leads me to observe something about the issue of poetry—and literature in general—in the universities. Our generation's own education grew out of some fundamental acknowledgment of poetry as a common discourse. Aside from spoken verse figuring in primary education, as I mentioned before, poetry figured centrally in the very basic introductions to higher literacy that used to be undertaken with great seriousness at colleges in the United States (they no longer are). Cleanth Brooks and Robert Penn Warren's remarkable and influential *Understanding Poetry* was first published in the mid-1940s. Its agenda included the close-reading for rhetorical comprehension, its deconstruction (for that is what it was) of lyric personae, its attention to the way complex games could be played with language for good or ill. The book spawned many academic clones, some of them diluted and some not, but they were all used in introductory freshman courses as part of a committed training in true literacy. To be able to write a few pages on a short, complex lyric poem without averting one's gaze from the text and simply retailing nth-hand biographical information or reporting the profoundly unimpressive impressions of a naive reader was one kind of training in paying attention to what has been written. It went hand in hand, of course, with analogous training in expository matters: informal logic, the study of what information was and how to be responsible to fact, the notion that there were fraudulent uses of language other than direct lying, and so forth. But a short poem remained a model text, short but complete, for rhetorical and intellectual and—if the students were lucky in their teacher—spiritual exercise. My point is that the poets of my generation were confronting these poems in classes mostly of people whose academic and subsequent general lives would not be occupied with poems, but who would on the other hand not be unfamiliar with them.

This is part of a chapter on the history of reading in the later twentieth century in the United States. But I cite it for what it meant for writers of poems, which was complex and interesting. Even as one observed and shared in a middle-level apprehension of poems and was aware that there was some kind of academic construction of the history of literature (which may or may not have had any relevance to the history of poetry), one was becoming aware of some private business with poems, some ulterior relation. But this relation was not subversive of the others—subversion being the operation of choice for contemporary reductive and usually joyless professors of literature—but supported by, in order to transcend, them.

This has now pretty much come to an end. Poetry is rapidly becoming marginal in the concerns of professionalized academics in departments of literature today. How and why this has happened is also complex and interesting, although a cultural criticism of this particular instance of the institutionalization of knowledge is not my current subject. And thus I will not address how or why (suggesting for example, that there is no stronger threat to an ideological discourse than what poetry can do) but note only that this has happened and that my generation of writers was partially defined by precisely how this was not then the case. But it might be appropriate to note one strange dissonance: during three or four decades the teaching of and about poetry, and professional writing about it that was both scholarly and interpretive—and that, incidentally, was often written with character, flair, and grace—flourished in universities. At the same time, there spawned the mass of creative writing programs and the academic culture of the workshop, which by and large excluded the rigorous and informed and even imaginative study of poetry that went on in the academic courses.

Thus there is again (and see "O Heavy Verse!" in this volume) the issue of the institution of the writing workshop, which has so rapidly—and in my opinion, so virulently—spread during the past forty years through American universities. This has been interestingly definitive; whereas very few poets in our years ever even took a "workshop," this sort of class has become—for worse, I feel, rather than better—almost as conventional as required freshman hygiene courses were at men's colleges at the time. I suppose what was important for us was that our poet-teachers were teaching literature in colleges, not conducting free-form group therapy sessions called workshops. John Crowe Ransom, Allen Tate, Mark Van Doren, Robert Frost, Yvor Winters, Josephine Miles—and there were quite a few others—were transmitting a literary culture, a culture of reading, a marvelous kind of critical attention that can isolate details and moments and moves and even words, and rejoice in what large movements they can effect. Reading—particularly poets' reading—is a very private matter, and nobody can go traveling with you in the realms of gold; but the experience of being confronted with an unfamiliar and unidentified poem, handed out in a class not just of twenty-year-old self-crowned laureates, but future medical workers, scientists, and political theorists as well, and led by a man or woman of letters (poet, novelist, or indeed critic) was like being a kind of Argonaut. Perhaps, then, because—no matter what our backgrounds—we all acquired early on a good deal of what neo-Marxists teaching English today call "cultural capital," there was no need of the largely ineffectual relief program that writing classes can only at their very best dole out, too little, too late.

We began to write, in a milieu in which the reading, writing, and discourse of poetry was not professionalized. Our readers were—as they are largely not now—people who knew and cared and thought about fiction and dramatic literature and movies (before the professorial agenda of "film" came into largely tedious being) and philosophy and political economy, rather than being merely what the arts administrators call poetry audiences. (And not that these, by the way, are by their narrowing of scope thereby more concentrated of knowledge and perception, and thereby more penetrating, which might be some recompense.)

Our generation was lucky in living and working in a period in the history of our culture generally in which the word "excellence" was seldom used publicly, as it is today, because there was no anxiety about it. Excellence—indeed, even modest competence—is a value that has been largely shelved by public institutions. Anyone involved with true art in any institutional way in the United States today will always, in claiming a commitment to excellence, be protesting too much. When we were starting to work, there were no arts councils to undermine the notion of excellence by substituting other agendas. We all got, and expected, less institutional help. Bureaucratic patronage is of a particularly dangerous kind, for the issue of connoisseurship is seldom present or even acknowledged to exist. You could flatter a vain duke in the dedicatory epistle of a Renaissance poem without writing the following poem down to him. (Rather, indeed, you flattered him by aiming above his head, as if he were that high.) Democratic largesse—unless it is more attentively dispensed than it has been in this country (rather than, say, under the Arts Council in Britain)—can undermine the realm of aesthetic judgment. Admittedly, for some decades the economy allowed people to live in cities, modestly and in safety. Being able to avoid—because there weren't any and because we could afford it—the institutional traps whose bait is now more necessary to life was a kind of privilege in itself. In the end, I think we were lucky in the cultural milieu in which we started out and which helped in enabling us to be variously good at what we did.

CHAPTER TEN

Discovering Wallace Stevens

In thinking about writing this rather personal account, I got out my old copy of *Transport to Summer,* bought in the Columbia University Bookstore in 1947 when I was a sophomore; I saw to my amusement and pique, half-surprised, half not at all, that some of the pages in "Notes toward a Supreme Fiction" remained uncut. What this could mean, and what it had to do with my own discovery of the Wallace Stevens we talk about now but who wasn't quite invented then, is what I discuss in this chapter. ("Discovery," as Charles Berger has pointed out, tends to mean "knowledge" in Stevens's work—partly perhaps, it might be added, because of its various legal uses. I employ it here not only with the inescapable resonances of Keats's mental galleon, but with some of that other sense as well.) I suppose these remarks will constitute very old-fashioned belletristic musings, although the form of them might seem consonant with a fashionable mode of historical cultural criticism unwittingly undermined by a supposedly authenticating anecdotal personalism. I hope, at any rate, that my few anecdotes may be Stevensian ones—that is, parabolic—and not extensions of mere dotage. And while it would be odiously pretentious to dedicate this chapter, I nevertheless want to mention Holly Stevens, whose death still feels all too recent, whom I had known for thirty years, and whose devoted and sophisticated executorship were so important for the history of the reception of the poet's work.

For a short while, I want to become an ignorant boy again, and see, if not the sun, then the text of the sun with an ignorant eye, as I first saw it. It is hard to sense, when you are a young reader, the degree to which you are inventing the wheel, discovering the already discovered, or merely developing a largely unshared affection. Julian Symons, writing of Stevens in 1940 in England, could declare that "in America, he is regarded as the best American-born poet writing today, next to Eliot" (the *Harvard Advocate* Stevens issue of December 1940 not having appeared). And yet it nonetheless remained the case that, in 1952, the then assistant publicity director at Knopf—indeed, someone at whose apartment I first met a young poet bearing a copy of his first book, a few years older than myself, James Merrill—when asked by me who were the poets Knopf published, said proudly "Steve Allen" (Steve *Allen* [!?!]). I suppose that scarcely remembered "television personality" had composed some comic or sentimental verses, but the lady could at least have mentioned John Crowe Ransom or Wytter Bynner, whose books were advertised on all the dust jackets of books like *Parts of a World* and *Ideas of Order.* Not a word about Stevens, although Columbia was about to give him an honorary degree.

We have begun to get it right, perhaps, at the Sorbonne, but forty-five years or so ago, modernist poetry was not taught at colleges (and perhaps, as Lionel Trilling argued, not to totally bad effect). The Sorbonne that is getting it right was barely at work when I started to read Stevens. Landmark essays were those of Blackmur, of course (not the original review of *Ideas of Order,* 1936–37 but the later "Examples of Wallace Stevens"), valuable for rhetorical criticism but strangely seeing so little of the matter of what we would call the poetry; of Yvor Winters, as so often the case with him, for being exactly, dead wrong, not merely slightly off; Marius Bewley's absolutely crucial essay (in *PR* 1949—I first read it a couple of years later); and Randall Jarrell (the 1951 earlier piece). In 1959 I met Harold Bloom and was astonished by his broad and deep knowledge of Stevens's poetry. I suppose I date my wider and deeper knowledge of Stevens from the next few years, in which I talked constantly with him, and through which I was able to appreciate the important work of the next twenty years: the essays edited by Marie Borroff in 1963, his daughter Holly's *Letters* in 1966, Vendler in 1969, then Bloom's own book in 1977, the essays in Robert Buttell's volume (1980), including particularly Isabel MacCaffrey on "Le Monocle" and the first inklings of what would be Eleanor Cook's wonderful study, Charles Berger's *Forms of Farewell,* and Joan Richardson's splendid biography.

But I was at college from 1946 to 1950, and perhaps I should say something about the kind of reader I was—the kind many of us were, back then when there used to be a world of readers of literature, only a small fraction of whom trained themselves to profess the study of it in universities. Fiction and poetry written during the previous half century was read in unedited and annotated texts, unframed by canons of critical tradition and, at most, highlighted by some exploratory essay in one of the major U.S. quarterlies or a pronunciamento in

Scrutiny. In those days you read in wonder and willing suspension of definition; you had only half a sense that you might have wandered, in your reading, into an allusion, sometimes; in those days you could carry about a great load of remembered language, prose as well as verse—language that you lived around and with and could call up and had called up for you—and yet, you didn't know what it all meant. This was certainly true of proverbial bits of Shakespeare and, even more particularly, of Scripture—by which I mean KJV, whose seventeenth-century English was full of words that easily deceive their later cousins and twist constructions into riddles. We all read enough so that unfamiliar words became familiar, sometimes needing a dictionary, sometimes accruing meaning by mere continued acquaintance. (There were also syntactic puzzles, for example: one of the quatrains of Fitzgerald's *Rubaiyat* that fascinated me in childhood and that I always remembered, concluded in two latinate lines that were beyond con-strual for me for years: "And those who husbanded the golden grain / And those who flung it to the winds like rain / Alike to no such aureate earth are turned / As, buried once, men want dug up again." But that never drove the lines out of my head; perhaps, indeed, the puzzlement helped them stay there.)

And so with the wonderful particular puzzles of modernist poetry. The first lines of Stevens I ever encountered, at the age of about fourteen, were the Harriet Monroe-Alice Corbin Henderson anthology *The New Poetry* that Macmillan had published in 1917: "Peter Quince at the Clavier"—one could almost add, "of course!" (Also included were the five-stanza "Sunday Morning" and a poem there entitled "In Battle," the fourth of the suite called in *Opus Posthumous* "Poems from 'Phases.' ") The book was my mother's, and although she was an expansive schoolteacher, she was witty, with a one-liner on many literary subjects. The only poets I had ever heard of in it were Eliot, Frost, Robinson, and Rupert Brooke. The only poet in it on whom my mother ever commented was Eliot (there represented only by "Portrait of a Lady"). Of "Prufrock" she remarked that it was far better for the women to be coming and going talking of Michelangelo than of mink coats and mah-jong. Meanwhile, engrossed in the poem's rhythms, knocked out by the opening simile of the etherized patient, I found her observation impressive, but quite unhelpful. I was learning to deal with the fact that whereas "sawdust restaurants with oyster-shells"—and on each table, an inevitable Chianti *fiasco* with the drippings of many candles on it—were my idea of barely accessible sophisticated entertainment, perhaps there was a world elsewhere that found them wanting, even degrading.

But Pound was another name with which I was familiar—if only because of the early twentieth-century writer Gelett Burgess, in his cautionary verses for children about exemplary malefactors called Goops (in this enterprise he was an earlier Dr. Seuss, an American Hilaire Belloc), which I had as a child. In them, Burgess seems to have been obsessed with E. P., as there are three of his Goops named respectively Ezra Pond, Ezra Pounce, and Ero P. Pounds. Pound's name appeared to me in the Monroe-Henderson anthology as a preposterous echo. I remember particularly his "Villanelle: The Psychological Hour" and being puzzled by the fact that it wasn't a villanelle (I had written one for the school paper), nor could it be assumed that one was being partially quoted in the rhetorically bracketed, italicized lines *"Beauty is so rare a thing / So few drink of my fountain."* Despite the puzzlement, I had, as a bookish, nervous, funny, shy boy, some sympathy with the scene in the poem in which the author, having "over-prepared the event," vainly awaits the visit of two newly made friends who don't show up: "With middle-ageing care / I had laid out just the right books. / I had almost turned down the pages." Middle-ageing? it seemed to me familiarly adolescent. Pound was, as Gertrude Stein remarked, "a village explainer, great if you were a village, if not, not," and I was—my whole generation of American writers then was—a village. From my earliest encounters with his work, I heard a querulous, comfortingly insecure voice talking to me, and I never found his poems, even when studded with unfamiliar allusions and manifesting puzzles like the missing villanelle, really problematic.

All this meant that Stevens's name was one among many, and I didn't know he was supposed to be more interesting than all the candidates for a future ubi sunt litany his poems reposed among. But "Peter Quince at the Clavier" was a different matter. I *did* recognize the allusions in it; but *how* they were being alluded to was quite mysterious. I had not thought of Harold Bloom's sense of the relation to "A Toccata of Galuppi's"—and perhaps to the musician speaking as he played to a dear living lady, with such hair, too. I still have never heard Handel's 1749 *Susanna* oratorio, but I guess I imagined the noise of the arriving and fleeing Byzantines to be something like the well-known music for the entrance of the Queen of Sheba from his *Solomon*. The utterly irresistible fiction and gentle diction drew me in and then stopped me short utterly with the trope of logical connection in "Music is feeling, *then,* not sound." And, even more, not yet having an inkling of the kind of problems with metaphor I'd later learn to take as the ground rules of Stevensian grammar, I wanted to protest, "No. metaphorical music isn't sound, but literal music remains so." Exactly; but I couldn't see then how the trope had delicately usurped the name of the mere actuality. And then the grammar itself: Susanna's music "plays on the clear viol of her memory," but was that ambiguous "memory" *souvenir* or *mémoire,* the stored information or the diskette?

It was Conrad Aiken's Modern Library anthology of Twentieth Century American Poetry (the 1944 version) that, along with Brooks and Warren, recommended by a friend, I bought for myself in high school, was most important for me. The Stevens in it consisted of "Peter Quince," "Sunday Morning," "Le Monocle," "Thirteen Ways of Looking at a Blackbird," "Domination of Black,"

"Sea Surface Full of Clouds," "To the One of Fictive Music," and "Cortege for Rosenbloom." This was all the Stevens I knew, for the next few formative years, until, at Columbia, I bought the recently reset *Harmonium, The Man with the Blue Guitar* (in a wartime printing on dreadful wartime paper) and *Transport to Summer,* all in 1947–48. But just before acquiring *Harmonium,* I had read Yvor Winters's *In Defense of Reason* and thereby acquired some additional puzzlement. I remember reading him on the snow man—and therewith, the poem. Winters's discussion of it had to do with ways of scanning free verse, and I dimly realized then that his markings of primary and secondary stress could mean nothing more than emphatic notations—like the kind radio announcers used to prepare their "continuity"—or copy—with in those days. But he said nothing about the *syntax*—that one long sentence whose complex periodicity embraced negations of negations, which made it so hard for a reader to know where he or she stood. I had known Oscar Wilde's celebrated one-liner ("one must have a heart of stone not to laugh at the death of little Nell"), and I was able to cope with the initial "One must have a mind of winter / Not to . . . [etc.]." (Although "It did not give of bird nor bush / Like nothing else" was very off-putting, tonally.) But of what the poem was about, was up to about constructing consciousness, he had nothing to say. And I myself couldn't begin to grasp its importance until I had read and brooded about "It Must Be Abstract." It seemed as if for Winters in that discussion (unlike Frost, of course), that sound was itself quite senseless. Worst of all, whatever "a mind of winter" could be (something more than "a wintry mind," surely), it kept bothering me that I had no way of knowing whether to have it was a good or bad thing.

And here was another crux. With Eliot, you knew where you were in an atmosphere thick with negative valorization of all the personages in the poems, sensitive, impotent Prufrocks and brutishly forceful Sweeneys. Even with Pound, despite his few residues of Browningesque dialectic (save in the case of "Mauberley," which was probably all about his own ambivalences, anyway) you could tell the good guys from the bad guys. I never could, with respect to protagonists in particular, and other personages, conditions, mental states, in Stevens. It caused me to suspend, somewhat unwillingly, my belief in a poem's power to focus my feelings and judgments in its version of the world. I remained puzzled for a long time; it was the richly puzzling grammar, the unique kinds of sound pattern and, when I could discern it, wordplay. But generally it was individual lines, which for my unknowing ear themselves raised "loquacious columns by the ructive sea."

Then, too, for me, there were what I felt to be perhaps trivial, and certainly private concerns, for example, the puzzling matter of occasional rhyming. This always haunted me, particularly in "Le Monocle" (as opposed to "Sunday Morning" where there are, emphatically, none)—putting greater syllabic stress on "this much-crumpled *thing*" and, particularly, "I wish that I might be a thinking *stone*" (as opposed to "a *think*ing stone"—and therefore as opposed to, say, a Pascalian thinking reed, which I didn't encounter until a junior in college.) Also, the very *mode* of "The Man with the Blue Guitar" allows couplets to be rhymed or not, even as blank verse can be stopped or enjambed. This continues to haunt me, as late as in such moments in "The Auroras of Autumn II" where the nonce rhyme falls resonantly across two tercets: "A cold wind fills the beach. / The long lines of it grow longer, emptier, A darkness gathers though it does not fall // And the whiteness grows less vivid on the wall." In my old age, I hear echoes of Robinson's "Luke Havergal" in these lines, and throughout, the nonce rhymes are like breaking into a kind of song, or at least humming along while you work.

I remember clearly a few isolated episodes. In 1948–49 a group of about eight undergraduates meeting in Jason Epstein's room in a Columbia College dorm for a couple of hours in order to go over "Sunday Morning"; and that spring in *Columbia Review* we put out a Stevens issue with three essays on him, including a devoted explication of "Esthétique du Mal" by someone who became a distinguished medical scientist and teacher. It was "Esthétique du Mal," actually, which I now realize was the only later poem of any major proportions after *Harmonium* that, aside from "The Idea of Order at Key West," I had been able to read. That and "Of Modern Poetry" and "The Poems of Our Climate," which I liked but underread at the time, came to me in 1950 when I acquired F. O. Matthiessen's wonderful *Oxford Book of American Verse* with its selection of twenty-five poems by Stevens. He newly published *Transport to Summer,* in which I had marked "Late Hymn from the Myrrh Mountain" (I had originally read it in the *Quarterly Review of Literature*) as being more comfortingly *Harmonium*-like. From the uncut pages of "Notes" I mentioned earlier I infer that I never read it through until I did so in the *Collected Poems* some eight years later. But that central poem is the startling—and for me, now, angelically necessary—masterpiece.

Some of the shorter poems in *The Auroras of Autumn* I read with Richard Howard, in his copy, when we were seeing each other almost every day in 1951. I remember him reading from "This Solitude of Cataracts": "To be a bronze man breathing under archaic lapis // Without the oscillations of planetary pass-pass"—Richard, whose French was even then prodigious, of course picking up the *passe-passe*, but loving the pure riddling thrust of the coined English. Also, from the puzzling "St. John and the Back-ache"—"I Speak below / The tension of the lyre," which we could only mistake then for reticence, an abnegation of the heroic, a modernist retraction; for as elaborate ephebes, we were constantly tightening the lyre's strings to the breaking point. The "below" as a profound depth, rather than the lowered volume of a poetic sotto voce would take me twenty years to grasp—it is indeed a very difficult poem. I remember intoning to him the final line of "On an Old Horn"—*played* on it, not, as one might imagine some Anglo-Saxon riddle, inscribed on it in runes—that final line that really sums up the poem's conclusion, at least as Stevens summed it up in the now well-known letter to Hi Simons: "Now, a final toot on the horn. That is all that matters. The order of the spirit is the only music of the spheres; or, rather, the only music; or in other words, 'Pipperoo, pippera, pipperum . . . the rest is rot.' " To which I added, "Look! he even declines nonsense." But this was a high outside fastball to Richard, who immediately returned, "No, indeed, accepts it." But what hit me most was a vague sense of familiarity, thinking of the end of a very famous poem that starts out with the first half of this last line and concludes with the end of it, Verlaine's *Art Poétique* ("De la musique avant toute chose. . . . Et tout le reste est littérature"). Be that as it may, such puzzlements and conjectures remained totally private and, we believed, idiosyncratic with us then.

By the early fifties I was still absorbed in W. H. Auden and did not realize at the time (not having read through "Notes toward a Supreme Fiction") that the lines from "In Praise of Limestone," a poem to which I was devoted, were aimed at Stevens, even as "X," in the latter's "Creations of Sound," were at Eliot (they might apply, even more in some ways, to Auden):

. . . The poet,
  Admired for his earnest habit of calling
The sun the sun, his mind Puzzle, is made uneasy
  By these marble statues which so obviously doubt
His antimythological myth.

At the very time when poets like Howard Nemerov were showing some of Stevens's rhetoric in their own verse, writers of my own, younger generation were alluding to it either wittingly ("Thirteen Ways of Looking at a Blackbird" became an all-too-common paradigm for easy variation) or perhaps unconsciously. For example, David Ferry had written an undergraduate thesis on Stevens at Amherst for that remarkable teacher Reuben Brower in 1948. I recall some lines of his from a 1955 poem invoking Watteau's "Embarkation for Cythera," in which "Thinking of her [that is, Venus], each lady / Fingered her necklace, and sweet music tattled / From the spinet of her desire." But it was a year later that I encountered the first *deeply* Stevensian resonance in one of my near-contemporaries (aside from Elizabeth Bishop, whose 1955 *Poems* I had just begun to read, but with no ability to hear yet what her responses to Stevens were like). Whether these lines were a conscious response to those of Auden just quoted, I have never inquired:

The mythological poet, his face
Fabulous and fastidious, accepts

Beauty before it arrives. The heavenly
Moment in the heaviness of arrival
Deplores him. He is merely
An ornament, a kind of lewd
Cloud placed on the horizon.

(John Ashbery, perhaps hearing all that in it, significantly omitted it from his later *Selected Poems*.) I would not hear the Stevens in, and below, these lines for a few years. But clearly, something had happened, not so much in the history of modern literature, as in ongoing poetic history. Stevens had started to become available in other ways, and it was in the following years that I can say I really started to read him with the kind of late reason that informs our discourse about him now.

CHAPTER ELEVEN

O Heavy Verse! The Shopwork of the Workshops

Colin Clout, Spenser's fictional version of himself as poet, sings in the *November* eclogue of *The Shepheardes Calender* an elegy for one Dido, who "lyeth wrapt in lead"; its intricate stanza turns on two refrains: "O heavie herse" (the decorative structure designed to hold candles above the heavy coffin and, perhaps, the funeral obsequy—the verbal decorative structure—itself) is one of them. The other is "O carefull verse" ("carefull" meaning sad, rather than guarded or meticulous, as it does today). Colin Clout's song is composed at an important moment for the foundation of poetry in English, in one of the most radical and experimental books of the sixteenth century. But I have deliberately misread and conflated these paired refrains, in addressing some of the problems of our own literary moment, a moment at which—given the self-consuming history of the literal, avant-garde—radical and experimental moves run the greatest risk of being tired and retrograde per se. It is the heavy verse of mere literature, rather than what enables poetry to become airborne, which I have not discussed elsewhere in these pages. In doing so now, I shall be concerned with verse and the poetry that is often not written in it. Verse of some sort involves patterns that do what Roman Jakobson famously called "organized violence" to ordinary, unstructured distributions of sound and even graphic elements of ordinary language. It is a necessary condition for poetry, but not a sufficient one. And for the reader who may think that "verse" is an attribute only of what he or she will call "formal poetry," a reminder at this point that verse is a matter of scheme, not of trope, of pattern and not of poetic fiction. So that, of course,

Devoid of fiction, fable, charm or curse,
These lines, not poetry, are merely verse.

I shall also be concerned with recent poetry in a literary situation. On the other hand, I shall not deal here with the deeper poetic question of the internalized state of the sociological, institutional history of literature, which poets secretly write for themselves and in which they live their inner lives of reading.

For true poetry has always occurred, from our Homeric and biblical scriptures onward, in a literary context. Poetic texts seem chained to literary event as soul seemed to be, for some medieval Christians, to body. (Professors of literature today tend more and more to be concerned only with the institutional body of literature.) All utterances that aspire to be poems—by announcing themselves to be such, even deviously, by arranging themselves in some extraordinary or ordinarily unusual way—are indeed literary texts. But most contemporary verse (and this has been true on every day since the invention of printing, at least) is not poetry. It seems astonishing that the liberations of modernism, so sophisticated about what would not do any more, never grasped the more than Trotskyist doctrine of permanent revolution or, in literary terms, continuing revision. Alexander Pope could praise Lord Burlington for the moral quality and consequence of his taste in introducing neo-Palladian architecture into eighteenth-century England. But he also knew at the same moment to warn him against the academy of academic journalism, as it were, that his innovations would unwittingly inaugurate. Now, what did modern poetry inaugurate, with brio and originality, that has now become mere product?

The contemporary equivalent of the cheesy sentimentality associated formerly with the rhymed jingle of greeting card verse, might be called rusty irony, today associated with the easy flabbiness of a ubiquitous form of short-lined free verse. The moral importance, for modernist poetry, of formal originations like free verse lay to some degree in the revisionary difficulty of the unexpected-looking. Whatever a vers libre poem was, or was not, it was certainly not jingle. The twentieth-century equivalents of the mere rhymers, who have always crowded around poetry and caused poets to despair, were the authors of jingles embodying popular pieties. Just as a stand had to be taken against the emptiness, and particularly the vulgarity, of those pieties, so the jingle had to be denounced in practice. It did not follow that all true poetry was henceforth to be in various free verse systems; although the major poetry of W. C. Williams and D. H. Lawrence indeed inhabit two very different free verse houses, the great poems of Yeats, Frost, Hardy, and most of Crane and Stevens do not. To "mount to Paradise / By the stairway of surprise," as Emerson's Merlin urged, was a call for sublimity and, prosodically, for supersession. But it did not specify, save to the hopelessly literal pen of the modern jingler, the floor at which one had to arrive. Indeed, many passed the levels of first revisions of accentual-syllabism, and went on to other ones.

True poems are never cast in forms, nor trivially "use" them, or whatever (ordinary language about form and content is often very misleading). Rather, they reinvent something about them. Poems are always making parables about their form, about the way in which poetry is half-created by, and half creates, its patterns and structures. I have shown in detail elsewhere how, in true poetry, the schemes of form become trope. We might add that figures of linguistic contrivance become figures of thought and even of will. From the standpoint of poetic composition itself, we might say that where pattern was, meaning will be. But ideological discussions of appropriate form—an obsession with which has marked much minor American poetry since Poe's time—seem evasions, unwitting and certainly always unacknowledged, of a central problem of meaning—of "subject," and of the ends and means of poetry as opposed to those of other modes of writing. The central question of figurative as opposed to literal language is suppressed in polemic about style. If the one parable we can perceive in the form of a poem or even a line is "This is not Brand X," or "This is the New, the Authentic," or "This is not influenced by what I learned to read from, except perhaps for what looks exactly like this," the text in question will merely be labeling itself. It will not be much of a parable. But when Milton makes a moment of linear chiasm a metaphor for the desperation of self-referentiality (Satan's "Hell within him, for within him Hell / He brings"), or Robert Frost uses the same structure as a trope of mirroring, and thereby meditative, reflection (in "Spring Pools"), this is a different matter. Frost himself said that "every poem is an epitome of the great predicament; a figure of the will braving alien entanglements." And, earlier in that same essay, "Every single poem written regular is a symbol small or great of the way the will has to pitch into commitments deeper and deeper to a rounded conclusion and then be judged for whether any original intention it had has been strongly spent or weakly lost. . . . Strongly spent is synonymous with kept." This can be read as prosodic crankiness, limiting the "written regular" to iambic pentameter. It would then be as frivolous as W. C. Williams's or Charles Olson's crankiness about iambic pentameter being all washed up, and as false. But there are many ways poems have of being "written regular," and it is their successful struggle with their own structures of alien entanglement that makes them figures of the human will. This is as true of the best Williams poems as of the best of Frost's. More importantly, it rules out mere jingle, whether of easy rhyming or flabby vers libre, the contemporary mode of Emerson's "tinkle of piano strings." It is tempting to call this tiresome formal mode of heavy verse "clunk"; in any case, the point is that the goddess Dullness has abandoned yesterday's jingle for today's clunk. The smooth uses of jingle were in greeting cards and public inscriptions and minor hymnody and the verse embodying secular pieties; the smooth uses of clunk appear today in little magazines, and from the graduates of most poetry-writing workshops.

The inept use of jingle was exemplified by the inadvertent hilarities of William McGonagall, "Poet & Tragedian," or what used to appear regularly in the now vanished Poesy Department of the *New Yorker*. Many readers and producers of clunk today would find McGonagall's rhetoric and diction amusing. Very few would even hear his hilariously inept scansion in, say (and one could select any lines at random from the *Poetic Gems* of 1890) the opening stanza of his "Jottings of New York: A Descriptive Poem":

O mighty city of New York! you are wonderful to behold,
Your buildings are magnificent, the truth be it told,
They were the only thing that seemed to arrest my eye
Because many of them are thirteen storeys high.

McGonagallesque doggerel is marked in particular by the use of rhyme without proper accentual-syllabic scansion. It is particularly sad to find a recent generation of ineptly rhyming clunkers—some of them pretentiously brandishing the banner of what calls itself a New Formalism—who cannot hear the relation in English (let alone in Russian) between rhyme and stress-pattern. Over the past fifteen years I have observed the following: In teaching a graduate course in Spenser's *Faerie Queene,* I usually assign as an exercise the composition of three Spenserian stanzas. These are not necessarily linguistic and stylistic pastiches, but ordinarily embody a modern equivalent of some pattern of rhetorical deployment familiar from the poem (a bit of narrative, an inset lyric, for a descriptive catalogue, for an analysis of a concept, interpreting some emblem, etc.) There were always students in the class (still, I'm surprised and grateful to report, a minority) whose lines simply didn't scan, and whose rhymes were merely the assonance, commonly mistaken for rhyme (flies/died, slow/hose, etc.), that may result from hearing only modern rock lyrics and not having rhymed verse in one's memory. Invariably, the students with tin ears were those who wrote verses and fancied themselves as poets as well as scholars and critics in training. I continue to ponder the significance of this.

The pervasiveness of clunk also wears down one's trust in a writer's abilities. Ordinarily, when a poet writes an egregiously unmetrical, unrhyming line, or violates in some way the private conventions that the poem itself has established within the framework of public (metrical, generic, etc.) ones, the reader assumes that he or she has intended this. The critical attention is then directed toward the particular occasion in the poem of this aberration—How is it acknowledged by the poem itself? How does it particularly work? and so forth. But it is hard to keep one's trust when it becomes increasingly difficult to tell whether the aberration is intentional or not. Perhaps a generic example might be of use here. Consider coming across a poem in stanzas like this one (these examples are all formal dummies):

(A) These lines are unscannable by
Any syllable or accentual count
But nonetheless arranged in what looks like
    a sapphic stanza.

The less you know, the easier it is to deal with these lines. The accentual-syllabic version of the Greek or Latin used by many poets in German and English is unmistakable to the ear:

(B) Taken into English, the long and short of
Ancient meters marked instead, in an up and
downbeat, just this never-varying pace of
      classical sapphics.

Similarly, a pure-syllabic adaptation of it (Auden introduced this in the case of alcaic meters as well) would be determinate:

(C) Each line will have eleven syllables and
Only eleven, which you can count but most
Probably will not discern by ear (the last
    Line will have just five).

In either of the last two cases, one can determine whether a line ended where it did by design or because of an error. And in the first instance—the free verse arranged to invoke or suggest sapphic stanza form on the page—I have always assumed the poet knew precisely what he or she was doing. This would mean that if the verse had any more character and power than that of the flaccid expository dummy in example (A), it would make effective use of the resources of free lineation (here, limited roughly by typographic length: 3 x regular; 1 x shorter, and indented) to underline syntactic elements, to call up the ghosts of momentary rhythmic cadences, and so forth. But today, one finds so much verse written with so leaden an ear that it's hard to be sure of the intention any more—(A) could easily be the work of younger poets really trying to write a sapphic stanza whose cadences they were unable to hear. Being able to hear rhythm and rhyme doesn't mean that one will or should write poetry in either accentual-syllabic or strict syllabic verse. It is a necessary skill for writing good free verse as well.

    I should probably add here that some of the younger generations of poets whose work I most admire do indeed write iambic verse, often rhymed, seldom to the exclusion of other modes as well. I am thinking in particular of Rachel

Hadas, Karl Kirchwey, George Bradley, Rachel Wetzsteon, and Greg Williamson; but I know they would shun the ideology and reductive agenda of anything like "new formalism," having too much skill to fetishize it, and too much knowledge of and respect for the privileged character of individual voices.

We must thus expand the domain of clunk to cover a new doggerel of ineptitude, whether in free verse or the handling of rhyme and rhythm. The inept use of clunk is found in the pious, personally sanctified utterances of the newly authenticated amateur. This category would include the schoolchild (and I'll return to this matter later on), the born-again scribbler, the prisoners who have been led to believe that coherent, well-argued prose must be unattainable by their wretched capacities, and possibly the enemy of the human spirit as well. They have been taught (by clunkers who know nothing but clunking and must contrive opportunities to teach that) to suppose that with the key of clunk America can unlock its heart. (And so it was with the "open sesame" of jingle that the task was performed so easily in the era through which modernism raged with the obvious objection that this couldn't be poetry.) That good free verse is hard to write, that clunk comes from the same tin ear and plastic image of the muse as jingle once did, is hard for most writers, teachers, and, alas, critics to understand as it was fifty years ago for them to see that smooth scansion and inevitable rhyme were not music, nor neatly disposed similes poetic. It is true now, as then, as ever, that a poem is easy to write if you don't know how; it is perhaps only that today, the "you" would include more of the population. Ambrose Bierce, somewhere around the turn of the century defined (in *The Devil's Dictionary*) "blank verse" in a way that, with the first three words removed, holds true for vers libre clunk today:

> BLANK VERSE, *n.* Unrhymed iambic pentameter—the most difficult kind of English verse to write acceptably; a kind, therefore, much affected by those who cannot acceptably write any kind.

Bierce himself wrote well-crafted satiric verse, and like so many writers of any kind up through World War II, could employ it as easily as prose. And it also remains true that acceptable pieties—the slightly ironic-sentimental, emotionalizing, secularly religious, vaguely left-wing pieties acceptable to the dwindling fragment of the public that still reads poetry—authenticate the academic forms of clunk associated with them.

Novelty is, as we have seen, merely repetitive; true originality is revisionary. As I have suggested in an earlier chapter, the great poetic texts have always alluded more complicatedly to prior poems than do the productions of literature. There is nothing as stale as yesterday's news, which is why poetry is not concerned with literary news, with what X feels, or A appears to be like some morning, or what We and Y all condemn. It must at the very least acknowledge something of the history of assertions about what one feels. It must reveal some awareness that any statement about inner states is figurative; that the history of seriousness has inextricably tangled up the moral directions "Within" and "Beyond"; that every great poem helps to reshape the ground rules of what is literal and what is figurative; that there is a natural history, a geological evolution, of metaphor and of linguistic frame, not to engage which diminishes the nobility of the mind and the life span of the utterance. The fashionable verse literature—the proliferating gossip columns of clunk—is composed on nature walks along artificial turf. But one gets to that phony wild by way of a literalizing mistake, following, as if it were not a trope, the sign that points "To the Road Less Traveled By" or "To the Stairway of Surprise." They who troop there, believing themselves to be wandering, are making no journey to the imaginative life. They gather already pressed flowers, each labeled "new variety." They demand of their spirits no proof, no test, and unlike Pamina and Tamino, they walk no grim passage between the menacing powers of fire and water. They write well, but they do not change the world by interpreting it. Innocent? *No.* Ignorant? *Yes.*

When we use words in ordinary discourse, "pass the butter (not the margarine)," "I meant the *sea* (not this chlorinated pool)," we are using them for the meaning *with* the meanings they have. But there is another kind of meanness here. We need to use words even, as we sometimes, alas, use other people. But for poetry, words are more than utensils. They have lives, histories, and moods. We begin to engage their being when we become aware that there is more to them than what they mean in the sense of how they are used. We are introduced to the being of words most often by playing with them. "I see the sea; the whole picturesque beach scene has been too often seen"—we play with the words by kidding them about their chance resemblances, pretending to hold them accountable for accidents not of their negligent contriving. But this is what the theorists would call *synchronic* play: it depends, as I suggested earlier (pp. 16–17), upon what the words are now, as if they had never had childhoods, stormy adolescences, and identity crises. It is a mode of playing that engages forms and patterns, of the ascription of semantic guilt by alliterative association, of the rhyming that makes fellow prisoners and strange bedfellows both of twins and enemies. It is the first stage of approach to the true being of words, this playing with them. We can't after all kid a utensil, joke with and thereby instruct a frying pan; and to acknowledge verbal being by doing so to a word, we are doing something not unlike acknowledging the humanity of the living human body.

But it is the second, or *diachronic,* stage of the approach to the life of the word that engages the past. Once one has learned to play with, to misuse, mistake, and misprize the present meaning of a word, its own history, lived out against the background of the history of human consciousness, becomes real. It is no matter to us, when we meanly use them, that the almost antithetical "black" and "bleach" are not only alliteratively available as dance partners, but are indeed distant etymological cousins. But the wonder in their lives is how two descendants of the same patriarch could wander such divergent ways. When we consider that, in our previous wordplay, the "scene" is named by a word that once meant a tent, then part of the classic Greek stage, then what was painted on it, then what was played against it or before it, an animated film of metaphor and metonymy is unreeled before us. What it is in our modern meanings of "scene" that has come out of its original tent is still covered by our framing pictorial (in one sense) or literary (in the other) consciousness.

But this kind of misuse, of mistaking, of almost psychoanalytically disturbing the present with the continuing life of the past, is poetic thought. Even our useful utensil, the word "word," constantly resounds—if one is not poetically deaf—with the struggle between two fraternal meanings: that which we write or print with a space (or say, with a morphemic boundary) on either side, or whatever it is we are indeed writing or printing or saying—utterance generally. By and large the first brother has popularly, and synecdochally, won out over his sibling, who, though not much older, is more archaic. Thus, less-educated readers think that whenever an older text speaks of a wingèd word, a password, or whatever, it has to refer to something that can either be a mono or a poly syllable. But I have digressed into mere words parabolically; every word itself is a poem, as Emerson knew, in the imaginative space of its history. And this is itself a parable about all poetry, about why true poetry as opposed to the rest of literature must be distinguished for its diachronic engagement. It is along the time dimension that the imagination projects itself most strongly, preserver and destroyer both of a moment in the history of human vision. It is this, too, that associates poetry with human freedom in the highest sense.

The almost weary invocation of Santayana's observation about ignorance of the past condemning one to repetition of it may still remind us of something very important. In our most pointed poetic fantasies, our available horrific projections of the limitations of human freedom by inhuman action—from Zamyatin's great anti-Utopia, *We* (1925), through Orwell's revision of it and through countless versions since—the opening, into a possible human future, through the walls of the totally totalitarian world, is the window into the past. And that is the window that is most tightly closed and barred: the library is locked or destroyed. Books are burned in order to destroy a possible future. In the revisionary quality of poetic imagination, the invocation of a journalistic or a literary novelty can at best be a diversionary tactic to suck in the critical secondary, as it were, to do an end run around the present. Literature is the game of the week, of the season; poetry is the life of the seasonal cycle itself. Whether sentimental or ironic, we continue to have a vast production of heavy verse in

America today. ("Production" is used advisedly here, against what an English critic has recently referred to as the "cottage industry" of verse in her own country.) The profession of poet has replaced the poetic calling in many instances, and in some wonder at this, I'd like to look again at the circumstances under which young writers have been starting out to write and publish—indeed, the very circumstances that shape their conception of what a poem is and that seem to distinguish them from, at least, a generation even a dozen or so years older than theirs.

I shall in fact be discussing only a small part of a generation, for there are very young writers who are already being somehow antithetically reformed even as I write. And on the other hand, having published a book or two of verse does not necessarily make one a poet, but merely an author of one or two or four books of verse. (Twenty years ago most writers seemed to know this; today the notion seems to be repressed with narcissistic *pudeur*.) Among these authors there may, or may not—as in England, say, between Gower and Skelton—be some poets. I have in previous pages been concerned with poetic history and not the annals of literature. But the relation between these two kinds of stories has always been part of the matter of the first of them. That is, the conditions of literature have always provided the climate in which poetry blooms or blasts. Being written, printed, and read by at least someone who will then write, these matters of sociology and economics are necessary, but not sufficient, conditions for literary art, whether in verse or prose. For there to be poetry, there must be literature in verse (alas), the small amount of true poetry aside. And yet it is the *literature,* and even the poetry *as* literature, which literary history has to map, and of which young writers are most aware. Fashion keeps the true poetry from being sorted out publicly, promoting the changing hemlines of literature with all the demonic power that fashion always has. Like the devil himself, fashion's greatest skill is to convince us, when most under its influence, that it does not exist or at least apply to ourselves. (In dress, this is probably beneficial. In the life of the mind or the ways of the heart, it is a disaster.) And so I ask myself again, what have been the literary conditions in which poets under forty in this country have been writing?

First off, a chronicler of literature in verse would observe the sheer growth in the number of books of verse published in the United States every year, the expansion in the number of little magazines publishing nothing or almost nothing but verse, the large number of university presses with poetry series of one kind or another, some of them publishing six or seven books a year. The change of scale—as opposed to the situation that prevailed in the 1960s, for example—is enormous. Wesleyan University Press started publishing four books of verse a year just about then, at a time when there was only the Yale Series of Younger Poets releasing one book a year, chosen by a poet of the major status and critical intelligence of W. H. Auden. Wesleyan did so because of having a great deal of money that the press's tax-exempt status required them to spend and a sense—quite correct, it now seems—that many important books were remaining unpublished because of the reticence of trade publishers to publish verse for financial reasons (and perhaps because of poor taste or ignorance). But as Darcy Wentworth Thompson reminds us in that most poetical of biology books, *Growth and Form,* if persons were built like fleas, they could not jump hundreds of feet into the air but would instead collapse under their own weight. Scale can alter all, and the hundred or so volumes issued every year by trade and university publishers (I leave aside small presses that publish nothing but volumes of verse) may be a mixed blessing. There is a Gresham's Law of art, in which the mediocre drives the good out of circulation; sophisticated critical work has to be done to sort things out, taxonomically first, in order that there may then be reasonable praise or blame. (And the quality of public reviewing during these years has been disastrous. Younger poets have been reviewed by each other without a critical agenda. "Bad artists," we are reminded by Oscar Wilde, "always admire each other's work. They call it being large-minded and free from prejudice.") But one of the long-lived pieties of modernism involved the programmatic nullification (actually, only a denial) of genre in poetry and painting. One of the results of this is that anything with a jagged right-hand edge is called a *poem.* (If you'll remember, this was Jeremy Bentham's criterion for poetry, scorned laughingly throughout the nineteenth and twentieth centuries, which has returned with a belated hideousness.) It is as if one were to speak seriously of "American novelists writing in the 1930s like William Faulkner and Pearl S. Buck" (both Nobel laureates, after all) or of "contemporary novelists like Iris Murdoch and Judith Krantz"—at least some of the MLA membership could still (at any rate, fifteen years ago—but I'm not sure today) giggle. But if one were to mention, say, "poets like Elizabeth Bishop and X" (for which you may substitute anyone each of you *knows* to be the analogue of Pearl S. Buck) there will be no laughter. And not because the same breath does appropriately contain them both, but rather because it is not permitted to differentiate taxonomically between the very finest American poet perhaps since Wallace Stevens and a purveyor of fashionable sentiments to a constituency of the moment. There are interesting cultural reasons for this, which I shall not go into now, although some of them are of the gravest importance. (For example, what are in fact the hymnodies and gospel songs, the ad hoc liturgies, of post-Christian religious sects in America today—political, racial, sexual, or enthusiastic of other more narrowed agendas—are not acknowledged as such, even as the religious character of the sects themselves are not. And yet imagine, in speaking of the 1860s, talking of "poems by Emily Dickinson and Dwight L. Moody.")

In any event, anything in verse has been a poem (exercising a right defended by the Literary Civil Liberties Union) for the past fifteen years or so. And yet in

1920, say, an enlightened lecturer on poetry would have to point out to a middle-brow audience that poetry was not necessarily what rhymed. (Chaucer, Spenser, Milton, Pope, and Shelley all, of course, strove to point that out as well.) But only Emerson, a later name on that list, might have anticipated our critic of sixty years ago by offering an easy elementary example: a vers libre that summoned up supreme fictiveness with as much incantatory power as accentual-syllabic measure could, given of course the necessary gifts of the wielder of it in each case. Today, mutatis mutandis, the general culture's ignorance has—as always—gobbled up the antithetical example and made it deadeningly primary. The result is that today, people who don't know what a poem really is will write free verse, even as they would have written Hallmark greeting card jingle back then. But like the changes of scale I mentioned earlier, this is no mere turnabout. The trouble is that amateur, inept free verse is harder for most people to distinguish from the skillful, adept sort than the clunky jingle was from good rhyme. (As evidence of this, consider the demise and impossibility today of the *New Yorker's* old Poesy Department, mentioned earlier. Bad free verse hides the fact of its incompetence, whereas doggerel wears its failure on its sleeve. If one didn't care deeply about democracy, one could argue that bad writing is itself a figure for the failure of representative government and decently egalitarian societies. But if one does, than one can only bemoan bad writing as cooperating with other causes of weakening and possible failure.)

Free verse—it was observed earlier—is very easy to write if you don't know how. Good poets know how. They have invented their own systems for themselves, as tropes, in fact, of earlier ones. But most bad poets cannot even have the satisfaction of learning a skill, a craft, of being able to get better, to expand their musicorhetorical hearing, to exercise at the very least the kind of wit that allows complex linguistic structures to make jokes about language and *thereby* about the rest of the world. One common mode of clunk is the contemporary equivalent of *abab*-rhymed common meter—a thirty-em typeset line not too egregiously varied. It is the received form of what, whether funny or not, would have been *light verse*. When funny, it could be and was deployed by masters of nuance, timing, playful intelligence, and antithetical wit—I think of Cole Porter, Ogden Nash, Samuel Hoffenstein, Dorothy Parker; and I would still rather read the vers libre of archie the cockroach than of Carl Sandburg. (The American poets under forty are at least probably blessedly too young to have heard him revered as a poet.) When sentimental, it could at least be smooth if boring and trivial. There is still wonderful comical verse around, such as the epigrams of J. V. Cunningham, the fine pranks of George Starbuck, the visionary wit of Kenneth Koch, but not that of the unskilled. Light verse that isn't even funny is heavy verse. And for the past fifteen years, younger poets' literary universe has been weighed down with it.

There are many historical reasons for the deadly sameness of verse, an atmosphere within which true poets under forty must struggle to breathe. One of these is obvious: verse has become literally academic. That term was first used in the later 1950s by a few propagandists to mean anything not in free verse, preferably written by someone who had taken a higher university degree. It has since acquired a legitimate referent. For in recent decades things called creative writing workshops have blossomed everywhere, in schools, colleges, churches, prisons, and so forth. It is their function not to try artificially to construct the *paideia,* which all poets naturally evolve for themselves—that profound and mysterious secret inner academy of reading and listening, of hearing what was read without totally understanding, in order that true poetic misunderstanding might develop, of self-imposed scales and five finger exercises, leading up to one's own *gradus ad parnassum.* Unhappily, it is not their function to supplement the loss of freshman composition classes of the older sort in which a canon of reading as well as of elocution was expounded with some authority. It is most often their function not to show young people who want to write verse what true poetry really is, how it is put together, what putting together is, and how to try to do it and get better at it. It is their function *not* to teach acquirable skills, which might indeed be usefully learned by anyone—how to write verse, for example; how poems have been put together in countless ways; how to read poems as great poets of the distant and recent past seem to have read them. You cannot teach people to become poets; they must, like all the poets of the past, learn that by themselves. But you can teach them certain procedures, and avail them of certain information, and even expand and focus their attention, so as to help them to perform that self-instruction. Workshops (taught by people who were produced by workshops, etc.) instead have aimed at the production of heavy verse.

Mark Strand, whose knowledge of the academy of poetry is wide, has observed that—not having the honest work of correcting metrical solecisms, weak rhymes, unvaried rhythms, inept collocations of metrical and syntactic units, poor phrasing, uncontrolled pace, the good musical work, in short, of ear training to get on with—the conductors of such workshops must deal with the inner lives of the participants. They must treat of authenticity and expressiveness and related important questions, which, however, cannot begin to matter until everything else has been learned. The difference between poetry and merely very good writing in verse will depend in part—although darkly so—upon such issues. But until the writing has been good and gotten better for some time, there is no context for them. It cannot matter poetically whether something ineptly wrought is sincere or phony, and the latter instance, more problematic, is at least prima facie more interesting. At very best, then, the matter of the diction appropriate to a particular style of heavy verse, or perhaps some strictures about *content* (as if what Blake called a cloven fiction—here of content and form—could be poetic matter, or anything more than a weakly professorial one), might emerge. Richard Howard, a poet different in every way imaginable from Mark Strand, who takes a similar dim view of workshops, discovered to his horror some time ago that most of the students in a graduate (a graduate!!) creative writing class he was asked to teach hadn't read any great, or even major minor, English poetry. True poets have always been shaped by what they read early, and it is the nascent imagination that produces the impulse to write verse. But if one has only read bad poems, one cannot know what a good one is. And yet the academy of the writing workshop is in its way deadeningly formalist. I remember a vagrant villanelle refrain that Donald Hall mentioned to me about forty years ago: "The mold is there, you only have to pour." That there is nothing to the making of molds; that one need not make one's own molds; that what fills the mold is poured into them, and not secreted internally by its living form—in these assumptions, and in the drive to have their participants come up with *product* rather than with a more poetical ear and eye, the verse mills are worse than diploma mills.

Formalism is most often accompanied by blindness, not to *content* (which is itself a formalistic chimera) but to the fictive. The literary world of heavy verse is heavily literal minded and holds a callow view of the complex relations of literature to the rest of life. That view is clouded by an unproblematic and unmediated mimetic and expressive theory—poetry is a flat mirror and/or glowing lamp at once, and in either case there is no work to be done save with Windex. Poetry is truly, I think, what Spenser called "a world of glass." But that very phrase generates several tropes at once: the hemispherical mirror, itself a figure of the globe of the world, producing a representation belonging to it and of its substance—a world of mirror and of mirror glass. A world of trope, and not of, say, hundreds of thousands of lines of heavy verse in which the first person singular pronoun is literally employed by solemn writers who have not been led by fashion (as previous generations were, for better, I believe, than worse) into writing "songs," what Yeats designated as "words for music perhaps," dramatic lyrics. For in real poetry, the most autobiographical-sounding "I" is always in alia persona somehow, whereas in versified journal or journalism, it is about as literal as it can get. But this matter of deadening literalism is not peculiar to the literary verse of the generation under discussion. It was merely that ars poetica in the past, the lively display of musical skill, the kind of spiritual energy that the play of pattern both draws upon and elicits, somehow mitigate the deadliness. If they cannot breathe life into cold public statues, they can make them more like us by putting funny hats on them. Wit—and ironically half-acknowledged, half-abashed contrivance—are not poetry. But in the name of poetry, better these than sincerity, than "relevance" to some institutional agenda. Yet how is one to learn this except from the endless work of trying to understand great poetry when one is young? And of coming to terms with that understanding when one is older?

I have momentarily forsaken a historical commitment. In closing, I shall at least pinpoint a few more crucial matters with which a literary chronicle of contemporary verse might deal. I have already mentioned the matter of poetic ear. This comprises tone, speech rhythm, the cadences of phrasal and clausal structure, and their interaction with the schemata of verse structure (accentual-syllabic or "free"), all the antithetical fables propounded in the undersongs of the sound of what is being said. Sensitivity to these, and a vocal response to them, has always been both a means and a partial end of poetic education. The teaching of recognizable and identifiable verse patterns—how to recognize them, how to perceive what different poets and poems do with and "in" them is, as I am arguing, not only useful but—when the teacher is her or himself competent—possible. One trouble with the teaching of verse writing today is that there is no useful conventional terminology for the description, taxonomy, and analysis of different modes of free verse. The metrical—and rhythmic, syntactic, rhetorical—modes that frame the vers libre (to take some of the most powerful poetry of the last forty years) of Robert Penn Warren, Elizabeth Bishop, May Swenson, John Ashbery, A. R. Ammons. W. S. Merwin, James Wright, and Mark Strand differ, often in the extreme. And yet there is insufficient received analysis of their operation and effects.

The era of heavy verse has also experienced a loss of voice. I am not referring here to theoretical attacks on the presence and function of voice and voicing by certain kinds of academic theory fashionable over a decade ago. More important is the way in which public elocution of coherent prose—even the meanest news copy on television—has decayed remarkably in the last two decades. What Robert Frost called the "sentence sound"—the auditions of meaning ranging from sheer syntax all the way to tonal nuance—has faded from public discourse. Listeners to books on tape will have noticed how, when a novel is read by an American actor, the following most often occurs: while the *verso* dialogue is read perhaps convincingly, any passages of narrative or descriptive *prose* will frequently be ineptly recited. The wrong words, or even syllables, will be stressed; even simple compounds, let alone any kind of periodic sentence, will often be bungled. And there seems to be no quality control, whether in a recording studio or a TV or radio studio. At the same time, high literary theory has expended so much ceremony on the exorcism of authorial "voice" that vocation, its presence and consequences, has fled the study of texts. And yet all our memory theaters are as full of music as of retrievable topoi. It is by way of the music that specific utterance, rather than elements of lists or narratives, are remembered. Heavy verse is doomed to be particularly unmemorable, whereas even light verse has always sneaked in to the palaces of memory through the musicians' entrance.

Our culture's present distaste for knowledge is another matter, but how that has affected the condition of writing poetry is too complex to discuss now. The ease with which critical discourse treats the rich problem of difficulty is another matter of significance, and more so than the problem of the sheer bulk of print-out, with which I started. It will remain a powerful and refreshing mystery how the handful of true poets who will emerge from this generation of writers will have managed to survive their easy access to Parnassus (which used to be on a high hill until they moved it), the early training and encouragement (grade schools now celebrate paratactic prose fragments, grateful, perhaps, to get *any* writing from the unreading young, as *poems,* in a kind of demented travesty of Suzuki-method). At the same time, the memorization and oral recitation of poetry, which was a crucial part of primary school curricula in the past, has virtually disappeared. One of the effects of this is that schoolchildren are protected from contamination by the audible realm of verse, and the short lines they write echo nothing of what they may have heard. Instead, a student will be applauded for writing a brief, inconclusive, unpointed sentence—however expressive of feelings or some kinds of knowledge—expositionally paratactic and isolated, with no way of pursuing the consequences of the sentence in and for other ones. (Most schoolchildren are not so fortunate as to have been exposed to the way Kenneth Koch has taught poetry to very young people, teaching them to play rather than urging them to express.) These little "poems" (for what else, I suppose, is a morsel of heavy verse to be called?) are written out in short, unjustified lines. And this prevails at a time when even what is palpably *prose* (I exclude loose rubric, captions, fragments of cataloguer or ad copy) is more and more often set unjustified because of typographical fashion.

Given all this, and the professional schools of heavy verse—an equally small handful of true critics will emerge as well, and thus the poets will be harder to identify. That they will be there is, as I said, a refreshing mystery, and an ancient one.

PART III

The Work of Poets

CHAPTER TWELVE

Whitman's Difficult Availability

We have yet had no genius in America, with tyrannous eye, which knew the value of our incomparable materials, and saw, in the barbarism and materialism of the times, another carnival of the same gods whose picture he so much admires in Homer; then in the Middle Age; then in Calvinism. Banks and tariffs, the newspaper and caucus, methodism and unitarianism, are flat and dull to dull people, but rest on the same foundations of wonder as the Town of Troy and the temple of Delphi, and are as swiftly passing away. Our logrolling, our stumps and their politics, our fisheries, our Negroes, and Indians, our boasts, and our repudiations, the wrath of rogues, and the pusillanimity of honest men, the northern trade, the southern planting, the western clearing, Oregon, and Texas, as yet unsung. Yet America is a poem in our eyes; its ample geography dazzles the imagination, and it will not wait long for metres.
—THE POET

It did not. Eleven years after Emerson concluded his essay "The Poet," there appeared a remarkable volume, prefaced with an echoing declaration that "the United States themselves are essentially the greatest poem," and likening itself and its "forms" to "the stalwart and wellshaped heir" of him whose corpse has just been carried from the house. *Leaves of Grass* was published by the author himself during the week of Independence Day 1855, and a few days later the corpse of his own father, Walter Whitman Sr., left its house at last. Self-published, self-reviewed (more than once), self-proclaiming, self-projecting, self-inventing, the *corpus,* the *opera,* the body of work and life of Walt Whitman Jr. gave birth to itself in an astonishing volume, augmentations, revisions, and rearrangements would occupy the poet's creative life.

The 1855 *Leaves of Grass* comprised twelve long stretches of a new sort of free verse, untitled, unglossed, and generically unframed, including the great poems now known as "Song of Myself," "The Sleepers," "Faces," "I Sing the Body Electric," "A Song for Occupations," and "There Was a Child Went Forth." Its title was—and remains—as deeply problematic as its appearance. Are the leaves literally the pages of books—not "those barren leaves" that Wordsworth's speaker wanted shut up to free the reader for the texts of nature, but pages that were paradisiacally both green and fruitful? Or are they rather metaphors for the poems, here not the "flowers" of old anthologies, but green with newness? Are they the leaves that, broadcast by the wind, served the Cumaean Sybil for her prophetic pages? Are they revisions of the oldest poetical leaves of all, those figurations of individual lives in Homer, Virgil, Dante, Milton, and Shelley, and is the grass likewise also that of all flesh mown down by death in Isaiah and the Psalmist? Are they *leavings*—residues of the act of "singing," departures for worlds elsewhere that are always regions of here? And in what way are the leaves-pages *of* grass: made of, about, for, authored by? "Leaves of Grass"—hard words, putting body, life, text, presence, personality, self, and the constant fiction of some Other, all together.

The poetry, like its title, looks easy and proves hard. Who was this and to whom was he talking? Was this "you" he invoked variously a version of himself, a companion, a muse, a reader? Why should a reader care about "Walt Whitman," "one of the roughs," even if he did regard himself as being "so luscious"? What appeared difficult and problematic immediately included the centrality of body, the placing of homo urbanus at a visionary frontier, the homoerotic realm as a token of both independence and connectedness, the confused addressing of reader, body and soul by a nonetheless unfractured voice, the innovative formats for the framing of metaphor. Now, just a hundred years after the poet's preparation of the "deathbed" edition of his works, these issues seem virtually classical. Nevertheless, Whitman's growing and ongoing book, insisting on its role and nature as the poem of Democracy and the poem of the great poem of "these United States," defies easy characterization the more one reads it. The poet insists that he stands for all America—that he is America, and lest you not believe him, he will play out that theme in energetically crowded detail. It is difficult because of its celebration of self-possession in scattered multitudes of tropes of self-dispersion, or in confusing images of the incorporation of wonderful arrays of particulars; it is difficult in its propounding the song of body, in compounding a body of song. And, as always, it presents us with the perpetual problem of the Old and the New, the Early and the Late. When Milton at the beginning of *Paradise Lost* proposes that his adventurous song will accomplish "Things unattempted yet in prose or rhyme," his very words are those—as I have mentioned in the essay in this volume called "Originality"—of a successful precursor (Ariosto) flamboyantly making the same promise. Whitman implicitly allows that celebrations and singings had indeed gone on in the past ("the talkers were talking, the talk of the beginning or the end," by which he means the Bible was bibling); still, he declares,

There was never any more inception than there is now,
Nor any more youth or age than there is now,
And will never be any more perfection than there is now,
Nor any more heaven and hell than there is now.

He demands to be taken literally and requires to be taken figuratively. ("I and mine do not convince by arguments, similes, rhymes, / We convince by our presence," he chants, which has to be either a lie or a metaphor.) What the poet of "Song of Myself" invokes as "O perpetual transfers and promotions!" are his tropes and his hyperboles, his profoundly nonliteral tallyings and ecstatic reportage, his episodic pictures fading in and out of parable. Robert Frost—that most un-Whitmanian of major twentieth-century American poets—characterized the essentially poetic as "saying one thing and meaning another, saying one thing in terms of another, the pleasures of ulteriority." Whitman's metropolis of ulteriorities hums and buzzes with lives and busynesses, but below its streets are pulsing countercurrents. His proclamations of openness ("Unscrew the locks from the doors! / Unscrew the doors themselves from their jambs!") only concern outer layers of closure, for the most important matter inside the house remains ever safe, as he proclaims and concedes in "As I Ebb'd with the Ocean of Life,"

. . . before all my arrogant poems the real Me stands yet
    untouch'd, untold, altogether unreach'd,
Withdrawn far, mocking me with mock-congratulatory signs
    and bows,
With peals of distant ironical laughter at every word I
    have written,
Pointing in silence to these songs, and then to the sand
    beneath.

This "real Me" or "Me myself" is an elusive being. For all the openings and accessions and outreachings propounded in the poems, it can never really bear to be touched, save by the mothering presences of night or the sea, perhaps, and thereby by death. Whitman's difficult ulteriorities are often reversals of this sort. When he announces his expansions, containments, and incorporations, he is frequently enacting a contraction and a withdrawal. Likewise with Whitman's varying figures of the filling and emptying of the Self and the Everything Else, the "I contain the XYZ" and the "I leak out into the XYZ." They are as easy to mistake as are his purported identifications of Self and Other, which D. H. Lawrence shrewdly observed had nothing to do with feeling and sympathy ("Agonies are one of my changes of garments, I do not ask the wounded person how he feels, I myself become the wounded person").

In "Song of Myself" the singer is very shifty about his mode of *standing for,* whether in the relation of the poet's "I" to the massive particulars he so ecstatically catalogues and inventories or to the other components of his being—his soul and his "real Me," not at all of one substance with the authorial father. The Personal, the Individual, instead of the Collective—but so overwhelmingly adduced that it is easy for the dulled reading spirit to glue all the vibrant particulars into a slab of generality. For enough people to be able to be in a crowd, each without losing self-identity, self-respect, and dignified particularity, would be to transform the meaning of "crowd" utterly. Whitman is a remarkable celebrant of dignity and confounder of shame; the only shame he feels is, manifestly, the moment at the end of "Song of Myself" (sect. 37): "Askers embody themselves in me and I am embodied in them, / I project my hat, sit shame-faced, and beg" where his riot of inclusions entraps him in the begging that would have been so sinful in his Quaker upbringing. (But it is this moment that leads to the remarkable self-recognition and recovery in section 38.) More generally, his implicitly pronounced shame is at shamefulness itself.

"Do I contradict myself? / Very well then, I contradict myself," he slantingly avers toward the end of "Song of Myself," but there is no paradox of self-reference here, and that is one of the things that makes this poem such a hard one. Starting out with the work of "loafing," which is more than the trivially paradoxical industry of idleness, the speaker poses quirkily, a *flâneur,* or dandyish observer of the life of the city street whose sympathies are always effortlessly outgoing:

Apart from the pulling and hauling stands what I am,
Stands amused, complacent, compassionating, idle, unitary,
Looks down, is erect, or bends an arm on an impalpable
    certain rest,
Looking with side-curved head curious at what will come
    next,
Both in and out of the game and watching and wondering
    at it.

Along with Whitman's celebration of bodily projection comes an ambivalence about old stories. "As if the beauty and sacredness of the demonstrable must fall behind that of the mythical!" he exclaims in the 1855 preface; but it is just the complex mythopoetic elevation and concentration of the "demonstrable" that his poetry effects. Wordsworth had, at a crucial moment in his preface to *The Excursion,* proclaimed the betrothal of ancient myth and the quotidian:

Paradise, and groves
Elysian, Fortunate Fields—like those of old
Sought in the Atlantic Main—why should they be
A history only of departed things,
Or a mere fiction of what never was?
For the discerning intellect of Man,
When wedded to this goodly universe
On love and holy passion, shall find these
A simple produce of the common day.
—I, long before the blissful hour arrives,
Would chant, in lonely peace, the spousal verse
Of this great consummation.

The Excursion, *800–810*

Whitman, subsequently but more audaciously, comes "magnifying and applying" in section 41 of "Song of Myself" as a collector of old images of "the supremes," the obsolete gods, buying them up at auction, reproducing them, "Taking them all for what they are worth and not a cent more, / Admitting they were alive and did the work of their days." He even uses them for a poetic coloring book: "Accepting the rough sketches deific to fill out better in myself (*by* myself, *with* myself), bestowing them freely on each man and woman I see. . . . / Not objecting to special revelations, considering a curl of smoke or a hair on the back of my hand just as curious as any revelation." By the end of the section's ode to the Olympus of Everything ("The supernatural of no account"), the poet himself, "waiting my time to be one of the supremes," half-astonished, acknowledges his own role as the sole originator. In a powerful vision that colors in the rough sketches that both the first chapter of Genesis and the opening invocation of *Paradise Lost* have become for him, he feels his near rape of the primordial darkness and chaos into which prior myths of the universe have now sunk: "By my life-lumps! becoming already a creator, / Putting myself here and now to the ambush'd womb of the shadows." He can also move from the acutely "demonstrable"—the detailed vignettes of sections 10 and 12 of "Song of Myself"—to the puzzlingly "mythical," as in the beautiful parable of section 11, with its twenty-eight young men who are also days of the month, and the lunar lady who comes to join them in the spray.

   Oddly enough, a chief difficulty of his poetry for every reader comes not from his ecstatic vocabulary, his self-descriptive "barbaric yawp" but in Whitman's hard ordinary words. These include basic verbs of motion, like "drift" and "pass," located somewhere between "sing" and "sally forth." There are also complex terms like "vista," which can mean (1) what is seen, (2) the point or place from which one sees it, (3) the structure of mediating or intervening opacity past or through which one does the seeing. There are rarer but stunning verbs like "project," which has both physical senses (to throw or cast out or away, to jut out from, to make something jut out from, to cast images or patterns onto a surface, etc.) and mental ones (transitively, to plan, contrive, devise; to put before oneself in thought, to imagine). The interplay of these senses helps energize that remarkable moment in "Out of the Cradle Endlessly Rocking" when he calls out to the bereft, widowed mockingbird, "O you solitary singer, singing by yourself, projecting me," (to which, darkling, he listens and reciprocates with, "O solitary me listening, never more shall I cease perpetuating you").

Most famously problematic has been the matter of Whitman's free verse and his formal innovations generally. A map of the "greatest poem," the United States themselves, shows us shapes formed by natural contours—seacoasts and lake shores, demarcating rivers and so forth—and by surveyed boundary lines, geometric, unyielding, and ignorant of what the eye of the airborne might perceive. Whitman's poem of America purported to have dispensed with all surveyors, with arbitrary strokes of a mental knife that score out legal fictions like state boundaries or city limits. It declared that all its component lines, stanzas, and structures would be shaped only by the natural forms they organically exuded. Which meant, as in every great poet's high ulterior mode, that the art that shaped them would teach older formal paradigms and patterns to dance, rather than negate them utterly. As a poet, you can only, in Wordsworth's phrase, "Let nature be your teacher" after yourself having taught nature how to speak. Very complex are the linear and strophic patterns in which Whitman would claim to "weave the song of myself" ("Song of Myself" section 15, where he fuses melodic lines and horizontal warp threads of a growing fabric), and their formal modes as well as their complex articulations of those modes are all in themselves subtle and powerful formal metaphoric versions of more traditional ones.

This revisionary character can be more easily observed at the level of trope or fiction than at the realm of scheme or formal pattern. Some of his greatest imaginative figures—leaf, grass, bird, star, sea, flowering branch, city, river, road, ship, the Wanderer, the Original—have all the freshness and imaginative power that only come from the revision of traditional figurations. And often the rhetorical deed of a poem or movement in a poem will be ceremoniously to enact such a revision, as when, for example, the poet substitutes his domestic, American, erotic, spring-blooming lilac for the more traditionally emblematic flowers on the funeral hearse of the Lost Leader in "When Lilacs Last in the

Dooryard Bloom'd": "O death, I cover you with roses and early lilies, / But mostly and now the lilac that blooms the first." He is hereby also substituting his own kind of poetry (text and bouquet, poesy and posy, having been associated since antiquity); and the original gesture earns its memory of "Lycidas" and "Adonais" by also mourning a complex mythological personage on the occasion of the death of an actual person. Or there is the substitution of the native American mockingbird for the romantic nightingale and skylark. These are simple and manifest instances of a phenomenon occurring throughout Whitman's poetry.

In its formal aspect, Whitman adopts almost unvaryingly an end-stopped line, characteristically connected to its near companions by anaphora (formulaically repeated opening word or phrase) or parallel syntactic form in a ramified growth of subordinate clauses (the familiar formats of his fascinating array of modes of cataloguing). In context, his form is as identifiable as a quantitative or accentual syllabic line would be, not marked by a tally of its parts but by the way it is shaped to be part of an epigram, a strophe, an aria, or sonata-form like "movement," or a block of stipulations. There are his strophic forms, sometimes, in his later work (as in "Eidólons" or "Dirge for Two Veterans" or "Darest Thou Now, O Soul") suggesting in their format classical stanzas, more often some form of ad hoc rhythm developed by linear groupings, as in the opening of "Song of Myself" no. 6. (There a pattern of two and then one, three and then one, four and then one develops in the responsive suppositions rising in answer to the child's—and the reader's—"What is the grass?")

And always, there is the marvelous deployment, throughout lines and strophes, of the rhythms of speech as well as the totally unspeakable rhythms generated only by writing, the cadences of the inventoried, parallel modifying phrases and dependent clauses (who *talks* like *that?*); the mannered, Frenchified noun-adjective inversions; the rhythmic jolts provided by intrusions of weird diction. The rhythmic patternings of long and short lines, aligned, variously interjected, refrained, extended, receding were not exactly, as Whitman put it to his friend Horace Traubel, analogous to "*the Ocean*. Its verses are the liquid, billowy waves, ever rising and falling, perhaps wild with storm, always moving, always alike in their nature as rolling waves, but hardly any two exactly alike in size or measure, never having the sense of something finished and fixed, always suggesting something beyond." But the fixer and finisher, the poet himself, is far more crafty a puller of waves than the coldly regular moon. He might just as well have likened his long anaphoric catalogues to urban crowds through which the reader himself will pass, jostling, pushing, sometimes striding, sometimes pausing.

A word or two about Whitman's basic form of cataloguing: it exhibits a variety of structural modes. In the third strophe of "Song of Myself" no. 31, for example, the little list begins with the generality "In vain the speeding or shyness," then reiterates the qualifier "In vain" to introduce each item in the list of ascending entities (in archaeological time and humanly scaled space—from "plutonic rocks" to the auk). The conclusion is the burden of this song: "I follow quickly, I ascend to the nest in the fissure-cliff," which itself follows quickly on the last line, as well as on the whole series of ineffectually evasive beings, all of which the poet "follows quickly." But it is as if the particular following—the climb up to the high point to the nest of the great bird—becomes a momentary archetype of all the others. And one great function of the list may have been to explore fully the meaning of "the speeding or shyness." Without the array of instances, it could not be grasped; fully informed by the items of the catalogue and the musical patterning in which they are unrolled, it becomes a unique phrase, Whitman's—and the reader's—own. What is not a central matter is the extent of Whitman's lists, but rather their internal structure, the narrative of their development, the ways in which they are—as in this case—variously framed by enveloping initial predications or shape their own closures by the framing gesture of the last entry.

Consider the great catalogue of specifications preceding the "I tread such roads" in "Song of Myself" no. 33. Starting after the declaration that "I am afoot with my vision," there are nearly eighty lines of *where*s ("Where the quail is whistling . . . / Where the bat flies . . . / Where the great gold-bug drops . . . / Where the brook puts out . . ." etc.), *through*s, *upon*s, *pleas'd with*s that make up subsections of their own. Through these and beyond, the whole passage itself treads roads of country, city, farm, factory, wild and domestic animal, marine nature and industry, and moves toward a hyperbolic envelopment. Its electrifying last entry functions like the dancing figures on Achilles's shield in *The Iliad*, which seem to sum up the whole story of the making and describing of the vision of human life represented on it:

Speeding amid the seven satellites and the broad ring, and the
     diameter of eighty thousand miles,
Speeding with tail'd meteors, throwing fire-balls like the
     rest,
Carrying the crescent child that carries its own full mother
     in its belly.

The concluding line is packed with complex figuration: the "new moon with the old moon in its arms" (from "Sir Patrick Spens" and Coleridge) invokes the barely discernible full sphere shadowed within the bright crescent, being connected—through the literal Latin sense of "crescent"—to the curved form of the enwombed fetus. It concludes, sums up, and reaches beyond the preceding elements in the list with a marvelous image of containment.

From the Homeric list of ships and the biblical genealogies, through the rhetorically rough inventories of goods; the blazons of erotic details of a desired body, the stacks of clauses and conditions and contingencies on a contract or lease; the inventories of rescued necessities by a Crusoe or Swiss Family Robinson or of what Tom Sawyer received in barter for the whitewashing; the wondrously detailed names of those who came to Gatsby's parties—the rhetoric of cataloguing in our literature has encompassed everything from the high heroic to the low quotidian. Whitman's catalogues often consist of lists of ramified predications. Sometimes their litanies of specimen instances are his sort of chanting of the laws—as only in biblical times and rituals—of the Great Poem of America as a self-acknowledged legislator of the world. Generally they are transcendental: they include and metaphorically revise these and other nonliterary modes of inventorying. With Whitman, lists become basic topoi, places in, by, and through which his poems develop themselves. Through their internal structures and rhythms of syntactic and semantic grouping, they articulate their own boundaries and purposes.

Not only is Whitman the poet "afoot with his vision" in the poem, but throughout his life, in his constant textual revisions as well. The nine subsequent editions of *Leaves of Grass* after 1855 not only rearrange material in the preceding ones but add many new poems, subtract a good many, sometimes reinsert a previous subtraction. The leaves of the book remain green and growing throughout his life. There is an academic industry of interpreting the continual changes Whitman made in his work from 1855 to 1891, with a number of different interpretive agendas, each running roughshod over the partial applicability of the others. There is the school whose central agenda is the matter of varying explicitness about homosexuality; another of developing explicitness about poetic intention; those who see greater obliqueness, increased second-guessing of a growing audience, and so forth. Such impulses can indeed all seem to be at work differently, at different times and places in the text. Whitman's evolving thoughts on formal structures are reflected in his renumbering—and thereby reconstituting—of strophes and sections ("Song of Myself," unnumbered and unnamed in 1855, falls into 372 numbered strophes—ranging from couplets to full odes—in 1860 but does not acquire its calendrical division into 52 sections until 1867.) Likewise interesting in this regard are the opening and form of "Out of the Cradle": the sheer play of retitling generally, sometimes reframing, sometimes clarifying an intention, sometimes obscuring or transforming one; the addition of clusters in later editions; the segmentation, in 1856, into genres of poems, and so forth.

The history of Whitman's reputation seems to me to be less interesting than the history of any reader's reaction to the poetry. But generally one may say that the Poem gets reinterpreted into the Works of the Bard. "Song of Myself," with, again, the ambiguous resonances of the grammatical construction (composed of, by, to, about, for, myself? "of myself" as it might be "of itself?" etc.) starts out untitled in 1855, becomes "Poem of Walt Whitman, an American" (which introduces the ambiguous "of"), and "Walt Whitman" thereafter until 1881, when it assumes its familiar title. New leaf-forms—asides, communiqués from Parnassus, blurbs for the universe, position papers, self-commissioned laureate verses, ghosts of leaves that are really only *Albumblätter,* etc., start filling up the pages. They work their way into thematized sections—he calls them "clusters" from 1860 on—as part of a program to extend his formal metaphor of organic structure from line to strophe to poem to poem-group to the ever-growing oeuvre itself. "Chants Democratic," "Leaves of Grass" (a synecdochal subtitle), "Enfans D'Adam," "Calamus" (again, like "leaves," a complex figure, blending the stiff phallic rush or cane, the musically tuned pipe cut from a reed, the writing-reed, the green, growing, and emphatically fragrant plant, into an object of erotic, musicopoetic instrumentality), "Messenger Leaves," these appear in the 1860 text. Some fall off and die in later editions, others continue to flourish and are joined by newer ones, often when entire books, like the volume of Civil War poems, *Drum Taps and Sequel* of 1865, are subsequently "annexed" to later editions.

Sometimes putting a previously published poem into a new cluster in a later version of the book amounts to a gloss on that poem. So with, for example, the gnomic "Chanting the Square Deific" with its four strophes erecting a weird pantheon composed of (1) Jehovah-Brahma-Saturn-Kronos, (2) Christ-Hermes-Hercules, (3) Satan, and (4) a subsuming Santa Spirita identified with the bard himself, who ultimately squares the circle of "the great round world" itself. It first appeared, along with the beautiful little "I Heard You Solemn-Sweet Pipes of the Organ" in the *Sequel* to *Drum-Taps* (1865–66), but by 1871 it had been gathered into the cluster entitled, from the second poem in it, "Whispers of Heavenly Death," as if implicitly perhaps to avow its cold agenda. "As Adam Early in the Morning" originally appeared in 1860 as the last poem (15) in the "Calamus" cluster, but without the first two words; the added simile may only make manifest what was latent in the original use of the word "bower," but it certainly brings to the little poem an additional assertion of Originality—it is as if Whitman were now off to name all the animals for the first time. Sometimes it is only a privileged glance at a manuscript that reveals some of the heart of Whitman's revisionary process. That traditionally formed emblematic poem "A Noiseless Patient Spider" emerged from a passing simile in a meditation on unexpressed love on an occasion of unseized erotic opportunity; in the published poem, the matter of a street pickup is put through what Hart Crane called "the silken skilled transmemberment of song" and becomes a greater matter of the soul's far-flung "gossamer thread" catching somewhere, of the song being heard.

There is also the effect, noted earlier, of the many retitlings. In some of his notebooks, Whitman projects poems with titles like "Poem of Kisses" or "Poem of the Black Person," where, as in his overall title, the *of* is fruitfully ambiguous.

Most original with him is the simple compound form, for example, "Sundown Poem" (the original title of "Crossing Brooklyn Ferry"; canceling it dims the prominence of the westwardness of the crossing from Brooklyn to Manhattan underlined by the occasion and allows the alternative directions of so many trips and crossings to emerge) or "Banjo Poem" (one of these projected—what would that have been like?). The two great shore poems—odes of the figurative littoral—"Out of the Cradle Endlessly Rocking" and "As I Ebb'd with the Ocean of Life" that dominate the "Sea-Drift" cluster were differently titled. The first was originally published as "A Child's Reminiscence," then "A Word out of the Sea" (with the subtitle "Reminiscence" at the start of the second strophe, and with an additional line before the present third one: "Out of the boy's mother's womb, and from the nipples of her breasts," thus giving Whitman's familiar Quaker designation of September, "the Ninth Month midnight" an additional significance). The second was initially "Bardic Symbols," then no. 1 of the cluster entitled "Leaves of Grass" in 1860 (again, with the added opening "Elemental drifts! / O I wish I could impress others as you and the waves have been impressing me"), then "Elemental Drifts," and finally, when those two lines were canceled, the present incipit title it now bears.

But we also sort through Whitman's leaves and form our own readers' clusters, generic groupings that seem to emerge among the finished poems as if from unstated or unavowed intentions. Walk Poems; Panoramic Poems; Talk Poems; Optative Exhortations (including the brilliant and sardonic "Respondez!" an ironic inversion of that mode originally entitled "Poem of the Propositions of Nakedness," and dropped after the 1876 edition); Poems of Pictures—following the fragmentation of that never-printed early manuscript poem "Pictures" (it survives both as the tiny "My Picture-Gallery" and, more importantly, throughout all the poems, starting with the well-known vignettes of sections 9 and 10 of "Song of Myself").

Then there are the musical odes, such as the midpoint chant of "Song of Myself" (section 26), "Italian Music in Dakota," the splendid "Proud Music of the Storm," "That Music Always Round Me," "I Heard You, Solemn-Sweet Pipes of the Organ," section 5 of "A Song for Occupations," section 3 of "Salut au Monde!" and of course, "I Hear America Singing." These tend to use Whitman's catalogue format in a unique way; their prototype is a pattern of layered lines of verse each embodying a polyphonic voice, instrumental, vocal, or "natural" (the wind in the trees, birdsong, sounds of moving water, etc., to which Whitman adds the noises of human work and enterprise, constructive, destructive, or whatever). This is a device that persists from Spenser through the romantic poets. Whitman employs it in a poetic revision of musical polyphony, even extending the symphonic format beyond phonetic materials to include specimens of all human activity. Section 15 of "Song of Myself," for example, opens with a Whitmanian duet: "The pure contralto sings in the organ loft, / The carpenter dresses his plank, the tongue of his foreplane whistles its wild ascending lisp" (and how Homeric this last half-line!), but then continues with about sixty varied glimpses of What Is and of What Is Done, musical relations between parts having been only an introductory paradigm for a more general organic assemblage of "the beauty and sacredness of the demonstrable."

Here and there throughout the poetry lurks a notion that the Poem of America—whether in the notion of the United States as "greatest poem" or in *Leaves of Grass* itself—had already been written by Walt Whitman in some earlier phase of consciousness and self-projection. It is not only among the animals, in whose selectively described moral condition ("Not one kneels to another, nor to his kind that lived thousands of years ago, / Not one is respectable or unhappy over the whole earth") the poet finds "tokens of myself." (It might nevertheless be added that Walt Whitman did not eat his young, or remain incapable of knowledge of death or acknowledgment of anything.) It is rather about all his inventoried and chanted phenomena that he surmises, "I wonder where they get those tokens, / Did I pass that way huge times ago and negligently drop them?" Still, his continuous "transfers and promotions" remain his greatest generosities and sympathies, his widest- and farthest-reaching hands or filaments: "And there is no object so soft but it makes a hub for the universe" means, of course, that the imaginative faculty that can construe as a hub a caterpillar, or a drop of sweat, or a hair on the back of a hand—and can construct the right concentric circles radiating from it—is the breath of Democratic life itself.

Democracy, for Whitman's poetry, begins with questions of "representation"—that is, of metaphor. His literal is elusively figurative, and his favorite figure—synecdoche, the part for the whole, the whole for the part, the container and the things contained variously figuring one another—is itself metaphoric, and even more ulterior. American democracy entails a representative government and a deference toward a body of opinion with a propensity to slacken toward self-identifications of the synecdochal sort. We clamor for public officials who are members of whatever group of which we constitute ourselves; we want to be represented by a lump of our region, district, race, sect, caste, or ethnic strain (but seldom of our intelligence, our moral nature, our imagination, our prudence, our regard for others). A system of metaphoric representation (and British Parliament, or perhaps our Senate—rather than our House of Representatives—has been more like this) would have us wish the best and most skilled advocate to argue and negotiate for us (which is a different business from singing), even if he or she were nothing like a neighbor, a workmate, a cousin, or a fellow congregant who would know our song by heart. Such a representative would *stand for* us in another way.

Whitman's affirmations thus always engage our Democratic paradoxes: that if there is to be no selfishness there must be true self-containment. Responsibility starts with the mutual obligations among the components of one's own identity; acknowledging the dignity of things and beings requires a zoom lens to home in on the minute and otherwise help get by the false worth of mere magnitude. Self-respect, as Whitman liked to say, mocks and dissolves aristocracies. American Democracy is both uniquely equipped for, and uniquely in need of, interpreting itself. Its own bodily and empirical constitution is framed anew in all the languages of many sorts of lives—from "the blab of the pave" to the complex poem of celebration that takes back with one hand what it gives with another, perpetually claiming that reading it poses no problems and thereby generating a multitude of them, yet always extending the ultimate perpetuating connection of poet and reader, interpreter and reinterpreter, citizen and citizen. Like his own great poem of poems, "Democracy" said Whitman in *Democratic Vistas* is "a word the real gist of which still sleeps, quite unawakn'd."

CHAPTER THIRTEEN

Arduous Fullness: On Dante Gabriel Rossetti

It is well over a hundred years since the death of Dante Gabriel Rossetti, and for something like the last sixty of these he has been, like his younger friend Swinburne, a remarkably underrated poet. This critical neglect was in some measure the result of the antiromantic stance of Anglo-American literary modernism. William Butler Yeats acknowledged Rossetti's role as a "subconscious influence" on the following generation, but it is still startling for modern readers to hear his voice lurking in those canonical modernists Eliot, Pound, and Frost. (Few know, I believe, that Rossetti found, meditated upon, and was struck by the passage from Petronius's *Satyricon* that Eliot later used as the final epigraph for *The Waste Land,* for example.) It was precisely Yeats's supposedly utter repudiation of the old adornments of that following generation—his own—in favor of "walking naked" that remains a central myth of modernist literary history. And yet how much of that nakedness is to be found in some of Rossetti's poems is still surprising. Ezra Pound praised Rossetti, early on, as a translator who made available medieval materials before Pound's own modernist medievalism—presumably more tough-minded—had treated them suitably. But certainly Rossetti's very great sestina, translated from Dante Alighieri's "Al poco giorno ed al gran cerchio d'ombra," with its ringing concluding stanzas

Yet shall the streams turn back and climb the hills
Before Love's flame in this damp wood and green
Burn, as it burns within a youthful lady,
For my sake, who would sleep away in stone

My life, or feed like beasts upon the grass,
Only to see her garments cast a shade.

How dark soe'er the hills throw out their shade,
Under her summer-green the beautiful lady
Covers it, like a stone covered in grass

is more powerful than any of Pound's versions of the poetry of Guido Cavalcanti.

We can observe that Rossetti's discovery of perfect end-words—those crucial recurring elements of the sestina form—for the Italian ones uncannily also allows analogous phonological relations to flourish among them. "Shade," "hills," "grass," "green," "stone," "lady" (in the order in which they appear in the first stanza) perfectly translate *ombra, colli, erba, verde, pietra, donna*. But they mirror the internal affinities of the original words: *om*bra—d*onna* (sh*ade*—l*ady*) for example, and *er*ba—*ver*de (here the assonance is picked up by the alliterative *gr*ass—*gr*een). Similarly, the syntactic boldness, in the lines quoted above, of "would sleep away in stone / My life" (for "che mi torrei dormire in poetra / Tutto il mio tempo") uses the enjambment to distance the deferred object from the verb even more, and imply that the "in stone" is part of the verb "sleep" itself. This is a Miltonic stroke, even as it is what the rhetoricians might call the tmesis of the syntax of "this damp wood and green" (for "questo legno molle e verde," where that same construction usually found in Italian poetry is absent). Rossetti could easily have written "this wood damp and green," but preferred, in a more intense mode, to remind one of the Italian grammar and at the same time conduct the reader through the two orders of predication in the case of the wood, emerging after the fact of the dampness into the returning, refrainlike terminal word *green* (as if to say, "this damp wood and—yes, here we go again—green"). But wherever one looks at Dante's original, one marvels at both the fidelity and the beauty, supposedly incompatible in translation, of what is an astonishing English poem of its own.

Pound writes of Rossetti, whether in blame or praise, as if the latter were nothing but a stylist and a literary historian from whom some good things could be learned and some bad ones avoided. Pound writes as if imagination were only rhetorical ingenuity, as if the substance of poetry and its mythologies of love and death, self and other, quest and loss existed only in the diseases of bad critical discourse. But the essence of what Pound is blind to in his work Rossetti reveals, brilliantly and darkly at once, in a miniature ars poetica, a poem of poetic craft. The prefatory sonnet written in 1880 to introduce his major poetic work, *The House of Life*, at first glance purports to deal merely with the sonnet form itself:

A Sonnet is a moment's monument,—
    Memorial from the Soul's eternity

To one dead deathless hour. Look that it be,
Whether for lustral rite or dire portent,
Of its own arduous fulness reverent:
   Carve it in ivory or in ebony,
    As Day or Night may rule; and let Time see
Its flowering crest impearled and orient.

A Sonnet is a coin: its face reveals
   The Soul,—its converse, to what Power 't is due:—
Whether for tribute to the august appeals
   Of Life, or dower in Love's high retinue,
It serve; or, 'mid the dark wharf's cavernous breath,
In Charon's palm it pay the toll to Death.

But this is more than merely an exercise in a genre—the "sonnet-on-the-sonnet"—continued from Wordsworth and Keats. Rossetti's "moment's monument" is the monument *of,* or produced by, a moment's vision and work and also the monument *to* the very brevity of that moment. Rossetti's sonnet is always, no matter what its putative "subject," the cry of its own occasion. The sculptural fable of art and life is revised from that of a freestanding figure, in the octave, down to the carved relief of a coin, in the self-characterizing sestet. It is an antique coin, still of great value; but as with all ancient coins, the matter of payment for the Stygian ferry creeps into the accounting as it does in Rossetti's closing. His bottom line, as it were, reveals what had been implicit among the other transactions—with Life and Love—all along. This sonnet, conspicuously reverent "of its own arduous fullness," is about poetry altogether. The epigraph to the sonnet sequence *The House of Life*—itself a discontinuous frieze of moments' monuments—is thus a reminder of final costs, of the way in which the whole procession of life itself is always being viewed with an averted gaze.

    In its central concern for human meaning, for the existential role of fable in our lives, the miniature bas-relief of Rossetti's coin (cut by the hand of the artist, caressed as art by the hand of the antiquary, passed on from hand to hand in ancient trade) thus constitutes a monument more significant and more mighty than the guarded, scaled-down decorations, the enamels and cameos that Pound and Eliot adapted from the French poet Théophile Gautier. The painter-poet's late romantic half-personifications of Life and Death were far less attractive to subsequent twentieth-century poetry than the dismantled figurines of irony and pity of the later poet as sculptor. Once the modern reader can penetrate a high, post-Keatsian gesture, Rossetti's poetry will be felt not as "pre-Raphaelite" but rather as tough, creatively problematic, rejecting easy or fake answers to ultimate questions, masterfully coping with the central modern problem of treating the great in the small. Indeed, if Rossetti's poems seem sweetmeats to a reserved, modernist taste, there is yet a hard nut to crack within, whereas Pound's poetic rhetoric is like a candy with a hard surface that quickly melts away to the fudge within.

The whole of *The House of Life* is problematic in several ways; its title (an astrological trope? a more general postbiblical figure of a consecrated space? a place *in, made of, belonging to, dedicated to,* etc., Life?) and its very lack of sequentiality are hard to deal with. This is more like an anthology of sonnets, written over a thirty-year period, brooding on eros and art, lit by the flaming presences of three female personages—a Beata Beatrix out of Dante, a Proserpina-Pandora figure, and a Lilith, these last two being pure Dante Gabriel, and in whom we may discern reflections of, respectively, Elizabeth Siddal, the poet's wife, a suicide in 1862; Jane (Mrs. William) Morris; and Rossetti's model and housekeeper, Fanny Cornforth. The poems range from the direct and naturalistic to the highly and manifestly allegorical, from the postcoital bed of "Nuptial Sleep" or the nature poetry of "Barren Spring" or "Autumn Idleness" ("The deer gaze calling, dappled white and dun, / As if, being foresters of old, the sun / Had marked them with the shade of forest-leaves" sounds, as Rossetti does often, like Robert Frost), where the hidden allegory is almost Emersonian, to poems like "Passion and Worship." Here a pair of personifications that might easily have come from the early Italian poets are reinforced by a traditional neoclassical distinction between the qualities of their musical attributes. Passion has a wind instrument, Worship a string; the particular harp and archaically designated "hautboy" are importations from pictorial iconography:

One flame-winged brought a white-winged harp-player
  Even where my lady and I lay all along;
  Saying: "Behold, this minstrel is unknown;
Bid him depart, for I am minstrel here:
Only my strains are to Love's dear ones dear."
  Then said I: "Through thine hautboy's rapturous tone
  Unto my lady still this harp makes moan,
And still she deems the cadence deep and clear."

Then said my lady: "Thou art Passion of Love,
  And this Love's Worship: both he plights to me.
  Thy mastering music walks the sunlit sea:
But where wan water trembles in the grove
And the wan moon is all the light thereof,
  This harp still makes my name its voluntary."

While "wan music trembles in the grove" is a fine visual correlative for the acoustic actualities of harp music, the sound of an early oboe, which Rossetti had probably never heard, is so thin and nasal and even braying that the instrument's role is purely emblematic. From classical times on, the wind-string distinction has corresponded to the contraries of energy and reason, will and wit (in Elizabethan terminology), Dionysian and Apollonian. Rossetti's pictorializing of the musical sound is effective in the case of the strong music of Love's white messenger; the word "hautboy," on the other hand, is purely iconographic.

Even more abstractly so is the celebrated image of the monochord, in the sonnet of the same name, which amused Swinburne and which William Michael Rossetti, in his notes to the edition of 1911, sought to dissolve completely from the poem, by arguing that the name of the archaic instrument alone, the word itself, invoked "an unspeakably mysterious bond between the universe and the soul of man." Originally published as a separate sonnet of 1870 called "Written During Music," the poem began: "Is it the moved air or the moving sound / That is Life's self and draws my life from me." When included in *The House of Life,* the first line was rewritten and the octave went as follows:

Is it this sky's vast vault or ocean's sound
    That is Life's self and draws my life from me,
    And by instinct ineffable decree
Holds my breath quailing on the bitter bound?
Nay, is it Life or Death, thus thunder-crown'd,
    That 'mid the tide of all emergency
    Now notes my separate wave, and to what sea
Its difficult eddies labour in the ground?

Even though the symbol of the archaic, largely didactic, instrument is retained in the title, the musical context has indeed vanished.

Rossetti was so much more capable of being overwhelmed by the poetic power of great art than were most nineteenth-century critics (save, of course, John Ruskin and Walter Pater) that he was unable, in his own painting, to transcend illustration to the degree that the major painters associated with the pre-Raphaelite brotherhood were (Ford Madox Brown, the best, and, before he went to the bad, John Everett Millais). His canvases have come in time to assume the true color of their provinciality, of their earnest half-amateurishness. Even a return to trivial but profitable favor and mindless, tasteless judgment in the contemporary art market of figurative illustration will not do much for the stature of Rossetti's painting. Not so for the poems; they look better every year. Aside from the central canon of his work—*The House of Life,* the sonnets for pictures, "The Stream's Secret," "Jenny," "The Sea-Limits," "Sudden Light," "Love's Nocturn," "Eden Bower," "Troy Town," "The Orchard Pit," fragmentary as it is—there are such poems as that splendid short lyric "The Woodspurge," whose poetic "action" is that of a radical reconstruction of an available emblem into a far more powerful metaphor. The speaker, grief stricken in a bleak windy outdoor scene, collapses forward in despair ("My hair was over in the grass, / My naked ears heard the day pass"—which is poetic language astonishing enough in itself). But then

My eyes, wide open, had the run
Of some ten weeds to fix upon;
Among these few, out of the sun,
The woodspurge flowered, three cups in one.

From perfect grief there need not be
Wisdom or even memory:
One thing then learnt remains to me,—
The woodspurge has a cup of three.

The flower is claimed here by no iconographic fancy; there is no trinitarian device, no allusion to ideal triads, lurking here. The *thisness*, as Gerard Manley Hopkins might have had it, of this unique perception of the wild flower's structure at that moment outlasts, for the speaker, any moralization of his own feelings. The epistemological moral only is left, which the reader, doing his own poetic work, must go on to draw. "The Woodspurge" not only embodies a Joycean epiphany, in which "a sudden light transfigures a trivial thing" (as Pater, mediating between Rossetti and Joyce, was to put it) but also unfolds the very action of a modern short story (from *Dubliners,* say) in miniature.

This prematurely modernist mode in Rossetti is frequently accompanied by a tone, diction, and rhythm that are far more direct and colloquial than those of the high rhetoric of poems like *The House of Life*. Consider that—for me—strangely charming sonnet called "A Match with the Moon":

Weary already, weary miles to-night
　　I walked for bed: and so, to get some ease,
　　I dogged the flying moon with similes.
And like a wisp she doubled on my sight
In ponds; and caught in tree-tops like a kite;
　　And in a globe of film all liquorish
　　Swam full-faced like a silly silver fish;—
Last like a bubble shot the welkin's height
Where my road turned, and got behind me, and sent
　　My wizened shadow craning round at me,
　　And jeered, "So, step the measure,—one two three!"
And if I faced on her, looked innocent.
But just at parting, halfway down a dell,
She kissed me for good-night. So you'll not tell.

The first seven lines and the last three are, once again, almost pure Robert Frost, the last one astonishingly so. This is, of course, to say how much Rossetti Frost had absorbed quite early on, but it is also to point out how misunderstood is the received view of Rossetti's language among those who haven't reread him. That he was an erotic poet who suffered the attack of a prudish fool named Buchanan is well known; but that he was a direct poet of nature has been largely forgotten. Even in some of his earliest poems, Rossetti can render with a potent and even astonishing precision the effects of natural sound—and, even more remarkably, urban and industrial noise—both within and upon the landscape in which the sounds arise. Consider, for example, that remarkable and remarkably unappreciated series of poems written on the train journey that he and Holman Hunt took to France and Belgium in 1849. *A Trip to Paris and Belgium* (sent to his brother, William Michael) combines blank verse journal and epistle with sonnets and a few inset lyrics, the first covering the travel by rail between London and Bruges, and the rhymed poems largely recording and commemorating stops and places. The handling of landscape moving by outside a train window is brilliant throughout these poems (the sequence opens, in "London to Folkstone," with "A constant keeping-past of shaken trees, / And a bewildered glitter of loose road"); the silent film unrolling alongside the train begins to be underscored with the audible only when the elements of the landscape themselves register the noise of the passing engine and cars:

And, seen through fences or a bridge far off,
Trees that in moving keep their intervals
Still one 'twixt bar and bar; and then at times
Long reaches of green level, where one cow,
Feeding among her fellows that feed on,
Lifts her slow neck, and gazes for the sound.

Later, passing into open country from between brick walls, he registers the "short gathered champing of pen sound," and even seems to feel, "close about the face / A wind of noise that is along like God." Still further on, in the sonnet "In the Train, and at Versailles," he registers the onset of silence after the noise of travel as something palpably filling the room of the landscape:

. . . A great silence here,
  Through the long planted alleys, to the long
  Distance of water. More than tune or song,
Silence shall grow to awe within thine eyes,
  Till thy thought swim with the blue turning sphere.

In "On the Road," a subsequent blank verse section, the very silence itself is audible: "A dead pause then / With giddy humming silence in the cars"; some lines later in the same poem, the traveler reports "A heavy clamour that fills up the brain / Like thought grown burdensome; and in the ears / Speed that seems striving to o'ertake itself." The first of these clauses might perhaps remind us that Rossetti was indeed carrying Browning (at least *Sordello*) with him on this trip; the second is a representation that seems more of the 1920s.

The finest section of the sequence is "Antwerp to Ghent," and in it the blanketing effect of the droning, continuing noise of the train on other sounds is wonderfully portrayed:

The darkness is a tumult. We tear on,
The roll behind us and the cry before,
Constantly, in a lull of intense speed
And thunder. Any other sound is known
Merely by sight.

The casual, often conversational, journal-entry quality of the blank verse (I have discussed elsewhere how lines like "Our speed is such the sparks our engine leaves / Are burning after the whole train has passed" remind one of the blank verse of Frost's eclogues) give these observations the virtues of the pencil, rather than of the more resonant brush.

In contrast with the naturally visual realm of these epistolary blank verse passages, the purely visionary demesne of a poem like "Love's Nocturn" draws upon medievalized mythology, which it then revises. This mysterious and difficult poem about erotic dreaming is in the form of an office of Love (the title suggests the liturgical term, rather than the name of the musical composition first used by John Field) as the god of dreams. At the outset he is invoked as "Master of the murmuring courts / Where the shapes of sleep convene," and the poem itself starts out in a region of consciousness in which sight and hearing begin to dissolve into each other in sleep. The poet petitions Love to send his sleeping lady a dream of himself, and in a later stanza introduces the role that audition, rather than vision, will play:

Master, is it soothly said
    That, as echoes of man's speech
Far in secret clefts are made,
    So do all men's bodies reach
Shadows o'er thy sunken beach,—
    Shape or shade
In those halls pourtrayed of each?

An old myth of echo becomes eroticized both in image and in function here, as parallel to the shadows of projected desire that exist as every man's double in Love's dream kingdom. It is this benign doppelgänger the poet hopes to meet—

"Groping in the windy stair, / (Darkness and the breath of space / Like loud waters everywhere,)"—and send into the sleep of his lady. But it is in sound rather than in sight or in dreamed touch that his "body's phantom" is to come to her:

Where in groves the gracile Spring
   Trembles, with mute orison
Confidently strengthening,
    Water's voice and wind's as one
    Shed an echo in the sun.

With this near-Clevelandism of romantic imagery, the blended voices of the *locus amoenus* figure also the mingling of shadow and echo, sight and sound. The poet's emanation continues to sing to her in the two musical modalities of absence and presence, longing and fulfillment:

Soft as Spring,
Master, bid it sing and moan.
Song shall tell how glad and strong
   Is the night she soothes alway;
Moan shall grieve with that parched tongue
Of the brazen hours of day:
Sounds as of the springtide they,
    Moan and song,
   While the chill months long for May.

Both of these melodies, the tones of song and of moan, are ultimately Keatsian (e.g., the "parched tongue"), as is the overall movement toward the usurpation of vision's kingdom by hearing. It is the specifically erotic milieu that is Rossetti's characteristic one. Even the Romantic cliché of the Aeolian harp—not as the strong Coleridgean or Shelleyan emblem of inspiration and imaginative response but as the languid image of nature reclaiming the suspended or abandoned instrument, a most ubiquitous trope—becomes a figure for relinquished desire. Toward the end of the poem, the speaker tells Love that if his lady's dreaming world is already occupied by another's shadow of desire, then his own must withdraw:

Like a vapour wan and mute,
   Like a flame, so let it pass;
One low sigh across her lute,
   One dull breath against her glass.

The "lute" is a purely visionary instrument, figuratively the lady's heart, abandoned and inaccessible as his instrument now. Any stringed instrument would do for the sigh across it, and the particular archaism here is part of the apparatus of the poem that is so redolent of the medieval Italian poetry he had already translated.

One of Rossetti's uniquely transformed genres is what scholars call poetic ecphrasis, the kind of poem that addresses a particular and actual work of art (rather than a notional one, like Homer's shield of Achilles, or the tapestries in book 3 of *The Faerie Queene*), the speaking pictures of verse giving voice, as it were, to the mute poetry of painting. Poetic language confronts the pictorial Other in an erotic or agonistic way, and images by interpreting. Ecphrastic poems (all too frequently on paintings by Pieter Bruegel the Elder) abound in most books of verse written in the 1980s and 1990s, but it was Rossetti who propounded the modern agenda for pictorial poems in English, long before the canonical anthology pieces by Rilke and Auden made the genre seem a modernist invention. Certain sections of *The House of Life* written for, and to, his own paintings aside, Rossetti produced some twenty-six poems—almost all sonnets—for paintings by Renaissance and later artists. The greatest of these is the sonnet to Leonardo da Vinci's *Virgin of the Rocks* (the version of the painting in London), with its rocks, caves, and shades of death; its foreground figures of Mary, her son, and the infant St. John, attended by the angel Gabriel; and its background caves opening out through close passages to distant, shining water. Rossetti's poem confronts the paradoxes of life and death, of entrances and exits, inherent in the scene's darknesses. Its own structures of questioning octave and answering sestet, both commencing with the word "Mother," trope the relation of foreground and background in the picture, and the difficult "pass" invoked in the ninth line (which sounds so much like Eliot's "Ash-Wednesday") points to a poetic passage—what Harold Bloom would call a "poetic crossing"—as well. It is significant too that the angel Gabriel is missing from the ecphrastic account, as if Dante Gabriel were replacing him as shower and teller. Almost as strong is the sonnet on the *Concert Champêtre* in the Louvre (then thought to be by Giorgione alone), a poem on which Pater so obviously drew for his celebrated meditation on the same painting in *The Renaissance*. But whether giving readings of pictures by Botticelli, Mantegna, Memling, Ingres, or Burne-Jones, or even some unspecified words on a windowpane, Rossetti's questioning gaze into the depths of art pierces always through to the heart of life.

CHAPTER FOURTEEN

The Poetry of Nonsense: Carroll's Quest Romance

A good bit has been written, some of it nonsense, about what Lewis Carroll designated—using the word in a rather different sense—his "nonsense" verse. I have in mind a range of views: those that accept at face value whimsy's claims for its own inherent frivolity; topical assaults on the puzzles of referentiality (to which Dodgson's contemporaries contributed); to recently fashionable positions, for example, Michael Holquist "What Is a Boojum? Nonsense and Modernism" (reprinted in the Norton Critical Edition of *Alice in Wonderland,* edited by Donald J. Gray; hereafter called Gray.) Since it seems to hold that the arbitrariness of linguistic meaning governs even sense, this essay's claims that the Snark is about nothing would either mean that it could be no less profoundly referential than any poem, or that the critic was at one with the naive reader of childhood whimsy. It should be clear that I do not include Elizabeth Sewell's *Field of Nonsense* in these objections, although remaining unhappy with its rhetorical scope. "The game of nonsense," as Sewell called it, is played, in *The Hunting of the Snark,* for very high stakes, even if the frame of the game insists that it is only penny-ante. It is not only a matter of quips and quibbles stuttered out frantically at the edge of the abyss, for the kind of criticism of Carroll loosely called Freudian is of limited value. But in that regard, one thing is certain: the major writers of the nineteenth century who wrote for the Muse of Childhood (Andersen, Carroll, Lear) all shared some sexual anomaly, a powerful apparatus of verbal repression, and, more important, a *poesis* that allowed the return of the repressed to blossom in wit and phantasmagoria.

It is hard to think of a writer so obsessed with the purity of discourse, and harder to find a better example—outside of actual dream work itself—of a text that so energetically discloses what the primary discourse of daily life struggles so to conceal. But we tend to forget that the originality of *The Interpretation of Dreams* lay not so much in its consequences for literary interpretation—the enabling of criticism to treat poems as if they were as personal, private, and obsessively coded as dreams—but in its discovery that dreams were as powerfully and obsessively organized, and as serious in their mimesis, as poems. Some of this has been discussed earlier (chap. 5); I want to add here that I feel the literary form of modern dreaming to be romance, rather than lyric or dramatic. The medieval convention of the dream vision, perhaps obliquely related to the narrative text in some book that the dreamer has abandoned, in falling asleep, for more weighty and original matter, gives way in poetic history to the intricately allusive, spatially oriented, transumptive structure of Renaissance romantic fable. But it is *The Faerie Queene* that is more dreamlike, in this tougher, Freudian sense of being overdetermined, than dream vision.

William Empson correctly observed (in his sage and serious "Child as Swain" in Gray) that *Alice in Wonderland* was more of a dream vision (with its concentration on the dreamer, her falls and changes of size, and the kinds of situation she encounters, at which the way in which she is behaving is usually at issue) than *Through the Looking-Glass.* (On the related issues of pastoral and romance, we may not actually differ; in English, Sidney and Spenser allowed the second of these modes to contain the first.) The latter has more the form of a romance, which relates it to *The Hunting of the Snark* (aside from the question of Carroll's association of that poem with "Jabberwocky," of which more later). This is not only because it has a quest story (ephebe-pawn to move through chessboard squares to be queened), nor because its episodes are mapped by its scheme, while its actual regions and places are more allusively allegorical than most of those in *Alice in Wonderland,* etc. *Through the Looking-Glass* also has an allusive relation to the earlier book. For example, Hatta and Haigha, the "Anglo-Saxon messengers" in chapter 7, are metamorphoses of the Mad Hatter and the March Hare (Tenniel's illustrations confirm this), although the narrative points only toward such associations as with Hengist and Horsa, say (and perhaps, as Harry Morgan Ayres suggested, with an Anglo-Saxon scholar named Haigh). The multiple allusiveness of the names and attributes of the characters in the second book is typical of dreams and of major romances like *The Faerie Queene.*

Similarly, the ways in which parody is employed in the two books are significant. In the first one, Alice continually finds herself subverting the education routines she is called upon by the adult creatures to perform. In the course of speaking a piece, she finds herself unwittingly parodying it, and the pieties of Isaac Watts come out full of nastiness, guile, and what Delmore Schwartz called "the scrimmage of appetite everywhere." (In the parody of "The Sluggard," the suppression, by reason of the Mock Turtle's interruption, of the final words— "But the panther received knife and fork with a growl, / And concluded the banquet by—" [inevitably—"eating the owl"] was clearly designed to be noticed by the amused children reading it.) But the inset verse in *Through the Looking-Glass* is generally more complex in its nature and in the role it plays in the narrative. Alice hears these poems and songs, rather than helplessly producing them, and the first of these, "Jabberwocky," remains a central subtext. The parodies here are of romantic poetry (Hood, Moore, Scott, and, of course, Wordsworth), the parodic modes ranging from univocal pastiche to revisionary satire so subtle and deep as to approach true poetry on its own, in a mode of the ridiculous sublime. Thus, in the White Knight's song (so framed by titles and metatitles that we should simply call it that), the remarkable conclusion goes beyond the mere parody of "Resolution and Independence" of its earlier published version. As the song of the absent-minded, poetical White Knight, whose access to the truth about his own originality is characteristically blocked (the tune of the song is *not* his "own invention," as Alice observes), its conclusion does a great turn on Wordsworthian involuntary memory generally:

And now if e'er by chance I put
  My fingers into glue,
Or madly squeeze a right-hand foot
  Into a left-hand shoe,
Or if I drop upon my toe
  A very heavy weight,
I weep, for it reminds me so
Of that old man I used to know—

The "for" in "I weep, *for* it reminds me so" is brilliant here, in that the joke about present and absent feeling aside, it does indeed lead to a catalogue of recollections, totally absent from the 1856 version of the parody reprinted in Gray.

Whose look was mild, whose speech was slow,
Whose hair was whiter than the snow,
Whose face was very like a crow,
With eyes, like cinders, all aglow,
Who seemed distracted with his woe,
Who rocked his body to and fro,
And muttered mumblingly and low,
As if his mouth were full of dough,
Who snorted like a buffalo—
That summer evening, long ago,
  A-sitting on a gate.

The White Knight seems never less ridiculous than when, in bidding Alice farewell on her last crossing into the square of the end of her quest and hearing that she has liked the song, replies "I hope so" (doubtfully), and "but you didn't cry so much as I thought you would." Just as it requires the larger genre of comedy to contain within its world a satirist, so it requires the realm of romance to contain within it a poet.

Alice in Wonderland does indeed occasionally move into the allusive mode of romance, for example, in the scene in chapter 8 in which Alice, finally reaching her longed-for garden, finds it full of English history. The gardeners painting the white roses red are enacting a child's confusion about Yorkist and Lancastrian roses succeeding each other; the gardeners seem to have wandered in from *Richard II* (act 3, scene 4); and the Queen of Hearts, whose garden it is, eventually appears as a sort of Bloody Mary, ordering beheadings left and right. In *Through the Looking-Glass,* the transformed topoi are more evocatively shadowed. The wandering wood or forest of Error in *The Faerie Queene* (book 1, canto 1) is the place where a lady and a lion roam, and where you can lose your moral way. Its avatar is the wood behind Ludlow Castle, in Shropshire, as it is figured in the dangerous forest in *Comus,* through which another virginal Alice (Alice Egerton, masquing the Lady) must be safely conducted. The wood where everything and every person loses its name is a strangely redeemed version of these forests, in that because of its dislocations and crises of identity, what may be a unique event in the two *Alice* books is enabled. Physical contact between Alice and the other personages and creatures is usually unpleasant or at least inconvenient. But as Alice moves through the wood with the Fawn she has encountered there, and who has forgotten its nature along with its name, a familiar emblem (Lady with Lion—Lady with Unicorn) takes on another aspect: "So they walked on together through the wood, Alice with her arms clasped lovingly around the soft neck of the Fawn, till they came out into another open field, and here the Fawn gave a sudden bound into the air, and shook itself free from Alice's arm." In a sudden burst of returning knowledge, Alice loses her "dear little fellow-traveller," and the sole moment of affectionate and gratifying touching in her two fictional worlds (aside from the contact between girl and kitten in the outer frame of the looking-glass realm) comes to an end. In the episode preceding her arrival in the forest of anonymity, the gentleman sitting opposite Alice in the railway carriage is dressed in white paper, which is certainly an allusion to official parliamentary documents (and thus may have provided the cue for Tenniel's caricature of Disraeli in his illustration of the scene). This scene partakes of the bungled history lesson in the Queen of Hearts' garden, but the episode of the wood feels far more like high romantic fable.

The looking-glass world is generally more mythopoetically active than what is down the rabbit hole. In *Alice in Wonderland* creatures from phrase and fable, sometimes with topical allusiveness to the court of Dodgsonian girls, share epistemological status with natural ones; and save for the baby who becomes a pig (having had its animal nature totally elicited by too much rubifacient and erotic pepper), it is Alice who metamorphoses, at least in size, and thereby in condition. The one exemplary instance of the generation of what a modern nominalist like W. V. Quine (who once remarked that he didn't want anything more in his philosophy than there were in heaven and earth) would call a "queer entity" is itself almost didactic and occurs in a scene of instruction. The Gryphon in chapter 9 is a creature of classical mythology and medieval heraldry, and his companion, the Mock Turtle, is created not by the poetic magic of "nonsense" or of allusive revision, not puns or anagrams, but by an otherwise fruitless algebraic mistake. The elementary error of misplacing parentheses is demonstrated as if in some invalid enthymeme: There is mock turtle soup; therefore there are mock turtles (from which the soup is presumably made). But the error is one of confusing what is, logically, "mock (turtle soup)"—which is what the name means—with "(mock turtle) soup." (This lesson is taught again in *Sylvie and Bruno Concluded,* when Bruno, counting pigs in a field, announces that there are "about a thousand and four"; when instructed in the notion of rounding out he protests that there are about a thousand spread over the field and four "here by the window," and that it was only the four that he could be "sure about." Again, misplaced parentheses: [about a thousand] and [four] vs. [about] [a thousand and four].) Perhaps the most profound antithetical joke about the education of Victorian girlhood made in the Mock Turtle's account of his school under the sea is the apparently trivial one about the Gryphon's (not, appropriately, the Mock Turtle's) Classical master, "an old crab," who taught "Laughing and Grief." The joke is not merely the superficial pun on "Latin and Greek," nor the more interesting allusion to Comedy and Tragedy, but instead lies in the matter of expressions of emotion being "taught" or conventionalized. One can imagine Dodgson's great ambivalence with respect to this; it is at once anti-Darwinian in one sense and a triumph of nurture over nature, and at the same time sounds a menacing note to the effect that the giggles and tears of the beloved Muse-children might have been acquired contrivances—an almost Blakean notion.

But in the second book, the mythopoetic imagination is always more deeply at work. There is the matter of memory and secondariness, which I touched on earlier. *Through the Looking-Glass* in fact remembers and transforms elements in the first book (the middle-class Gryphon and Mock Turtle, beside the sea, are replaced by the working-class Carpenter and Walrus by the seaside in Tweedledee's ballad, for example). Chess has provided an allegorical milieu since the Middle Ages, and the child as pawn in the adult world of strategy, progressing by direct degrees to an adult role herself, is a more complex romance protagonist than a dreamer shuffled among cards. And finally, the matter of language itself is constantly foregrounded in the looking-glass world, with much more being made of the relation of names to things, and, even more central, in the theory of the "portmanteau word" in Humpty Dumpty's scholia on "Jabberwocky," which applies to the whole history of modern romance, from the nature of naming in *The Faerie Queene* to the very fabric of *Finnegans Wake*, not to speak of the hieroglyphic language of half-concealing, half-disclosing Freudian dream work.

And yet we tend to forget, I think, that Humpty Dumpty's explication of the miniature quest-romance of "Jabberwocky," bringing reason to rhyme as it does, represents nonetheless one of the many sorts of deflection or evasion with which Carroll frames so much of his "nonsense" verse. When she first deciphers the mirror writing of the text of the ballad in the first chapter, Alice observes that "it seems very pretty . . . but it's *rather* hard to understand." This might apply to much poetry. But she concludes, "however, *somebody* killed *something:* that's clear, at any rate—." Yes, somebody killed something, and this is precisely what Humpty Dumpty, in his pursuit of etymological glosses, neglects to observe. "Jabberwocky" is a great heroic tale, and the son, the "he" of the poem, is one with the tribe of Cadmus and Beowulf and Siegfried and Redcrosse, and his song of sallying forth, preparatory meditation, conquest, and triumphal return is framed in the identical stanza of prologue and epilogue, a cluster of stage set details that Humpty Dumpty (who "can explain all the poems that ever were invented—and a good many that haven't been invented just yet"—he is some kind of generative grammarian) so memorably annotates. But Alice's initial response remains absolutely central, and Humpty Dumpty's philology averts its gaze from what she knows.

Carroll's other quest romances in verse, such as the Pig-Tale in *Sylvie and Bruno*, likewise seek to deflect attention from their mode of conditional heroism, but in different ways. The pig who "made his moan . . . Because he could not jump" sits alone "Beside a ruined Pump" in a scene of picturesque melancholy (even "made his moan" is a Spenserian-Keatsian locution); he comes to grief when he mistakes the advice of a frog in the matter of athletic training, till "Uprose that pig and rushed, full whack, / Against the ruined Pump" (the stanza's last line adds: "It was a fatal jump!"). But there is no moral, and he is memorialized only by the frog (sitting "on the ruined Pump"), silent, because with the death of the pig, he would get no fee for his jumping lessons. But the refrainlike "ruined Pump," like the "A-sitting on a gate" of the White Knight's song, has the last, echoing word.

It was nominally Humpty Dumpty's theory of the portmanteau word and the linguistic allusions to "Jabberwocky" that caused Carroll to say in the preface to *The Hunting of the Snark* that it was "to some extent connected with the lay of the Jabberwock." I should, however, prefer to observe with Alice that, in the case of the bedeviled Argonauts of the *Snark, some people* went after *something:* that's clear at any rate. The realms of "nonsense" verse and child's dream world are alike for Carroll in legitimating high romance, and the nonsense verse elements in the unfolding of the quest of the Snark are a necessary part of its *poesis.* Nonsense verse deflects attention from its sense by pretending to be silly, even though the maker of it may be as sincere in this pretense as the dreamer is in an intention to sleep on undisturbed by anything meaningful. The method in the madness need not call for an uncovering of repressed material alone. In *Sylvie and Bruno,* the mad gardener's song that runs throughout is sometimes keyed to the narrative in a variety of ways (passing figures in a stanza of the song—like the Elephant that practiced on a fife—are actualized in the story, for example). But the paradigmatic structure of the stanzas—"He thought he saw X; He looked again and saw it was Y; 'Z', he said"—suggests that "Z" is a response only to Y. But often it applies to both. Thus:

He thought he saw a Rattlesnake
  That questioned him in Greek:
He looked again, and saw it was
  The Middle of Next Week.
"The one thing I regret," he said
  "Is that it cannot speak!"

A Hermetic serpent asking sphinxlike questions about the future metamorphoses into a prophesiable future, but the serpent is no oracle. What is regrettable is that the Middle of Next Week cannot speak now (only, as it were, *then*) and the Rattlesnake will not speak answers, at any rate, which amounts to much the same thing. Even frightening portents seldom deliver true prophecy, save by the most twisted and figurative of readings.

Behind the nonsense of *The Hunting of the Snark,* then, lies its serious quest story. W. H. Auden, both in *The Enchafèd Flood* and in a series of lectures on the Quest in literature, included the voyages of the Snark hunters and Edward Lear's *Jumblies* among the company of *Moby-Dick* and "The Narrative of A. Gordon Pym," and by calling attention to its generality he did something useful in combatting misplaced literalisms among interpreters. Of the history of detailed readings of the poem, I should say that F. C. S. Schiller's celebrated parodic commentary of 1901 (originally in a parody issue of *Mind* and reprinted in its entirety in Martin Gardner's *Annotated Snark*) remains the best, not because the Snark is read jokingly as a Hegelian Absolute, which at least outjokes whimsy into something nearer the truth than "nonsense," but because some of its mock glosses of particular stanzas are better and more memorable than solemn ones might be. Just as some sort of Borgesian fiction about, say, a

Shakespearean crux may ring truer than a serious, half-reasonably grounded scholarly "suggestion," so (of a resonant stanza—fit 4, st. 5):

I said it in Hebrew—I said it in Dutch—
  I said it in German and Greek;
But I wholly forgot (and it vexes me much)
  That English is what you speak!

"The accounts of the Absolute in German and Greek are famous, while the Hebrew and Dutch probably both refer to Spinoza, who was a Dutch Jew, although he wrote in bad Latin. The forgetting to speak (and write) English is a common symptom of the Absolute." Leaving aside the matter of these being the Baker's lines to the Bellman, and the "it" being his metaphysical vulnerability to Boojums, totally transcended *(aufgehoben)*, Schiller's gloss nonetheless, like those of Humpty Dumpty or of Bentley on Milton, points to a real question of why just *those* languages, and not the more usual French or Latin, for example. And in general, thinking in fact of the Snark as a Black Hole of mystification, some Greco-German Absolute, will let one do better with the rest of the poem than most suggestions will.

But if one is to read cues as clues, the canonical one, repeated six times, is certainly there. Once it has been introduced by the Baker's uncle, and reiterated by the Bellman, the famous stanza heads all of the last four fits:

They sought it with thimbles, they sought it with care;
  They pursued it with forks and hope;
They threatened its life with a railway-share;
  They charmed it with smiles and soap.

I suppose I should say right off that the "it" of these lines is probably something less than the Absolute, but has been magnified by neurotic terror into something that, for the quest story, will do as well. Female sexuality—a distorted version of *das Ewig-Weibliche,* the "eternal feminine" of *Faust* for a spirit that remained blocked by the sexuality—seems to be the point here. (This was the view of W. H. Auden, advanced in conversation about thirty years ago, and without reference to or discussion of the relevant passages.) Thimbles, care (the effect of the whimsical zeugma here and in the next line is only momentarily to deflect attention away from the concrete entities of care and hope employed in the hunt); forks, hope: the domestic objects and the inner states marshalled in a kind of courtship. The world of the broker is alien and intrusive in that of the Victorian *gynacaeum.* The smiles and soap make amends for this. The fear of the less than erotically secure of being "softly and suddenly" swallowed up in an abyss of femininity is materialized in the last glimpse of the unnamable Baker:

They beheld him—their Baker—their hero unnamed
    On the top of a neighboring crag,

Erect and sublime, for one moment of time.
    In the next, that wild figure they saw
(As if stung by a spasm) plunge into a chasm,
    While they waited and listened in awe.

fit 8, sts. 4–5

The name of the Snark—Carroll himself suggested the portmanteau snail + shark—is full of suggestions of snarling and snagging, as in the stanza commencing with the magnificent line (consider the final word)

Then the bowsprit got mixed with the rudder sometimes
    A thing, as the Bellman remarked,
That frequently happens in tropical climes,
    When a vessel is, so to speak, "snarked."

fit 2, st. 7

—but here the sense is of a vessel spooked as well. If the Snark is indeed like a viscous mollusk with teeth in it, however, it is also like a snake in the dark. "Just the place for a Snark" is the voyager's paradise of land where, quite properly for quest-romance, the poem starts in the middle of the journey.

But even the Bellman's instructions in the second fit (stanzas 15–20), and his recitation of the "five unmistakable marks" by which a Snark may be known are significant about femininity. Snarks taste "meagre and hollow, but crisp: / Like a coat that is rather too tight in the waist, / With a flavour of Will-o-the-Wisp." Snarks get up too late, don't get jokes nor tolerate puns, are fond of bathing machines, and are (and here Dodgson would least like to think about what Carroll is writing) ambitious. And some are Boojums, at which the Baker faints to end the fit. I find it interesting that the third fit immediately thereafter commences with a stanza that heralds the repeated clue-quatrain in its perfect syntactic paradigm:

They roused him with muffins—they roused him with ice—
    They roused him with mustard and cress—
They roused him with jam and judicious advice—
    They set him conundrums to guess.

fit 3, st. 1

The alliterative jam and just counsel in the third line seem to anticipate the "Little birds are feeding / Justices with jam" in the introductory verses to the Pig-Tale in *Sylvie and Bruno Concluded*. In any event, twice more (in fits 4 and

5) is the syntactic paradigm repeated, hammering it into consciousness in the poem—if not into truth—by its own "rule of three." The most significant repetitions in the poem are those of the alliterating B's of the ten voyagers, all bachelors, whose chart of the sea is "a perfect and absolute blank" and who are doomed, in pursuing the strange Snark, to encounter in it the more horribly alliteratively *heimlich* Boojum after all. (In the digressive episodes, the Banker is maddened by the Bandersnatch, but the Jubjub bird, also imported from "Jabberwocky," is a highly moral, although desperate and passionate, creature, the contemplation of which leads to a benign scene of instruction and a consequent friendship between Butcher and Beaver.

Yet it is ultimately the Bellman and the Baker who matter most. The former, having something of the "drowzy charm" of Milton's Bellman in *Il Penseroso* (from which Carroll quotes in his preface), is one of the poet's surrogates in the poem; the Baker, with his forgotten name and abandoned forty-two parcels (the years of Dodgson's life—I am sure that a scholarly conjecture is right in this), is more clearly the major one (see *The Annotated Snark*). With such a central protagonist vanished, there is nothing more of the poem to be said. Carroll's continued insistence that the whole poem started with the *vers donné* of the last line— "For the Snark was a Boojum, you see"—may be a little like Poe's account of the composition of "The Raven" in what it directs attention away from. Certainly the Baker's fear is as much a driving force in the poem's workings as the Bellman's questing, but neither Captain Ahab nor Coleridge's Mariner seem pertinent here, insofar as character and motivation are concerned. And yet, in the end, the Hunting of the Snark, the quest itself, is seen to have had the power of character and motive that even its central characters do not. And it remains one of the major quests of our romantic literature, having become part of our conceptual landscape. Whether we think of Spenser's Guyon, believing he knows what the Bower of Bliss really is as he sets out to destroy it, or of a sleuth in any modern detective story, every Snark—and here I should rather put the question of engulfment aside, and return to the joked-about Absolute—will always turn out to have been a sort of Boojum. The line that came into Carroll's head, and that required the whole verse romance to give it meaning, ends up by having become true, true of all our stories and of, alas, all our lives. Which is what real nonsense is for.

CHAPTER FIFTEEN

A Poem Lost and Found:
Jean Ingelow's Successful "Failure"

Literary discoveries can be of two sorts. Manuscripts or lost books can turn up in attics or cellars. Christopher Smart's *Jubilate Agno,* written in an insane asylum during the years surrounding 1760, "turned up" to be published first in 1939; this great poem would probably have been preserved originally as primitive psychiatric data and only entered literary history at a time when modernist poetic theory could tolerate an ode of such revolutionary form and so learned and ecstatic a texture.

Often, interesting texts lie buried not in trunks of old papers but in once-popular books, thousands of copies of which may survive on secondhand shelves. In this instance, the same sorts of shifts of taste that consigned them to oblivion, now working in another direction, bring them to light. In general, modernist literary criticism tended to prefer a minor seventeenth-century poet to a minor Victorian one; only in the past decade and a half have the central concerns of the most sophisticated poetic criticism been absorbed with the nineteenth century in England. And in this revisionary light, some lost masterpieces will likely be recovered. While doing some reading on Victorian children's books, I recently came across a startlingly moving poem by a once-famous poet whom I had only previously known in college as a clutterer-up (along with copies of Stephen Phillips's *Marpessa* and Owen Meredith's *Lucille*) of the poetry sections of Fourth Avenue bookshops. This find had lain hidden not in an attic, but in a darkened reputation.

Jean Ingelow provides an unusual instance of one of those blocked poetic imaginations of the nineteenth century upon which the Muse of Childhood smiled for a moment. Born in Boston, Lincolnshire, in 1820, she lived there, then in Ipswich, and, from 1863 until her death in 1897, in London. She was a famed poet; her various volumes of verse sold upward of two hundred thousand copies in the United States alone, and her "High Tide on the Coast of Lincolnshire," a historical effusion concerning the year 1571, was a huge success. It is generally in the mode of historical ballad popularized a decade or so earlier by Longfellow and, earlier still, by Felicia Hemans, save that it is tricked out with occasional Chattertonian archaic spellings and forms. The poem's virtue among Ingelow's other verse may have been that it was relatively short (280-odd lines—her poems tend to run into the low thousands), and its concluding lines, in which the narrator recalls in reprise the call of his wife, drowned in the flooding tide, to her cattle, must have had the same kind of réclame in their day as the opening of Ginsberg's "Howl" in recent decades:

Quit your pipes of parsley hollow,
  Hollow, hollow;
Come uppe Lightfoot, rise and follow;
  Lightfoot, Whitefoot,
From your clovers lift the head;
Come uppe, Jetty, follow, follow,
Jetty to the milking shed.

This mode is not for us, although a version of it is still ubiquitous in ironic-sentimental closures of cheap TV films, etc. In all the rest of Ingelow's verse, the only lines we could read with acknowledgment of more than trivial competence are here and there in a few sonnets (whose narrow room often concentrates the versifier's deeper attention), such as at the conclusion of a meditation upon "An Ancient Chess King":

    Thy masters are all dead;
  My heart is full of ruth and yearning pain
At sight of thee; O king thou hast a crown
  Outlasting theirs, and tell'st of greatness fled
Through cloud-hung nights of unabated rain
And murmurs of the dark majestic town.

Perhaps one might also note the use of the refrain, slightly modulating, through the eight stanzas of "A Winter Song," in which a mother tells of the death of her husband on a winter night:

  Came the dread Archer up yonder lawn—
  Night is the time for the old to die—
But woe for an arrow that smote the fawn,
  When the hind that was sick unscathe went by

—and awaiting the return of her fallen, or at least prodigal, daughter for a final paternal blessing. The father dies, the girl doesn't show up, the mother searches for her in the woods and, in the last stanza,

By night I found her when pent waves steal
  (Night is the time when the old should die),
But she lay stiff by the locked mill-wheel,
  And the old stars lived in their homes on high.

Ingelow was put forward for the Laureateship on the death of Tennyson in 1892, and at first glance she might appear to have been the one candidate over whom the appointment of the ridiculous Alfred Austin might have seemed appropriate. But it is almost impossible to believe that the latter produced a poem as good as one that the occasion of Miss Ingelow's fairy tale elicited. *Mopsa the Fairy* appeared in 1869, four years after *Alice in Wonderland* (whose fantasies of change of scale and birth it seems to echo) and three years before *Through the Looking Glass* (whose queening of the fairy pawn or young initiate and final banquet scene it seems to anticipate). It is remarkable for the structure of its quest romance and the realm through which its mortal hero, Jack, and his fairy child, Mopsa (marsupially carried in his pocket until she reaches her first stage of growth), travel. The particular Fairyland in question is surrounded by contingently actual regions of moral significance; misused boats are redeemed for use in visionary journeys (there is something of Shelley's *Alastor* here), and bickering washerwomen, clockwork automata of a satiric cast, etc., all keep the realm of moralizing on the borders of Fairyland itself. It is only there that "Whatever you *can* do you *may* do" (as in all the classical and postclassical treatments of the Golden Age), and where no questions may be asked about what lies behind phenomena (as Milton's Raphael cautioned Adam against asking).

But the most remarkable presence is that of the Apple-woman, a surrogate for the poet herself. In Fairyland, she is "the woman whom they love because she can make them cry," a mortal who has been trapped in the imaginative realm because she chose as an adult to wander into it. In the book, she sings all the songs that Miss Ingelow composed for the story, largely echoing Scott or Burns. The following, for example, is excellent Burns ("a laverock on the lift" = a lark in the air):

It's we two, it's we two, it's we two for ay,
All the world and we two, and Heaven be our stay.
Like a laverock in the lift, sing, O bonny bride!
All the world was Adam once, with Eve by his side.

Miss Ingelow's mother was Scots, and the songs the Apple-woman sings are those of a poetical nurse. It is only at the end of their journey through Fairyland that Jack and his Mopsa, now a queen, can absorb the poetic functions of the now-departed older woman; Mopsa, blindfolded and in the terrifying presence of Jack's fairy Double, tells a tale of origins and ancient faults and exile in the language of the parables of the Gospels. Jack is allowed the poetic achievement of the Tennysonian:

One morning, oh! so early, my beloved, my beloved,
All the birds were singing blithely, as if never would they
      cease;
"Twas a thrush sang in my garden, "Hear the story, hear the
      story!"
   And the lark sang, "Give us glory!"
   And the dove said, "Give us peace!"

at which we are given the very Red Queen-like interjection: "What the dove really said was, no doubt, 'Give us peas.' All kinds of doves and pigeons are very fond of peas").

It is the verse epigraph to the last chapter of the story, "Failure," however, which gives us some clue to what Jean Ingelow was about in *Mopsa*. This is the astonishing poem I mentioned earlier, a post-Keatsian sonnet about Orpheus and Eurydice that evokes both Jack's loss of Mopsa to the Pluto of his own fairy Double, and the eternal sorrows of poetical belatedness. It seems to me to be one of the finest short poems of its time:

We are much bound to them that do succeed;
  But, in a more pathetic sense, are bound
  To such as fail. They all our loss expound;
They comfort us for work that will not speed,
And life—itself a failure. Ay, his deed,
  Sweetest in story, who the dusk profound
  Of Hades flooded with entrancing sound,
Music's own tears, was failure. Doth it read
Therefore the worse? Ah no! So much to dare,
  He fronts the regnant Darkness on its throne.—
So much to do; impetuous even there,
  He pours out love's disconsolate sweet moan—
He wins; but few for that his deed recall;
Its power is in the look which costs him all.

The direct echo ("sweet moan") of Keats, the extremely Keatsian adaptation of Milton's syntax in lines five through eight, the possible allusion to Smart's *Song to David* in the "dare" and "do," are all most rich. But the overall sense of quest romance as the quest of, for, and by poets is most remarkable in its application to *Mopsa the Fairy*. It was Jack's kiss that allowed Mopsa to grow into queenly size; she returns his kiss to him, and him to Nature, at the end of the tale. The "failure" of the sonnet and of the chapter title is that of all such poetic quests. Its corresponding success lies in the way in which it has prepared the mortal traveler for the privileged life that lies beyond the mere fact of his return.

Mopsa the Fairy would be a remarkable book even if it had not occasioned what is surely one of the major lost poems of the nineteenth century. The fact that it did so is one more instance of the anomalies of what Harold Bloom called poetic influence. It is only in writing about herself as the poetic ephebe Jack that Jean Ingelow could recover a Keatsian power upon which she never can manage to draw in verses elsewhere. Her mythology of Fairyland is a poetically enabling one; it is only part of the Orphean failure that most commentators upon it have failed to see how serious the poet was.

CHAPTER SIXTEEN

Meredith's Poetry

"He was one of those whose wit can shake / And riddle to the very core / The counterfeits that Time will break." When George Meredith died in 1909, these lines of Thomas Hardy honored the departed writer as a satirist of circumstance, like the living one who thus praised him. They certainly appear to apply at first to Meredith the novelist, and to his theory and practice of social, institutional, and erotic comedy. But the author of such splendid ironic interweavings as *Beauchamp's Career, The Egoist,* and *The Ordeal of Richard Feverel* — knotty as their prose and their sensibility have seemed to the modernist temperament, which has often preferred the moral macramé of farce — began writing as a poet, and continued to do so throughout his life. But unlike Hardy, whose poetic career took over after the end of his novelistic one, Meredith's books of poems were intermittent, and between 1862, when the volume containing the magnificent ironic sonnet sequence *Modern Love* appeared, and the *Poems and Lyrics of the Joy of Earth* of 1883, there were no published volumes of verse. Meredith cared more, by the mid-1880s, to be praised for his poems than his prose. Rossetti and Swinburne, with whom Meredith at his best can be on a par, both admired his poems and seem, as most reviewers never did, to have grasped their power.

Meredith is even more problematic — although perhaps even better — as a poet than as a novelist. He is best known for a number of poems, including the splendid and heavily anthologized sonnet, "Lucifer in Starlight," the resonance of whose final line, "The army of unalterable law," seems to come from oscillations between two senses of its figure (is the army in the service of or peopled by momentarily personified elements of "unalterable law"? Also see p. 99, above in "Of *of*"). Then there is the beautiful Theocritean idyll, "Love in the Valley," with its surging trochaic lines (but very free with extra unstressed syllables) alternating with a *dum* da da da *dum* da da da *dum* da da da *dum*—and yet so wonderfully varied in the different syntactic and rhetorical patterns disposed among them. Thus the opening stanza

Under yonder beech-tree single on the green-sward
  Couched with her arms behind her golden head,
Knees and tresses folded to slip and ripple idly,
  Lies my young love sleeping in the shade.
Had I the heart to slide an arm beneath her,
  Press her parting lips as her waist I gather slow,
Waking in amazement she could but not embrace me:
  Then would she hold me and never let me go?

and, later on,

This may I know: her dressing and undressing
  Such a change of light shows as when the skies in sport
Shift from cloud to moonlight; or edging into thunder
  Slips a ray of sun; or sweeping into port
White sails furl; or on the ocean borders
  White sails lean along the waves leaping green.
Visions of her shower before me, but from eyesight
  Guarded she would be like the sun were she seen.

The inexorable, purely accentual four-beat rhythms, the pastoral delight in the air of continuing erotic promise, the profusion of pictorial moments, all combine in a poem that is simply gorgeous.

"Modern Love" is a celebrated masterpiece, a thorough ironic revision of the Renaissance sonnet sequence through "Conception of a newly added chord"—two extra lines so as to make of the form a structure of four quatrains rhymed *abba*. Its milieu is a novelistic pattern of Husband (sometimes the speaker), Wife, Other Woman, Other Man, its outcome the dissolution of marriage. It even plays against traditionally invoked autobiography in forming the mythology of sonneteering (even as Rossetti would be doing it with his three female figures as versions of his own three women in *The House of Life*). Meredith's wife had run off with the painter Henry Wallis, the friend for whom Meredith had been the model in his famous "Death of Chatterton" some time before. The strong final poem closes with a heavily quoted affirmation of skepticism:

But they fed not on the advancing hours:
Their hearts held cravings for the buried day.
Then each applied to each that fatal knife,
Deep questioning, which probes to endless dole.
Ah, what a dusty answer gets the soul
When hot for certainties in this our life! —
In tragic hints here see what evermore
Moves dark as yonder midnight's ocean force,
Thundering like ramping hosts of warrior horse,
To throw that faint thin line upon the shore!

And it is instructive to compare the final image here with the one at the end of
the beautiful autumnal poem 17 ("We saw the swallows gathering in the sky"):

The pilgrims of the year waxed very loud
In multitudinous chatterings, as the flood
Full brown came from the West, and like pale blood
Expanded to the upper crimson cloud.
Love, that had robbed us of immortal things,
This little moment mercifully gave,
Where I have seen across the twilight wave
The swan sail with her young beneath her wings.

"The Woods of Westermain," too, is a great poem, but it has for the past fifty
years been read primarily by graduate students studying Victorian literature
who have had their attention called to the post-Darwinian *tristesse* of the clearing in the forest where "old-eyed oxen chew / Speculation with the cud" and
where the wanderer through the mythology of forests is urged to "Read their
pool of vision through, / Back to hours when mind was mud." G. M. Trevelyan,
in a not unpopular little book first published in 1906, was more appreciative
than many critics, but he muddled Meredith's poetry with what he took to be
his philosophy. Modernist taste was perhaps prefigured in Wilde's remark
(regarding the novels he admired so, but this applied to some of the verse as
well) about a style "quite sufficient of itself to keep life at a distance"; but Wilde
continued, "By its means he has planted round his garden a hedge full of thorns,
and red with wonderful roses."

A reassessment of Meredith's poetry is long overdue. One would have
thought that the strong feminism of "A Ballad of Fair Ladies in Revolt" would
have attracted more discussion, for example. Such fresh looks are frequently
occasioned by new texts. There has been no systematic edition of which I am
aware since 1911, although there was a selection edited by Trevelyan in 1955, and
a separate edition of "Modern Love" with a good commentary by C. Day Lewis

in 1948. Cecil Lang's selection in his generally excellent anthology called *The Pre-Raphaelites and Their Circle* (2d ed., 1975) has less of Meredith than one might have liked. Phyllis Bartlett's exhaustive two-volume edition, published by Yale University Press in 1978, came at a somewhat ironically appropriate time. The ongoing revision, in literary history and criticism, of the relation between English and American romanticism puts the problematic aspects of his poems—which his contemporaries had pretty much divided up between infelicities of style and awkwardness of thought—into a new light. It is not just that we can hear today the Wallace Stevens of "Le Monocle de Mon Oncle" in such lines as these (from "Modern Love," 37)—

A quiet company we pace, and wait
The dinner-bell in prae-digestive calm.
So sweet up violet banks the Southern balm
Breathes round, we care not if the bell be late:
Though here and there grey seniors question Time
In irritable coughings

or "Bands of her limpid primitives / Or patterned in the curious braid" (not to speak of the explicit echo of the title of Meredith's "Ballad of Past Meridian" in the later poem of middle-age love). It is not just that Robert Frost probably read Meredith as heavily as he did Rossetti, as we hear in the anticipations of "The Most of It" and "Never Again Would Birds' Song be the Same" in "but his lyric had a tone / As't were a forest-echo of her voice." In a Frostean reading of Meredith's own line "The Whither whose echo is Whence," we are in a better position today to see the antecedents of his major poetic strain, as well as to isolate that strain from some of the more confused rumblings and chirpings of the literature in verse—occasional poems, ballads, mythological idylls, and narratives—which, even more than his maddening syntax on occasion, put off the modern reader.

That strain is the voice of the poet "in deep woods / Between the two twilights" (but, we might add, heavily mindful of both of them). In his 1851 *Poems*, two early instances of Meredith's continuing reworking of the romantic image of the Aeolian harp of nature itself—the wind in the trees singing not merely its own white noise but the song of a figurative wind-harp—mark out the two directions in which his poetic oeuvre would develop. "Twilight Music" is a piece of minor Tennysoniana; "South-West Wind in the Woodland," in unrhymed tetrameters, anticipates the milieu of most of his finest verse, a sophisticatedly—and delicately—allegorical sylvan realm in which vision can attend the wedding of nature and consciousness. Much of his best poetry is by way of being epithalamion to that marriage, even as "Modern Love" sang the soured aubade for its imperfect human simulacrum ("But not till Nature's laws and man's are one, / Can marriage of the man and the woman be," he remarked elsewhere). The source of his wood notes, I believe we will come to see, is not so much in Tennyson and Browning, whom he elsewhere imitates, and rarely builds upon (the end of the sonnet on old age is an exception: "Yea, to spread light when thy proud letter I / Drops prone and void as any thoughtless dash" is splendid super-Browning).

It is Emerson. From specific echoes—such as the "We are the lords of life, and life is warm" of "Modern Love" 30, which becomes even more deeply ironic when read against its source in the verse epigraph to Emerson's "Experience"— to larger tonal influences, indeed, to the very way in which Meredith slips in and out of various ways of mythologizing nature is more like a governing tradition in American poetry than has, I think, ever been noticed. As a poet, he seems to feel most imaginatively healthy in a symbol of forests, as it were,

Here all say,
We serve her, even as I:
We brood, we strive to sky,
We gaze upon decay,
We wot of life through death,
How each feeds each we spy;
And is a tangle round,

I hear Emerson, too, in "The Lark Ascending," particularly in this fine passage:

Was never voice of ours could say
Our inmost in the sweetest way,
Like yonder voice aloft, and link
All hearers in the song they drink.
Our wisdom speaks from failing blood,
Our passion is too full in flood,
We want the key of his wild note
Of truthful in a tuneful throat,
The song seraphically free
Of taint of personality,
So pure that it salutes the suns
The voice of one for millions,
In whom the millions rejoice
For giving their one spirit voice.

And that previously thought "philosophical" (like Swinburne's "Hertha," I suppose) strange "Earth and Man," with its strangely patterned, often quite disjunct quatrains, seems haunted by Emerson too, not just in diction, as when talking of human consciousness' "fables of the Above" and "gapped readings of the crown and sword," but ("he" is Man and "she" Earth throughout)

And ever that old task
Of reading what he is and whence he came,
Wither to go, finds wilder letters flame
Across her mask
The thing that shudders most
Within him is the burden of his cry,
Seen of his dread, she is to his blank eye
The eyeless Ghost.

And the final stanza:

Meanwhile on him, her chief
Expression, her great word of life, looks she;
Twi-minded of him, as the waxing tree,
Or dated leaf.

All Meredith's poetry might be said to be of human nature, taken in two senses of the phrase: the nature of humanity and the humanized, interpreted presence of nature that surrounds, but is half-created by, consciousness. On the other hand, there is a major body of what is traditionally thought of as rural, rather than urban, observation—indeed, it is almost central to him. "The Woods of Westermain" and the lesser "Forest History" map out the field of imagery for this body of nature-poetry, which is filled out by such poems as "The Lark Ascending," "Tardy Spring," "Night of Frost in May," "Winter Heavens," "Dirge in Woods," "Hard Weather," "The Thrush in February," "Woodman and Echo," "Seed Time," the wonderful "Meditation under Stars," the strangely Emersonian "Hymn to Colour," and "Woodland Peace," among others. In characterizing Dante Gabriel Rossetti's poetry in "A Later Alexandrian," Meredith beautifully drew the boundaries of a region, full of shadows of Tennyson, which he would himself avoid: "The moon of cloud discoloured was his Muse, / His pipe the reed of the old moaning waste." Meredith's strongest poetic activity would remain in what the title of his strongest single book was to call "a reading of earth."

The Yale edition of Meredith's poetry is exhaustive, primarily from a bibliographical viewpoint. The late Phyllis Bartlett, who died when the first galleys were being delivered, was primarily interested in gathering all the collected, uncollected, and unpublished poetry with as much information as possible about their occasions. One cannot tell what her critical concerns would have been; although the edition includes critical as well as textual notes (the latter more elaborate and apparently more complete), they are primarily historical glosses and indications of allusion, very rarely wrong (e.g., "hallali" in "Forest History" is not Meredith's own neologism—he has, indeed, many—but perfectly good misspelled German for the hunter's halloo at the death), often biographically useful. Among the lesser poems are some minor treasures—the Hardy-like "Martin's Puzzle," the strange "Jump-to-Glory Jane," which would read rather better as a Robert Frost blank verse treatment of Ludwig of Bavaria that Kingsley Amis might well have included in his *New Oxford Book of Light Verse,* a lot of very good translations from the German romantic lyric, the ironically feminist "Ballad of Fair Ladies in Revolt," and, among the unpublished notebook material, an occasional gem like this untitled quatrain: "I seize in a central knot, / I grasp in a spark of fire, / The circle of a thought, / The round of a desire."

This is primarily an edition for scholars and libraries, and I hope that a good selection from it might be made available soon. Meredith, Rossetti, and Swinburne are wonderful poets, whose imaginative power and moral force, as well as—particularly with the first two—influence on twentieth-century American poetry are only now beginning to be appreciated, perhaps as they could never really be by their contemporaries.

CHAPTER SEVENTEEN

"Far Space and Long Antiquity": Trumbull Stickney's Autumns

Trumbull Stickney died young, at thirty, in 1904, leaving behind him a largely ignored book of verse and some remarkable poems in manuscript. His work was kept alive, after his death, by other poets. The edition that his Harvard friends William Vaughan Moody and George Cabot Lodge, both poets themselves, prepared in 1905 was crucial. But the remarkably sensitive selection of his work by Conrad Aiken in successive versions of his Modern Library anthology of twentieth-century American poetry was also very important indeed. Aiken invoked him as "a forerunner" and as "the natural link between Emily Dickinson and the real twentieth-century 'thing.' " Edmund Wilson wrote a short but intense essay on him in 1940; but interestingly enough, it was in England, in 1968, that there first appeared a good collection of more than seventy of his poems, both published and from manuscript, four years before the only American text of his work.

Joseph Trumbull Stickney came from an expatriate New England family. Born in Geneva, he grew up, like someone in a Henry James story, in London, Italy, and Switzerland. He studied classics—and perhaps became romantically involved with an older woman—at Harvard (graduating six years before Wallace Stevens); he returned to France to study at the Sorbonne, where he took the first doctorate in Greek ever awarded to an American. The final year of his life was spent teaching Greek at Harvard and in suffering the physical pain of a brain tumor, from which he died the following spring. His Harvard was that of Santayana; his émigré Europe that of his friends Henry Adams and Bernard

Berenson. His poems—save for his verse drama *Prometheus Pyrphoros* and some dramatic fragments—all sonnets and strophic lyrics full of a revised romantic Hellenism and a formal sense stronger than their rhetoric, needed half-apologizing for under the strictures of modernism. But in the light of American poetry's coming to terms with its romantic origins in the later part of this century, his work appears more central than before.

Stickney's vision was transformed by the actual landscape of Greece, which he visited, for the only time, in the next-to-last summer of his life. The rugged Arcadian (not the Virgilian mythological Arcadia) mountain scenery, read through post-Wordsworthian filters, becomes for him a vision that cries out for meditation, in an ironically anti-Wordsworthian turn. Thus, for example, his fine poem on Mt. Lykaion (the great mountain in the northern Peloponessus sacred to Zeus as wolf) starts out with one kind of fiction—the columns and eagles he read about in Pausanias, the second-century A.D. historian (who himself, by the way, was reporting hearsay). But then it moves into another mode:

Alone on Lykaion since man hath been
Stand on the height two columns, where at rest
Two eagles hewn of gold sit looking East
Forever; and the sun goes up between.
Far down around the mountain's oval green
An order keeps the falling stones abreast.
Below within the chaos last and least
A river like a curl of light is seen.
Beyond the river lies the even sea,
Beyond the sea another ghost of sky,—
O God, support the sickness of my eye
Lest the far space and long antiquity
Suck out my heart, and on this awful ground
The great wind kill my little shell with sound.

The monumental columns (traces of "long antiquity") exist only in text; but in the eye's plain experience, the "far space," the nest of Emersonian circles—river, sea, sky—figures the dissolving limits of transcendence. And the combined voices of poetic past and physical present seem louder than can be borne. The eye's "sickness" here—that clouding of the eyeball's (again, Emersonian) transparency—brings an imaginative health, however, in poems like "Near Helicon," another of his late "Sonnets from Greece." Here the overpowering ghosts of Wordsworth and Keats, haunting the sonnet for Stickney as much as the mythology of the particular landscape he is contemplating haunts its visual presence for him, emerge in order in the sestet:

To me my troubled life doth now appear
Like scarce distinguishable summits hung
Around a blue horizon: places where
Not even a traveller purposeth to steer,—
Whereof a migrant bird in passing sung
And the girl closed her window not to hear.

(Helicon, sacred to Apollo, is the dancing place of the Muses, but the mythology is closed off in this poem by the actual landscape.)

Stickney never simply replays romantic motifs. He is always aware of how late he has come to Greece, to poetry, to—indeed—his own American imagination. Consider how he muses on the columns of the temple of Poseidon at Sunion, the end of the cape near Athens, built in propitiation of the god of the sea who lost out as patron to Athena, but whose powerful presence is attested to by all capes and small islands. (On one of these columns, incidentally, Byron carved his name, which can still be read.) But the figure Stickney makes of these columns partakes of the same sort of revision of the ubiquitous romantic trope of the Aeolian harp that haunted nineteenth-century German and American poetry. Starting with Coleridge's image of nature itself as "one organic harp, divinely framed," this can be traced through Emerson and Thoreau (who wrote constantly in his journals of his "telegraph harp"—the wind making a literal Aeolian harp out of telegraph wires) to Hart Crane's Brooklyn Bridge cables. In Stickney's "Sunium," the columns are played upon both by the hand of the wind and by light itself, even as the strength of the traditional image is in time consumed by the very poetic light—that of the sun, and thus Apollo's—that has played upon if for more than 150 years of metaphor:

These are the strings of the Aegean lyre
Across the sky and sea in glory hung;
Columns of white thro' which the wind has flung
The clouds and stars, and drawn the rain and fire.
Their flutings now to fill the notes' desire
Are strained and dubious, yet in music young
They cast their full-blown answer far along
To where in sea the island hills expire.
How bravely from the quarry's earthen gloom
In snow they rose amid the blue to stand
Melodious and alone on Sunium!
They shall not wither back into the land.
The sun that harps them with his golden hand
Doth slowly with his hand of gold consume.

The columns' "flutings" are both the vertical striations (in the term's architectural sense) and the musical sounds, now of wind and stirring mixed. The powerful and elegant chiasmus of the ending (harps—golden hand / hand of gold—consume) is by no means archaistically decorative, but itself sets up a momentary trope of reciprocity.

Nine years earlier, Stickney had merely copied Shelley's exhortation to the west wind ("Make me thy lyre, even as the forest it") in an untitled sonnet that also began with a direct quotation ("though inland far we be") from Wordsworth's "Immortality Ode":

Tho' inland far with mountains prisoned round
Oppressed beneath a space of heavy skies,
Yet hear I oft the far-off water-cries
And vast vague voices which the winds confound.
While as a harp I sing, touched with the sound
Most secret to its soul, the visions rise
In stately dream.

And yet only a year after this, at the age of twenty-one, he can undo another romantic myth—of the seashell as a sort of ear-mouth that speaks prophetically of the sea. (Wordsworth and Landor had quarreled over which of them had first introduced it to poetry.) Yeats had, a decade before Stickney's poems, invoked this commonplace in "Go gather by the humming sea / Some twisted echo-harboring shell"; thirty years later, Hart Crane would invigorate it in "As steadily as a shell secretes / Its beating leagues of monotone." It is almost as if, in "On Some Shells Found Inland," the young Stickney were lamenting, not just their distance from the Yeatsian humming sea, but their meaningless status as relics of romantic poetry:

These are my murmur-laden shells that keep
A fresh voice tho' the years be very gray.
The wave that washed their lips and tuned their lay
Is gone, gone with the faded ocean sweep,
The royal tide, gray ebb, and sunken neap
And purple midday,—gone! To this hot clay
Must sing my shells, where yet the primal day,
Its roar and rhythm and splendour will not sleep.
What hand shall join them to their proper sea
If all be gone? Shall they forever feel
Glories undone and worlds that cannot be?—
'Twere mercy to stamp out this agèd wrong,
Dash them to earth and crunch them with the heel
And make a dust of their seraphic song.

But these are not the speaking shells that the poet has himself borne inland. They engage a recapitulation of the eighteenth-century geological speculations occasioned by thinking about seashells on inland mountain tops, which had such profound later repercussions for nineteenth-century religious thought about the literal historicity of the bible. For Stickney, the shells were emblems of poetic figuration that must be reconstituted, but he had not yet realized that the dust into which they are ground in despair must become part of a limestone, as it were, from which new emblems and new figurations can be carved.

The poems he wrote upon finally seeing the Greek landscape, which had been the stuff of literature for him theretofore—poetic, and minutely scholarly text—keep breaking out into supplication. Like the last lines of the poem on Mt. Lykaion, they ask for imaginative strength with which to cope with the relations between what he sees, has read, has heard, and both knows he feels and feels he knows. At the end of the first of three sonnets on Mt. Ida, his prayer to the sacred place asking for poetic power is couched in terms hardly neoclassical, but in those of American romantic Hellenism that in some ways parallels his friend Henry Adams's gothicism:

O Ida, snowy bride that God espoused
Unto that day that never wholly is,
Whiten thou the horizon of my eyes,
That when the momentary sea aroused
Flows up in earthquake, still thou mayest rise
Sacred above the quivering Cyclades.

To "whiten the horizon" of his vision—is this to "widen" it? or to narrow its focus for greater concentration? The grandeur of Hölderlin's earlier construction of Greece involved complex religious displacements and transfers of belief. For Stickney, the matters of poetry, of work and *métier* (his classical scholarship), and of a first glimpse that is in itself a complex re-vision, all add density to his American fascination with the meaning of landscape.

As Edmund Wilson indicated in his essay, the elegantly strong closure of sonnets like the one just quoted was characteristic and could tighten up the language at the end of the poem to a pitch that even a modernist taste could acknowledge. Thus the image of Delos (the central island of the Cyclades invoked above) emerges exuberantly in the last line of an untitled sonnet that starts out portentously (watered-down Pater? watered-down Nietzsche?), moves through the beautiful image of the rainbow of promise broken as a lyre with broken strings, and breaks forth itself into a resonant final line:

Live blindly and upon the hour. The Lord,
Who was the Future, died full long ago.

Knowledge which is the past is folly. Go,
Poor child, and be not to thyself abhorred.
Around thine earth sun wingèd winds do blow
And planets roll; a meteor draws his sword;
The rainbow breaks his seven-coloured chord
And the long strips of river-silver flow:
Awake! Give thyself to the lovely hours.
Drinking their lips, catch thou the dream in flight
About their fragile hairs' aerial gold.
Thou art divine, thou livest,—as of old
Apollo springing naked to the light
And all his island shivered into flowers.

And again, at the end of the sonnet "Tho' Inland Far" quoted above—

    the mellow evening falls;
Alone upon the shore in the wet light
I stand and hear an infinite sea that calls.

The rhythm of the penultimate line here—and the vowel-and-consonant patterns of lines 6–8 in the previously quoted sonnet—all manifest Stickney's remarkable ear for verse, which seems unmatched in its mode since Tennyson.

Throughout the brief history of Stickney's poetry, the imaginative movement was from text to place, from poetic topos to geographic location. But when the sense of place is fully achieved, it is never bare of historical significance or of poetic illumination. Just as "the far space and long antiquity" doubles the visual present with the dimension of visionary myth—rather than merely historical time—to overpower the poet's sight on Mt. Lykaion, so the wind blowing past his precursors—past Hölderlin, past Leopardi and Ugo Foscolo—can be heard on nearby hills in his later lyrics.

Dying still in his own late spring, he never escaped from what he calls in one sonnet "the tone / Of memory's autumnal paradise." In another poem, his Decembering urban vision—trees and chimneys intermingled—focuses on an image of belatedly revived desire that seems self-descriptive of the "rich belated flower" of his own poetry; in "The Melancholy year is dead with rain" memory and desire are associated not with T. S. Eliot's relentlessly unhopeful April of "The Waste Land," but with the autumnal condition generally, and with the refrain of rainfall to which he would return, as will be seen, at the end of his finest poem. But at the close of this sonnet what appears to blossom is his own poem:

So in the last of autumn for a day
 Summer or summer's memory returns.

So in a mountain desolation burns
Some rich belated flower, and with the gray
Sick weather, in the world of rotting ferns
From out the dreadful stones it dies away.

(These ferns return again in the cycle of love poems called "Eride" when "Desire /
Revives like ferns on a November fire.") Poetic as well as erotic desire is shadowed
by the past for Stickney. A garden speaks of this in "An Athenian Garden":

The burned and dusty garden said:
"My leaves are echoes, and thy earth
Is packed with footsteps of the dead.

"The strength of spring-time brought to birth
Some needles on the crooked fir,—
A rose, a laurel—little worth.

"Come here, ye dreaming souls that ne'er
Among the immortals of the grave:
My summer is your sepulchre."

Some of his more moving poems embrace topographical prospects, like those
of American landscape paintings of the later nineteenth century, framed with a
touch of ironic distancing. "In Ampezzo" is one of these—it starts out with a
half-avowed echo of Milton's "Lycidas" ("Yet once more O ye Laurels") to
underscore its own derivative hesitation, as if all the old poems, as well as the
landscape, lay before him.

Only once more and not again—the larches
Shake to the wind their echo, "Not again,"—
We see below the sky that over-arches
Heavy and blue, the plain

Between Tofona lying and Cristallo
In meadowy earths above the ringing stream:
Whence interchangeably desire may follow
Hesitant as in dream,

At sunset, south, by lilac promontories
Under green skies to Italy, or forth
By calms of morning beyond Lavinories
Tyrolward and to north.

Here, in the northern mountains of Cortina d'Ampezzo, is Stickney's inland scene again, in which he tracks the signs of the landscape to the sea, even as the echo of Milton's word "over-arched" (for the Tuscan shades in book 1 of *Paradise Lost*) calls up a landscape far to the south. This poem ends quite beautifully in contemplation of the distance from its mountainous prospect to a sea itself enisled—never has its name been more literalized in its landed surroundings than in the short line of the penultimate strophe here:

Just as here, past yon dumb and melancholy
Sameness of ruin, while the mountains ail,
Summer and sunset-coloured autumn slowly
Dissipate down the vale;

And all these lines along the sky that measure
Sorapis and the rocks of Mezzodì
Crumble by foamy miles into the azure
Mediterranean sea:

Whereas to-day at sunrise, under brambles,
A league above the moss and dying pines
I picked this little—in my hand that trembles—
Parcel of columbines.

The poet plucks the day, and the poem, from the moment of sunrise, which is also the dawning of the sea's ultimate hegemony.

The overambitious *Lieder* style of "Eride" (from Eridanus—the river Po— made into a local river muse in grand poetic tradition; the actual muse may have been a Jewish girl the poet knew in Paris) colors another of these autumn visions, but in another sort of place. The opening of its fifth section frames a moment typical of Stickney's best poetry, an instant in which the autumnal scene itself, rather than a self-assessing speaker, summons up the remembrance:

Now in the palace gardens warm with age,
Of lawn and flower-beds this afternoon
The thin November-coloured foliage
Just as last year unfastens lilting down,

And round the terrace in gray attitude
The very statues are becoming sere
With long presentiment of solitude.
Most of the life that I have lived is here,

Here by the path and autumn's earthy grass
And chestnuts standing down the breadth of sky:
Indeed I know not how it came to pass
The life I lived here so unhappily.

Palace gardens were the poet's playground as a child—he seems to be evoking the Luxembourg gardens here—and the color of Verlaine's "vieux parc, solitaire et glacé" washed as it were into the engraving, here arises from childhood memories.

Another longer meditative poem is "Lakeward," in which yet once more the young poet's Horatian control of his verse is patent, as in these stanzas that start out with a prospect of boulders that

Stand to the burning heaven upright and cold.
Then drawing lengthily along their shoulders
    Vapours of white and gold

Blow from the lowland upward; all the gloaming
Quivers with violet; here in the wedge
The tunnelled road grows narrow and outcoming
    Stealthily on the edge

Lies free. The outlines have a gentle meaning.
Willows and clematis, foliage and grain!
And the last mountain falls in terraces to the greening
    Infinite autumn plain.

The flow of syntax here through the line and stanza breaks (like that in the third through the seventh lines of "On Some Shells Found Inland," quoted earlier) and the interruptions of the eye's scanning process work together almost cinematographically. The "representative versification" (in Samuel Johnson's phrase) of the penultimate long line is also very fine indeed. But they are all suffused with the light of earlier poetry.

Stickney's ecphrastic sonnets come from Rossetti in some measure, rather than from Gautier or Baudelaire. In his poem on a piece by Rodin called *L'Illusion, fille d'Icare,* his title (rather touchingly, given the vague strain of incestuous longing in many of his poems) misremembers Rodin's, and substitutes perhaps the "sister, lovely in my sight" of "Mnemosyne," to associate her with Illusion. The sonnet's "moment's monument," its brief memorial, is of a myth even more belated than Keats's Psyche:

On Rodin's "L'illusion, Soeur d'Icare"

She started up from where the lizard lies
Among the grasses' dewy hair, and flew

Thro' leagues of lower air until the blue
Was thin and pale and fair as Echo is.
Crying she made her upward flight. Her cries
Were naught, and naught made answer to her view.
The air lay in the light and slowly grew
A marvel of white void in her eyes.
She cried: her throat was dead. Deliriously
She looked, and lo! the Sun in master mirth
Glowed sharp, huge, cruel. Then brake her noble eye.
She fell, her white wings rocking down th'abyss,
A ghost of ecstasy, backward to earth,
And shattered all her beauty in a kiss.

The unrolling of the little narrative is continuous here through the sonnet's room, as contrasted with the way in which Yeats, in his famous "Leda and the Swan," revises the Rossettian pattern by confining his description of the scene to the octave, retreating into an interpretive distance in the first half of the sestet, and, finally, distancing himself so totally that the verb tense changes to the preterite in the last three lines. And there is an untitled sonnet (usually referred to as "On Sandro's Flora") that is half-conscious of Rossetti's sonnet on the same picture.

Stickney's verse drama, *Prometheus Pyrphoros* (fire-bearer), has some memorable moments; one is Prometheus's account of his ascent of Olympus as he "floundered up the dumb dead humid night" and, later on, in a short song of Pandora's:

As an immortal nightingale
I sing behind the summer sky
Thro' leaves of starlight gold and pale
That shiver with my melody,
Along the wake of the full moon
Far on to oceans, and beyond
Where the horizons vanish down
In darkness clear as diamond.

Even here, there occurs Stickney's characteristic moment of reading the signs in landscape to track them seaward.

Among the smaller fragments, some of which Lodge and Moody collected, are two that, a little more than a decade after Stickney's death, might have been claimed by Imagist aesthetics as complete little poems. One may be so by design; it is obviously supposed to be "from" a pastiche of Jacobean drama, which poets from Beddoes through Swinburne and T. S. Eliot had adored and studied. Indeed, to the antiromantic modernist, it reads like something Eliot might have quoted in an essay on John Webster:

Sir, say no more.
Within me't is as if
The green and climbing eyesight of a cat
Crawled near my mind's poor birds.

The mediated but uncompromising assault of the cat's gaze fixes, in this powerful image, that only half-mad fear that one is going mad, a fear that marked some eighteenth-century British poets in particular. As such, the fragment seems a complete poem—a moment of Browning, perhaps—and it may indeed have been written—like many of the epigraphs George Eliot composed for her chapter headings—as a "fragment" to begin with. This second one, more likely planned either as the opening of a quatrain, or part of something longer in *terza rima,* or very possible the start of a villanelle, nevertheless constitutes a perfect three-line poem, finer than anything of its sort until early Stevens, powerfully concise:

I hear a river through the valley wander
Whose water runs, the song alone remaining.
A rainbow stands, and summer passes under.

This is a beautiful revision of Heraclitus's trope of time and river and banks, and it governs the other figures here—of water under the bridge of the rainbow, of the song or poetic discourse of the concrete but visionary stream. These are, in almost haiku-like fashion, quite disjunct; yet the connections of rhyme, and the phonological patterns within the last two lines, themselves form bridging structures.

In the lines about the Athenian garden, full of burnt-out summer, it is not ruins that are at issue, but Miltonic and Shelleyan leaves, echoes themselves of older metaphors—"barren leaves" in both Wordsworthian and Whitmanian senses. As we saw, those lines attempt to unroll some new metaphor of "birth" from "earth" in the terza-rima, but the poem collapses at the end into a banal anecdote of children playing in the dust, "with pail and hoe": desert is momentarily redeemed as sandbox. Stickney was unable in his middle twenties to set these dead leaves "turning in the wind," as Stevens does in "Domination of Black" (1916), and thereby turning, troping again, the very tradition of the leaf image (from Homer through Shelley and Whitman) itself. But Stevens at thirty could probably not have written Stickney's absolute masterpiece, "Mnemosyne," composed in his middle thirties.

Ultimately, this is his one major poem. In its very structure it so animates the sense of the past as to turn it in the wind of imagination, somehow to reinvent the concept of remembering. Sometimes one feels that only Proust lies between it and much of James Merrill. It also marks Stickney's most powerfully and fruitfully autumnal moment. The opening line—"It's autumn in the country I remember"—returns throughout the poem to mediate between the unfolding tercets. For four of its occurrences it is both refrain for the preceding three lines and subtitle for the following three. Janus-like in looking ahead and backward, it is lingeringly ambiguous in its syntax: for example, "It is autumn now in the country that I remember"? or "I remember that it is autumn in the country"? or even "It is autumn in the country. I remember.")

It's autumn in the country I remember.

How warm a wind blew here about the ways!
And shadows on the hillside lay to slumber
During the long sun-sweetened summer days.

It's cold abroad the country I remember.

The swallows veering skimmed the golden grain
At midday with a wing aslant and limber;
And yellow cattle browsed upon the plain.

It's empty down the country I remember.

I had a sister lovely in my sight:
Her hair was dark, her eyes were very sombre;
We sang together in the woods at night.

It's lonely in the country I remember.

The babble of our children fills my ears,
And on our hearth I stare the perished ember
To flames that show all starry thro' my tears.

It's dark across the country I remember.

There are the mountains where I lived. The path
Is slushed with cattle-tracks and fallen timber,
The stumps are twisted by the tempests' wrath.

But that I knew these places are my own,
I'd ask how came such wretchedness to cumber
The earth, and I to people it alone.

It rains across the country I remember.

Masterful here are the modulations of the off-rhyming words in each tercet (save for the inevitably autumnal "ember," which, we also remember, composes the final syllables—here also impregnated with the autumnal—of "September," "November," and "December.") They are matched by the semantic variation of the predicates in the refrain, once *autumn* departs literally from the line ("autumn in . . . cold abroad . . . empty down . . . lonely in . . . dark across"). And after the poignant ellipsis of the refrain itself before the last tercet, it returns with the final "rains across" (the only time its verb is not merely the copula), filled as much with the wind and the rain of Feste's song at the end of *Twelfth Night* as of Verlaine's "il pleure dans mon coeur." The "sister lovely in my sight" is perhaps both biblical (from the Song of Songs—"my sister, my spouse") and Baudelaireian ("mon enfant, mon soeur" of *L'invitation au voyage*). But to "stare the perished ember / To flames" is a full revisionary resurrection of the scene that Shakespeare implicitly conjures up in his great autumnal sonnet 73 ("That time of year thou mayst in me behold") and that Gaston Bachelard so charmingly mythologized in *The Psychoanalysis of Fire*.

The neoclassicism of the poem's title is totally transcended in that Menomsyne—memory, the mother of the Muses—has indeed begotten here a new muse, the ad hoc spirit of an autumnal poetry far removed from Keats's. She presides over Stickney's strange sense of displaced landscape (the memory of a European-American oscillating back and forth); perhaps she is a female counterpart of the Roman god of Autumn, Vertumnus, whose name is marked by *vertere* (to turn) and whose nature is to turn the weather, the vegetation, the year itself. And *vertere*—which gives us *verse*—is the Latin counterpart of the Greek word that gives us the "trope" that is poetic life. In a poem like this, a moment of glorious originality opens up.

It is impossible to say what Stickney would have gone on to become, what kind of poet and with what kind of development, what the outbreak of World War I when he was forty might have meant for him imaginatively, and so forth. His friends Moody and Lodge never showed the formidable skills and resonant ear that place Stickney, as belated Keatsian, somewhere between Rossetti and that usually unacknowledged disciple of Rossetti, Robert Frost. "Mnemosyne" concludes with a strong movement away from the internalization of landscape, and with the homely native image—"It rains across the country I remember"—derived from the immediate parks and gardens of European cities and palaces, but transformed into that central scene of American poetry, the landscape within which—but necessarily out of which—we all grow up.

CHAPTER EIGHTEEN

Spoon River Anthology: *A Late Appreciation*

Spoon River Anthology is one of those remarkable, seemingly sui generis American books, like William Carlos Williams's *Spring and All,* or John Dos Passos's *U.S.A.,* that seems to mark milestones in the long, strange course of our country's trying to understand itself. It creates a fictional community through the short dramatic monologues spoken by its deceased inhabitants, rather than by overt description. The town is more like Edwin Arlington Robinson's Tilbury Town (something like his own home of Gardiner, Maine)—and certainly like Sherwood Anderson's *Winesburg, Ohio*—than like Sinclair Lewis's Gopher Prairie (in *Main Street*) or Thornton Wilder's *Our Town* (Grover's Corners, New Hampshire) or, of course, Faulkner's Jefferson in his Yoknapatawpha Country. Its author was a Chicago lawyer, political progressive, literary figure (in the circle of Theodore Dreiser, Vachel Lindsay, and Carl Sandburg, among others), womanizer, and quite uninspired poet, who in the unique format, and under unique imaginative pressures, excelled himself by producing a masterpiece.

The volume appeared for the first time in 1915 and, in the expanded form in which we now know it (with thirty-five added epitaphs), in the following year, just three-quarters of a century ago. It was an immediate success, praised extravagantly—and alternately condemned—for its skeptical energy, erotic specificity, reforming nay-saying coupled with romantic transcendent yearnings, unfamiliar structure, and mode of verse. It went through seventy editions in many languages and remained a canonical work, which was itself widely and heavily anthologized. Over the years since World War II it seemed to wear less well, possibly because it was most widely known through snippets, separate portraits that appeared in anthologies but that would not allow any of the book's quasi-narrative and schematic structures to emerge. As individual "poems," the individual epitaphs have far less power than they do in context. But a fresh look at the whole volume today—and at a time when the sexual and political issues raised in it are totally tame, and a vernacular vers libre has replaced rhymed jingle as the mode in which "everybody" writes—reveals a splendidly durable, fascinating, and moving book.

An "anthology" is, in its literal Greek sense, a garland or bouquet of flowers, applied originally to a collection of epigrams compiled, on the basis of many earlier ones, in the tenth century A.D. (the so-called Palatine Anthology). The term subsequently became used for collections of verse by various authors (although in Elizabethan England they were called "miscellanies") and, significantly, in the title of the massive collection of American poetry, *An American Anthology,* edited by Edmund Clarence Stedman in 1900. But it is the little poems of the so-called Greek Anthology that Masters had most directly in mind, particularly the sepulchral epigrams of book 7. These are actual or, more usually, fictional epitaphs, sometimes of only one couplet, sometimes of greater length. Among them are the famous words of Simonides, quoted by Herodotus, for the Spartans killed at the battle of Thermopylae (480 B.C.); as they might be put in the standard English epigrammatic meter:

Tell them in Sparta, you who now pass by
That here obedient to their laws we lie.

Verse epitaphs like this one typically speak for the deceased, asking the passerby to—in the words of old-fashioned railway crossings—"stop, look, listen," to contemplate for a moment something of the life of the deceased as the occasion for a general *memento mori,* a reminder of death. Alternatively, it is the monument or grave marker personified that does the speaking. The dead on the Hill in Spoon River speak variously: directly, like the forsaken Mary McNeely ("Passer by, / To love is to find your own soul / Through the soul of the beloved one.") or to the reader figuratively, as "passerby" or "traveler"; to the citizens of the town (as if Simonides had written "O Spartans"); or to one another. Their rhetorical modes are various, and their verbal actions include confession, plea, naive and devious expression, ironic narrative, and wide-reaching parable. In the pairings and sometimes larger sequential groupings of speaking graves, the reader frequently comes upon a narrative constructed by the corrective view of the subsequent speaker. From the totality of these emerges the nature of the town itself and the way in which it is made to function as a representation of American life, both rural and urban.

The individual epitaphs were originally published in separate "garlands." The first one appeared in *Reedy's Mirror,* a St. Louis periodical, on May 29, 1914. It consisted of the framing poem "The Hill"—a traditional exercise in the medieval ubi sunt (where are they now?) formula, best known in the later nineteenth century through Dante Gabriel Rossetti's translation of François Villon's ballade with the refrain "And where are the snows of yester-year?" Following it, and under slightly different names, was the epitaph of Hod Putt, with which the complete anthology commences:

Here I lie close to the grave
Of Old Bill Piersol,
Who grew rich trading with the Indians, and who
Afterwards took the bankrupt law
And emerged from it richer than ever.
Myself grown tired of toil and poverty
And beholding how Old Bill and others grew in
    wealth,
Robbed a traveler one night near Proctor's Grove,
Killing him unwittingly while doing so,
For the which I was tried and hanged.
That was my way of going into bankruptcy.
Now we who took the bankrupt law in our respective
    ways
Sleep peacefully side by side.

(One notes the resonantly biting repetition of the phrase "the bankrupt law" to mean not the federal Bankruptcy Act of 1898 but rather the institution of the Law itself, having exhausted all its store of Justice). Also in this first garland were the epitaphs of the embittered wife Ollie McGee (although the soliloquy of her husband Fletcher, emerging as a spiritually parasitic monster in her monologue, tells his own reciprocal story when placed next to her in the anthology); the Unknown, a Wordsworthian boy continually expiating a gratuitous act; Cassius Hueffer, shuddering under a blandly falsifying inscription; the ironically paired revelations of two women, each protesting against inscribed misreadings of their lives—Serepta Mason:

My life's blossom might have bloomed on all sides
Save for a bitter wind which stunted my petals
On the sides of me which you in the village could
    see.
From the dust I lift a voice of protest:
My flowering side you never saw!
Ye living ones, ye are fools indeed
Who do not know the ways of the wind

And the unseen forces
That govern the processes of life.

and Amanda Barker:

Henry got me with child,
Not knowing that I could not bring forth life
Without losing my own.
In my youth therefore I entered the portals of
    dust.
Traveler, it is believed in the village where I
    lived
That Henry loved me with a husband's lover,
But I proclaim it from the dust
That he slew me to gratify his hatred.

Even in this small group, we can note the emergence of a pattern that would recur throughout the completed book: The portraits of Serepta Mason and Amanda Barker form a kind of loosely related diptych and, with the further addition of the analogously misconstrued Constance Hately in 1916, a grim triptych. It is the rhythm of the sequence of these polyptychs and of individual portraits variously isolated from or connected with others appearing earlier or later on that manifests the book's unfolding structure.

The way in which the reader gathers information about individual people and families, about the economic, political, and social structure of the town, or learns the other side of an apparently authoritatively stated story, or discovers that an apparently finished matter was really a loose end forms the basic fabric of the book. The opening diptych of Ollie and Fletcher McGee enacts a radical revision and warns us that our responses to and feelings about the personages talking from beyond the grave must school themselves in ironic wisdom. The four panels of the Pantier family and their son's schoolteacher, Emily Sparks, also look ahead to the stories of Dora Williams. ("The milliner's daughter made me trouble," says Reuben Pantier, "And out I went into the world," an episode she refers to, in her own epitaph later on, as "When Reuben Pantier ran away and threw me / I went to Springfield.") Her tale, and that of the milliner, her mother, will in turn engage those of Roscoe and Mrs. Purkapile. (The Pantier family's tale will be further glossed by the complaining question of the zealous and puritanical A. D. Blood—himself revealed as a murderer later on—"Why do you let the milliner's daughter Dora / And the worthless son of Benjamin Pantier / Nightly make my grave their unholy pillow?" as well as by the observations about them and the moral chemistry of marriages of Trainor the Druggist.) The five-paneled group starting with the rich and honored Washington McNeely's epitaph—with its emblematic cedar tree recurring in refrain—is another such, as is the series of three epitaphs starting with Tom Merritt's in which violence unfolds subsequently into judicial and moral horrors. The poetess Minerva Jones is raped by "Butch" Weldy, whose monologue ends a five-part sequence but is reengaged in the later story of Roy Butler. Weldy, long after having been blinded in an accident, serves as foreman of the jury falsely convicting Butler of a rape he never committed. This is the most frequent pattern of narrative connection, frequently involving the much-delayed discovery of an interlocking of lives.

Sometimes the diptychs frame an ironic contrast, such as those of the amoral newspaperman, Editor Whedon, and his devout progressive neighbor on the Hill and in these pages, Carl Hamblin (his epitaph contains a fierce excoriation of badly institutionalized Justice, and involves a brilliant rereading of her traditional emblematic blindness and sword.) Sometimes a sequence of several pairings develops an emphatic momentary narrative rhythm, for example, Else Wertman paired with Hamilton Greene's unknowing and thus tragically ironic boast about his ancestry (not knowing that Else, the peasant girl from Germany, is really his mother). This is followed by the paired philosophical meditation and violently unphilosophical story of Ernest Hyde and Roger Heston, followed in turn by the Sibleys, the eternally cuckolded preacher and his gnomic, chthonic, *Ewigweiblichen* wife, whose secret (quite shockingly for 1915, one would guess) lies "Under a mound that you shall never find"—perhaps an illegitimate child buried somewhere, perhaps an emblematic *mons veneris* itself under a burial mound.

This whole sequence manifests a pattern of revelations: the reader knows the unacknowledged mother of the rich family's son before his epitaph shows him to be miserably unaware of who he is; then Ernest Hyde's solipsistic meditation gives no hint of having witnessed a parable gone horribly wrong. Finally, in a mirroring of the Wertman-Greene pattern of discovery, Mrs. Sibley (she is given no Christian name, whereas, given the mystical cast of her little chant, a missing surname seems more appropriate) is revealed to the reader as a creature wholly other, the medium of a generation myth. She has no story to tell at all, but merely a quasi-liturgical string of anaphoras to intone: "The secret of the soil,—to receive seed, / the secret of the seed,—the germ," finally ending with "My secret: Under a mound, . . . etc."

And there are the parallelled but unpaired musicians, Fiddler Jones—that avatar of the grasshopper or cicada of the well-known Greek Anacreontic poem—and Blind Jack, with his higher, Homeric vision. But there are other less formal patternings that arise as well: the different modes of parable propounded by Samuel Gardner and Dow Kritt, Browningesque and Blakean respectively (and William Goode's seems almost a parable Robert Frost might have played with, but not so baldly). For underlying all the patterns of relation among the individual portraits is the tangle of lines of power emanating from the banker Rhodes and his judicial, clerical, and journalistic deputies. It is this structure, together with the relations outlined above—some thematic, some narrative, some rhetorical—that hold the book, and the fiction of the town, together.

An exemplary and powerful instance of the way in which one story will undercut another is that of Knowlt Hoheimer's little story:

I was the first fruits of the battle of Missionary
    Ridge.
When I felt the bullet enter my heart
I wished I had staid at home and gone to jail
For stealing the hogs of Curl Trenary,
Instead of running away and joining the army.
Rather a thousand times the county jail
Than to lie under this marble figure with wings,
And this granite pedestal
Bearing the words, *"Pro Patria."*
What do they mean, anyway?

The mild irony of the sadly familiar and frequent occasion for military enlistment is underlined sharply by the superb ending: poor Knowlt doesn't know what the Latin words "mean," because he doesn't know any Latin. Much less the rest of the famous tag from Horace ("dulce et decorum est pro patria mori"—Wilfred Owen, in a great poem about World War I, called it "the old lie") expressing the dubious sentiment that it's lovely and appropriate to die for your country. But he asks the question for Masters's intended sophisticated reader, who knows all that, but who must be made to ask a higher, moral question: what can "patria" mean if it kills its sons? All this is very effective. But then the story is glossed—although hardly authoritatively—by Lydia Puckett, the next speaker:

Knowlt Hoheimer ran away to the war
The day before Curl Trenary
Swore out a warrant through Justice Arnett
For stealing hogs.
But that's not the reason he turned a soldier.
He caught me running with Lucius Atherton.
We quarreled and I told him never again
To cross my path.
Then he stole the hogs and went to the war—
Back of every soldier is a woman.

Well, she would say that. And the real story remains midway between their versions of it, even as it embraces both his ironic question and her home truth.

There are even subtler juxtapositions, of a purely poetic rather than a narrative sort, as well. For example, the epitaph of the boy called simply "the Unknown" (pointedly not an Unknown Soldier—its Ancient Marineresque killing of a hawk strangely anticipates a major poem of Robert Penn Warren's) ends with the dead boy recounting how

Daily I search the realms of Hades
For the soul of the hawk,
That I may offer him the friendship
Of one whom life wounded and caged.

His short story is juxtaposed with the shortest of all the epitaphs, that of Alexander Throckmorton, who is hardly a presence at all, but a mere voice for framing one of the oldest of paradoxes:

In youth my wings were strong and tireless,
But I did not know the mountains.
In age I knew the mountains
But my weary wings would not follow my vision—
Genius is wisdom and youth.

Far more poignant than the contrast between two very different senses of lost youth here is the way in which the trope of the hawk, used parabolically by Throckmorton, seems to have flown in from the preceding poem. Such nuances as these are seemingly far from the agenda of the book's sardonic iconoclasm, for which symbols are usually degraded public images whose ideological function it is the task of realist vision to expose. Throckmorton's hawk is a rare instance of a powerfully puzzling metaphor.

Among Masters's citizens are all manner of men and women, practitioners of many trades and crafts, village atheists, philosophers and layabouts, many lawyers and several writers, including sad bad poets like Petit, and comically bad ones like Jonathan Swift Somers (his broadly Miltonic parody, *The Spooniad*, appears at the end of the volume, just before the unfortunate epilogue added in 1916, with its rhymed verse and weak echoes of Goethe and Shelley). Many of them are persons of the sort Sherwood Anderson would shortly afterward call "grotesques." There are several suicides, and a good many victims of murder, fraud, injustice, religious subjection, and spiritual death, and the procession of malefactors, victims, and wretches throughout the first half of the book is indeed a dismal one.

This view from the dark side of the Hill, as it were, suggests that the communitas of the town of Spoon River is maintained in two modes, public and private. In the public realm, courthouse (and understandably, there are a good many lawyers in Spoon River), church, press, and pulpit are the institutional instruments, with Thomas Rhodes's bank remaining always the center of power and control, even as the epitaph of the man himself occurs at the center of the book (in 1915, it was the 104th out of 210). Most of those in power are seen as morally corrupt, although in each sphere there are antithetical figures, usually lonely in some way. The private realm is that of the horrors, despairs, and human abuses of sexual and family life, and it is the internalized "institutions"— of erotic repression, guilt, fear, quiet and unquiet desperation, among others— which seem to move among these lives from the inside in response to the forces exerted by Money and Law from without.

But the moral map of the town is not drawn only on the projection of the turn-of-the-century muckraking reformer, with many of whose views Masters was indeed sympathetic (but indeed, with a mature skepticism of some of the simple pieties of populism, as in John Hancock Otis's view of Anthony Findlay, who follows him). He puts the epitaphs of "the fools, the drunkards, and the failures" first; it is from their stories we infer the character and operations of the villains. Toward the end of the anthology come the monologues of "the heroes and the enlightened spirits," although these seem inevitably less forceful than the earlier ones. (In between—in what he admitted was a Dantean progression—Masters placed the souls of what he called "people of one-birth minds.") Among the "enlightened spirits" are the amateur scientists; the astronomer; the village atheist; Father Malloy—the one cleric exempt from the charge of corruption; in the almost totally protestant town he is an exotic and spiritually rich outsider and counts for Masters as a secular flame and rock; the skeptic Schofield Huxley; and the prophets Isaiah Beethoven and Elijah Browning (and all these manifest the allusive naming, sometimes heavily ironic, in the latter part of the book, for example, Voltaire Johnson, Hamlet Micure.)

The collection concludes with the Apollonian invocation of Webster Ford (the name Masters frequently used as a nom de plume, and particularly for the authorship of the separate "garlands" of epitaphs he originally published), and is thereby to be considered his own notional epitaph. In addition, there is that of Percival Sharp. The distinguished poet May Swenson felt that this epitaph was also Masters's own; it certainly appears to be so in a stronger, perhaps because less literal, way. And it certainly embodies the Renaissance topos of poetic perpetuation, best known from Shakespeare's sonnet "Not marble, nor the gilded monuments / Of princes shall outlive this powerful rhyme." It starts out by considering the conventional emblems on its own and nearby grave stones:

Observe the clasped hands!
Are they hands of farewell or greeting,
Hands that I helped or hands that helped me?
Would it not be well to carve a hand

With an inverted thumb, like Elagabalus?
And yonder is a broken chain
The weakest-link idea, perhaps—
But what was it?
And lambs, some lying down,
Others standing, as if listening to the shepherd—
Others bearing a cross, one foot lifted up—
Why not chisel a few shambles?

This epitaph concludes "for myself I know / I stirred certain vibrations in Spoon River / Which are my true epitaph, more lasting than stone," which rings with the irony of this fictive inscription on the fictive tombstone of a notional person. It is indeed the "true epitaph" of Masters the poet, "more lasting" than any literal stone, or than all the rest of his minor, though ambitious verse.

Masters had published two minor volumes of poems, in 1898 and 1910, before his one major book. Subsequent to it, he brought out thirteen more, including *The New Spoon River*. A sequel published in 1924, it contains 318 new epitaphs, some of considerable interest, but many with less force and either individuation or interconnectedness than marked the original book. (One can't resist wondering whether the name of the final speaker, the ponderous aphorist Cleanthus Trilling, had not been inserted by a later wag to send up a pair of noted and influential academic literary critics who flourished in later decades.) After the immediate success of the first *Spoon River Anthology,* Masters moved to New York, where he continued to live and write thereafter, giving up his law practice in 1920 and subsequently publishing five novels, plays, several biographies, a memoir, and a history of the Sangamon river before his death in 1950. He was born in Garnett, Kansas, in 1868, but his family soon moved to Illinois, and he grew up in the region around Springfield. After a year at Knox College in Galesburg, Illinois (at which time he studied Greek and became acquainted with some of the classics), he returned to study law privately. In 1892 he moved to Chicago, gradually building up a good law practice and becoming more and more involved with the literary life of the city. It was in Chicago that he began writing, and eventually publishing, while still enjoying the intellectual challenge and the sociological insights gained from a legal practice sometimes made difficult for him by his radical views. "The law had been an X-ray to me, and many kinds of chemicals," he wrote later of the relation between his legal work and his imaginative literature.

While J. W. Mackail's elegant prose translations of *Select Epigrams from the Greek Anthology* (rev. ed., 1906)—which Masters had perhaps seen earlier but which his friend and editor William Marion Reedy had apparently given him in 1913—were perhaps an enabling force for him; so perhaps was a visit from his mother to Chicago in May 1914 a precipitating one. They talked much of "the whole past Lewistown and Petersburg," bringing up people and events he had forgotten and tracing "those persons to their final fates." Some days later, just after her departure, he started on "The Hill" and a few of the first portraits of what would be the anthology. But he was also conflating these impulses with another, long-abandoned one. A decade earlier, he had thought of a novel that might represent and embody an entire town. In his memoir, *Across Spoon River* (1936), he recalls asking "why not make this book the book I had thought about in 1906, in which I should draw the macrocosm by portraying the microcosm? Why not put side by side the stories of two characters interlocked by fate, thus giving both misunderstood souls a chance to be justly weighed?" But that very same earlier unwritten book had perhaps its own earlier source.

In 1903 Masters had entered into a law partnership with the subsequently illustrious Clarence Darrow, which lasted eight years. Darrow himself published in 1904 a book called *Farmington*, a strangely lyrical novel done as a set of sketches about a small Pennsylvania town. It probably influenced Masters strongly, at first in his desire to write that novel about a town in Illinois, and eventually in the transmutation of that intention in Spoon River. Darrow's chapter on the town's burying ground, creeping in time up a hill from the churchyard may have been particularly resonant, as in a moment like this:

> I think the first time my faith was shaken in anything I saw on a grave-stone was when I chanced upon a brand-new slab erected to the memory of the town drunkard by his "loving wife and children." The inscription said that the deceased was a kind and loving husband and a most indulgent father. Everyone in Farmington knew that the wife had often called in the constable to protect her from the husband; but still here was the stone. Yet, after all, the inscription may not have been untrue; indeed, it may have been more truthful than those that rested above many a man and woman who had lived and died without reproach.   *Farmington, 126*

This is the sort of conjecture that lies behind the epitaph of Chase Henry, Spoon River's town drunkard (one of the first published), and the wry observation of Judge Somers that he, the erudite lawyer, lies "unmarked, unforgotten, / While Chase Henry, the town drunkard, / Has a marble block, topped by an urn, / Wherein Nature, in a mood ironical, [and here, the high, inverted diction itself produces a tone ironical] / Has sown a flowering weed?" Generally, it raises the question of undecidable narrations, one that Browning's great *The Ring and the Book* raised for Masters with lasting effect, for it gives local narrative force to the diptychs and polyptychs and deferred pairings of epitaphs, one correcting, revising, making ironic in retrospect the special pleading of an earlier one, basically supplying the "plot" of the whole sequence, aside from what the author acknowledged to be the nineteen stories "developed by interrelated portraits."

Literary allusion and echo aside, historical allusiveness is everywhere present in the book, with a range of degrees and modes of irony, in the names of the dead citizens of Spoon River. Masters reported later that he had drawn most of the names "from both the Spoon River and Sangamon River cemeteries, combining first names here with surnames there," but the names on the Hill represent a broad spectrum of modes of fictional naming. There are the sorts of names from eighteenth-century drama and fiction, like those of Penniwit the Artist or Petit the (obviously minor and trivial) Poet (opposed to Theodore the Poet, more a self-portrait of Masters himself). There is the Dickensian-Dostoyevskian sort of fantastic name, which evokes, less literally but through near puns, something of character. It has been remarked that "Hod Putt," the opening portrait of the anthology, with his grim observations on bankruptcy, is indeed "hard put." There are the allusive associations of names like that of the town banker (evoking that of Cecil Rhodes, colonial entrepreneur of Africa) and the pointed irony of that of Robert Southey Burke, for example, alluding to the English romantic poet scorned by Byron and others for selling out to arch conservatism. Or there is the broad irony in the name of Georgine Sand Miner, the shallow, vengeful, and unproductive echo of the free-living and high minded pseudonymous French novelist. Or in that of W. Lloyd Garrison Standard, no moral kin of the great abolitionist.

The fictional community of Spoon River itself reflects the actual name of the river in central Illinois and the towns of Lewisburg, situated on it, and Petersburg on the Sangamon, from the latter to the former of which Masters's family had moved in his youth. There are in fact seven actual historical personages buried on the Hill, although two of them—Davis and Lucinda Matlock—are given a changed surname: they are Squire Davis and his wife, Lucinda (Wasson) Masters, the poet's paternal grandparents. John and Rebecca Wasson were indeed his great-great-grandparents. The other three figures are all constellated around Lincoln: his law partner and biographer, Herndon; his supposed early love, Ann Rutledge; and, most interestingly, a woman named Hannah Armstrong, whose story slightly fictionalizes the historical facts on which it is based.

When Abraham Lincoln lived in Salem, Illinois, from 1830 to 1836, he knew Jack Armstrong and his wife, Hannah. In 1857 their son William Duff Armstrong was indicted for murder in connection with a tavern brawl; on the basis of old friendship, Hannah wrote to Lincoln, by then a successful lawyer and at an important point in his political career, asking him to defend her son. He did so, winning the case, in the so-called almanac trial (by producing an almanac in court to discredit key prosecution testimony about the height of the moon at the time of the murder and by convincing the jury that the death had occurred in a drunken fall from a horse). Five years later, with all four of Hannah Armstrong's sons in the army (one, indeed, killed in action and one wounded) and she herself too reticent to write Lincoln in the White House, a common friend communicated with Lincoln to ask him to secure William Duff Armstrong's compassionate discharge; on September eighteenth of that year, the president sent Hannah Armstrong a telegram announcing he had granted the request.

This is, of course, not quite the story that Spoon River's Hannah Armstrong tells. There was no "Doug"; the letter of petition did not fail; there was no imploring trip to Washington, etc. Masters himself seems to have misremembered parts of it, despite his own friendship, between 1913 and 1925, with John Armstrong, William Duff's son. In his memoir *Across Spoon River,* he identifies him as "the son of Jack *[sic]*, who had been defended by Lincoln for murder." In recasting the story, though, Masters is not merely misremembering, but pointedly shaping an anecdote to its teller's sentiments. And despite Masters's iconoclastic attitude toward the traditional Lincoln hagiography in his unreliable and biased *Lincoln the Man* (1931), it helps place Lincoln at the book's historical center, like the poet himself, "Talking the while of the early days / And telling stories."

Prior to the *Spoon River Anthology,* Masters had written very conventional verse of a not particularly distinguished sort; and while Goethe, Emerson, Shelley, Browning, and Whitman were all extremely important for him, he had been unable to use his great precursors in the way that strong poets do (as Shelley had stood behind Browning, and both of those behind Thomas Hardy, for example). The interrelated monologues of Browning's *The Ring and the Book* were obviously influential for Masters, and indeed, he imitated aspects of it more obviously in his later work. In *Spoon River Anthology* we find frequent Browningesque rhetorical turns: Joseph Dixon, for example, is an incarnation of Abt Vogler, and his epitaph derives from Browning's music poems generally; the way the parables are strung out at the end of the Davis Matlock and Samuel Gardner poems, etc.

But as has been noted, J. W. Mackail's prose translations from the Greek Anthology seem to have had the precipitating formal effect on his writing, unrelated to matters of deeper influence. (Masters was extremely sophisticated in his knowledge of antecedent free verse in English—in talking of his friend Carl Sandburg, he correctly invokes the Matthew Arnold of "The Strayed Reveller," a poem that many modernist metrical cranks ignore, Ossian, William Ernest Henley, and the German romantics as well as Whitman.) He later described the metrical convention of the Spoon River epitaphs as "a kind of free verse that was free as iambic pentameter is free, where the lack of rhyme and the changing caesuras, and the varying meter give scope for emotion and music." In fact, a good deal of the "free verse" in this book is unrhymed accentual-syllabic verse, sometimes only occasionally varied by a shorter line. Obvious cases include Paul McNeely's invocation to his beloved nurse, Jane, which is all in tetrameters, or the accentual four-beat lines of "Bert Kessler," or of the Cavalier historian Jefferson McNeely, or the anapest-laden pentameters of Wallace Ferguson's Shelleyan meditation on Geneva. Or "Fletcher McGee," which is almost pure blank ballad stanza throughout (save for the first two stanzas in the conventional alternative 3343, the rest are all quite normal.) Or Mrs. Williams, the milliner, Autolycus-like, singing of her wares in emphatic dimeter. Or the hypocrite Elmer Karr grinding out his last six lines in pompous blank verse. Or the classical, often dactyllic pentameters of Thomas Trevelyan's Ovidian reminiscence. The rhythmic variations that keep sounding through these epitaphs give voice to them in a way that much subsequent free verse could not. It is interesting now to note that T. S. Eliot, in commenting negatively on Masters's use of free verse in *Spoon River* in his "Reflections on *Vers Libre*" written two years after its appearance, compares it unfavorably with George Crabbe's use of tight couplets for equally "prosaic" material, which, in Masters's case, he characterizes correctly as not being "of the first intensity; it is reflective, not immediate; its author is a moralist, rather than an observer." It is perhaps characteristic of Eliot not to have heard not only the Browning and Shelley in Masters's verse; but it is less so to have missed the embedded accentual regularities. But in any case, Masters thought of the formal mode of his book as extending, rather than shallowly and—like some American poets of the next fifteen years, modernistically—affronting, poetic continuity. It is perhaps just that he was able to put his Browningesque impulses to best work in the collected dramatic monologues of these inscriptions, and to write with greater rhythmic interest and power than when he had kept too literally to older modes of variation to "give scope for emotion and music."

In other ways, too, the poetic language of the anthology is far less simple, colloquial, and "modern" than has been observed. When poetic inversions occur, they are often sophisticatedly enlisted in aid of a pointed effect. Lucinda Matlock's "Rambled over the fields where sang the larks" should by all rights by "where the larks sang"; but the immediate context is an allusion to an Edenic context, and the lines establishing it are pure Milton:

I made the garden, and for holiday
Rambled over the fields where sang the larks
And by Spoon River gathering many a shell,
And many a flower and medicinal weed.

Or, again, the Miltonic mode—this time, of enjambment—in the first two lines of the epitaph of the prostitute Rosie Roberts, "I was sick, but more than that,

I was mad / At the crooked police, and the crooked game of life," with its discovered revision *mad at = angry,* for *mad = insane*. There are also many echoic
fragments appearing here and there; thus, at the end of "Sexsmith the Dentist"
(whose profession is established, it seems, merely to give him the terms for a
final metaphor) we get two lines suggesting a Kipling ballad (read these as if the
line preceding them ended in "old"): "Why a moral truth is a hollow tooth /
Which must be propped with gold."

Webster Ford's epitaph concludes the collection and functions as a kind of
envoi for Masters's own work. The name of the speaker of this Apollonian invocation combines those of the Jacobean playwrights John Webster and John
Ford. This poem is mythopoetically quite complex, being centered on the story
of Daphne and Apollo as a fable of the origins of poetry in defeated erotic desire.
But it also brings in, at its opening, Mickey M'Grew, the "man-of-all-work in
Spoon River," someone whose gesture of bravura caused his death by falling. He
is associated by implication with Phaeton or Icarus as an Apollonian failure,
with fallen aspiration. This is contrasted with Webster Ford's own inspiration:

> Do you remember, O Delphic Apollo,
> The sunset hour by the river, when Mickey M'Grew
> Cried, "There's a ghost," and I, "It's Delphic
>   Apollo";
> And the son of the banker derided us, saying "It's
>   light
> By the flags at the water's edge, you half-witted
>   fools."
> And from thence, as the wearisome years rolled on,
>   long after
> Poor Mickey fell down in the water tower to his
>   death,
> Down, down, through bellowing darkness, I carried
> The vision which perished with him like a rocket
>   which falls
> And quenches its light in earth, and hid it for
>   fear
> Of the son of the banker, calling on Plutus to save
>   me?
> Avengeful were you fore the shame of a fearful
>   heart,
> Who left me alone till I saw you again for an hour
> When I seemed to be turned to a tree with trunks
>   and branches

Growing indurate, turning to stone, yet burgeoning
In laurel leaves, in hosts of lambent laurel,
Quivering, fluttering, shrinking, fighting the
    numbness
Creeping in to their veins from the dying trunk and
    branches!
'Tis vain, O youth, to fly the call of Apollo.
Fling yourselves in the fire, die with a song of
    spring,
If die you must in the spring. For none shall look
On the face of Apollo and live, and choose you must
'Twixt death in the flame and death after years of
    sorrow,
Rooted fast in the earth, feeling the grisly hand,
Not so much in the trunk, as in the terrible
    numbness
Creeping up to the laurel leaves that never cease
To flourish until you fall.

This, like so many other passages in the book, falls into strongly accentual five-
beat lines. The last four of Ford's epitaph make up an almost perfect unrhymed
sapphic stanza that invokes the whole book's preceding "leaves of me":

Too sere for coronal wreaths, and fit alone
For urns of memory, treasured, perhaps, as themes
For hearts heroic, fearless singers and livers—
Delphic Apollo!

In modern America, the pure heroic has become impossible, but there was a
modernist time during which the conjunction of rage at evil and injustice and
overleaping hopefulness constituted a sort of democratic nobility of the spirit.
Spoon River Anthology partakes of this. And in addition, it has by now become
so much part of the American literary landscape that nature has begun to imitate it. I recall a friend's telling me—to my initial disbelief—of a brief epitaph
on a tombstone in a Key West cemetery: "I told you I was sick." It sounded like
a line by a Borscht Circuit stand-up comic. But the inscription—I have since
been assured—is indeed there. And all one needs to do is imagine for oneself a
continuation of its story for two dozen lines or so. It stops being unwittingly
funny, and reveals its true origin, on the Hill, in Spoon River.

CHAPTER NINETEEN

Marianne Moore's Verse

In considering Marianne Moore's poetry, I want to address the question of her intricate and original prosody, although the sorts of discussion of form and rhetorical means in most reviewing of poetry today might give me pause in so doing. Writers of verse and some of their sectarian apologists—ideologues of rhyme and accentual-syllabism on the one hand and of some particular mode of vers libre on the other—have so written about the matter of style that, as I have previously suggested, the central question of the nature of poetic fictions is totally suppressed. Whitman guessed that the grass, one of his central tropes, was "the flag" of his "disposition," but some of his self-proclaimed acolytes would want to brandish an academic requirement for free verse as the banner of a faction. If Emerson's prophecy in "The Poet" and Whitman's fulfillment of it in the 1855 *Leaves of Grass* was right, then any follower of Whitman couldn't write like *that* and manifest anything but that betrayal of poetic following, the political follower or clone.

I have also pointed out that apologists for academic vers libre (canonized, taught in the schools of verse writing, etc.) confuse the issue by calling accentual-syllabic verse "formal." Thereby they divert attention—perhaps even their own—from their own formalism and deny that all good free verse has formal structure and power, although its forms and ability to play with language are themselves a figure, rather than a literal extension, of those of accentual-syllabism. An additional implication is that form cannot frame, identify, or gloss a mode of poetic discourse. Worst of all, it seems to deny that form, for a true poet rather than a versifier, is both generative and allusive, and that while students must learn that verse is not poetry—that poetry is a meter-making argument, as Emerson put it—the secret knowledge of poets is of how much argument-making meter there really, and almost inexpressibly, is. But this is such a personal and awkward matter that poets often avoid it or else say very misleading and often self-misrepresenting things about their private modes of voice when they do indeed consent to do so.[1] I hope it will not be wrong to try to invade some of Marianne Moore's formal privacy for a while.

Moore's formal practice is personal in so obvious a way that it is easy to misconstrue its nature and function. Her first book, *Observations,* has a few short residual accentual-syllabic poems ("To an Intra-Mural Rat," "Reticence and Volubility," "A Talisman," etc.) and some long poems in two different modes of vers libre, for example, the long, unwinding strip of that grand poem "Marriage"—a strip, varying from twelve to about thirty picas in width, unrolling like a path jointly trod or a term of years viewed as a corridor, not as a chamber, its extent, rather than a more obvious openness, constituting its trope of possibility. Or, on the other hand, there is the more problematic, accordion-pleated movement of "An Octopus" or "Sea Unicorns and Land Unicorns," in which some lines are so long as to require turnovers in the typesetting of the 1924 volume. But it is here that Moore's idiosyncratic isosyllabism emerges as a dominant system for her, providing the pattern of rises, turns, and landings of her particular Emersonian "stairway of surprise."

We might consider a few short poems that are characteristically generated in—and *by*—her schemes in that system. And I should like to consider how her use of them is as original as her way of dealing with the phenomenal world and how her isosyllabism, with its manner of framing English verse and its partitions of written language, correspond in the mixture of familiarity and strangeness with her segmentations—as B. L. Whorf put it—of nature. But first some observations about syllabism generally and about some of the problems it raises for interpretation.

Counting syllables alone in constructing lines of verse is so conventional as to seem natural in languages without tonic stress like modern French and Japanese, or even in those like Czech, Finnish, or Italian (all unrelated), with a clear but clearly predictable stress (initial in the first two, penultimate in the last). But it is quite as foreign to English as Greek quantitative prosody was to Latin when Ennius adapted it. The accommodation by strictly accentual Germanic meter— the four-beat alliterative line—of French syllabism at the time of Chaucer yielded, as we know, the great mixed metaphor of accentual-syllabism. But our system is one in which the accentual will tend to dominate, extra unstressed syllables but not stressed ones being allowable by the ear. Strict syllabism, on the other hand, is phonologically mysterious in languages with phonemic or problematically prominent word-stress. It might be likened to the quantitative experiments of the Elizabethans, who could, by the use of rules applicable only to the spelling system of written English, assign ghostly "quantities" to syllables without regard to phonology and produce lines often of puzzling beauty and effectiveness.

For example, a well-known anonymous sixteenth-century translation from Ovid's *Heroides* sounds, some archaisms aside, like the one mode of beautifully paced modern end-stopped free verse:

Constant Penelope sends to thee, careless Ulysses.
Write not again, but come, sweet mate, thyself to revive me.
Troy we do much envy, we desolate lost ladies of Greece,
Not Priamus, nor yet all Troy can us recompense make,
Oh, that he had, when he first took shipping Lacedaemon,
That adulterer I mean, had been o'erwhelmed with waters.
Then had I not lain now all alone, thus quivering for cold,
Nor used this complaint, nor have thought the day to be so
    long.[2]

Yet these various six- or seven-stressed lines, without any regular cadential closure, are, according to a secret rule, perfect Latinate hexameters.

A prosodic system, then, can engage the written language with various consequences for the spoken language therein encoded. This makes for the fundamental problematic of the borrowed system of strict syllabics, first written in English by Moore and Robert Bridges (probably quite independently of one another) and subsequently by W. H. Auden, Richard Howard, and others. The linguistic problem of defining a syllable varies in speech and writing, raising the question—in writing alone—of a syllabic rule. (Is the word *motion* to be considered di- or tri-syllabic, and does the consequent interpretation thus allude implicitly to the accentual-syllabic verse of the seventeenth, or the nineteenth and twentieth, centuries?) Moore, for example, often archaizes in this way or even more egregiously, as in "Nevertheless": "within the fruit—locked in / like counter-curved twin"—where the archaic spelling "curvèd" would be necessary for the hexasyllabic measure, and where its introduction, given the strong rhyme anyway, moves it toward iambic trimeter. But this brings up once more the central question: while the scheme is phonologically neutral, the audible rhythm of any line or lines is ad hoc a fulfillment but not a prescription of the syllabic rule. Thus, two lines of ten syllables each might be:

This line will be inaudibly measured,
But this line's heavy stresses can be heard.

The first sounds like a tetrameter—for example, "This line will be inaudibly measured," which tempts us to go on, "Its rhythmical riches will always be treasured," and which temptation would stem from an aural misprision of the syllabic system. Yet if the poet were writing syllabic couplets of ten and twelve, this added line would both follow the syllabic rule and work, by a different rule, for the ear. Note also that my sample pair of lines "rhymes" in a syllabic system, *a la manière française,* and not in any normative one for English, in which only stressed syllables can carry a rhyme. Also, note that the shorter the line, the more likely it is to resound accentually, whether by design or not.

But written syllables "rhyme" in a frequently inaudible way, given the fact of vowel reduction—in languages like English or Russian—on unstressed syllables. The initial *a* in the first syllable of the word *about*—phonemically, / ə /—can be treated as if it were /a/ or even /ey/ by a syllabic rhymer. The word *syllable* can be heard as if "full," or ending in a "bell," or even standing mutely like a "tree" in a system like Moore's. There is a sort of visionary trope of phonology at work in this. Thus, consider a poem such as "A Carriage from Sweden" with an *xbbxx* rhyme scheme and internal rhymes in the first and last lines of the stanza, usually connecting (in the last lines) the first and last syllable in each one. The last line of stanza 2 goes: *"in*tegrity it is a ve*in"* (my italics), where "vein," monosyllabic for the eight-syllable count of the stanza's terminal line, momentarily breaks into two syllables of "ve-in" for the *rime riche.*

But the central rhythmic issue of syllabic verse remains the tuning in and out of the accentual, as in the two-line example given before. The following passages will be of interest in this regard:

Perch'd on the upland wheatfields beyond the village end
A red-brick Windmill stood with black bonnet of wood
That trimm'd the whirling cross of its great arms around
Upon the wind, pumping up water night and day
From the deep Kentish chalk to feed a little town
Where miniatured afar it huddled on the coast
Its glistening roofs and thrust its short pier in the sea.

Robert Bridges

Mid the squander'd colour
  idling as I lay
Reading the Odyssey
  in my rock-garden
I espied the cluster'd
  tufts of Cheddar pinks
Burgeoning with promise
  of their scented bloom
All the modish motley

of their bloom-to-be
Thrust up in narrow buds
on the slender stalks

Robert Bridges

Through the open French window the warm sun lights up the polished
breakfast-table, laid round a bowl of crimson roses, for one—a service of
Worcester porcelain, arrayed near it a melon, peaches, figs, small hot rolls
in a napkin, fairy rack of toast, butter in ice, high silver coffee-pot, and,
heaped on a salver, the morning's post. She comes over the lawn, the young
heiress, from her early walk in the garden-wood, feeling that life's a table set
to bless her delicate desires with all that's good, that even the unopened
future lies like a love-letter, full of sweet surprise.   *Elizabeth Daryush*

Fifty-odd years ago if you were going to see Shoshone Falls, the road was
not, God knows, slicked up for the wheeled hordes of Nature-lovers
gawking in flowered shirts from Hawaii, and little bastards strewing
candy wrappers as they come. No—rough roads then, gravel sometimes
and, too, lonesomeness: no pervasive stink of burnt high-test, like the
midnight memory of some act of shame long forgotten but now back in
sickening sweat.   *Robert Penn Warren*

When there are so many we shall have to mourn, when grief has been made
so public, and exposed to the critique of a whole epoch the frailty of our
conscience and anguish, of whom shall we speak? For every day they die
among us, those who were doing us some good, who knew it was never
enough but hoped to improve a little by living. . . . One rational voice is
dumb. Over his grave the household of Impulse mourns one dearly loved:
sad is Eros, builder of cities, and weeping anarchic Aphrodite.   *W. H. Auden*

One Rational voice is dumb. Over his grave
the household of Impulse mourns one dearly loved:
    sad is Eros, builder of cities,
and weeping anarchic Aphrodite.

W. H. Auden[3]

The first of the two quotations from Robert Bridges, the opening of his 1921
poem called "Kate's Mother," is in twelve-syllable lines with the accentual six
beats so frequently dominating that these read like blank alexandrines. This
effect is underlined by the internal rhyme in the second line and the enjamb-

ment of "huddled on the coast / Its glistening roofs," with the discovered transitivity of the verb reinforced by the reciprocal verb *thrust*. But note the second passage from Bridges, the opening of his "Cheddar Pinks" of 1924, the same year as Moore's *Observations*. Whatever accentual patterns resound through the parallel syntactic elements in the last four lines, for example, it is obvious that the movement of these lines depends upon what looks like an opening accentual promise being broken. The first two lines suggest that the next two will be something like "Reading moldy Homer / on the first of May," as I have elsewhere argued.[4] There is something programmatic about introducing the syllabic mode in this fashion. As we shall see, Marianne Moore frequently does almost the opposite, letting the poem unroll in pure syllabics, with occasionally prominent rhythmic patterns surfacing here and there, but with a pronounced accentual scheme for cadential closure.

It is always instructive to recast vers libre or isosyllabic verse as prose and consider what emerges in the scanning of the prose lines. The third sample, a pure-syllabic sonnet by the British poet Elizabeth Daryush (Bridges's daughter, in fact), starts out with all the characteristic cadences and periods of a certain mode of novelistic descriptive prose, but the last sentence resounds in clear, rhymed, iambic pentameter. As has been apparent, an iambic pentameter line is a perfectly possible instance of the isosyllabic design, just as a Keatsian pentameter, full of resonant alliterations, is an allowable but unspecified instance of iambic verse.

Included are two other samples of pure syllabism very different in effect from Moore's: Robert Penn Warren's totally prosaic octosyllabics (an experiment that this wonderful poet wisely never repeated) use the resources of the scheme not at all. But the opening of W. H. Auden's poem "In Memory of Sigmund Freud" sets up a movement that prevails throughout the longish poem. The stanza form uses two lines of eleven syllables, one of nine, then one of ten, set up and indented so as to look like, and allude to, a poem of Horace's in the alcaic stanza. The first two lines are heard in roughly accentual pentameters, the last two being lost in the drawn-out clauses of the periodic syntax. Only at the very end, the last strophe, which is included in its correct form, breaks out into the canonical cadence.

Moore's poems present a few additional problems, which I shall only list briefly.

1. She revises format totally from time to time (e.g., "Peter," which gets recast into free verse after *Observations*).
2. The frequent turnovers in the setting of the earlier books falsely suggest that the stanzaic form is other than what it is (e.g., the nineteen-syllable line ending each strophe of "Radical" is turned over but with the residue so indented as to suggest that it is a seventh line—the stanza has only six—of a varying number of syllables).

3. Her indention practice seems strange at first; traditionally, strophes of varying line-length indent in decreasing number of feet or, if all lines are the same length, to group rhymes. Moore indents to group rhyming lines, often only two to a six- or seven-line stanza, despite the greatly varying lengths.

4. The look of the stanza can sometimes seem functional, sometimes less emblematically allusive. The early poems keep looking like seventeenth-century lyric stanzas. Perhaps a prototypical one is that of Herbert's "Denial," which may have been an important poem for her. "The Fish" seems to swim down the page, but that poem isn't about fish in any case, and the title and strophic shape make a subtle joke about surfaces and depths, once one has read down to the heavy, dark bottom of things.

5. There are her indeterminacies, the variations, inconsistencies, violated stanzaic and linear schemes that, perhaps, like the *abrash,* or sudden violation of pattern, in certain oriental carpets, may be there as if to ward off the evil eye.[5]

And there is the matter of quotation, of the incorporation of found linguistic objects, in Moore's poetry. With Moore it is not a question of dealing with the inadvertent emblem that nature produces in some trivial occurrence, like the typographical error that yielded the mythological occasion of Elizabeth Bishop's "The Man-Moth." Nor are Moore's quotations like those of Eliot in which he reconstitutes a famous line or phrase by adding or subtracting, with a ringing ironic gesture—for example, the altered quotation of the first line of Oliver Goldsmith's famous song from *The Vicar of Wakefield,*

When lovely woman stoops to folly,
    And finds too late that men betray,
What charm can soothe her melancholy,
    What art can wash her guilt away?[6]

In the rather nasty treatment the poem gives to "the typist home at teatime" in "The Fire Sermon" section of *The Waste Land,* Eliot's quatrain (ll. 253–56) answers the question of Goldsmith's lines. But by shifting the first word of Goldsmith's second line to the end of the first one, he puts the "and" into stressed—and what will emerge as rhyming—position, giving it a more emphatic quality, a sense of *atque* rather than merely *et* in Latin. Moreover, the line becomes one of the pentameters of Eliot's mock-heroic, rhymed section of the poem, and for us, his equally famous lines, now about a woman he regards as being so wretched as to cast doubt upon the possibility of any such thing as a lovely lady existing, revise and scornfully complete the lost, simple matter of what was framed in Goldsmith's opening line:

When lovely woman stoops to folly and
Paces about her room again, alone,

She smoothes her hair with automatic hand,
And puts a record on the gramophone.[7]

Moore's quotations of bits of prose do indeed adapt them formally, in that they enter into her realm of syllabic counting in many of the poems, but without the blatant irony that accompanies the device in the example just quoted, in which seeing a new formal possibility implied finding something wrong with the sentiment it expressed. But she sees her quoted passages as potential pieces of her own discourse without *that* sort of ironic concern made prominent, and she reinterprets the passage, or generalizes from it, as if with any found linguistic object in the vernacular—quotations, private scriptural allusions, or citations from a vast bible of ordinary discourse. Also, the quoted texts are like her poetic elements, her syllables, insects or tiny organs of the natural history of written language; these fascinate her from the early poems on, and at first she begins to prize apart the written organ/organism. This botanizing or lepidoptery extends to the larger formats of poems themselves, I think, and graphic patterns of stanzaic forms, found on pages of books of poetry, await her inclusions and decontextualizations. And so too, to a degree, with her quoted material.

But before leaving this issue, it should be noted that Marianne Moore is quite capable of complex quotation of the sort that depends on a residue of the original text excluded by the fragment quoted. Two early examples: the indented quotation from Daniel Webster at the end of "Marriage," itself part of a quotation in Moore's poem (and hence the quotation marks)

"Liberty and union
now and forever"[8]

is made to apply in a strange way to the minimal polity of a couple in the poem, "that striking grasp of opposites / opposed each to the other, not to unity." But the suppression of the rest of the remark, which during my childhood schoolchildren knew, is quite telling: "one and inseparable" completes Webster's proclamation, but the wry originality of Moore's view of the polarizations of marriage has been too dialectical to allow for a trivial notion of the married pair as "one and inseparable." Out goes the last phrase, but with a strong gesture of its being thrown out to mark the event.

An even more complex return of an excised context occurs toward the end of "In the Days of Prismatic Colour" (*CP* 41–42):

Principally throat, sophistication is as it al-

ways has been—at the antipodes from the initial great truths. "Part of it was crawling, part of it was about to crawl, the rest

was torpid in its lair." In the short-legged, fitful advance, the gurgling and all the minutiae—we have the
classic

multitude of feet.

Moore's footnote identifies the quoted phrase as coming from the Loeb Library translation of the *Greek Anthology* (tr. W. R. Paton—actually it is not on page 129 of volume 3 as her note, unchanged from *Observations* on, states, but from epigram 129 of book 9, page 67 of Paton's third volume). The epigram in question concerns not some sort of centipede, but rather a large, thirsting dragon, so thirsty that, putting its jaws into the river Cephisus, it drank it up completely "and horrid gurgling sounded in its throat. As the water sank, often did the nymphs lament for Cephisus that was no more." The "gurgling" is sucked up into the poem, without acknowledgment, and perhaps the lament-ing nymphs are reduced to some of the "minutiae." In any event, a considera-tion of the source of the quotation here reveals the mythographic etiology of the tiny unpleasantness of the personified "sophistication," whose ancestor is a great dragon that consumes a river, perhaps a river of discourse, and perhaps even of poetry.

Most of the peculiarities of Moore's formal practice are apparent almost from the outset, not only in their flexibilities and determinedly ad hoc schemes, but in their revisionary relations to accentual-syllabic modes of rhythmic pat-tern, rhyming, and versification. (One might adapt Yeats's characterization of his own later dramatic lyrics and call much of her work "poems in rhyme per-haps.") An inspection of two short early poems will be of interest here. The first appears in the 1924 *Observations* as "Fear Is Hope." (Left out of subsequent edi-tions, it resurfaced as a poem called " 'Sun,' " first in *The Marianne Moore Reader* then, again revised, in *Tell Me, Tell Me* with some important changes and, typi-cally, a shifted pattern of indentation and no initial capitals.) Totally rhymed— the one unrhyming line in the first stanza rhymes within its analogue in the sec-ond one—and redolent variously of Donne and Herbert, the poem is nearly prototypical. It commences with a quotation, although, oddly enough, never identified with a note. Its title brandishes the kind of near-oxymoronic paradox so characteristic of Moore's moral discourse; it looks forward, as will be seen, to "What Are Years?" in this respect. Moments in it—for example, the fine phrase about the rising sun and its own inner light as a trope of human inner resources, "Splendid with splendor hid you come"—prefigure her deliberate teasing of specimens of language in the wordplay of the later poetry. But what I wish to point out in "Fear Is Hope" is the prominent accentual-syllabic cast of the verse, audible in spoken performance without forcing

"No man may him hyde
    From Deth holow eyes."
  For us two spirits this shall not suffice,
  To whom you are symbolic of a plan
  Concealed within the heart of man.
      Splendid with splendor hid you come, from your
          Arab abode,
      An incandescence smothered in the hand of an as-
          trologer who rode
  Before you, Sun—whom you outran,
  Piercing his caravan.

Sun, you shall stay
With us. Holiday
  And day of wrath shall be as one, wound in a device
  Of Moorish gorgeousness, round glasses spun
  To flame as hemispheres of one
      Great hourglass dwindling to a stem. Consume
          hostility;
      Employ your weapons in this meeting place of surg-
          ing enmity.
  Insurgent feet shall not outrun
  Multiplied flames, O Sun.[9]

One notices here that, in almost a deliberately Donne-like fashion, Moore seems to pun on her own name at an appropriate turn in the second strophe— "round glasses spun / To flame as hemispheres of one / Great hourglass dwindling to a stem" is, indeed, "a device / of Moorish gorgeousness" (so did she "weave" herself "into the sense"). It is, as has just been implied, a singularly Herbertian trope as well, turned yet once more: Sunday and mundane, doomsday and funday, sunrise and sunset woven together. The "you . . . symbolic of a plan" only emerges as the sun at the end of the stanza. (The revised version, " 'Sun,' " identifies the addressee in the title, displaces the "two spirits" of the early poem onto the figure of the sun itself, and, in the next line, demotes the concealment of the "plan" and most efficiently dissolves the "incandescence" into a far harder "fiery topaz."[10]) The "Fear Is Hope" of the title presents not an emblem that a strange, twisted associative chain—not of argument, but of that highly original discourse we now think of as Marianne Moore—talk—will come up with a reading of, but rather the motto, glossing the *impresa* of the rising sun.

In any event, the poem not only reads aloud well (T. S. Eliot remarked in 1923 that this was generally true of Moore's work) but, more specifically, the versification is itself audible, and pushes the syllabic mode toward its accentual pole. It has already been observed that very short syllabic lines tend to generate such an effect in any case, whether by design or not. But here it is not a question of, say, six-syllabled couplets like those of "nevertheless." The couplets closing the strophe here, their rhymes in fully stressed position, the past tense of "outran" / "caravan" yielding to the future of "outrun" / "sun," keep the seventeenth-century overtones ringing. What is problematic are the long lines, of fourteen and eighteen syllables respectively, which fall unambiguously into the accentual cadences of a fourteener and a paired pentameter and tetrameter with the rhyme being carried at the end of the second of these. It is this sort of accentual presence that keeps emerging and receding in the later poems, controlled by a range of metrical, graphic, and other rhetorical devices, for example, the clear accentual rhymed quatrain that emerges at the very end of "In Distrust of Merits" (*CP* 136–38), the established pattern of 7a, 7b, 7a, 6b having previously provided a purely graphological and typographical scheme, with largely inaudible rhymes. It breaks out into unambiguous cadence, as if the intention all along had been an accentual trimeter quatrain, rhymed *abcd:*

I inwardly did nothing.
   O Iscariot-like crime!
Beauty is everlasting
   and dust is for a time.

This poem, then, syllabic in scheme, is accentual-syllabic in instance, prominently rhymed—*aabccddcc, eebffggff,* with the strophes linked by the *b* rhyme—and weakly enjambed. Its format is also typical: indentation marks rhyming lines, but not equally measured ones, and unplanned-for turnovers occurring in the typesetting occasion the apparent hyphenations and ghost-lines "Arab abode," "trologer who rode," and, in the second stanza, "hostility" and "-ing enmity," which do indeed scan in having four syllables (whereas the first two do not). Whatever sense of stanza format—in both historically allusive and purely phenomenal, naturally historical, zoological dimensions—may have been at work in these early poems, the exigencies of printing may have fiddled with it somewhat.

On the other hand, "To a Chameleon," also from *Observations* and also reprinted much later, with tiny but significant changes (in *O to Be a Dragon*), is quite a bit more problematic in the way its accentual qualities allow a listener to retrieve the versification. A splendid little emblem-poem, it deftly moralizes the chameleon as an icon of the imagination's resourcefulness, a creature whose camouflage is yet one more instance of the kinds of arms, armor, carapace, protective spines, and even certain paradoxical outward fragilities that are her continuing tropes for inner resources. The chameleon is traditionally—at least from Andrea Alciato's *Emblemata* (1531)—the emblem of flatterers. *In Adulatores* is its motto, and the epigram in Alciato, and universally translated into vernaculars thereafter, tells us how the chameleon, always open-mouthed, feeds on air and changes in appearance by taking on different colors save red and white. So also, the comparison continues, flatterers of princes feed on the vulgar air *(aura popular)* and, gaping, devour all. But Moore seems almost to be revising this emblem without having known anything of it directly, other than proverbial chameleon-as-insincerity lore. She uses the trope interestingly elsewhere (in "St. Nicholas" and in the fine, early little poem on Disraeli called "To a Strategist," addressed as a "bright particular chameleon" who "regale[s] a shabby fence"), but here it partakes most of the general figure of hard, resourceful purity and integrity with which Moore seems so often to be allegorizing virginity. It is neither the easy tangibility of the creature nor its somewhat maculae appearance at stages in its change to which she speaks; indeed, the chameleon is to some degree of the tribe of the ermine, that sixteenth-century emblem of virginity. (As always, Moore writes like Belphoebe with the kind of moral imagination about the nature of her own armor that only an old, wise Amoret could have.)

Before examining the poem, I will add one more observation. Aside from some of the ways in which her unrolling, idiosyncratically periodic syntax overflows the frequently tightly syllabic cups and basins of her stanzas, running down through them like water in a baroque fountain, what makes some of her poems seem rather Horatian is her ongoing argument with Horace's Ode 1.22. Notwithstanding her confessed displeasure with Latin at school, students of her generation would have sung, to a slowly paced German melody, at least the first strophe of

Integer vitae scelerisque purus
non eget mauris iaculis neque arcu
 nec venenatis gravida sagittis,
  Fusce, pharetra
[He who is upright in life and pure of guilt
needs no Moorish darts nor quiver loaded, Fuscus,
with poisoned arrows.][11]

It is just those "Moorish darts" that, thrown aside in Horace's rhetorical disclaimer, so fascinate the Moore-ish mind; she picks up the mere external, facetious literalness that one kind of poetry abandons and refugees it in a new, dangerously literal-sounding kind of emblem, of the sort that she is herself, throughout her oeuvre, picking up, turning around, dissecting with "those various scalpels" of her attention.

I shall come back to this Horatian quality shortly, but for now, the matter of the form of "To a Chameleon" requires attention. It starts out with the natural locus of the very colors of dark red and green, which the animal appropriates:

Hid by the august foliage and fruit of the grape vine,
  Twine
 Your anatomy
 Round the pruned and polished stem,
   Chameleon.
  Fire laid upon
 An emerald as long as
 The Dark King's massy
One,
Could not snap the spectrum up for food as you have done.[12]

The fourteen syllables of the opening line resist a stress-ordering, and the rhyme (on the unstressed final syllable of "grape vine") is picked up for the ear only because of the way in which the monosyllabic line "Twine" calls for attention. But as the poem untwines, what is essentially its binary epigram of exhortation and explanation ("O X, do Y; for Z is the case"), a characteristically curious thing happens. Disregarding line length, we observe that the poem's rhyme scheme is *aabxccybcc*, but once the muted rhyme of "grape vine" / "Twine" has gone by, all we *hear* is another, less muted "Chameleon" / "Fire laid upon," a diameter couplet. But accentual, and prominently so, the poem uncoils from the syllogism of its first half into strong couplets

  Chameleon.
  Fire laid upon
An emerald as long as The Dark King's massy One,
Could not snap the spectrum up for food as you have done.

—two dimeters and two fourteens. (The alternative word order, "could not snap up the spectrum for food as you have done," would have given a six-beat last line and destroyed the inset accentual and rhyming cadence.) The poem itself, as symbolic chameleon, breaks out in a change of color past the midpoint, when fire gets laid on the silent darkness. In the revised form of the poem, Moore was careful, along with making the initial letters all lower-case, to hyphenate "grape-vine," to ensure that it would not be intentionally interpreted as the spondee that disyllabic compounds in the process of formation in modern English remain before finally, as it were. Combined with a capitalized *august* with its shifts of stress and designation, a spondee there would have pushed the line into the stance of a fourteen, like the last one. This is a tiny although prominent and epigrammatic case of what might be called the momentary allegorizing of what is rhetorically purely a scheme, and thereby representational neutral. Major poetry always does this. It is not a matter of what has often been talked of as the expressive effects that verse, framing rhyme, mimetic rhythm, what

I. A. Richards called the "interanimation of words," frequently generate. Rather, it is a question of the scheme operating at another level, becoming momentarily opaque—rather than merely doing its expressive work, however subtly and strongly—and then being allegorically interpreted by—though not explicitly in—the course of the poem.

Let me give some examples. Milton works this way with syntactic devices, with the tension between Latinate and English word-order, with his variety of enjambments, and so forth. William Carlos Williams, in a poem called "The Right of Way" in *Spring and All,* explores a range of ways by which enjambment can create a new meaning in a sentence or clause by playing with a syntactic ambiguity whose very existence has been hidden in its implicitness and only revealed in its deployment:

> In passing with my mind
> on nothing in the world
>
> but the right of way
> I enjoy in the road by
>
> virtue of the law—[13]

it starts out. These line breaks employ the scheme of cutting syntax and serving up unexpectedly shaped slices of it. But they do not trope the scheme. Only at the very end of the poem does this happen, and with great wit. The word *enjambment* in French, with its visible leg, means striding across, or straddling.

Williams's poem has been taking a little walk, straddling the fences it finds at line-endings, and thereby exercising its own "right of way." Only in the last two lines is this figuration established, with an enjambment of a sentence *au sujet d'enjamber,* a cut that looks sharply surgical, but then, with the *contre-rejet* (as French prosody calls the straddled opening of the next line), immediately is sutured:

> Why bother where I went?
> for I went spinning on the
>
> four wheels of my car
> along the wet road until
>
> I saw a girl with one leg
> over the rail of a balcony

A joke, perhaps, but a deep one for ars poetica. Similarly, we might look at a beautiful quatrain of Emily Brontë's, the penultimate one of her posthumously published "Stanzas." The first two lines, expository and reportorial, walk easily through their transparent pentameters. The second two, full of phonological incident and rhythmic excitation, unveil, successively, scenery and spirit:

I'll walk where my own nature would be leading:
   It vexes me to choose another guide:
Where the grey flocks in ferny glens are feeding;
   Where the wild wind blows on the mountain side.[14]

Smooth lines walk; rougher ones create noticeable place, the locus of both vision and freedom. The alliteratively chiasmic "grey flocks in ferny glens" is pictorial; the spondaic build-up of "wild wind blows on the mountain side" is a figure of boundlessness. Yet both, by their position in the quatrain, partake of the figure of opacity as place to be reached, if only by the medium of the regular pace of walking.

What is the scheme, then, that Marianne Moore is troping in this little poem? The chameleon hidden in the foliage and fruit of the vine emerges at first as being twined around it. The accentual rhyming pattern of the chameleon poem emerges into audibility from its own pure-syllabic camouflage. The scheme in question is Moore's own—her stanzaic patterns, which, in their fixity, allow of many motions when in use. A final matter is that of the form as *format*. It is not that the typographical pattern produced by aligning rhymed lines is anything like a shaped or figured poem like the Hellenistic *technopaignia*, Herbert's altar, or *calligrammes* by Apollinaire or May Swenson. Instead, to use Marianne Moore's own words in 1926 about e. e. cummings, such a stanza represents "a kind of verbal topiary-work . . . not a replica of the title, but a more potent thing, a replica of the rhythm—a kind of second tempo, uninterfering like a shadow."[15] Not a chameleon-shaped stanza, in short, but a symmetrical form one reads into and then out of. In fact, it is rather like the stanza pattern of Herbert's emblematic "Easter-Wings." And in the slightly shifted indentation of the later version, this pattern is made more apparent, even at the cost of violating the alignment of the rhymed lines—long/short, short/long—of the opening and closing "couplets":

Hid by the august foliage and fruit of the grape-vine
  twine
    your anatomy
      round the pruned and polished stem,
        Chameleon.
        Fire laid upon
      an emerald as long as
    the Dark King's massy

one,

could not snap the spectrum up for food as you have done.

Herbert's stanzaic pattern scans a movement from longer lines down to the words "thin" and "poor" at the center of the two stanzas, where Moore has "Chameleon" and "Fire laid upon." Moore's poem glosses the pattern of diagonal descent through long and short lines—aligned as Herbert, who indented by line length, could not contrive—into a revealed center and then out again into accentual audibility. Her shape narrows and thins, but it is not troped as such. Nor is it true that the schematic emergence of the accentual rhythm and the audible rhyme from pure-syllabic hiding are generally troped this way in her work. Indeed, the tuning in and out of phonological pattern, the occasional accentually marked internal rhymes, are usually transparent, not opaque.

Thus, the breaking-out of audible short concluding couplets in the last two of the three stanzas of the fine poem "What Are Years?" (*CP* 95) is not itself emblematic of a pattern of action in the poem. But the foregrounding of the rhythmic process as the structure is worked through is related in another, non-mimetic way to its argument. (I use *argument* here not in its modern logical sense, but in the older one—most familiar through Milton and Emerson—of poetic substance or *mythos*.) Its "firm stanzas hang like hives," in Stevens's words, though not here, as with Dante's, in hell.[16] The bees of phrase buzz in and out; the looser, more problematic part of the argument overflows the first of the strophes into the second, while the third, fully possessed of its central trope, is self-contained. Nothing in the strophic scheme (brackets here stand for indented positions)—

6a]
6x
7a]
8x
4x
9x
7x
6b]]
6b]]

tells us much about what might be done with it, save that, in any poem of Moore's we will not see the stanzas used as narrative moments or as phases of an unfolding or turned aspects of a central trope. But let us turn to the poem itself. Its title poses a question of a puzzling sort: it must be glossed over before it can be answered. "What are years?" Well, that would depend upon what "years" are. . . . The first strophe opens in a traditional mode of not-quite-answering:

What is our innocence,
what is our guilt? All are
   naked, none is safe. And whence
is courage: the unanswered question,
the resolute doubt,—
dumbly calling, deafly listening—that
in misfortune, even death,
     encourages others
     and in its defeat, stirs

   the soul to be strong? He
sees deep and is glad, who
   accedes to mortality
and in his imprisonment rises
upon himself as
the sea in a chasm, struggling to be
free and unable to be,
   in its surrendering
   finds its continuing.

   So he who strongly feels,
behaves. The very bird,
   grown taller as he sings, steels
his form straight up. Though he is captive,
his mighty singing
says, satisfaction is a lowly
thing, how pure a thing is joy.
   This is mortality,
   this is eternity.

Such a question, given as if in answer—perhaps to evade not a wrong answer but another sort of untruth—comprises a poetic scheme of its own, which I have discussed in detail elsewhere. Here it is used even more obliquely than usual: "innocence" and "guilt" are paired terms, immediately aligned and then perhaps crossed, with nakedness and safety in the next line. But there is no analogous dichotomy between aspects of *years*. Without the question of the title to puzzle us, we read on to the logically plausible next question about the sources of courage, until drawn up again by the first appositive glossing: "courage: the unanswered question, / the resolute doubt." The recursive reference of "unanswered question"—the title's, the first line's, perhaps the one about courage that the very phrase is in the act of helping to propound—is impossible to avoid.

That last question, extending its period through the inaudible syllabic rhyme of the unclosing couplet of the first stanza, untouched by any phonological disturbance, comes to interrogative roost only in the second strophe.

From there, the unanswering assertion, Latinate in syntax, Horatian in tone, moves to the figure of containment—the sea rising up in a narrowing chasm— that presents another feature of the relation of sea and rock unfolded at the end of "The Fish." As the stanza moves toward its close in "What Are Years?" accentual patterns start working prominently: "the sea in a chasm, struggling to be / free and unable to be"—here the chime of "be" with the earlier "sea" promotes its syllabic weight at line end and momentarily suggests that the verb is existential rather than predicative (in Italian, e.g., *essere* rather than *stare*). That suggestion is immediately quenched by the rhyming *contre-rejet* "be / free," although that very line continues something of the indeterminacy of the verb, this time because of the possibility of the previously established periodic syntax—as if "unable to be, / in its surrendering *[something]*." But no; the second "be" is of that same "be / free." The audible couplet "in its surrendering / finds its continuing" makes sure of that. All we could complete the "unable to be" phrase with is the understood "so." The rhythmic couplet, by the way, is prominent despite its absolute rhythmic ambiguity. Either line could be performed as if scanned either as a dactyllic dimeter

> *in* its sur*rend*ering

—or as a trimeter—

> *finds* its con*tin*uing.

In either case, both lines would get parallel stressing and, prepared for by all the preceding *sea*-ing and *be*-ing and *free*-ing, close out simultaneously sentence, strophe, moral paradox, and ultimately, purported answer to the question about courage.

The "so" opening the last strophe, together with the following "behaves," is elegantly ambiguous. The sentence can mean "thus it is that he who feels things strongly behaves himself, or behaves himself thereby." Or it can mean that "he who strongly feels so—that is, strongly also—behaves." And yet the poem's moral stance, apportioning those two readings perhaps to the parties of innocence and guilt, would ultimately reveal them as being identical. The caged songbird, parallel to the previously enchasmed sea, "steels / his form straight up." The assertive declamatory rhythm of this opening accumulates within and across its lineation. Accentually, we get a little unrhymed quatrain:

So he who strongly feels,
  behaves. The very bird,

grown taller as he sings, steels
   his form straight up.

The rhyme "feels" / "steels" is displaced by the rhythm (cf., "grown taller in singing, steels," which would cause the rhyme to resound), even as we in reading feel the "steel" to be displaced from the bars of the birdcage onto the frail creature imprisoned by them, making of his nakedness a kind of safety. And even as the sea rises up in its chasm, perhaps to produce a spectacular display at high tide, so the bird's "mighty" song rises above the poverty of satisfaction with his lot. The poem avoids the easy expedient of contrasting with the lowly (a biblical word, as Marie Borroff has suggested[17]) satisfaction, "how high a thing is joy." The chiastic pattern "satisfaction"—"lowly" / "pure"—"joy" not only contrasts but links purity and lowliness, yet not with an oversimple valorization of high and low. This is the purity that Moore continually celebrates.

In one of the *Soliloquies in England* called "Skylarks," Santayana observes, both of songbirds and young men training to be World War I aviators, that "the length of things is vanity; only their height is joy."[18] Moore's joy is neither of mere height nor of mere length, but of life, perhaps even weirdly, fulfilling itself in its limitations. All of this being the case is our mortality and thereby all the eternity that can be conceived. The final couplet perfectly matches its precursor at the end of the second stanza in rhythm and parallels the gentler paradox of surrendering being continuing with its own sharper and more final one.

Perhaps now that the strange, twisted argument has discovered its own end, we can confront the question of the title. What are years? Terms of imprisonment? As our own years increase, are we doing time or redeeming it? Are years for counting up? Counting out? Does their accumulation build up the prison of our days? Daryl Hine, in writing about verse form itself, observed how "glibly we speak of the sinister forces that shape our existence / When, were it not for their influence, most of our lives would be shapeless."[19] In the case of this poem, the shaping of its very utterance is exemplary. The way it moves through its syllabic frame is parabolic, while not in the least mimetic. The bird's singing is *not* invoked in lines that themselves suddenly break out into the song of accentual cadence, for example, which would have been a low, even more than a lowly, device. Accentual emergence in "What Are Years?" is not troped as song; it is rather employed en passant to probe syntactic and semantic depths and, almost conventionally in Moore, for closure, for resolution. She asks, at the end of a later poem called "Saint Valentine" (*CP* 233), "Might verse not best confuse itself with fate?" invoking the etymological sense of confusion as a mixed outpouring and reminding us yet once more that, for the true poet, verse is not a mold to pour thoughts into nor the badge of style that a literary politics might seem to require. It is rather character, and bodily voice.

NOTES

1. Stephen Cushman in *William Carlos Williams and the Meanings of Measure* (New Haven: Yale University Press, 1985) discusses these questions with superb insight and clarity. I also recommend this book for its splendid general discussions of the formal operations of free verse.

2. This text appears in William Byrd's 1588 book of madrigals. See the discussion of it in Derek Attridge, *Well-Weighed Syllables* (Cambridge: Cambridge University Press, 1974), 196–98.

3. These passages are from, respectively, Robert Bridges, "Kate's Mother" and "Cheddar Pinks," in *Poetical Works* (London: Oxford University Press, 1953), 514, 507; Elizabeth Daryush, "Still-Life," quoted in *In Defense of Reason,* Yvor Winters (Denver: Swallow Press, 1947), 148–49; Robert Penn Warren, "Part of What Might Have Been a Short Story, Almost Forgotten," in *Being Here: Poetry, 1977–1980* (New York: Random House, 1980), 51; and W. H. Auden, "In Memory of Sigmund Freud," in *Collected Shorter Poems: 1927–1957* (New York: Random House, 1966), 166–70.

4. See my *Vision and Resonance* (New York: Oxford University Press, 1975), 272–79.

5. As in the case of l. 2 of the second stanza of "Fear Is Hope," discussed below.

6. Oliver Goldsmith, *The Vicar of Wakefield,* ed. Arthur Friedman (London: Oxford University Press, 1974), 133.

7. T. S. Eliot, *The Waste Land,* in *Collected Poems: 1909–1962* (New York: Harcourt, Brace, and World, 1963), 62.

8. Marianne Moore, "Marriage," in *Complete Poems of Marianne Moore* (New York: Macmillan, Viking, 1967), 62–70. Hereinafter, poems from this collection are documented parenthetically within the text with *CP* followed by the pagination of the poem under discussion.

9. Marianne Moore, "Fear Is Hope," in *Observations* (New York: Dial Press, 1925), 15.

10. Marianne Moore, " 'Sun,' " in *A Marianne Moore Reader* (New York: Viking, 1961), 88.

11. Horace, "Ode 1.22," in *The Odes and Epodes,* trans. C. E. Bennett (New York: Macmillan, 1924), 64.

12. Moore, "To a Chameleon," in *Observations,* 11.

13. William Carlos Williams, "The Right of Way," in *Spring and All* (Dijon: Contact, 1923), 120. See the fine discussion of this poem in Cushman, *William Carlos Williams,* 48–50. For a more general theoretical consideration of the workings of enjambment, see Hollander, *Vision and Resonance,* 91–116.

14. Emily Brontë, "Stanzas," in *Oxford Anthology of English Literature,* ed. Frank Kermode and John Hollander, 2 vols. (New York: Oxford University Press, 1973), 2:1482.

15. Marianne Moore, "People Stare Carefully," in *Complete Prose of Marianne Moore,* ed. Patricia C. Willis (New York: Viking, 1986), 125.

16. Wallace Stevens, "Esthétique du mal," in *Collected Poems* (New York: Knopf, 1954), 315.

17. In her excellent *Language and the Poet* (Chicago: University of Chicago Press, 1979), 125.

18. George Santayana, "At Heaven's Gate," in *Soliloquies in England and Other Soliloquies* (New York: Scribner's, 1922), 116.

19. Daryl Hine, "Epilogue: To Theocritus," in *Theocritus: Idylls and Epigrams,* trans. Daryl Hine (New York: Atheneum, 1982), 139.

CHAPTER TWENTY

Modes and Ranges of a Long Dawn:
Robert Penn Warren's Poetry

If old statesmen make us sneer, old athletes and teachers make us applaud condescendingly, and old soldiers make us nervous, who is to be wise? Only old painters and poets, perhaps, those who can with profit and pleasure become their own grandfathers. (We all become our fathers, but not knowing what to do about all that becomes part of our continuing domestic tragicomedy.) The problem of wisdom in America was in heroic crisis prophetically earlier than our nation itself appeared to be. But, our imaginations being our best part, and the decline of the best always dragging down behind it the inert worst, this should hardly surprise. Poetry, observed Stevens, is a cemetery of nobilities, but the grass growing around the monuments, we might add, is wisdom.

Robert Penn Warren was one of our wisest men of letters, and became not only part of the literary landscape of America but, more significantly, part of the way in which we view that landscape. As the coauthor, with Cleanth Brooks, of perhaps the most influential textbook for the study of poetry in our time in America—great-great grandsons of *Understanding Poetry* are still being spawned—he helped generations of students learn that creating a reading of a poetic text can be as much an act of intensity and joy as composing one. In novels like *At Heaven's Gate, All the King's Men, World Enough and Time,* and that remarkable metasouthern novel, *Flood* (I list only my personal canon) he represented the more than complex fate of southern America—the non-Emersonian, old New World—as an emblem of universal, rather than of sectional, human conditions. Many of the themes handled in his novels, and occasionally embodied in their inset philosophical lyric sections, have reappeared in and among his poetry. The ruined and haunted pastoral of the American field, the deaths of fathers and mothers, the nightmare ever knocking at the child's door in the mind of the man, the failure of the American West as a measure of our more general failures, the saving shreds of affirmation, we see these becoming, in Robert Penn Warren's later poetry, not so much subjects, as regions of poetic experience.

It is his poetry, rather than his telling of tales, upon which I comment, and if not to treat him specifically as what Spenser called a poet historical, then nevertheless as one who "thrusteth into the middest, even where it most concerneth him . . . there recoursing to the things forepast, and divining of things to come." The paradoxes of American history and the profundities of some of its violences have served his vision of the enduringness of promise—even unto the breakers of promises—even under the most stained and faded of rainbows. "Such a subject"—Warren once wrote this of the Civil War "bloodily certified by actuality" for Herman Melville's poetry—"would serve his need only if the centrifugal whirl toward violent action was perfectly balanced by the centripetal pull toward an inwardness of apparently unresolvable mystery, or tormenting ambiguity." In many ways this describes the uses to which Warren's own poetry has put the historical anecdote, the tale of which he is always in some way the teller. Throughout the growth of his oeuvre, the expansions of narrative—parable, oblique anecdote, text for meditation—have marked his originations of form and new lyric genres. From *The Ballad of Billie Potts* and the internalized horrors of "Original Sin," he moved to the form of the historical episode reconstituted and redeemed in that remarkable extended eclogue *Brother to Dragons*. There, the novelist Robert Penn Warren becomes one of the governing presences in a poem whose end is, among other things, to teach some of the meanings of history to its other major presence, Thomas Jefferson.

In his poems since *Promises* (1957), the created moments of personal and public history grew more passionate and complex. The unreeling of story or of account became more a matter of what mythographers call the unfolding of myth. These newer, long suites of poems—chains of questionings, revisions of meditative position—constitute some of the most original poetry written in English. In form, too, they are unique; original structures of free verse, they rework and recall, but never trivially imitate, complex odelike rhyming schemes. They allow both narrative and an increasingly frequent mode of self-catechism (this surfaced first, I should imagine, in the remarkable "Ballad of a Sweet Dream of Peace" in *Promises*) to transform the programs of modern lyric. It is instructive, perhaps, to glance for a moment at the ways in which they evolved.

In Warren's early poems one finds the tight metrical and epigrammatic homages to seventeenth-century lyric that are epitomized in the allusive version of Marvell's garden of verses (a garden in which one would not dwell forever, but wherein, fifteen years later, my own generation played as poetic children). Warren's version of this was a garden

Where all who came might stand to prove
The grace of this imperial grove,
Now jay and cardinal debate,
Like twin usurpers, the ruined state.

(The touches of archaism here extend even to the older meaning of *prove* as "test.") But even in these earlier poems, the allusiveness is no mere stylistic or tonal marker. In the famous "Bearded Oaks," under the trees that are "subtle and marine,"

Upon the floor of light, and time,
Unmurmuring, of polyp made,
We rest; we are, as light withdraws
Twin atolls on a shelf of shade

the Shakespearean sea change from *The Tempest* extends to the Marvellian sea of grass from "Upon Appleton House," revised on the forest floor. But the very mode of wit is itself being self-consciously revised, and its light filtered through the poem's own meditative leaves, until the inevitable conclusion about time has moved far beyond a mere carpe diem. Indeed, the last quatrain is proleptically thematic for much of Warren's later poetry:

We live in time so little time
And we learn all so painfully
That we may spare this hour's term
To practice for eternity.

Later on in his work, the "hour's term" collapses to a far more intense moment, Hardy's moments of vision and beyond these; at the same time, the poems embodying them expand rhetorically into quasi narratives. Back in these same years in which he was still working with seventeenth-century echoes, Warren was engaging with certain lyrical-narrative forms developed by Hardy and, in particular, writing onrushing, run-on long lines that flooded the banks even of purely rhythmic scansion.

He himself had written of how important an early poem called "The Return: An Elegy" (1930) was for him, how uncannily it seemed to know more about his life—and his mother's nearing death—than he did as he wrote it. Formally, it does indeed look ahead to the strange, irregular odes of the years after 1965; rhetorically, it prefigures them in its way of arguing with itself, of interjecting mysterious bits of broken refrain. But like the poems in tight quatrains or more expanded balladry, it is still something of an echo chamber, whether half-consciously recalling Eliot, on the one hand

the old bitch is dead
what have I said!
I have only said what the wind said
wind shakes a bell the hollow head

By dawn, the wind, the blown rain
Will cease their antique concitation.
It is the hour when old ladies cough and wake,
The chair, the table, take their form again
And earth begins the matinal exhalation.

or, on the other, ironically quoting Elizabeth Akers Allen's celebrated parlor piece, and demolishing it with an Eliotic device of construing her second line as a pentameter, instead of the dactyllic tetrameter it is, by forcing it into a lowering couplet:

turn backward turn backward O time in your flight
and make me a child again just for tonight
good lord he's wet the bed come bring a light

There are moments of what might be called in at least two senses a middle style in *Brother to Dragons* that approach prophetic cadence. Of its memorable set pieces one is the song of chill, of the encroachment of winter:

And the year drove on. Winter. And from the Dakotas
The wind veers, gathers itself in ice-glitter
And star-gleam of dark, and finds the long sweep of the
      valley.
A thousand miles and the fabulous river is ice in the
      starlight
The ice is a foot thick, and beneath, the water slides
      back like a dream.
And in the interior of that pulsing blackness and thrilled
      zero,
The big channel-cat sleeps with eyes lidless, and the brute
      face
Is the face of the last torturer, and the white belly
Brushes the delicious and icy blackness of mud.
But there is no sensation. How can there be
Sensation when there is perfect adjustment? The blood

Of the creature is but the temperature of the sustaining flow:
The catfish is in the Mississippi and
The Mississippi is in the catfish and
Under the ice both are at one with God.
Would that we were!

This is the time of the literally and figuratively cold-blooded for whom violence and rage will not be heat. The language of the narration (the speech of
Robert Penn Warren in the poem) rises to a more overly prophetic strain a few
pages after:

And now is a new year: 1811.
This is the *annus mirabilis*. Signs will be seen.
The gates of the earth shall shake, the locked gate
Of the heart be stricken in might by the spear-butt.
Men shall speak in sleep, and the darkling utterance
Shall wither the bridge's love, and her passion become
But itch like a disease: scab of desire.
Hoarfrost shall lie thick in bright sun, past season, and twitch like fur.
The call of the owl shall discover a new register.
When ice breaks, the rivers shall flood effortlessly,
And the dog-fox, stranded on the last hillock,
Shall bark in hysteria among the hazel stems.
Then the bark shall assume a metronomic precision.
Toward the end, silence. The first water coldly fingers
The beast's belly. Then silence, He shudders, lets
The hind quarters droop beneath the icy encroachment.
But the head holds high. The creature shivers again,
And the rigid muzzle triangulates the imperial moon.
Until the spasm, the creature stares at the moon
With the aggrieved perplexity of a philosopher.

Here, though, as the prophecy gives way to a kind of moralized narration, we
find another sort of anticipation of the structures of the later poetry. It is interesting to observe the way in which the more regular cadences of this passage
give way, in Warren's 1979 revision of *Brother to Dragons*, to a muting of both
the meter and the grammar of the prophetic mode, and how the whole passage
with its powerful but problematic transition, is broken into two after "fur."
Other characteristic devices of the mixed modality of the later poetry have
included that puzzling, article-less form of title, sometimes mocking a newspaper headline (an early occurrence, in *Promises,* is "School Lesson Based on Word
of Tragic Death of Entire Gillum Family"; another, from the same book and

resonant more of a picture title, is "Mad Young Aristocrat on Beach"). In Warren's early poetry, the kind of irony this allusiveness would generate would be rather easier to pin down; in these later poems, from *Promises* on, the strange grammar is no longer a matter of establishing a distanced tone, but rather comes to invoke a whole range of tones: bitter, Olympian, sympathetic, detached.

So, too, the increasingly common formal scheme of isolating a cadential line from a strophelike structure as if to make it a stanza of its own, or have it stand in for a closing couplet in a sonnet, or a longer, more pastoral fade-out conclusion. He uses it in "Fall Comes in Back-Country Vermont" and throughout, to conclude sections in the Emerson poem, also from *Tale of Time*. This later, characteristic device of closure, the separated, single final line, neither purely epigrammatic nor partaking of lyrical coda, is deployed in a rich variety of situations. A typically complex instance of this occurs at the end of a poem I have always particularly liked, perhaps as much for the way in which it makes romance of a central epistemological moment as for what has seemed to me to be its mode of invoking another, very different modern American poem. William Carlos Williams's ode to the spring wind, beginning "By the road to the contagious hospital" (from *Spring and All*), celebrates in a strange, problematically modernist way the birth of a moment of realization: the cold wind felt at the beginning of the poem yields up its true identity as the breath of spring, in what is half-likened to a birth process. Buds that look at first like gnarled, perhaps even diseased, protuberances of bare stalk release the green shoots that "enter the new world naked, / cold, uncertain of all / save that they enter." Williams's usual undersong, the suppression of conceptualization in favor of the trope he calls "things," itself struggles against this poem's own metaphor of focusing an optical device (either microscope or field glass), as "One by one objects are defined— / It quickens: clarity, outline of leaf."

Warren's remarkable "Brotherhood in Pain" (from *Can I See Arcturus from Where I Stand?*—it is closely related to many of the poems in the "Speculative" section of *Now and Then,* which followed it in 1978) is far less reticent about its trope for that central act of consciousness so important to poets and so played down by philosophers, the act of *noticing*. The birth of an element of the external world is a painful one, but the pain is, inevitably, shared by subject and object; perhaps the grammar of "in pain" of the title is a revision of that of "[conceived] in sin," or "[conceived] in liberty":

Fix your eyes on any chance object. For instance,
The leaf, prematurely crimson, of the swamp maple

That dawdles down gold air to the velvet-black water
Of the moribund beaver-pond. Or the hunk

Of dead chewing gum in the gutter with the mark of a molar
Yet distinct on it, like the most delicate Hellenistic
    chisel-work.

Or a black sock you took off last night and by mistake
Left lying, to be found in the morning, on the bathroom tiles.

Or pick up a single stone from the brookside, inspect it
Most carefully, then throw it back in. You will never

See it again. By the next spring flood, it may have been
    hurled
A mile downstream. Fix your gaze on any of these objects,

Or if you think me disingenuous in my suggestions,
Whirl around three times like a child, or a dervish, with eyes
    shut,

Then fix on the first thing seen when they open.
In any case, you will suddenly observe an object in the
    obscene moment of birth.

It does not know what it is. It has no name. The matrix from
    which it is torn
Bleeds profusely. It has not yet begun to breathe. Its
    experience

Is too terrible to recount. Only when it has completely
    forgotten
Everything, will it smile shyly, and try to love you,

For somehow it knows that you are lonely, too.
It pityingly knows that you are more lonely than it is, for

You exist only in the delirious illusion of language.

To begin with, the objects of contemplation are by no means "chance," for they are all emblems of death, traditional or modern instances of what has been sloughed off, what time has caused, like bodies and life itself, to be cast aside. With the end of the sixth couplet, however, the poem's attention turns ironically aside ("if you think me disingenuous in my suggestions") to deal with a true "chance object," perhaps as if the latent memento mori in any monumental emblem, in any powerful figure from nature, had somehow to be purged before the ultimate matter of the relation of world and knowledge could be approached. As it is, this is no "spousal hymn," as Wordsworth called it, of that relationship, but the celebration of the birth of a sibling.

The "matrix" from which bits of reality are always being most timely ripped is, in its original sense, a womb, and in its derived one, a conceptual paradigm, and the two meanings themselves seem both conjoined and torn apart in the figure that embodies them. Whose womb it is—just *who* gives birth to any object (and who, implicitly, gives birth to the observer)—may be too terrible for the poem to contemplate. The repression of the nature of that mother may have something to do with the powerful further turnabout of the final line (a turnabout emphasized by the enjambed conjunction "for" at the end of the preceding couplet). Ordinarily, we should feel for the contingency of the external world, of the recently born observable piece of reality. But with something like metaphysical condescension, the object pities the subject, who cannot ever know its own birth, notice itself, or—and again, only implicitly—observe its own death. The subject's existence "in the delirious illusion of language" is the inferential quality of that existence, no matter how much pain it may be sharing with the world. And yet "language" has never been a primary issue in the poem until now (save for the fact that the "it" has, at birth, no name—only the subject, living and breathing the air of the realm of language, will have one for it). The powerful closing line reflects also the original and unique mixture of genres in the poem itself: meditative lyric, spiritual exercise, very brief narrative. All these modes "end" differently, and the operations of all three of those endings are effected in this one, which seems as well to close out all the issues of the poem itself.

In the 1970s and 1980s in particular, Warren's formal invention grew to meet the demands of new and varied forms of fabling. From the modernist dogma about tight form holding in check the violence of passion and revelation, he began to roam through old and new woods, like the John James Audubon of his own poem, a quester crashing through prosodic brush and drawing the blood of rhetoric in pursuit of greater precision and wider views. In that marvelous book *Incarnations* (1968), a poem like "The Leaf" could announce a period of late greatness in the work of a poet who knew, like Yeats, that old embroideries had to be shed. Yet this was a true poet, who knew that, after Yeats, "walking naked" could only be a literary enterprise, and not a poetic one. He knew that the far-from-barren leaves of the reclaimed image of the fig tree in "The Leaf" could alone authenticate the trope of late poverty in order that there be late fruition. This was to be the major poet of nature, one who could recall—as no wandering botanizer could catalog or pursuing hunter could overlook—

All day, I had meandered in the glittering metaphor
For which I could find no referent.

Nature in these late poems yields up its parables of delicacy and violence in subtle interrelations. Warren's hawk, the creature of range, high vision, and the
power of lightning descent upon particulars, wings through time as well as
across space. His long poem *Or Else* (1974) extended the questing of the
Audubon figure to new structures, modes, and ranges of voice. These continued to evolve in *Now and Then* (1978), in which the struggle with present phenomena kept yielding the vision of new twists in the troublesome riddle of
time. Beyond narrative, beyond the forms of meditative lyric, Warren's poetry
of the seventies and eighties suggests the deep storytelling of biblical commentary—tales told us in elucidation of the true story we all know but cannot com-
prehend. Robert Penn Warren's poetry has emerged as perhaps the grandest
part of his writing. His poems have become parts of our world. He now aston-
ishes us—as Cocteau said we had to be astonished—yet no longer with the
amazement of youthful fireworks (or as the French say, *feux d'artifice*), but with
the deep and continuing astonishingness of a long dawn.

CHAPTER TWENTY-ONE

Elizabeth Bishop's Mappings of Life

Geography III is a magnificent book of ten poems whose power and beauty would make it seem gross to ask for more of them. Its epigraph is a catechistic geography lesson quoted from a nineteenth-century textbook, claimed for parable in that seamless way of allowing picture to run into image that the poet made her own. In this instance, it is by her own added italicized questions about mapped bodies—of land, of water—and about direction, following the epigraph in its own language but now become fully figurative. The opening poem of Bishop's first volume, *North & South,* is called "The Map"; in all the work that followed it, the poet was concerned with mappings of the possible world. More generally, she had pursued the ways in which pictures, models, representations of all sorts begin to take on lives of their own under the generative force of that analogue of loves between persons that moves between nature and consciousness. We might, somewhat lamely, call it passionate attention. Its caresses, extended by awareness that pulses with imagination, are not only those of the eye and ear at moments of privileged experience, but rather at the times of composition, of representing anew. The mapmakers' colors, "more delicate than the historians'," are as much part of a larger, general Nature as are the raw particulars of unrepresented sea and sky, tree and hill, street and storefront, roof and watertank. Much of the praise given Bishop's work has directed itself to her command of observation, the focus of her vision, the unmannered quality of her rhetoric—almost as if she were a novelist, and almost as if love of life could only be manifested in the accuracy and interestingness of one's accounts of the shapes that human activity casts on nature.

But the passionate attention does not reveal itself in reportage. Love remains one of its principal tropes, just as the reading, interpreting, and reconstituting of nature in one's poems remains a model of what love may be and do. The representations—the charts, pictures, structures, dreams, and fables of memory—that one makes are themselves the geographies that, in our later sense of the word, they map and annotate. The radical invention of a figurative geography in *North & South,* the mapping of personal history implicit there, are perhaps Bishop's *Geography I;* after the Nova Scotian scenes and urban landscapes to the south of them in *A Cold Spring,* lit and shaded by love and loss, the grouped Brazilian poems and memories, rediscoveries even, of childhood yet further to the north, asked questions of travel. A literal geographic distinction, a north and south of then and now, gained new mythopoetic force; all that intensely and chastely observed material could only have become more than very, very good writing when it got poetically compounded with the figurative geography books of her earlier poems. *Questions of Travel* is thus, perhaps, her *Geography II.*

This book is a third, by title and by design, and, by its mode of recapitulation, a review of the previous two courses as well as an advanced text. Like all major poetry, it both demands prerequisites and invites the new student, and each of these to far greater degrees than most of the casual verse we still call poetry can ever do. The important poems here seem to me to derive their immense power from the energies of the poet's creative present and from the richness and steadfastness of her created past ("A yesterday I find almost impossible to lift," she allows in the last line of the last poem in the book). Yes, if yesterdays are to be carried as burdens, one would agree; but even yesteryears can themselves, if one is imaginatively fortunate, become monuments to be climbed, to be looked about and even ahead from, to be questioned and pondered themselves.

And so here with the monuments of the earlier Bishop poetry; the reader keeps seeing them in these later poems—in the background or in pictures hung as it were on their walls. Rhetorically, a villanelle echoes the formal concerns of the earlier sestinas and, at a smaller level, the characteristic use of repeated terminal words in adjacent lines, whether in a rhymed or unrhymed poem, continues to be almost synecdochic, in these poems, of the imperceptible slip from letter into spirit of meaning. The magnificent earlier "The Monument," echoed in this volume in part of "The End of March" (of which more later) resounds even through Bishop's wonderful translation of an Octavio Paz homage to Joseph Cornell—a string of boxed tercets. "12 O'Clock News" recapitulates a whole cycle of emblematic poems in her previous work, this strange prose poem being a kind of Lilliputian itinerary of the poet's own desk, a microcosmography of the world of work. The piece called briefly—but hardly simply—"Poem" is something of a meditation upon the earlier poem "Large Bad Picture," as well as, manifestly, upon the small good one that presents a view, a spot of time in

Nova Scotia, a moment in the past that is recollected from its fragments in the attempt to puzzle out an ambiguous sign, a representation of a *something* that may or may not be part of one's own life. (*Well, of somebody's,* we are tempted to go on in one of Miss Bishop's characteristic tones—there is no lack of human significance in the pictures of life in the world about which she broods, and the problem with them is rather one of mapping the directions in which they urge the viewer to turn.) The scene in this little painting has assembled itself out of contemplation, rather than commerce; the artist turns out to have been a great-uncle "quite famous, an R.A." The poet goes on:

I never knew him. We both knew this place,
apparently, this literal small backwater,
looked at it long enough to memorize it,
our years apart. How strange. And it's still loved,
or its memory is (it must have changed a lot).
Our visions coincided—"visions" is
too serious a word—our looks, two looks:
art "copying from life" and life itself,
life and the memory of it so compressed
they've turned into each other. Which is which?

But "vision" is, of course, not too serious a word (as, I suppose, "serious" is too unvisionary a one). A major rhetorical device in American poetry of the past century and more has been a mode of evasion of the consequences of visionary seriousness; it can take the form of a pretending, for example, whether in Hawthorne or Frost, that anecdote is merely that and not myth showing a momentary face, a defense of whimsy or skepticism. Stevens's way was to pretend to a theory of just that sort of pretending, to discuss the ground rules by which experiences and names for them play with each other. Elizabeth Bishop is not obviously Stevensian, even when she makes figures of figures (as in that wrenching early epigram, "Casabianca"); and in her celebrated and profoundly original diction there are few echoes of the whole of harmonium (save perhaps for the trace of "Disillusionment of Ten O'Clock" in her "Anaphora" from *North & South,* where day "sinks through the drift of classes / to evening, to the beggar in the part / who, weary, without lamp or book / prepares stupendous studies"). Her personal mode of rhetorical questioning, of demands for truth directed toward the mute objects she has herself invented, is certainly an analogue of Stevensian turnings in the wind of the leaves of imagery itself. These questionings ("Are they assigned, or can the countries pick their colors?") occur in her earliest poems, and continue to quicken all her fictions, giving the breath of life—as do Stevens's "qualifications"—to her molded figures and scenes. Bishop's characteristic mythopoetic mode is one in which description, casually and apparently only heuristically figurative, bends around into the parabolic. What happens in the latter part of "At the Fishhouses" is possibly the locus classicus of this movement in her work; the almost painted scene offers up its wisdom not with the abrupt label of a moralization, but gradually, as images of place begin to be understood—almost to understand themselves—as images of the condition of consciousness itself.

It is that poem that seems to lie in the background of the powerful "The Moose" in the new book. Although its anecdotal frame might suggest "The Fish" as a prototype, the nonviolent encounter with the animal presence here is very different and far more profound: a bus ride southward from maritime provinces of the past is halted at the end of the poem as a she-moose emerges "out of / the impenetrable wood / and stands there, looms, rather, / in the middle of the road." Underscored by a deceptively disarming cadence of lightly rhymed stanzas of six trimeter lines, the account of the bus ride becomes parabolic with its ability to contain the past rather than merely to observe traces of it through the windows; a sort of Sarah Orne Jewett dialogue between two ancestral voices emerges from the backseats of the bus and the poet's mind as they move toward Boston, and the great creature appearing out of the woods, at a kind of border between the possibility of one sort of life and that of another, comes into the poem as a great living trope of the structures that get wrecked in crossing such borders—"high as a church, / homely as a house / (or, safe as houses)." The appearance of the creature is a phenomenon at once unique and paradigmatic, an "embodiment" in momentary dramaturgy of Something in nature analogous (the antlerless form?), which came of the poet's crying out to life for "original response" ("As a great buck it powerfully appeared"). The moose's powerful appearance is too important a manifestation, as always in Bishop's poetic world, to occasion the squandering of poetic diction. Even the gently ironic homeliness of the chorus of other travelers (" 'Sure are big creatures.' / 'It's awful plain.' / 'Look! It's a she!' ") echoes point by point the narrator's admittedly guarded mythologizing ("high," "homely," "safe") and with the effect of domesticating even more the awe and the pressure of significance. We are tempted to think of her language at the most sublime moments of her travel talks as "cold" or "casual," but it is neither of these. Her great originality has always washed other kinds of voice away, and notwithstanding her "Invitation to Miss Marianne Moore," in *A Cold Spring*, to descend as a tutelary muse upon her, Miss Elizabeth Bishop's work seems as self-begotten as any in our time. What seems cold in her language is warmed by the breath of its own life.

And yet it is not to compromise the originality of "The Moose" to point how it seems to answer a prior text, but in the way in which only the most original poetry ever does. Robert Frost's "The Most of It," the protagonist of which, who "thought he kept the universe alone," could only elicit echoes from nature in answer to his voice—a sort of pre-Friday Crusoe, in fact; what he wanted from the world was not his "own love, back in copy-speech / But counter-love, original response." But all that comes of what he calls out is "the embodiment" of it, "powerfully" appearing as "a great buck" that swimming across the lake on the other side of which he stands, "stumbled through the rocks with horny tread, / And forced the underbrush—and that was all." The female moose, Bishop's answer to Frost's conditionally answering appearance of a (male) buck, herself appears in answer, not to the poet's cry to nature for acknowledgment, but to the preceding five stanzas of

an old conversation
—not concerning us,
but recognizable, somewhere,
back in the bus:
Grandparents' voices

uninterruptedly
talking, in Eternity.

It is no wonder that she is imaged with respect to church and house. Frost's dissatisfaction with mere echo for his protagonist itself enacts a revision of Wordsworth's Boy of Winander, standing "alone / Beneath the trees or bathe glimmering lake," blowing "mimic hootings to the silent owls / That they might answer him." Bishop's maternal moose, social, domestic, powerfully appearing in a way antithetical to that of Frost's buck, is crucially different, too, in that she interrupts a journey, rather than being part of a staged scene.

A word might be said, too, about the possible revisionary force of Bishop's only villanelle, "One Art," in this same volume. Her two other uses of French lyric forms, "A Miracle for Breakfast" and "Sestina," both use the patterned repetitions of the terminal words, as all good modern sestinas do, to tell a counterstory of their own. The availability of the villanelle for contemporary poetry was certainly accomplished by William Empson, and his villanelles with the refrain lines "It is the pain, it is the pain endures," "The waste remains, the waste remains and kills." Perhaps it is the latter of these, "Missing Dates" with its final meditation on how "It is the poems you have lost, the ills / From missing dates, at which the heart expires" that is directly answered in Bishop's poem. There, specific matters of the art of losing and a catalogue of its accomplishments respond to Empson's gnomic generalities:

[Empson,] The art of losing isn't hard to master;
      So many things seem filled with the intent
      To be lost that their loss is no disaster.

The meter requires "To *be* lost," which makes the sense even sharper, and even more clearly frames the refrain line that, unlike the first of the two refrains (the poem's opening line) will, in itself, suffer losses throughout its repetitions—only the word "disaster" will remain (like Empson's "waste"), alternating with its negation ("no disaster"—"will bring disaster"—"wasn't a disaster"—and then the final "(Write it!) [for, say it!] like disaster." "One Art" is, of course, troped here by another—the art of writing, even of one's losses—and due acknowledgment is paid to the first by the elegant deployment of the latter, revising the villanelle form into a form of losing.

Of the two major masterpieces in *Geography III,* the astonishing longish poem called "Crusoe in England" engages some of the larger meditative consequences of this self-sufficiency. It is a great dramatic monologue of the famous Solitary returned to a world of memory and discourse, the larger isle of England, "another island, / that doesn't seem like one, but who decides?" It is as if the narrator had come from an island of myth (the fable of what one was? what one made and made of one's life?) to our overhearing and growing suspicion that he had been as responsible for the lay of the land upon which he had been cast up as for his own survival in it. As usual, a tone of detached gazetteering (again, suggesting the distanced detailings of "The Monument" and, even more, the narrative cadences of "The Riverman") colors a stanza of frighteningly powerful vision:

The sun set in the sea; the same odd sun
rose from the sea,
and there was one of it and one of me.
The island had one kind of everything:
one tree snail, a bright violet-blue
with a thin shell, crept over everything,
over the one variety of tree,
a sooty, scrub affair.
Snail shells lay under these in drifts
and, at a distance,
you'd swear that they were beds of irises.
There was one kind of berry, a dark red.
I tried it, one by one, and hours apart.
Sub-acid, and not bad, no ill effects;
and so I made home-brew. I'd drink
the awful, fizzy, stinging stuff
that went straight to my head
and play my home-made flute
(I think it had the weirdest scale on earth)
and, dizzy, whoop and dance among the goats.

Home-made, home-made! But aren't we all?
I felt a deep affection for
the smallest of my island industries.
No, not exactly, since the smallest was
a miserable philosophy.

The very island is an exemplar, a representation; it is a place that stands for the
life lived on it as much as it supports that life. Its unique species are emblems of
the selfhood that the whole region distills and enforces, and on it, life and work
and art are one, and the homemade Dionysus *is* (rather than blesses from without or within) his votary. "Solitude" itself is a forgotten word in this place of
isolation. Terrors of madness assaulted, even as they necessitated, the retreat
into poetry of the Crusoes and Castaways of William Cowper, solitaries to
whom the very tameness of the animals was frightening as a mark of wildness
that had never known the human, nor ever learned to fear and be fearsome; solitaries who would "start at the sound" of their own voices. But for Bishop's
Crusoe, madness is not the problem, particularly the eighteenth-century madness kept at bay by faith. The one mount of speculation on his island is named
"Mont d'Espoir or *Mount Despair"* indifferently (for Defoe's Crusoe, "Despair"
only), and he is rescued from one insulation to another in a different, colder sea
enisled, "surrounded by uninteresting lumber."

But one cannot begin to do this splendid piece justice in a brief essay; it is
the centerpiece of the book's geographies and a poem of the first importance.
So, too, is "The End of March," a beach poem in which, again, "vision" is not
too serious a word, a strange, late domestication of the poet's earlier Nova
Scotia seascapes. But this time it is not a meditation on a scene so much as a
movement against a scene, a classic journey out and back, toward a treasured
image of imagined fulfillment, along a stretch of beach that yields up none of
the comforts of place ("Everything was withdrawn as far as possible, / indrawn:
the tide far out, the ocean shrunken"), past objects from which meaning itself
has withdrawn. The goal is never reached, and the walk back presents glimpses
of an almost infernal particularity:

On the way back our faces froze on the other side.
The sun came out for just a minute.
For just a minute, set in their bezels of sand,
the drab, damp, scattered stones
were multi-colored,
and all those high enough threw out long shadows,
individual shadows, then pulled them in again.
They could have been teasing the lion sun,
except that now he was behind them.

This moment is itself, in its replacement of a wrecked hope, a splendid monument to a poetry that has always remained measured, powerful in imagination and utterly clear—radiantly and distinctly—in its language. If it seems to manifest rhetorical or eschatological withdrawals, these are never movements away from truth, or even from the struggle for it. Miss Bishop's poems draw themselves in when they do, like wise and politic snails, from the rhetorics of self-expression, the figures of jealousy and pity, the boring industry of innovation. Withdrawn or not, so many of her poems have moved themselves into the few unoccupied corners of perfection that seem to remain, that we can only end as readers where philosophy is said to begin, in wonder.

CHAPTER TWENTY-TWO

May Swenson's Massive Panoply

"One must work a magic to mix with time / In order to grow old." May Swenson's poetry made that magic, and more. She was one of our few unquestionably major poets; of the generation of Bishop, Roethke, and Lowell, she remains one of the strongest for me as I grow old, a remarkably original writer whose loss I still mourn (she died in 1989, at the age of seventy-six) and whose work I continue to celebrate. The last book published in her lifetime was entitled *In Other Words* (1987); its own "other words"—those of poetry itself, of her deep and high-spirited allegorizing of what has come to pass, of what, in her own resonant formulation were "things taking place"—are typically full of formal invention, interplays of genres, and powerful emblematic vision. Her poetry was as American as apple pie in its ongoing revision of Emerson's observation (in *Nature*) that "It is not only words that are emblematic; it is things which are." This mutual interdependence of signs, of interchangeable tokens and types, has remained important for a number of twentieth-century American poets. Among these are Marianne Moore (typically) and Elizabeth Bishop (occasionally—as in a poem like "The Man-Moth" in which a typographical error is taken as some palpable *lusus naturae* might have been by a seventeenth-century poet). For in the next dialectic turn, words can, in their poetic opacity, become as emblematic as things, once they are freed from their daily work in the marketplace of our discursive economy. May Swenson remains very much in this tradition. Her poetry's modes of interpreting, glossing, conjuring, calling up, and her forms of spell and enchantment were all enacted with uncanny rhetorical power. Her verse itself—rhymed, free in various modes, internally rhymed with unnotated rhythmic patterns, playing to eye and ear at once—confounded trivial classification. She invented marvelous *calligrammes* in both iconic and abstract shapes; indeed, her poetry gives new meaning to the concept of shape itself. Her patterned poems, whether in that sui generis book *Iconographs* or elsewhere throughout her work, were always making specific local parables and at the same time propounding a more general one—about inscriptions that seem to be aware of, and take account of, their own appearance. And thereby, too, her poems seem ever to be meditating profoundly on the many meanings of the words *character* and *nature,* and of their interplay.

An early poem, "Any Object," could serve, like Robert Herrick's "Argument of His Book" or Frost's "Pasture," as a gateway to her work:

any Object before the Eye
Can fill the space can occupy
the supple frame of eternity

my Hand before me such
tangents reaches into Much
root and twig extremes can touch

And we are reminded again how the similarly shaped ramifications of root and stem branchings suggest a circular relation of source and result each returning to the other. The poem ends, with a splendid assertion of her own Emersonian originality, in the expansion and elevation of the minute poetic particulars with which she starts:

then every New descends from me

uncoiling into Motion i
start a massive panoply
the anamolecular atoms fly

and spread through ether like a foam
appropriating all the Dome
of absoluteness for my home

As at the start of "Any Object," perceived form always seems to call out to her for interpretation beyond acknowledgment of its natural function, as if emblematic signification were one of the very operations and processes of nature itself. Hers is a modern version of the Renaissance doctrine of signatures read in all things. Whether the "any object" from which—or by which—she starts is a given or conventional one, or a chance occurrence, it is a significant part of what there is, and its particular significance demands celebration. This will frequently involve that basic poetic strategy of re-vision, of revealing a new or alternative mode of signification.

Consider, for example, her wonderful little poem that turns the Arabic numeral forms into hieroglyphic pictograms, reversing millennia of evolution of abstract signs, "Cardinal Ideograms"—the cardinal numbers, not the ordinals, which even in their combined form (1st, 2d, 3d, etc.) are polluted with abbreviated linguistic supplements. And also, "cardinal" in the sense of being first, general, almost universally used in all languages despite having different "readings" in them (e.g., 4 reads as *four, quatre, vier, tessera, arba,* or *empat,* depending upon whether your language is English, French, German, Greek, Hebrew, or Malay.) Thus "1 A glass blade or cut. / 2 A question seated. And a proud bird's neck"—even the tiny matter of the difference between the "or" connecting the two readings in the first case and the "and" in the second reflects some difference in the relation between those readings themselves. There are more comfortably whimsical readings such as "5 A policeman. Polite. / Wearing visored cap." "7 A step. / Detached from its stair" is followed by the longest. It is a composite, in which subsequent interpretive readings are conceptually layered, moving from two different modes of emblem through a bit of poetic topology, which, among other things, elegantly revises the oldest of emblems, the serpent with its tail in its mouth as a picture of eternity:

8 The universe in diagram:
A cosmic hourglass.
(Note enigmatic shape,
absence of any valve of origin,
how end overlaps beginning.)
Unknotted like a shoelace
And whipped back and forth,
Can serve as a model of time.

This little stanza (or section? or epigram?—the model for this poem, particularly in the dramaturgy of its movement, denumerable sequentiality aside, from emblem to emblem seems to be Stevens's "Thirteen Ways of Looking at a Blackbird") points to another matter. In its sense of the relation between scientific models and poetic metaphors, Swenson's poem reveals the sophistication of her attention to systematic knowledge of nature as opposed to mere bursts of anecdotal awareness, far better informed than some vulgar invocation of "relativity" might manifest. That temporality can be pictured spatially is of serious interest to any concern for the whole matter of representation. And Swenson's poetry always trembles with that concern.

The phrase "valves of origin" evokes Emily Dickinson, the particular character of whose importance Swenson constructs in her remarkable "Daffadildo" and it is instructive to see how, in another case, Swenson responds to Dickinson's "Split the Lark—and you'll find the music" with her wonderfully reciprocating "The Secret in the Cat." It is at once a mock anatomy and a mock naughtiness of childhood. These are the first three stanzas:

I took my cat apart
to see what made him purr.
Like an electric clock
or like the snore

of a warming kettle,
something fizzed and sizzled in him.
Was he a soft car,
The engine bubbling sound?

Was there a wire beneath his fur,
or humming throttle?
I undid his throat.
Within was no stir.

This poem has a wonderful ear for the overtones of the sounds its own words are making, and the vagrant rhyming sequence *purr—snore—soft car—fur,* after moving past *throttle—throat,* returns to a full rhyme again; this last line is itself such a full echo of Dickinson's diction and syntax that it almost needs the full authoritative control of speech and sentence sound (as Frost called it), to assure us that this was deliberate. So, too, by the way, with the poem's conclusion:

Whiskers and a tail:
perhaps they caught
some radar code
emitted as a pip, a dot-and-dash

of woolen sound.
My cat a kind of tuning fork?—
amplifier?—telegraph?—
doing secret signal work?

His eyes elliptic tubes:
there's a message in his stare.
I stroke him
but cannot find the dial.

Here, the first and last lines of the final stanza resound so strongly the tone of the Dickinsonian three-beat short line. And yet the stanza is carefully constructed to flatten that echo and give us a vers libre-sounding ending. It is just this sort of control of the resources of modern American verse, and exercised in such an original way, that typifies Swenson's unique gifts. In general—as was observed earlier—her handling of verse defied trivial classification. The biology of words themselves figuring so importantly for her imaginative world, all their phonological and graphological aspects have equal status as natural phenomena. It is not surprising that her versification and deployment of formal structures of both traditional and highly novel kinds derives from the immediate source, in her own engines of execution, of the poem itself.

This is not to say merely that she writes in no consistent unvarying formal mode nor that, even more importantly, she propounds no aesthetic or cultural ideology about various notions of what poetic form might be. It is also not only that—as uniquely perhaps with Thomas Hardy—the form of a particular poem will be completely ad hoc to the occasion of writing it. That occasion can sometimes, indeed, call for the engagement of conventional modalities: in "Any Object" quoted earlier, the associations—for seventeenth-century poets—of lightness and whimsical wit called up by rhyming tercets of shorter lines are determinedly overridden by the weight of the poem's manifesto. But in general, her linear and stanzaic patterns remain free of emblematic associations or literary-historical affiliations. In Hardy's case, a wide range of available formal options were always circumscribed by the boundaries of rhymed accentual-syllabism. Swenson was a later twentieth-century American poet with the history of early and late modernist formal and rhetorical conventions behind her. Her poems are formed in ad hoc patterns and structures that are not only generically but systemically ad hoc. (As she observed in a note on her volume called *Iconographs,* "It has always been my tendency to let each poem 'make itself'—to develop, in process of becoming, its own individual physique.") She will write vers libre of many different sorts, accentual-syllabic rhymed quatrains, say, poems written in interesting combinations of these (not, say, in the late Beethoven quartet "movement" pattern of Eliot's *Four Quartets* but in strange, often simultaneous and superimposed patterns). She loves to bury rhymes, and sometimes whole iambic rhyming lines, in unmeasured but typographically patterned verse, for example. An early poem called "Almanac," framed in a free verse line of about forty characters per line, keeps ringing out rhymes from its concealed music box and, as in the first stanza, concluding in a rhymed tetrameter couplet hidden in the last line and a half of free verse:

The hammer struck my nail, instead of nail.
A moon flinched into being. Omen-black,

It began its trail. Risen from horizon
on my thumb (no longer numb and indigo)
it waxed yellow, waned to a sliver that now
sets white, here at the rim I cut tonight.

There is no classifying term for this organizing principle, nor does it have any history of appropriate or signifying use. Swenson's sense of the principles by which words may be patterned and worked into spells, charms, songs, inscriptions is as personal as is her sense of the words, and of the things in the world they designate, and of what—in the realms of thought, belief, and understanding—those things themselves designate or at least stand for. Her poems are put together seemingly as particular acknowledgments of other particular patterns and relationships seen and felt and heard.

Something of the relation of ear and eye—of linguistic sound in the inward or auditory ear and inscriptional shape—can be seen in her significantly problematic title *Things Taking Place*. It was a working title of her earlier collection eventually published in 1963 as *To Mix with Time*, and indeed eventually reappeared in the name of what still remains her major selection, *New and Selected Things Taking Place* (and certainly a *Complete Poems* is long overdue from a responsible publisher), and its peculiar resonance is characteristic. The ambiguity of the phrase "things taking place" (= *things happen* and *things take [their] place or places*) invokes time and space in its alternative constructions. Very good poems are always "taking place" in a temporal order of the ear and in a spatial order of the eye, but in Swenson's case, the way in which these dimensions coextend seems dazzling.

In Other Words is a book typical of Swenson for an artistry so sure and so *charming* (in its older senses of singing and en-chanting as well) that its precise workings are hard to see. One of two little poems looking rather like children's games (the second, "A Nosty Fright," is composed entirely of such Spoonerisms) is a case in point. The first one, "Summer's Bounty," plays with one simple linguistic fact of English: we form compound words most naturally on the Germanic (and in fact, Greek) model by jamming them together, but the French incursions into the Germanic base have nonetheless left residues of romance compounding, the prepositional phrase, e.g., seafood vs. fruits-de-mer. (This is discussed in detail on pp. 96–98) By romancing—as it were—the common, compounded names of the fruits of the earth (notice that our biblical phrase chooses the romance option) Swenson turns a mere catalogue of edibles into an exuberant litany of strange metaphors (e.g., the opening quatrain: "berries of Snow / berries of Goose / berries of Huckle / berries of Dew"). The poem works its way through berries, apples ("of Crab . . . of May . . . of Pine . . . of Love," etc.), through quatrains listing nuts, beans, melons, cherries, always capitalizing the prepositional objects to further estrange them from their humdrum designatory role. The final, rhymed, quatrain runs through other categories, composing a coda to the whole list, the poem, the day of summer itself:

glories of Morning
rooms of Mush
days of Dog
puppies of Hush

Let words play with each other and they will do the imagination's work. As she herself observed in the preface to a selection of her poems that she'd made for children and that highlights the matter of puzzle and riddle in all poetry: "Notice how a poet's *games* are called his "works"—and how the "work" you do to solve a poem is really *play*. The impulse and motive for making a poem and for solving and enjoying a poem are quite alike: both include curiosity, alertness, joy in observation and invention." Very, very good poetry does indeed make temporary poets of its readers, even as the inventiveness of poetry is itself so often a kind of interpretation.

I first encountered May Swenson's unique sensibility—her own "curiosity, alertness, joy in observation and invention"—not in her poems, but in a short story published in a periodical called *Discovery* in about 1955. It was called "Mutterings of a Middlewoman" (writing this title, I recall today Dorothy Parker's "a girl's best friend is her mutter") and recorded a satiric vision of the office life of a New York business of its day (a more visionary look at the assaults of such life on personhood is her early poem called "Working on Wall Street" from this same period); in particular, though, was its wonderful treatment of the early stages of a secretary's encounter with an electric typewriter. It was marked for me by the total absence of any vulgar Luddite or antitechnological rant or even bias, and I was not surprised, as I began to read and learn to appreciate her poems, to discover the interest they revealed in scientific and even technological conceptions. I suppose that only W. H. Auden and, more to the point, A. R. Ammons among the older generations (or Richard Kenney and Debora Greger among the younger ones) have manifested these concerns not only for natural history but for the interpretations of natural fact in post-Linnaean biologies.

Many of her poems on animals have the kind of power one finds in those of Edward Thomas and even the great ones of D. H. Lawrence (a poem like "Lion" from the early volume *Another Animal,* or the astonishing "Motherhood," or the owl poem called "The Snowy" from 1988). Her previously mentioned preoccupation with finding emblems in natural fact remains unrelenting throughout, but her moralization, always poetic, moves in at a point alternative to either a structural or functional account of some phenomenon, or to either a Darwinian or Lamarckian causal story (as opposed, say, to the chain of metaphysical conceits that the latter basic hypothesis affords Richard Wilbur in his charming "Lamarck Elaborated"—as in the penultimate stanza: "The Shell of balance rolls in seas of thought. It was the mind that taught the head to swim"). A little poem called "What's Secret," for example, observes in its opening line one phenomenon seemingly general in vertebrate life. But then it goes on—in a major mode that extends from Sir Thomas Browne through Emerson to our day—to natural mythmaking (I quote from the text of Swenson's *Iconographs* all the poems of which are designed to be set in a typewriter font):

What's Secret

```
   Always the belly lighter than the back.
  What grows in the shade pales,
 what's secret keeps tender.

  In version saves the silk of innocence.
Fierce melanosis of the adult coat
From whips of sun. The overt coarsens,

stripes and grins with color.
 Exposure, experience thicken half the beast
  who, shy as snow, stays naked underneath.
```

The volume entitled *Iconographs* is outstanding among the very few attempts to write serious poetry of what I might call an inscriptional sort. By this I mean not what is usually loosely called "concrete poetry"—which is most often a mode of graphic art—but rather a poem the precise typographic form of whose inscription (down to font and size of type) cannot be translated or adapted. Ordinarily, the manuscript version of any poem can be printed in any number of ways without altering any of the author's basic intentions about form. Consider, say, a sonnet, for which the author chooses an optional format (indented *b*-rhymed lines in octave, stanza-break space, *c*-, *d*-, *e*-rhymed lines in matched indentations, etc.); whether the poem is set in serif or sans serif, a face relatively condensed or not, etc., will certainly affect the "look" of the poem on the page and engage questions of visual taste on the part of the reader if he or she is at all aware of matters of typographic design. But it will not engage the poet's particular options of sonnet format in the least. A concrete poem will make discriminations about absolute matters of design as only a designer or graphic artist might. Swenson's "Iconographs" are all composed and printed in

an elite typewriter font and arranged in an array of patterns on the page, sometimes iconic—wave forms, a bottle formed by a void generated by the typed
lines, a DNA helix, a trellis whose verticals are always formed by the cross-word
"rose" (or its derivatives) and "blue"—and sometimes abstractly or expression-
istically shaped. Their range of attention to visual matters is very wide indeed.
The kinds of shape and pattern and typographical turn they exhibit are all based
on the typewriter (before word processing), which is almost an homage to a
muse or a Ouija board through which the voices of pattern talk to her. One of
several marine poems is called "Beginning to Squall" and plays with the emerging conceit that an uppercase "P" is a half-submerged uppercase "B." Another,
very different, in fairly conventional-looking stanzas of six long lines pairs the
strophes by a mirrored indentation scheme (3 indented + 3 flush left, 3 flush left
+ 3 indented). It is a profoundly meditative ecphrastic poem starting from a
frivolous kitschy, postcard; "Merry Christmas. You're on the Right" begins

```
    I'm looking at these two raffish child-angels
    by Raphael, a section of his sky this corner
    transaction cropped for close-up on a picture card.
Sunwarmed, well-fleshed, naked except for wings,
(the plum-red bows unpleating from their shoulder-blades,
so short they couldn't hold a robin up are pure

    convention), they rest their elbows on a beam . . .
    that looks like wood, not light—some plank in middle
    heaven they've reached for perch, or, breaking surface,
reached arms up over, like raft or rafter. There
they dawdle, hips immersed, unseen from behind,
kissed, blown on, spanked by waves that could be either

    wind or water.
```

Raphael made raffish may have been one of the starting points here. In any case,
the poem ends up on the page with what, rotated through ninety degrees, will
resemble three pairs of conventionalized angelic wings (even as the mirrored
pairings of stanzas speak to the matter of the paired angels).

   The poem called "The Shape of Death" is quite uncanny, being laid out in a
perfect square twenty-six lines by fifty-four typed characters, with a blank line
between two blocks of twelve and thirteen lines, all justified right and left, but
with a strange, hard to read, not quite "amorphous" river of blank space
roughly dividing the square into irregular quarters. Milton calls Death, Satan's
son and grandson, a "shape, / If shape it might be called that shape had none /

Distinguishable"; and Swenson's shape will not accommodate any trivial iconomorphic form. It is instructive to consider this poem in relation to her earlier "Satanic Form," which, beautiful and powerful, looks forward to those of the later typewritten book while yet remaining in a traditional mode, apart from the visual element resulting from the typographer's formatting. It consists of a catalogue of menacing entities, "forkmarks of Satan," in short lines successively moving one pica to the left as they creep down the page. The pattern reaches its farthest extension in a longest line that inverts the negative valorization of the preceding list and initiates an antithetical expanding catalogue in lines that are reciprocally indented again. The moment of turn is very strong (I quote these seven lines from the very middle of the poem):

> the needled hands the 12-eyed face
> against the open window past which drops the night
> like a dark lake on end or flowing hair
> Night unanimous over all the city
> The knuckled fist of the heart opening and closing
> Flower and song not cursed with symmetry
> Cloud and shadow not doomed to shape and fixity
> The intricate body of man without rivet or nail

—and there is a heavily Blakean echo in the last line here. In a poem like this one, we can see how Swenson's patterns can become emblems even of epistemological concerns, and of states of thought. And here, as throughout her poetry, the shadows of form are always being given the substance of deep significance.

Anyone knowing and loving May Swenson's writing will recall, from another early poem, her unanswered question. It can form a fitting conclusion to this *hommage:*

Body my house
my horse my hound
what will I do
when you are fallen . . .

James Merrill, in one of his last poems, shows one of the concerns he shared with her for seeing eternity, if not just in a grain of sand, then in a tiny mark of ink. His "Body" muses on that word's letters, on "how like a little kohl-rimmed moon / *o* plots her course from *b* to *d*," on *y* as an unanswered question or questioner, ending by enjoining the reader to ask, in turn, "what the *b* and *d* stood for." While Swenson might have observed that, like birth and death, their initial letters turned their backs upon each other, it is hard to keep these two poems entirely apart. May Swenson's last version of her "Question" is put in its closing lines:

With cloud for shift
how will I hide?

But no matter how faded and wrapped in cloud a person's dead body may be, the body of a poet's work continues always to grow as we understand it more and more.

CHAPTER TWENTY-THREE

The Scarred Most Sacred:
Some Remarks on Geoffrey Hill

Nothing, said Emerson, is got for nothing, and in initially confronting an important poem by England's major poet of our time, we must give up certain things. One of these is any appetite we as readers may have for quick laughs, pleasant chatter, or nostalgic evocation, even in its high modes. Hill's poetry is very often difficult, intense, and compact. And while it provides, as all good poetry does, its own continual interpretive underscoring in what in the past has been called the music of its language, his poems do not take time out to explain themselves. Another thing Geoffrey Hill's poetry won't do for us is to present surfaces for the convenient attachment of glib labels. Take for example the question of what people who really don't know much about poetics call "formal poetry": all verse has form of some sort, and to treat the question of what tonalities one writes in or what instrumentation a poet employs, as a political matter is most often the result of having nothing much to say about the most important poetic questions. True poets all know how private are these instrumental matters, which will have what are for them crucial public consequences. Hill has written both free verse and elegantly controlled rhymed iambic verse, and like all serious poets, the issue of form has nothing to do with ideology or literary gossip—so-called new formalism or naked poetry or whatever. Any good teacher could use the free verse of his "September Song" in a classroom as examples of masterful technique; every line-break in the poem answers to some matter of precise signification, and in far more subtle ways than those of either trivially surprising or dully nullified enjambment. The carefully cadenced prose-poems of the *Mercian Hymns* develop, as the medievalist Nicholas Howe has shown, a poetic mode derived not directly from the rhythms of Anglo-Saxon poetry but from its syntactic structures—appositions, in particular—and some of its rhetorical particularities. But Hill would probably not want—nor would any true poet really want—to be enlisted in the ranks of some battle of the styles.

Yet there are other sorts of difficulty with his poetry. He is never easily ironic, in that late modern mode that is so cheap as to be close to the sentimentality it so trivially scorns. It is so truly poetic it won't dilute itself in bits of surrounding self-generated journalism—the kind of thing that most bad poets write when their attempts at poems are full of stories about what they were doing that morning when they set out to write these lines. To expect, that is, touching and amusing letters from the poet to his or her college roommate—again, the standard form of what most people call a poem in the United States today—is to find that Geoffrey Hill will only perplex.

His very kinds of poems are also very much his own. Hill often favors the poetic sequence, and many of his cycles of poems, both longer and shorter, have been meditations on history. In his work in general a sense of religion is shaped by history and a sense of history by religion. And yet he is a religious poet in no creedal or sectarian sense, and questions of belief in his poetry will often concern the boundaries of utterance itself, what seems epistemologically unsaysable and morally unspeakable. He contemplates unsainted martyrdoms, uncanonized by churches or by historians' doctrines.

Geoffrey Hill was born in Worcestershire in 1932, educated there and at Keble College Oxford where he took a first-class honors degree in 1953, the year after Fantasy Press brought out a first pamphlet of his poems. For some time he taught at the University of Leeds; in 1981 he moved to Emmanuel College, Cambridge, where he taught and lectured for the university's English faculty until coming to the United States in 1987, where he became one of the university professors at Boston University. Of his books, *For the Unfallen* was published in 1959, *King Log* in 1968, the remarkable *Mercian Hymns*—infused as it is with a spirit of the continuity of the fundamental culture of the Midlands—in 1971. These were all collected in *Somewhere Is Such a Kingdom* of 1975. Next was *Tenebrae* in 1979, and *The Mystery of the Charity of Charles Péguy* in 1983. His book of essays, *The Lords of Limit,* appeared in 1984. He has been awarded among other prizes the Hawthornden Prize and the Heinemann Award, and in the United States, the Loines Award from the American Academy and Institute of Arts and Letters. In 1972 he was elected a Fellow of the Royal Society of Literature.

I first heard of Hill from Donald Hall, at Harvard in 1955 or so, but it wasn't until a few years later that I read his remarkable early poem "Genesis," with its now famous opening lines "Against the burly air I strode / Crying the miracles of God," quite overcoming me with its almost Blakean sense of the inherence of the Fall in the very Creation, with its terrifying vision of nature springing into life already reddened in tooth and claw, reminiscent of the moment in book 10 of *Paradise Lost* when the creatures turn against each other. Each day of creation darkens the matter of life more:

And the third day I cried: "Beware
The soft-voiced owl, the ferret's smile,
The hawk's deliberate stoop in air,
Cold eyes, and bodies hooped in steel,
Forever bent upon the kill."

But the visionary's attempt to escape from the realm of blood to a cold, oceanic version of Yeats's sailed-to Byzantium makes him return, by week's end, to the world: "By blood we live, the hot, the cold, / To ravage and redeem the world: There is no bloodless myth will hold." This was all the more remarkable at a moment when most of the new British poetry I was finding attractive was of a very different sort, marked by a return to an almost eighteenth-century poetry of statement, an abandonment of modernist difficulty. Geoffrey Hill's poetry was not at all like this. At the end of "God's Little Mountain," the speaker descending from the hill of an incompletely vouchsafed vision concludes "For though the head frames words the tongue has none. / And who will prove the surgeon to this stone?" The stone may indeed have been like that of Revelation 2:17—"I . . . will give him a white stone, and in the stone a new name written, which no man knoweth save that he receiveth it." But the question was as much directed inward by the poet to himself as to the reader, and some of the tasks—of interpretation of first and last things as they present themselves in privileged glimpses of ordinary ones, and of giving voice to those interpretations—seemed particularly applicable to the very poems of his I was reading. Shortly after the appearance of Hill's collection called *For the Unfallen,* another friend, the critic Harold Bloom—whose views about poetry were about as polar to those of Hill's early admirer Donald Hall as could be found—assured me with sweeping emphasis that Geoffrey Hill was the one true poet in England. That both of these writers could perceive Hill's position as a poet with the powers of Hardy and D. H. Lawrence and yet themselves exhibit absolutely no apparent affinities was really remarkable. Not about them, but about the poet we they were speaking of.

One of the easiest of Hill's poems—to read, to admire, and even to perceive the brilliant artistry of—is one in which he now shows negative interest. (He has as far as I know refused permission in the past to anthologize it.) "In Memory of Jane Fraser" is beautifully constructed, tactfully managed at every point (I could even point, I suppose, to the casual-looking syntax of the last line, which itself frames one of those moments of closure that turn to a momentary picture—not obviously "of" what one had been saying, but on reflection, pointing into the heart of it):

She died before the world could stir.
In March the ice unloosed the brook
And water ruffled the sun's hair.
Dead cones upon the alder shook.

Here the word order at first sounds inverted and slightly archaic, but of course it is not—"shook" isn't modified by "upon the alder" and the word order is perfectly modern and compact—it is this kind of instant of stylistic puzzle that leaves us as readers meditating on the metaphorical puzzle of this emblem. I shall say no more about this poem, not wishing to discomfort the author, save to remark that happy is the poet who can afford to think less than well of a poem of his or her own that is this good.

But we might profitably dwell a moment longer on some of the other things that emerge when we put Hill's lines under microscopic poetic scrutiny. When Spenser in a poem called *The Teares of the Muses*—in which he is lamenting how much bad poetry there is in England in 1590 (when there was more good poetry being written than perhaps at any other time)—has the muse of love poetry, Erato, urge all the others to "change your praises into piteous cries / And Eulogies turn into Elegies," he plays rather openly on the sounds of the two words, suggesting that the second is the product of some kind of negation of the first. When Hill directs our attention to the processes by which words follow each other resonantly, as well as significantly, he is making those very processes tell more of his story. Thus "Patience hardens to a pittance, courage / unflinchingly declines into sour rage" he observes in his wonderful poetic sequence *The Mystery of the Charity of Charles Péguy*—it is as if a moral version of grammatical declension were at work on concepts, even as sound changes between near-homonyms move toward reduction and diminution. (It's interesting that Spenser's very pair of words, but this time passed through French, "éloge and elegy" are at the very end of this poem wedded, rather than phased along a descent, reminding us that there can be occasions for the mutual entailment of mourning and praising.)

But the whole of Hill's *Péguy* cycle exhibits this pattern. The poem itself appeared in 1983 in England. It had some affinities with his *Tenebrae* of some years before, but the Arthurian ambiance of those sonnets (and their powerful parrying of Tennyson, kept just at bay) is superseded in this new poem by the *matere*—as the medievalists call it—of World War I, the poetic province of Owen and Rosenberg and Brooke and other poets of their generation, on the one hand, and the prose of David Jones's *In Parenthesis,* on the other. It exemplifies several senses of the phrase that gives its title to one of Hill's essays on questions of poetry and belief, which characterized poetry as "menace and atonement." Its own title alludes to that of Péguy's *Le Mystère de la charité de Jeanne d'Arc* (she was a central figure in that French writer's three long poems) and is concerned with the consequences of poetic and spiritual vocation, and with their poetic tropes of action and their deadly literalization into violence. Péguy is, for Hill's poem, a version of one of his own saints-innocents. The socialist and "self-expatriate but adoring" Catholic (as Hill puts it in a note) had engaged in violent polemic against his sometime Drefusard ally, Jean-Léon Juarès, and whether or not as a consequence of this, the latter was assassinated in a cafe in 1914, at the brink of the outbreak of the war. That same year, Péguy was killed in a beetfield on the first day of the Battle of the Marne.

Hill's poem starts out with a shot that resounds within the work with greater consequence than the one at Sarajevo in 1914.

Crack of a starting-pistol. Jean Juarès
dies in a wine-puddle. Who or what stares
through the café-window crêped in powder-smoke?
The bill for the new farce reads *Sleepers Awake*.

History commands the stage wielding a toy gun,
rehearsing another scene. It has raged so before,
countless times, and will do, countless times more,
in the guise of supreme clown, dire tragedian.

In Brutus' name martyr and mountebank
ghost Caesar's ghost, his wounds of air and ink
painlessly spouting, Jaurès' blood lies stiff
on menu-card, shirt-front and handkerchief.

Did Péguy kill Juarès? Did he incite
the assassin? Must we stand by what they write
as by their camp-beds or their weaponry
or shell-shocked comrades while they sag and cry?

One of the masterful things about this sequence is the way in which it can start out with a moral question most writers would have had to struggle, in the course of a work, to derive. These opening lines cut to the matter of atonement, for which poetry must make its own pledge of unification. Hill's other, more familiar mastery is apparent everywhere in his firm stanzas, quatrains that move through their own purgatorial changes of rhyme scheme and frame that superbly tough and resonant diction that this major poet has made his own. Time and again he will strike overtones of the pitch of loaded words, never with the crude ironic purposes of debunking, but in a more autumnal kind of sadness. Thus in a 1914 battlefield scene

Inevitable high summer, richly scarred
with furze and grief; winds drumming the fame
of the tin legions lost in haystack and stream!
Here the lost are blest, the scarred most sacred.

—he works up glimpses of shatter heroics that go beyond Wilfred Owen's simple characterization as the "old lie" of *dulce et decorum est pro patria mori*. Here are—in a series of phonetic witherings that reverse the evolution of "sacred" from "scarred" in the final line just quoted—the "guerdon," which becomes embodied in cruelly needless loss ("Chinese" Gordon—as he was called—dying at Khartoum), the shriveling of "patience," the declination of "courage":

solitary bookish ecstasies, proud tears,
proud tears, for the forlorn hope, the guerdon
of Sedan, "oh les braves gens!" English Gordon
stepping down sedately into the spears.

Patience hardens into a pittance, courage
unflinchingly declines into sour rage,
the cobweb-banners, the shrill bugle-bands
and the bronze warriors resting on their wounds.

He does this often throughout the sequence of ten odes, "éloge and elegy" both, where "Dear lords of life"—sadly diminished from Emerson's—move through the inexorable powers of "the lords of limit"—a phrase of Auden's that Hill uses as the title of his volume of essays. We hear these phonetic echoes of moral reductions in his invocation to the "bristly-brave gentlemen"

of Normandy and Loire. Death does you proud,
every heroic commonplace, "Amor,"
"Fidelitas," polished like old armour,
stamped forever into the featureless mud.

push on, push on!—through struggle, exhaustion,
indignities of all kinds, the impious Christian
oratory, "vos morituri," through berserk fear,
laughing, howling, "servitude et grandeur."

The sequence keeps coming back to the contention between the cycle of violent action and verbal fiction that lies at the heart of its author's concerns:

. . . no wonder why
we fall to violence out of apathy,

redeemed by falling and restored to grace
beyond the dreams of mystic avarice.

But who are "we," since history is law,
clad in our skins of silver, steel and hide,
or in our rags, with rotten teeth askew,
heroes or knaves as Clio shall decide?

"We" are crucified Pilate, Caiaphas
in his thin soutane and Judas with the face
of a man who has drunk wormwood. We come
back empty-handed from Jerusalem

counting our blessings, honestly admire
the wrath of the peacemakers, for example
Christ driving the money-changers from the temple,
applaud the Roman steadiness under fire.

We are the occasional just men who sit
in gaunt self-judgment on their self-defeat,
the élite hermits, secret orators
of an old faith devoted to new wars.

There is a strange touch of Auden in the fourth and fifth stanzas quoted here; but nobody save Hill could elicit the ironic nuances of "for example . . . temple." Equally characteristic is the Shakespearean play on the ambiguous syntax of "orators / an old faith devoted to new wars"—not only is there the typical falling in the rhyming transition from "orators" to the horrible literalization of their rhetoric in "wars," but the insistence that it is the faith itself—not merely its defenders—that is "devoted to new wars." Similarly, in the next stanza, where the "élite hermits" are now seen as shirkers from active service (in the military sense of *embusqués*)—

We are "embusqués," having no wounds to show
save from the thorns, ecstatic at such pain.
Once more the truth advances, and again
the metaphors of blood begin to flow.

And again, in the last line here, the central notion is embodied; the poets' metaphors will flow (metaphorically) like the blood so literally flowing that troped by those metaphors (so that in a way the actual blood of those dying in the "new wars" is a sort of transumption of the metaphor—a horrible literalization of it).

This reminds us of how the whole poetic sequence is a passionate and controlled elegy for a major mode of heroic poetry and for the celebration of active ideals (and again I think of Auden, as Hill seldom makes me do, in his setting poetry to its task). Like all major modern poetry, Hill's is grounded in its retractions and lit by the bonfires where the false faces of nobility are burned. But these retractions are themselves of imaginative proportions that are as heroic as things get.

A final look at the similar way Hill makes the sounds of words in relation to each other propound their own local parable: in one of the poems of the sequence called "Of Commerce and Society" when, talking of celebrated disasters and the dead they left, he is poetically wary of the wrong sort of immortalizing, the wrong way of remembering and dealing with history. He calls "Auschwitz, / Its furnace chambers and lime pits / half erased," "half-dead" and adds "a fable / Unbelievable in fatted marble." In that great mode from Spenser through Keats and Tennyson, the poet whose words are more like characters and actors than like objects or utensils leads them through their roles; the failure of "fable" when it becomes, half-rhymingly, "unbelievable" is caused by the expansion of its phonemes or speech sounds into those of "fatted marble," thus telling once again one of poetry's most important tales that continually needs repeating: fables, parables, metaphors, the fictions by which poetry makes certain truths known, become mere statuary when they are institutionalized, when they are interpreted down into principles, however heroically misconceived. Hill here is significantly as one with Wallace Stevens in distrusting metaphor frozen into the merely monumental.

But his own special distrust touches on how far poetry may itself go even when authentic. "Annunciations," that brilliant and intensely difficult poem, seems to involve that question; and even when he tentatively accords poetry its role in the exposition of a theodicy, it is very guarded, as in the last quatrain of the final poem in "Of Commerce and Society":

There is, at times, some need to demonstrate
Jehovah's touchy methods that create
The connoisseur of blood, the smitten man.
At times it seems not common to explain.

Hill's poetry is full of the consciousness of "smitten men" and of the imagination of disaster. It is also continuingly attentive to the relation of words and deeds, when they seem to become each other, when they are mistaken for each other, when horror or beauty may result.

INDEX

"Forest History," 220; "Hard Weather," 220; "Hymn to Colour," 220; "Jump-to-Glory Jane," 221; "The Lark Ascending," 219, 220; "A Later Alexandrian," 220; "Love in the Valley," 216; "Lucifer in Starlight," 215–16; "Martin's Puzzle," 221; "Meditation under Stars," 220; *Modern Love*, 215–19; "Night of Frost in May," 220; *The Ordeal of Richard Feverel*, 215; *Poems* (1851), 218; *Poems and Lyrics of the Joy of Earth*, 215; "Seed Time," 220; "South-West Wind in the Woodland," 218; "Tardy Spring," 220; "The Thrush in February," 220; "Twilight Music," 218; "Winter Heavens," 220; "Woodland Peace," 220; "Woodman and Echo," 220; "The Woods of Westermain," 217, 220

Meredith, Owen: *Lucille*, 210

Merrill, James, 8, 60, 145, 153, 232, 297; "The Book of Ephraim," 49; *The Changing Light at Sandover*, 49; "The Mad Scene," 91; "Mirror," 44–49, 57; *Water Street*, 48

Merwin, W. S., 8, 146, 173

Miles, Josephine, 150

Millais, John Everett, 194

Milton, John, 6, 24, 41, 58, 85, 102, 162, 170, 178, 213, 247, 263; *Areopagitica*, 84; *Comus*, 84, 203; "Lycidas," 183, 228; "Ode on the Morning of Christ's Nativity," 62n3; *Paradise Lost*, 25, 32, 33, 36, 65, 69, 84, 91, 98–99, 106–7, 108, 139, 179, 181, 212, 229, 296–97, 301; *Paradise Regained*, 58; *Il Penseroso*, 134, 209; sonnet 23, 83

Monroe, Harriet, and Alice Corbin Henderson: *The New Poetry*, 148, 154, 155

Montaigne, Michel de, 74, 107

Moody, Dwight L., 169

Moody, William Vaughn, 222, 231, 234

Moore, Thomas, 202

Moore, Marianne, 144, 146, 250–68, 288, "A Carriage from Sweden," 253; "In the Days of Prismatic Color," 257–58; "In Distrust of Merits," 260; "Fear Is Hope," 258–59; "The Fish," 256, 267; "Marriage," 251, 257; *Marianne Moore Reader*, 258; "nevertheless," 260; *Observations*, 251, 255, 258, 260; "An Octopus," 251; *O to Be a Dragon*, 260; "Peter," 255; "Radical," 255; "Reticence and Volubility," 251; "St. Nicholas," 261; "Saint Valentine," 268; "Sea Unicorns and Land Unicorns," 251; " 'Sun,' " 258, 259; "A Talisman," 251; *Tell Me, Tell Me*, 258; "To a Chameleon," 260, 261–62; "To an Intra-Mural Rat," 251; "To a Strategist," 261; "What Are Years?" 258, 265–67, 268

Morris, Jane (Mrs. William), 193

Moss, Howard, 144

Mother Goose, 29–30, 34

Murdoch, Iris, 169

Nash, Ogden, 170

Nemerov, Howard, 144, 158

New Yorker, The, 163, 170

Nietzsche, Friedrich Wilhelm, 16, 17, 26, 226

Nineteenth-Century American Poetry, 148

Novalis (Friedrich Leopold von Hardenburg), 78, 91

Olson, Charles, 162

Opie, Iona and Peter: *Oxford Dictionary of Nursery Rhymes*, 29

Orwell, George, 147, 167